INTELLECTUAL PROPERTY IN ASIAN EMERGING ECONOMIES

To Desta Yimam and all our relations

Intellectual Property in Asian Emerging Economies

Law and Policy in the Post-TRIPS Era

ASSAFA ENDESHAW
St Mary's University College, Addis Ababa, Ethiopia

ASHGATE

Published by
Ashgate Publishing Limited
Wey Court East
Union Road
Farnham
Surrey, GU9 7PT
England

Ashgate Publishing Company
Suite 420
101 Cherry Street
Burlington
VT 05401-4405
USA

www.ashgate.com

British Library Cataloguing in Publication Data
Assafa Endeshaw, 1950-
Intellectual property in Asian emerging economies : law and policy in the post-TRIPS era.
1. Intellectual property--Asia.
I. Title
346.5'048-dc22

Library of Congress Cataloging-in-Publication Data
Assafa Endeshaw, 1950-
Intellectual property in Asian emerging economies : law and policy in the post-TRIPS era / by Assafa Endeshaw.
p. cm.
Includes bibliographical references and index.
ISBN 978-0-7546-7459-7 (hardback) 1. Intellectual property--Asia. 2. Intellectual property--Government policy--Asia. 3. Agreement on Trade-Related Aspects of Intellectual Property Rights (1994). I. Title.
KNC370.A97 2010
346.504'8--dc22

2009042948

ISBN 9780754674597 (hbk)

Mixed Sources
Product group from well-managed forests and other controlled sources
www.fsc.org Cert no. SA-COC-1565
© 1996 Forest Stewardship Council
FSC

Printed and bound in Great Britain by
MPG Books Group, UK

Contents

List of Tables

About the Author

Dr Assafa Endeshaw (PhD, LLM [London], LLB [Addis Ababa]), specializes in information law (intellectual property policy and information technology law). He has authored *Intellectual Property Policy for Non-Industrial Countries* (Dartmouth, 1996), *Intellectual Property in China: The Roots of the Problem of Enforcement* (Acumen, 1996), and *Internet and E-Commerce Law: With a Focus on Asia-Pacific* (Prentice Hall, 2001). Previously, he was a legal attorney and advisor in government departments and a researcher and consultant in a law firm in Ethiopia. Subsequently, he taught at the Nanyang Business School of the Nanyang Technological University, Singapore, during 1994–2004, first as Lecturer and later as Associate Professor of law. He then took up the position of Reader in Information Law at the School of Legal Studies of Wolverhampton University, UK, in 2004–7, and again at the Department of Law of Oxford Brookes University, UK, in 2007–8. He currently teaches at the Law School of Dire-Dawa University, Ethiopia. He may be contacted at AssafaEndeshaw@yahoo.com.

Preface

The literature on intellectual property (IP) law and policy in developing countries (DCs), including the emerging economies, particularly those in East Asia, has been expanding at a furious pace. This is in keeping with the rising importance of IP in international trade, subsequent to the conclusion of the Agreement on Trade-Related Aspects of Intellectual Property Rights (TRIPS) in December 1994. Nonetheless, the level and scope of the discourse in IP policy has not necessarily changed at the same speed.

On the one hand, a huge proportion of the literature dwells on the compatibility of new laws adopted in DCs with TRIPS and the lack of implementation of those laws. The repetitive nature of the theme can be gleaned from a perusal of the literature across, and about, DCs. On the other hand, the coverage of policy issues has been torn between bland assertions of the importance of IP for DCs and increasingly shrill voices upholding the contrary view. The polarization of views is not particularly new, although the manner in which the supporters of the status quo present their arguments has undergone a certain transformation: They have resorted to natural rights theories and the deployment of economic, political and military power to make DCs continue to adhere to forms of IP generated by the most advanced nations.

This book departs from the catalogue of writings that elaborate on legislative changes in DCs following TRIPS and recommend more changes and adaptations *ad nauseam*. It aims to critically review the recurrent debate on IP law and policy in DCs (particularly the East Asian emerging economies) carried out in the last decade; to identify the still unresolved policy issues, and to propose alternative approaches that resonate with the needs for transformation of the economic and social reality of those economies. It seeks to draw lessons to be learned by researchers, policy makers, legislators and the business sector in general and concludes by putting forward proposals for reform.

Assafa Endeshaw

List of Abbreviations

ASEAN	Association of South-East Asian Nations
DC	Developing Countries
FDI	Foreign Direct Investment
FoD	'Group of Friends of Development'
FTA	Free Trade Agreement
IP	Intellectual Property
MFN	Most Favoured Nation
MNCs	Multi-National Corporations
NICs	Newly Industrializing Countries
TRIPS	Agreement on Trade-Related Aspects of Intellectual Property Rights
UNCTAD	United Nations Conference on Trade and Development
USTR	Office of the US Trade Representative
WIPO	World Intellectual Property Organization
WTO	World Trade Organization

Chapter 1
Overview

Introduction

Asia is a vast continent with a huge diversity of countries, cultures and political–economic systems. However, only a small number of those countries have managed to achieve a measure of economic progress, becoming known variously as 'Tiger economies', 'emerging economies' or 'newly industrializing countries'. A veritable avalanche of research has been generated to understand the underlying causes and policy frameworks in the economic and political fields that have presumably led to those achievements. Studies into Asian laws and how they have managed, if ever, to keep up with the economic 'miracles' have not been as extensive or popular. Far more restricted in magnitude and scope have been inquiries into the more specialist area of intellectual property legal developments in Asia.

As with other nations across the world that sought to catch up with advances in Europe and North America by imitating the paths the latter had followed, appropriately dubbed 'modernization', Asian nations had either borrowed or adopted Western intellectual property (IP) laws. The state of IP laws in Asia (whether newly imported or left behind by colonialism) remained very much unchanged until the 1960s and 1970s when the view began to spread among the developing countries (DCs) that acceding to the increasingly strident demands of Western countries and corporations to reform their IP laws would serve their objective of attracting foreign capital and technology. The pervasiveness of such a belief is demonstrated by the fact, for instance, that China managed to introduce Western-style IP laws, lock, stock and barrel in a space of a decade in the hope of avoiding any barriers to the inflow of foreign technology and capital. Both East and South East Asian 'Tiger' economies took similar actions to thwart any possible disadvantages of criticisms levelled against them on account of the gaps left between their IP laws and that of Western countries.

Soon, however, the pace of reform in IP law-making picked up. What had begun as an attempt to transform the domestic IP laws in view of a perceived internal need to promote their self-interest gradually became a compulsion to do so for other more pressing reasons. Having come to the decision, in the 1960s and 1970s, that it needed to protect its lead in the world economy by tightening the laws regulating technology flows, the US took the uncompromising stance of raising standards of IP and their enforcement as codified in the Agreement on Trade-Related Aspects of Intellectual Property Rights (TRIPS) under the World Trade Organization (WTO). Increasingly, the US became more vocal in its critiques of the level of IP and enforcement across the world and, more specifically, in the emerging economies. The Office of the US Trade Representative (USTR) took it upon itself to conduct annual reviews from 1995 onwards[1] of, among other things, the state of IP law-making and enforcement in virtually all countries, with emphasis on those with an industrial and commercial significance in the export sector. The annual reviews became a signal of US intentions towards other trading nations; in particular the grouping of countries under the labels of 'priority watch list', 'watch list' and the like served as a warning of what measures the US might take in retaliation for perceived shortfalls by the respective countries. The fear of loss of access to the US market that such open pronouncements exposed the various nations to could not but lead to frenetic activity in the repeated revisions or new additions of IP laws everywhere, particularly in Asia where the dependence on the US market has always been massive. Asian governments had to hasten to acquiescence to any form of change demanded by the US (more often), the European nations (intermittently) and Japan (to a lesser extent). The consequence has been an unceasing flurry of law-making and revision in all countries to bring their laws and practices in line not only with TRIPS but also with other standards that have found favour in the major industrial powers since then.

An illustration of how the inclusion by the USTR of any country in its annual 'black list' might, if nothing else, speed up the law-making and enforcement process is that of China. The USTR issued on 30 April 1996 the names of countries likely to attract US retaliatory (so called the 'Special 301') action and designated China the sole 'priority foreign country', allegedly because it had failed to implement the 1995 agreement it had reached with the US. The US followed this in May 1996 by drawing up a list of Chinese exports to the US which would be hit by tariffs of US$3 billion unless China put an end to suspected production of pirate CDs and barriers to import of US audio, video and software products. China sought to counteract this by announcing its list of US products that it would slap with tariffs. The tit-for-tat threats of trade war were finally averted with the Chinese side agreeing on 17 June 1996 to do what the US demanded.

Much of the criticism of IP in emerging countries of Asia and elsewhere in the decade after TRIPS were based on the view that they were 'not TRIPS consistent'. Most Asian countries had to comply with TRIPS by 1 January 2000 as they were considered DCs. A number of emerging economies among them (China – though not a member of WTO yet – along with Hong Kong, the Philippines, South Korea and Taiwan) had done so by the stated deadline, although a few still had bits and pieces left in the area of protection for circuit layouts, trade secrets, simplification of procedures for acquisition of IP rights and tightening of enforcement mechanisms (customs control, for instance). Not surprisingly, Japan led the way, although it too had some remaining gaps that exposed it to some criticism. The most extensive

1 The annual reports of the Office of the US Trade Representative (USTR), known as 'National Trade Estimate Report on Foreign Trade Barriers', are available at http://www.ustr.gov/reports/index.html.

changes were made in Hong Kong, in view of its impending reunification with China and the apparent British desire to present a *fait accompli* to China.

More recently, however, criticisms have started to be levelled at the IP laws of emerging economies for their alleged failure to reflect bilateral obligations assumed by those nations when they signed 'free trade' agreements with the US. The latter type of agreement has become instrumental in injecting 'TRIPS-plus' standards across a range of countries, including a few in Asia, considered of economic or trade importance to the US.

General Features of IP Changes in Asia

A large proportion of treatises on IP in Asia is confined to explanation and manipulation of technical rules in the black-letter law tradition. Yet, IP is notoriously linked to, and mirrors, economic and technological developments or aspirations towards such. Any serious study of how IP changes in Asia came about or failed needs thus to grasp the parameters of economic and technological developments in the respective nation as well as the general framework for IP law-making and enforcement. Just as it is never easy to jumble all Asian nations together and establish their economic and technological needs and how they might resolve any attendant problems, any assumption that those nations should embrace and implement a set of identical IP laws and to prescribe such to them will doubtless be meaningless. Add to this the fact that the majority of Asian nations remain bogged down in rudimentary economic and technological problems and, left to themselves, would not believe the adoption of IP laws that have found favour in the more advanced among them (Japan) might usher in a quick fix to those problems.

As a matter of fact, the diversity in Asia expressed in terms of a handful of newly industrializing nations together with a large number of non-industrial ones has produced a divergent response to the question of accession to TRIPS, and further extension of IP subsequent to that agreement (whether through 'free-trade agreements' or in other ways). The huge dependence of Asian emerging economies on the US for market, capital and technology made sure that accession of nearly all of Asia to TRIPS would take place without much fuss. If any disgruntlement and disappointment with the lack of any 'policy space' within TRIPS to incorporate domestic Asian concerns appeared, it was after the accession and in light of developments in a new round of trade negotiations under the WTO.

The rising wave of discontent as to why Asian nations were not allowed to decide at their own pace to evolve IP policies for their socio-economic transformation only emerged with the opening up of TRIPS for revision under the auspices of the WTO. Indeed, Asian nations have, for a long time, understood that the incorporation of laws into the statute books was not identical with their implementation. Regardless of whether they were politically willing to implement those laws, a multiplicity of factors had intervened to forestall such a prospect. For one thing, the vast disparity in economic and technological standings with advanced nations where IP was found to be relatively relevant did not inspire confidence in them that they would benefit from the usual gap filling or modifications of existing premises of their own IP laws. Secondly, many Asian nations did not feel that the peculiarity of their domestic interests was addressed by laws that matched developments in Western Europe and North America.

Nonetheless, they did not go to the extent of rejecting wholesale transplantation of foreign IP laws by embracing the lessons learnt in studies of the evolution of IP in the advanced economies (e.g. Penrose,[2] Grundmann[3] and Endeshaw[4] echoing Seidman[5] and Trubek and Galanter[6]), namely that the making or enforcement of IP laws appropriate to countries should be founded on an understanding of the role of law in development and the necessity of translating economic and technological policies into laws that facilitate development. As a matter of fact, the fundamental question of whether any form of IP in Asia should be devised and continuously updated to facilitate the development of technology as well as the economic prerequisites for such an outcome never really surfaced in any official communications by governments or at the increasingly frequent conferences by heads of states (the Asia–Pacific Economic Cooperation, APEC, for instance). It was not therefore unexpected for Asian nations not to clamour for an approach in IP law-making of formulating concrete principles and rules to help transform their economies. The fear of retaliation by the US and hope that adorning themselves with the latest IP laws might thwart such threats and even lead to transfer of technology and inflow of capital put paid to any ideas of charting any national approaches towards a more relevant IP system.

The huge influence that the main trade partners of Asia, namely the US, Japan and the EU, have on developments in Asia, in particular through their constant critique of the level of IP protection available to their corporations, led to constant pumping of the IP systems with additions and trimmings often suggested by those powers. According to one commentator:

> The history of the West's relations with East Asia over the past century and a half is replete with examples of the impact of might, even when it has not made right. And one would be disingenuous when assessing intellectual property

2 Edith T. Penrose , *The Economics of the Internatinal Patent System*, Johns Hopkins Press: Baltimore, MD, 1951.

3 Helge E. Grundmann 'Foreign Patent Monopolies in Developing Countries: An Empirical Analysis', 12 *Journal of Development Studies* 186, 1976.

4 A. Endeshaw, *Intellectual Property Policy for Non-Industrial Countries*, Dartmouth: Aldershot, 1996.

5 R.B. Seidman, *The State, Law and Development*, Frances Pinter: London, 1978.

6 D.M. Trubek and Marc Galanter, 'Scholars in Self-estrangement: Some Reflections on the Crisis in Law and Development Studies in the United States', *Wisconsin Law Review* 1062, 1974.

> developments in the ROC and Korea – and even in Japan and the P.R.C. – to ignore the impact of threats to limit access to the American market.[7]

Another commentator added in the same vein:

> Europe and the United States have an important stake in accelerating the adoption and enforcement of stronger intellectual property in Asia … If the US and Europe combines their market power [in Asia – as major export markets for Asian goods] to push for stronger intellectual property in Asia, they would send a doubly strong message about the importance of this issue for first world investors, and probably speed up enforcement efforts.[8]

The perennial question for Asia in general and for emerging economies in Asia in particular is how and when they might start to plug the inflow of external (foreign) IP developments without any real examination, modification or pronounced reservations and move towards tailoring their own laws to address domestic requirements in tune with their cultures and aspirations.

Aims of the Book

Intellectual Property in Asian Emerging Economies scrutinizes the existing legal and institutional structure relating to IP in emerging economies of Asia and proposes the direction and forms of possible reforms in light of the failure of the system already in place. It lays down alternative plans of future action that governments and civil society within those countries would be expected to implement.

In particular, this book will point to the differentiation that needs to be maintained in the making or implementation of laws across countries and cultures by contrast to the current dominant perception that all nations should think alike and behave alike in IP terms, if not in others as well. It will also underline that emerging economies must take stock of their own internal peculiarities, needs or problems and set out to craft a legal and institutional structure in tune with their own state of social and economic conditions. However, the threat of trade sanctions, political and military pressure has compelled nations to abandon making their own laws and, instead, copy versions of the laws of the major industrial nations. Indeed, many countries have to work hard to establish what is expected of them across a range of policies, laws and institutions rather than what they might need for themselves.

---

7 W.P. Alford, 'How Theory Does – and Does Not – Matter: American Approaches to Intellectual Property Law in East Asia', 13 *UCLA Pacific Basin Law Journal* 8, Fall 1994; available online from Lexis-Nexis; accessed on 13 October 2000.

8 B. Callan, 'US and European Efforts to Enhance Intellectual Property Protection in Asia: A Logic in Cooperation', *IPAsia*, 35–8, November 1997, at 35.

Intellectual Property in Asian Emerging Economies also highlights the attempts of those economies to fake compliance with the wishes and demands of the industrial nations instead of working out *autonomously* policies and laws appropriate to their requirements and in line with their capabilities. The consequence is that, preoccupied as they are with the perennial pressure to copy IP laws and institutions of the industrial nations, these countries cannot effect any real changes in their own domestic laws and institutions. This has generally resulted in a state of paralysis in law-making and enforcement in these nations.

The book will also show that the continuous rise in expectations of IP owners in the industrial nations, particularly the big powers, that the rapid spread of their laws to emerging economies and DCs amounts to a promise to execute them instantly has generated illusions. For many a multinational company operating in DCs, including emerging economies of Asia, the state of IP enforcement has remained patchy or non-existent. Governments such as those of the US and EU thus continue to put pressure on DCs to implement the IP laws on their statute books. Yet, DCs have discovered that they can hardly afford, or willingly commit, to implement laws that do not conform to their requirements.

Moreover, the book will argue that the industrial powers' perception that treaties should be upheld, that DC governments should fulfil their obligations lest they fell prey to trade sanctions and external political pressure, serves only to heighten the state of misunderstanding between the two sides and to lead to confrontations in international fora such as the WTO (Doha Round). It adds that the confrontation is made worse by the dominant literature in IP which ignores the specific problems that afflict the enforcement of IP in the non-industrial and newly industrializing nations of the world but pushes for more of the same regardless of the brewing dissent and backlash against the status quo. Even where a section of the literature accepts the need for reforms, its prescriptions are piecemeal (focusing mainly on education or institutional capacity building) and come to an end shortly after barely scratching the surface.

Finally, the book explores the growing recognition that the transformation of the DCs in the economic and technological fields may be desirable even for the industrial nations. The crises that bedevil the world economy every so often, the latest being the one which erupted in 2007/8, could be averted or overcome through an expansion of the market in emerging economies, the DCs in general and ultimately the global market. The impasse in the IP field could also be resolved if both industrial and developing nations accept the necessity for a joint approach to achieve mutual benefits.

Organization of the Book

Intellectual Property in Asian Emerging Economies is organized in two parts. Part I (in Chapters 2–7) deals with post-TRIPS issues in IP law-making, while Part II (in Chapters 8–13) examines the backlash against post-TRIPS extensions of IP.

Chapter 14, by way of a conclusion, suggests the possible future directions of IP law- and policy-making in Asian emerging economies.

Chapters 2 and 3 inquire into the IP law-making process in a selected number of Asian emerging economies (the Association of South East Asian Nations, ASEAN, and China, respectively) in view of their expected compliance with TRIPS. The author decided against a similar treatment of IP developments in India, mainly because that country is an interesting and distinct case all by itself and would deserve an independent study. Moreover, the relative complexities of its legal history and tumultuous relationships with the major industrial powers would not lend themselves to a brief account that fits the limited space available here.

Chapter 2 focuses on policy grounds in the making and constant revision of IP laws in five countries of the ASEAN (namely Indonesia, Malaysia, the Philippines, Thailand and Singapore), often referred to as the emerging economies of that block, as well the legal rationale behind the variations in the local laws as well as among them and the adoption or rejection of specific formulae. The setting for the interplay of all the issues to be raised and considered is the likelihood of success in the formulation of an ASEAN-wide IP system, as has been framed by the member states. Chapter 3 dwells exclusively on developments in China in view of its rapid absorption of foreign IP laws by way of completing the 'modernization' of its laws and gaining entry into the WTO. It discusses how China's emergence as an economic powerhouse and its adoption of the most up-to-date IP laws have not necessarily obviated criticisms of the low level of its enforcement of those laws and continuing mismatch between the IP laws and the domestic demands on them.

Chapter 4 takes up the harmonization of IP in ASEAN. Most of ASEAN have put in place IP laws that were originally either inherited from the colonial past or adopted later as part of the urge to modernize. Although a desire has been expressed, through the 'ASEAN Framework Agreement on Intellectual Property Co-operation', adopted on 15 December 1995, to unify their IP systems, that agreement has not been followed by any detailed plans yet. The chapter seeks to examine the prospect for ASEAN of adopting a single regional IP system within the context of the international system and by reference to the intra-ASEAN divergent economic and social circumstances. It argues that ASEAN will not be able to trail blaze in terms of formulating IP policies and laws that conform to domestic requirements as they would be forced to embrace international developments in the IP sphere willy-nilly; nevertheless, they might succeed in introducing a single administrative machinery for ASEAN based on the stated developments.

Chapter 5 surveys the prospect for developments in IP law-making beyond TRIPs and at the behest of the major industrial powers. It looks at the instance of the new demands on the major economic powers and the pharmaceutical companies to alleviate the chronic problems of development in general and AIDS in particular, and how the debate has thereby widened. It contends that, while piracy is a global problem, rampant even within the industrial countries themselves, the incidence of piracy in DCs be better characterized as the main direct consequence of the forcible incorporation of incongruent or inappropriate IP laws into their statute books. It argues further that the role of emerging economies and DCs in IP law-making has vanished for the most part and that piracy in those countries is partly the flip side of their inability to craft IP laws in aid of their national economic and cultural pursuits and partly as an ideologically motivated label (hence a misnomer).

Chapter 6 scrutinizes Asian perspectives on post-TRIPs issues. It starts with the premise that Asian countries have, for the most part, slavishly imitated the IP system long entrenched in, or newly introduced by, the major industrial powers. It notes that, in recent years, governments, industry groups and academic scholars in the major industrial countries have sought to restrain further expansion in IP in view of its arguably deleterious effects on innovation, investment and competition. Asian emerging economies have also started to respond to the same problem, although in the limited contexts of health, traditional knowledge and the environment. Moreover, their approach lacks coherence as well as breadth, thereby hindering the emergence of a common position in their negotiation vis-à-vis the developed countries in the new round of negotiations (Doha and afterwards). This chapter examines the efforts of the Asian economies in confronting the stated problems and the possible paths for the emergence of a common position among them.

Chapter 7 opens by examining the role of IP law in Asia in light of the euphoric references to the 'tiger economies', the 'Asian Miracle' and the 'Asian Century' by comparison to the conditions in Africa. It argues that, although the disparity between Asia and Africa, both in terms of past achievements and future prospects, might appear to make a comparison of the respective roles of IP in Asia and Africa implausible, there are a few common features that are shared by Asia and Africa.

Both Asia and Africa are vast continents with a multiplicity of nations, histories and cultures. Their laws have largely originated from, or been heavily influenced by, foreign or colonial traditions. The equation of 'modernization' to 'Westernization' has propelled their legal developments in the direction of imitations, copying and full-scale transplants of further Western legal forms and jurisprudence. In the realm of IP too, despite the specific differences in the way that the laws may have evolved in each nation, the general patterns are broadly alike.

The chapter attempts to establish an analytical framework to fill the gap between the two sets of nations in terms of the significance of IP. It points to the congruity of the IP laws to the specific economic and social conditions of those nations as well as the existence or absence of industrial transformation among them as the most critical issues in the analytical framework.

Chapter 8 inquires into whether and how Asian nations have succeeded in managing the disconnect created between the protection of IP internationally and the circumstances in which they, together with most non-industrial or developing nations, were forced to forego their domestic interests and accede to treaty obligations without being given corresponding minimal benefits deserving of sovereign contracting parties. It starts with a survey of the common misperceptions about the role of IP. It then attempts a brief appraisal of the conflicting interests and forces that condition the level, or lack, of IP law-making and enforcement in Asia. Next is a brief look at the external pressure on Asian Non-ICs in both IP law-making and enforcement, followed by tracing the signs of change in IP enforcement in Asia. The chapter concludes that, despite some emerging signs of change in attitudes and levels of IP enforcement, the very same issues will remain at the forefront of IP in Asia and as a major source of dispute with the US and, to a lesser extent, the EU and Japan. It stresses that progress will continue to elude all parties, whether Asian or foreign.

Chapter 9 argues that, subsequent to the introduction of TRIPS as part of the rules governing the global trading system (WTO), the enforcement of such rights has become a focal point of confrontations between the developed industrial nations and the developing countries (especially the emerging economies). It refers to the mounting external pressure on Asian and African nations, as on other nations elsewhere, which has taken the shape of annual reports of culprits and pirate nations. The tirades against the culprits extend to threats of retaliatory, action particularly by the US and more and more by the EU and Japan.

The chapter contends that, in spite of the support for or opposition to this stance taken by commentators and policy-makers, including those in developing nations, two principal issues tend to be suppressed or ignored. Firstly, the role of IP in economic or social development is not perceived to be dependent on who bears the costs of enforcement. Secondly, it is often overlooked that the problem of IP enforcement in the end merges with the general problem of the establishment of the rule of law, of the recognition of civil rights and their implementation in practice. This chapter seeks to examine these issues in order to fill the relative void in current thinking.

Chapter 10 discusses the IP clauses in bilateral free trade agreements (FTAs) between developing and developed countries in terms of whether a high level of IP protection will damage the DCs, including those in Asia, and affect multilateral trade negotiations as well as present enforcement difficulties. It reviews the FTAs negotiated by the EU, Japan and US and compares those of South Korea and Singapore in the context of their domestic policies and economic needs. It also examines to what extent the FTAs stipulate a higher level of protection than TRIPS and whether those levels are sustainable in the emerging economies and beyond.

Chapter 11 opens the discussion of whether the newly industrializing nations in Asia, and indeed beyond, are serious about the enforcement of IP by referring to the irony of Western reports of any changes in IP among these nations being replete with calumny and backhanded attacks of deficiencies and wilful dereliction of obligations on their part. The chapter discerns three main tendencies in current Asian IP law: an attempt by nations to keep abreast of any additional demands of the industrial powers and to introduce all manners of new laws or revisions of old ones considered to be important for foreign investors; a continuation of Asian reluctance to confront foreign nations (chiefly the US and EU) as regards the form and contents as well as enforcement of such laws; and a desire to keep costs of the IP system down and help local businesses benefit from better access to such a system. It concludes that foreign, particularly US, criticism and attendant heavy-handed moves to compel Asian nations to implement IP laws are being viewed more and more through Asian eyes as crossing the boundaries of propriety and might easily backfire.

Chapter 12 reviews the burgeoning resistance of the DCs to the persistent attempts of the major industrial powers to push through the newly initiated (Doha) round of international trade negotiations without addressing their needs for 'development' in general, and their demands to revisit the role of TRIPS in their economies and cultures in particular. It then scrutinizes the proposal put forward by Brazil and Argentina articulating a 'development agenda' for the World Intellectual Property Organization (WIPO) and the responses of the major industrial powers. The chapter concludes by highlighting the fallacious propositions that permeate the 'WIPO Development Agenda', namely that the international IP system culminating in TRIPs can still facilitate the transformation of DCs and that it possesses sufficient flexibility to be amenable to the needs of such nations.

Chapter 13 studies how IP might impact upon the 'digital divide' (a shorthand to refer to any perceived inequality in the use of information and communication technologies). It argues that the growing uncertainty and confusion about what exactly constitutes IP and the extent to which society can afford to grant and protect them has begun to impact negatively on science and innovation, economies and cultures, across the globe. It then attempts to bring together, and critically assesses, the various strands of views on possible way(s) of bridging the digital divide in terms of current IP law and policy and in light of any emerging trends. The chapter concludes that, while IP does contribute to the digital divide, some of its critics fail to recognize the paramount role of the economic and social environment within which it has developed; consequently, any proposals for overthrowing IP leaving that environment intact will remain fanciful.

Chapter 14 attempts to pull together the strands of analyses undertaken in the course of the book and to sketch the possible directions for formulation of alternative policies in IP law for developing nations in general and the emerging Asian economies in particular. It contends that the major step in formulation of such policies should be an understanding of the factors, both internal and external, holding back the enforcement of IP in Asia; only then should any reform of IP laws and their institutional trappings be considered.

PART I
Post-TRIPS Issues in Intellectual Property Law-Making

Chapter 2
Intellectual Property in ASEAN: A Survey

Introduction

The intellectual property (IP) laws in the newly industrializing countries (NICs) belonging to the Association of South East Asian Nations (ASEAN) have undergone fast changes in the last two decades. All Asian nations have been hard pressed to undertake substantial changes in their existing laws and to upgrade them in light of their outstanding obligations under the World Trade Organization's Agreement on Trade-Related Aspects of Intellectual Property Rights (TRIPS), as well as the ever-broadening international IP regime.

This chapter focuses on the policy grounds in the making and constant revision of IP laws in five countries of the ASEAN (namely Indonesia, Malaysia, the Philippines, Thailand and Singapore), often referred to as the emerging economies of that block, as well the legal rationale behind the variations in the local laws as well as among them and the adoption or rejection of specific formulae. It might be noted that all five acceded to TRIPS on 1 January 1995. The additional setting for the interplay of all the issues to be raised and considered is the likelihood of success in the formulation of an ASEAN-wide IP system as has been framed by the member states (to be discussed in Chapter 4). The discussion of developments in each country will proceed alphabetically.

Intellectual Property in Indonesia

The first post-independence IP laws of Indonesia were the 1961 Trademark Act followed by the 1982 Copyright Act and, after some gap, the 1989 Patent Law, all of which replaced the Dutch colonial laws[1] in force in the respective areas.[2]

Trademark law

The 1961 Trademark Law (Law No. 21 of 1961, known officially as the Company Marks and Trademarks Law) did not recognize service marks nor certification

1 These were the 1910 law of patents, the Regulation of Industrial Property of 1912 (for trademarks) and the copyright law of 1912.

2 For a good collection of all the post-independence IP laws, including the regulations issued to implement them, see, Carl-Bernd Kaehlig and Gregory J. Churchill, *Indonesian Intellectual Property Law*, P.T. Tatanusa: Jakarta, 1993.

marks. The protectability of marks was not conditional on registration but on first use.[3] The registration of a mark would only create a presumption of being the first user and no more.[4] Non-use within six months after registration would lead to invalidation of the mark[5] as would non-use for three years.[6] The Registry was duty-bound to refuse to register marks that were identical or so similar to those already on the Register that they might confuse consumers. However, the 1961 Trademark Act did not recognize trademark licensing, but only assignment.[7] Parallel imports were not prohibited under the Act either. Trademarks were protectable for 10 years and renewable. It might be noted that the old law of 1912 allowed protection for 20 years.

The 1961 trademark law was replaced in August 1992 (through Law No. 19 of 1992, the Law on Marks) to extend protection to service and collective marks, as well as marks consisting of a combination of colours.[8] The 1992 law also regulated the licensing of trademarks. In line with international developments, the transfer of a registered mark was allowed separate from or together with the goodwill associated with it.[9] On the other hand, use by a licensee could be taken as proof of use in Indonesia; moreover, protection was available to such a licensee if it registered the licence at the Trademark Office. The previous requirement of prior use for registration was removed so that those who registered first would have prima facie ownership of a mark.[10] In addition, the Trademark Office could refuse to register marks that were similar to famous or well-known marks.[11] However, the criteria for determining whether the said marks should be well-known in Indonesia too had not been specified. Otherwise, the 1992 law had retained much of the previous law regarding such things as the duration of protection for trademarks.

Indonesia promulgated Trademark Law No. 14 of 1997 to bring the earlier law into line with TRIPS. The new law included more expansive protection to well-known marks. Yet a further law was issued in 2001 (Trademark Law No. 15) nullifying all previous laws. The new law essentially consolidated all previous laws and added a few novelties. Thus the 2001 trademark law raised the maximum fine for criminal violations while reducing the sentence for such. The protection of well-known marks still awaits the promulgation of further regulations proposed by the government.

---

3 Article 2(1), Trademark Law of 1961.
4 Article 2(2), ibid.
5 Ibid.
6 Article 18(1) (c), ibid.
7 Article 20, ibid.
8 Articles 1 and 2, The Law on Marks of 1992.
9 Article 41, ibid.
10 Article 3, ibid.
11 Article 88, ibid. and the Decision of the Minister of Justice of 2 May 1991 (No. M.03-HC.02.01) regarding the rejection of applications for registering well-known marks.

Copyright law

The Copyright Act (Law No. 6 of 1982) was imbued with the understandable influence of Dutch law and that of other European countries, but the attempt to keep to a level of generality in the formulation of rules rather than provide specific ones left much room for uncertainty and ambiguity. Thus, for instance, the definition of 'publication' was slightly different from those one ordinarily finds in copyright laws of many countries in that it refers to 'reading, announcement' and such like.[12] The types of protectable works were listed with no apparent common characteristics that are usually recognized in other countries' laws. Thus instead of making clear distinctions between the well-known four types of 'original works of authorship', that is literary, dramatic, musical and artistic works, on the one hand, and the derivative works (or neighbouring rights), on the other,[13] and amongst them, the Copyright Law of Indonesia provided a single long list. The lack of a clear basis in the groupings created in the Law, for instance to determine duration of rights granted, revealed a perplexing approach.

Otherwise, copyright came into existence by the mere fact of creation; however, it was possible to register copyright at the option of the owner.[14] The registration of a work created a presumption of ownership by the registrant.[15] In addition, the law recognized moral rights,[16] again a reflection of lingering Dutch influence. The work of a foreign owner of copyright would be protected if the work were first published in Indonesia or in accordance with treaty obligations of Indonesia.[17]

Among the exclusions from copyright, the most important were Indonesian laws and regulations, decisions of courts[18] and works generated by and on behalf of the government (unless some reservation was made earlier).[19] The fair use exceptions[20] extended to using works for lecture (educational) purposes or for performances for which no fees were charged, copying 10 per cent of a work for criticism or review, 'limited' reproduction for libraries and documentation centres and educational institutes. Yet, there was no indication as to what kind of limits there might be in the making of reproductions. Pursuant to Articles 15 and 16, some form of compulsory licensing was allowed for works that were not available

12 Article 1 (c), Copyright Law of 1982.

13 Understandably, the 1956 UK Copyright Act separated them as Part I and Part II works, respectively. This was abandoned later. Even continental law, which was the original influence in Indonesia, distinguishes between the two.

14 Article 29, note 12, above. In an apparent move to avoid any doubt of the optional nature of the registration facility, Article 29 was further amended in 1987 with a new sub-article (4), which stated that registration shall not be an obligation to obtain copyright.

15 Article 5(1), note 12, above.

16 Article 24, ibid.

17 Article 48, ibid., as amended in 1987.

18 Article 12, note 12, above.

19 Article 13, ibid.

20 Article 14, ibid.

in Bhasa Indonesia, or not reproduced there within two to three years from their date of publication elsewhere. On the other hand, any assignment of copyright was allowed if done so entirely; in other words, no partial assignment was permitted.[21] It is difficult to say what this entailed particularly as copyright was susceptible to exploitation through a multiplicity of forms, any of which might be bundled off separately to would-be licensees or assignees.

The copyright for material produced by an employee during the course of employment belonged to the employee; however, copyright would belong to the employer if the creation were made 'in connection with official service for another person in the scope of employment'.[22] The intended distinction appeared to have been between a general and specific assignment of an employee – hence, the employee had copyright in the former and the employer in the latter. However, that may have been purely conjectural. (Again this illustrates the ambiguity in the drafting that we have alluded to earlier.) It might be noted that this did not apply to government employees, because of the absence of copyright for materials originating from that source. The term of protection for copyright ran for life plus 25 years for classical works and only 15 for photographic and cinematographic works.[23]

The Copyright Law was amended by Law No. 7 of 1987 in response to US threat of trade retaliation and upon the declared recognition that 'infringements of Copyright have reached a dangerous level and can disrupt the order of social life in general and the desire to create in particular'.[24] The deadline set by the US for Indonesia to bring its copyright law in line with international conventions was 30 September 1987.[25]

By virtue of the 1987 amendment, the law incorporated computer programs as a category of creations 'in the field of science, art and literature',[26] obviously not quite in the same way as the well-known US formula (reproduced in TRIPS) of treating them as 'literary works'. A new exemption from copyright was also added: the making of a backup copy for computer software.[27] The 1987 law generally lengthened the period of protection;[28] thus, besides the classical allowance for life plus 50 years extended to the original groups of works, other works, whether derivative or not, such as sound and video recordings, would be protected for 50 or 25 years, computer programs being among the latter. The confusing manner in which 'works of authorship' such as adaptations were protected only for 25 years

21 Article 35, ibid.

22 Article 8, ibid.

23 Article 27, ibid.

24 Preamble to the Copyright Law No. 7 of 1987.

25 See, E. Upoff, *Intellectual Property and US Relations With Indonesia, Malaysia, Singapore, and Thailand*, Southeast Asia Program, Cornell University: Ithaca, NY, 1991.

26 Article 11(1) (k), note 17, above.

27 Article 14 (g), ibid.

28 Articles 26 and 27, ibid.

while translations were protected for 50 years or 'lectures' were only protected for 50 years owed its origin to the lack of a consistent basis for distinction (as already argued above).

The other key change was to stop the grant of a compulsory licence to private individuals although use by the government in cases of national requirements of development would continue.[29] The government issued a Regulation (No. 1 of 1989) stating the particular circumstances and the manner in which foreign works might be translated and/or reproduced for use in education, science, research and development on payment of remuneration to the right holder(s). An exception to the government's disavowal of copyright (mentioned above) was inserted in the new law to maintain copyright in prehistoric remains, historical and other national and cultural objects.[30] An additional change was the further tightening of the sanctions against criminal actions of infringement and the grant of special powers of investigation into copyright offences to a department to be established within the Ministry of Justice.[31]

Indonesia introduced amendments to the Copyright Law to make it TRIPS-consistent. The amendments (Copyright Law No. 12 of 1997) recognized the exclusivity of rental rights to computer programs and sound recordings and extended the protection period of computer programs to 50 years. Still, that was not considered sufficient and Copyright Law No. 19 of 29 July 2002 (which came into force in July 2003) repealed all earlier law on copyright. One novelty of the new law is in the provisions that meted out criminal penalties for 'piracy' and civil injunctions against 'pirates' as well as further extensions of protection for neighbouring rights such as sound recordings, particularly for activities involving renting and broadcasting of such works. Another is a provision (Article 10) granting the state copyright in cultural, historical and cultural artefacts as well as in folklore and 'works of popular culture' such as songs, stories, handicraft and dances. According to Article 31, such copyright is for an unlimited period. The new provision is however a culmination of years of searching for a solution in IP terms of a problem that Indonesia has always perceived in protecting its rich cultural heritage. Prior to this, the Cultural Heritage Law No. 5, 1992 (1), issued by way of implementing the Convention Concerning the Protection of the World Cultural and Natural Heritage of 6 July 1989 that Indonesia had ratified, provided legal recognition and devices for managing the sector.

Patent law

The Patent Law (Law No. 6 of 1989), which came into effect in 1991, excluded from protection inventions related to the production of food and beverages, new

29 Article 15, ibid.

30 Article 10(1), ibid.

31 Article 47, ibid.

types of animals or plants, and methods of treating animals and humans.[32] It unequivocally stated that the importation of a patented article or process would not constitute use of a patent.[33] Patents were valid for 14 years with possible extension for another two. A 'Simple Patent' (obviously another name for 'petty patent'), issued for inventions that fall short of the requirements for a patent and have 'practical utility value',[34] lasted for five years.

The patent law also allowed the issue of compulsory licence together with a stipulation as to the amount of royalty and the method of payment. This could be done through a court order where implementation of a patent had not taken place in Indonesia despite 'opportunities for commercial implementation.'[35] The government too was given power to use a patented product or process, subject to a Presidential Decision and the payment of compensation, where the patented product or process was considered important for national defence and security.[36] The decision of the government was final and could not be appealed from. Finally, the 1989 Indonesia patent law offered no 'pipeline' protection (that is protection against unfair commercial use of undisclosed test and other data supplied to the relevant authorities for licensing of drugs).

The US openly called for a change in the patent law. The 1997 Report of the USTR protested that 'Several areas of concern remain, including compulsory licensing provisions, a relatively short term of protection (14 years), and a provision allowing the import of certain patented raw materials. In addition, concerns remain regarding Indonesia's law and regulations on local working requirements and patent cancellation.' Inevitably, the patent law was further amended by Patent Law No. 13 of 1997; however a more comprehensive law, the Patent Law No. 14 of August 2001, was issued to replace (and consolidate) all prior law. Significant changes introduced by the new law are the lengthening of the patent term to 20 years per Article 8 (that for 'simple patents' to 10, per Article 9) and the removal of many aspects of the law the US objected to. Thus the exclusion from patentability for plant and animal varieties was deleted, although the provision for compulsory licensing was not removed totally.

Other IP rights

Until recently, trade secrets could only be protected in Indonesia through contractual provisions. However, Article 322 of the Criminal Code made it an offence for an employee to disclose information pertaining to his employer. There are no design rights or laws regarding plant or animal varieties yet.

32 Article 7, the Patent Law No. 6 of 1989.
33 Article 20, ibid.
34 Article 6, ibid.
35 Articles 81–93, ibid.
36 Articles 104–108, ibid.

Indonesia enacted a Plant Variety Protection law in 2000 and introduced three new pieces of legislation, the Trade Secrets Law, the Industrial Design Law and the Integrated Circuits Law in 2001, 'despite the continuing economic and political crisis' but in an apparent bid 'to regain trust and support from foreign investors and the international market'.[37]

Membership of treaties

In the international arena, Indonesia withdrew from the Berne Convention in 1958 and remained outside it until 1997 when it rejoined. Indonesia has had a reciprocal arrangement with some EU countries from 1 June 1988 regarding the protection of sound recordings. Copyright protection was similarly extended to US works, and not just to sound recordings alone, pursuant to the bilateral agreement signed on 24 March 1989 between them. Indonesia had been a member of the Paris Convention from 1950, even when its patent law was still the colonial version.

As part of its drive to conform to TRIPS, Indonesia acceded to the Patent Cooperation Treaty, the Berne Convention and the Trademark Law Treaty in 1997 as well as the WIPO Copyright Treaty (on 6 March 2002) and the WIPO Performances and Phonograms Treaty (on 15 February 2005).

Intellectual Property in Malaysia

Malaysian IP started in the different territories of its present day federal units at a time in the nineteenth century when Britain, as the colonial power, controlled them separately or in groups. Thus the Straits Settlements (made up of Penang, Malacca and Singapore, the latter joining the Federation in 1963 but leaving it in 1965) adopted the earliest copyright law, the Telegram Copyright Ordinance, in 1902. The law was designed to protect newspaper establishments which purchased news stories from abroad from unfair competition by rival newspapers. The Federated Malay States followed suit with a similar enactment in 1911. When the UK Copyright Act 1911 came out, the Straits Settlements incorporated it first through local legislation, the Copyright Ordinance of 1914. The Ordinance was later introduced into the Federated Malay States in 1930 and into other regions of present day Malaysia. The replacement of the 1911 Act in the UK by the 1956 Act gave rise to further adjustments and adoptions by one state or another of that latest Act. The result of this was that, neither in 1957, when Malaysia became independent, nor in 1963, when the latest additions to the federal structure were allowed, was there a single federal copyright law as such. That was achieved only

37 [Anonymous] 'Indonesia: Parliament strengthens IP legislation', *IPAsia*, December 2000/January 2001, at 13.

in 1969 when a new law, the Copyright Act 1969, was issued, superseding the diverse array of laws existing in the different states until then.[38]

Besides the divers types of copyright statutes (including those based on the UK Acts of 1911 and 1956 and others), a number of Designs, Trademarks and Patents Ordinances were issued in Malaya, Sabah and Sarawak at different dates (between 1949 and 1957) but with substantial similarities across the three states. The content of the Ordinances reflected faithfully the laws in force in the governing colonial state, namely the UK. Designs continued to be protected through first registration in the UK on the basis of the United Kingdom Designs (Protection) Ordinance in the three states. The trademark law provided for registration in two parts, including certification marks. Part B marks would only have been registrable if they had been in use for two years prior to the application. The use of the common law passing off action was also available to protect unregistered marks.

By contrast, the patent laws of the three states only allowed re-registration of UK granted patents. Applications even from Malaysia had to be submitted in the UK and a grant obtained there before a certificate of registration was given to the patentee in Malaysia. The Patents (Rights of Government) Act 1967 allowed the grant of an authorization by the state to government departments or individuals to use patented inventions. The Act was clearly intended to introduce a compulsory licensing regime but the novelty was only in one aspect: the user would not be liable to pay any compensation to the patentee.

A new set of IP laws was introduced for the whole of Malaysia by repealing the existing ones at various stages. Thus the Copyright Act 1969, the Trademarks Act 1976 and the Patents Act 1983 were issued by repealing either the respective British colonial ordinances or the laws enacted for what later became federal states.

Trademark law

The Trademark Act 1976 (Act 175) covered trademarks used in relations to goods.[39] Although marks could be in printed form or 'other visual representation',[40] colours were not supposed in themselves to constitute trademarks. Trademarks were defined in the same way as in the 1938 UK Trademarks Act. As per the repealed laws operating previously in parts of present day Malaysia (i.e. before the Federation), the Register was divided into two parts; marks already registered in that way would continue to be protected.[41] The registrability of marks was dependent on the same grounds as the 1938 UK Act and those grounds were expounded similarly.[42]

38 For a succinct account of the early period of Malaysian copyright law, see, Khaw Lake Tee, *Copyright Law in Malaysia*, Butterworths Asia: Singapore, 1994, at 2–5.

39 See Section 3(1) of the Trade Mark Act 1976 for the definition of 'trade mark'.

40 Section 3(2) (a), ibid.

41 Section 6(2), ibid.

42 Sections 10–13, ibid.

It was possible to register similar marks as associated marks[43] or as a series in one registration[44] (and hence considered to have the same legal effect[45]); the same held true for defensive marks.[46]

A system of appeals to the High Court has been in place in cases of refusal for registration of marks.[47] Also, opposition can be presented to any acceptance of a mark for registration (signalled by the advertisement of the mark).[48] The Act did not allow registration of colours as distinctive marks except where their use could become distinctive;[49] similarly an application was to be restricted to one class of goods.[50] Yet, prior use was no absolute requirement, only a proposal to use,[51] even if by an assignee or registered user.[52]

The duration of protection for trademarks was seven years and renewable for further periods of 14 years. The effect of registration of a mark was that it was prima facie valid[53] and in all respects valid after seven years from registration.[54] A continuous three-year period of non-use of a work might lead to removal from the register, as would a registration without a bona fide intention to use the mark.[55] Trademarks were assignable with or without the goodwill of the respective business but for this to be effective it needed to be entered in the register and notice of it issued through an advertisement.

The Trademark Act 1976 was amended through the Trademarks (Amendment) Act of 1994 (Act A881) which entered into force on 1 December 1997. The Amendment extended to 'services' the protection already available to goods. Most of the sections in the Amendment dealt with such a change in many sections of the 1976 Act. The division of the Register into part A and part B was retained.[56] The provision as to colour as a mark or the restriction in an application to a single class of goods was not changed either. However, the duration of trademarks was raised to 10 years,[57] while the renewal period was brought down to 10.[58] In line with the change in copyright law to accommodate international demands for protection

43 Section 22, ibid.
44 Section 24(1), ibid.
45 Section 24(2), ibid.
46 Section 58, ibid.
47 Section 25(5) and the following, ibid.
48 Section 28, ibid.
49 Section 13(1), ibid.
50 Section 25(2), ibid.
51 Section 25(1), ibid.
52 Section 26(1), ibid.
53 Section 32(1), ibid.
54 Section 37, ibid.
55 Section 46(1), ibid.
56 Section 9, the Trade Marks (Amendment) Act 1994.
57 Section 25, ibid.
58 Section 31, ibid.

of IP that could not have been recognized ordinarily under Malaysian law, the Amendment extended similar protection in the area of trademarks too.[59]

Malaysia issued further changes to the trademark law in 2000. The Trademarks (Amendment) Act 2000 abolished the division of the register into Part A and Part B, instituting a single standard for registrability ('capable of distinguishing'). It also introduced provisions for protection of well-known marks (Section 70B) as well as for refusal of registration of false or misleading geographical indications. The law has injected border enforcement measures (Part XIVA) in pursuit of similar requirements under TRIPS.

Malaysia has kept the common law of passing off for unregistered marks or other distinctive subject matter. The courts seem to understand this cause of action slightly differently than elsewhere. Thus in *Goodyear Tyre & Rubber Co. & Another* v. *Silverstone Tyre & Rubber Co. Sdn. Bhd.*,[60] the court refused to grant injunction for Goodyear on the basis that mere confusion of customers is not enough and that they should be able to recognize the source of tyres.

Copyright law

The Copyright Act 1969 (Act 10) recognized all categories of works except performances,[61] but the additional major difference from laws of other countries was that the term of protection would be life plus 25 years for most works and only 25 for 'neighbouring rights'.[62] Just like in the UK, materials generated by or under the directions of the government bestowed copyright on the latter.[63] A novelty in the law was the attempt to introduce a standard of copyrightability in terms of 'sufficient effort'[64] having been expended in making the work – a solution which would have saved English copyright law from going through the trouble of establishing such a requirement in a line of cases including *Football League* v. *Littlewoods*![65] Another novelty was the possibility of obtaining a non-exclusive licence, subject to the payment of royalties, for purposes of publishing and producing materials in the national language.[66] The fair use exceptions allowed, apart from the other well-known ones, any dealings with copyright works for purposes of research, private use, the use in libraries and educational institutions or the communication to the public of any work where no profits or admission charge are made.[67] Otherwise, Section 14(2) of the Act specifically forbade parallel importing.

59 Section 50, ibid.
60 [1994] 1 MLJ 348.
61 Section 4, the Copyright Act 1969.
62 Section 5, ibid.
63 Section 7, ibid.
64 Section 4(2) (a), ibid.
65 [1959] Ch.637.
66 Section 16, note 61, above.
67 Section 8, ibid.

The Copyright Act 1969 was replaced by the Copyright Act 1987 (Act 332) because of Malaysia's commitment to embrace computer software in its copyright law and the pressure of the UK and the US on Malaysia to make it tighten the same law as well as enforcement mechanisms against alleged growing piracy. Just like the previous Act, the 1987 Act follows the system of automatic recognition without requiring any deposit or registration. Besides defining 'computer program',[68] the Act assimilated it to 'literary work'. A further novelty was the definition given to publication in Section 4(1): making copies available 'with the consent of the author or of any person lawfully claiming under the author in a manner sufficient to satisfy the reasonable requirements of the public'. Of the category of works to be protected, listed under Section 7, performances were left out.

The requirement of 'sufficient effort' for copyrightability that was introduced in the 1969 Act was kept in the 1987 version.[69] Similarly was retained copyright in government generated materials.[70] Major changes related to the duration of copyright; the previous term was generally extended by 25 years across the entire range so that musical, literary and artistic works (save photographic works) would be protected for the life of the author and 50 years afterwards. Derivative works are protected for 50 years from publication. Government use, reproduction or adaptation of works with the payment of compensation are exempted from infringement action.[71] Individuals too could obtain non-exclusive licences to produce and publish a translation of a work in the national language on payment of royalties.[72] However, the grant of a compulsory licence is conditional on a number of requirements being met: proof that the said work has not been published in Malaysia within one year of first publication elsewhere or, if translated, has been out of print; that the applicant has sought authorization from the author but was denied; that the applicant could not find the owner; that the applicant pays the author royalties and preserves his moral rights.

For the first time ever (probably in view of Malaysia's ultimate objective of acceding to the Berne Convention), the 1987 Act recognized the moral rights of authors.[73] The Act also included criminal sanctions (fines and/or imprisonment) against infringers. Yet, of far reaching importance is the new section added in the Act iterating the enforcement measures (entry, removal, detention and forfeiture

---

68 Section 3 of the Copyright Act 987 defined it thus: 'an expression, in any language, code or notation, of a set of instructions whether with or without related information intended to cause a device having an information processing capability to perform a particular function either directly or after either or both of the following: (a) conversion to another language, code or notation; (b) reproduction in a different material form'.

69 Section 7(3) (a), ibid.

70 Section 11(1), ibid.

71 Section 24, ibid.

72 Section 31(2), ibid.

73 Section 25, ibid.

of an article) by the police authorities and controllers of copyright who have supervision powers over matters under the Act.[74]

The Act was modified by the Copyright (Amendment) Act 1990 (Act A775) both to clarify some provisions and incorporate changes in the interest of foreign (particularly US) proprietors of IP. A new Section 59A was inserted in the Copyright Act 1987, to make it obligatory for Malaysia to recognize works that had already been recognized in foreign countries; in a sense, this would exempt them from being disqualified under Malaysian laws if the latter are interpreted strictly and territorially.[75] The Amendment also made it possible for Malaysia to bring the earlier law in line with the soon-to-be adopted Berne Convention. Thus the definition of a literary work was amended to exclude official texts of the government, statutory and legislative bodies and judicial decisions.[76] Through an amendment of Section 13(b),[77] which was in any case ambiguous, 'performances, or showing or playing to the public' were instituted as exclusive to the right holders in the respective category of works. Further refinements were effected on the private and domestic use of sound recordings, films and other works too.[78]

A distinct change was the complete removal[79] of the allowances for the government to use any works without impunity (Section 24 of the Act). Section 36 of the 1987 Act which permitted some level of defence for parallel importation was changed to include actual or constructive knowledge ('ought reasonably to know') 'that the making of the article was carried out without the consent or licence of the owner of the copyright'.[80] A similar tightening of enforcement measures has been noticeable too; whereas police powers were to be used in cases of infringing copies surfacing or detected, now mere suspicion that they might be would serve as grounds for action.[81]

The new set of revised laws adopted in Malaysia were meant, according to a reported statement of the Domestic Trade and Consumer Affairs Minister, Abu Hassan Omar, on 14 June 1997, to 'attract new foreign investment to the country's high-tech industry'.[82] Still, a further change of copyright law was introduced through the Copyright (Amendment) Act 2000, in force from 2001, largely devoted to the protection of performers. The exclusive rights of performers extend to sound recordings, rentals, broadcasts and any reproductions. The new law also allows foreign proprietors to instruct agents to act on their behalf to prosecute copyright claims by removing the earlier restriction of such to locally registered entities.

74 Section 5, ibid.

75 See Section 21, the Copyright (Amendment) Act 1990.

76 Section 5(3) (e), ibid.

77 In its 1987 form it referred to 'Communications to the public'.

78 Section 13, note 75, above.

79 Section 8, ibid.

80 Section 9, ibid.

81 Section 13, ibid.

82 [Anonymous] *World Intellectual Property Report*, Vol. 11, No. 3, March 1997, at 88.

Patent law

The Patents Act 1983 (Act 291) has created an independent system of patent protection for Malaysia (although the influence of the UK Patent Act 1977 is apparent[83]). This is because it dispenses with the previous practice of re-registration of patents granted in the UK for inventions of universal novelty. Patents were valid for 15 years after grant[84] until the changes in 2003. The 1983 Act also provides for a system of protecting 'utility innovations',[85] defined as models of implements, tools or process which have practical utility, for a period of five years (and extendable once only for a further five years); however, the innovations do not have to be novel or involve an inventive step and the like, as inventions. The Act excludes from protection plant or animal varieties or 'essentially biological processes … other than man-made living' micro-organisms.[86] Furthermore, acts done only for scientific research are considered non-infringing.[87]

The Patents Act 1983 incorporates a scheme for compulsory licensing. For this to happen, it must be proved that, after three years from grant, the patent has not been worked 'without any legitimate reason', or that the article covered by it is being sold at high prices or does not meet public demand.[88] Any grant of such a licence will state the time limit within which the licensee must work the invention, the royalty to be paid to the patentee and the manner of payment.[89] As in specified laws of many countries across the world, the licence cannot be used for importation purposes. The government or its departments have also been empowered to make, use or exercise any invention without being encumbered by any payment or liability to the right owner; the unconditional manner in which this has been laid down suggests that it might not be long before some revision becomes necessary in the way that such has been effected in copyright law (in particular Section 24, discussed above).

Provisions that prohibit infringement and provide remedies in the Patents Act 1983 are similar to those one would find everywhere: civil and criminal remedies including penalties for false attribution of having a patent or for falsely declaring a patent being pending. Of far greater significance may be the special enforcement mechanism laid down in the Act. A public officer (which might also be a police officer) would be appointed to exercise the powers, specified in Sections 68–78, of arrest, search and seizure against suspected sources of infringement and offence.

83 A case in point is the determination of ownership and the provision for 'equitable remuneration' for employee inventors who have to give up the ownership to the employer. See Section 20(1), Patents Act 1983.

84 Section 35(1), ibid.

85 Section 17, ibid.

86 Section 13(1) (b), ibid.

87 Section 37(1), ibid.

88 Section 49(1), ibid.

89 Section 52, ibid.

The Patents (Amendment) Act 2003 has changed the patent term to 20 years from registration. It has also made changes in the formalities of filing and public inspection of applications. More important are the new provisions allowing parallel importation, the use of patented drugs for the purposes of developing and submitting information to the Drug Control Authority. The Act also trimmed the scope of compulsory licensing allowed earlier, including to the government. A new test of failure to obtain a licence from the patentee on 'reasonable commercial terms' has been established.

Other IP rights

The old Design (Protection) Ordinances in the federal units of Malaysia but based on the 1949 UK Industrial Designs Act have given way to the Industrial Designs Act 1996, in force in 1999. Apart from the usual provisions found in nearly all jurisdictions, the law provides for a maximum of 15 years of protection for qualifying designs, an indigenous law and registration facility.

Other additions to the menu of IP laws are the Geographical Indications Act 2000, the Layout Designs of Integrated Circuits Act 2000 and the Optical Discs Act 2000. The latter provides for the licensing and regulation of the manufacture of optical discs. Manufacturers have obligations to use identification codes on such discs to enable tracking of any possible infringement activities.

Trade secrets are still protected under the common law following from long-established English law rules. They may of course be protected through contractual obligations. By contrast, no animal or plant varieties are yet covered by any law.

Membership of IP conventions

As far as membership of international treaties goes, Malaysia joined the Paris Convention on 1 January 1989, the Berne Convention on 1 October 1990 and the Patent Cooperation Treaty in 2006.

Intellectual Property in the Philippines

The Philippines has had, for much longer than any country in ASEAN, the full gamut of IP laws that one might consider appropriate for a developed nation. The antecedents of these laws were the Spanish laws of IP extended to the Philippines through a Royal Decree of May 1887; these laws continued in effect under the US colonial authorities by virtue of the treaty of transfer of sovereignty between the US and Spain. Subsequently, the US reorganized the administrative machinery for IP (1901) and replaced the patent law through a 1913 Act which transplanted US patent law to the Philippines.[90] The copyright law too was changed in 1924 (Act No. 3134). US works became protectable by virtue of the patent and copyright laws thus passed under US tutelage. The 1935 Constitution (Section 4) embraced a variant of the famous US provision which laid the ground for the protection of works of authors and inventors. This was followed after the Second World War and with the full independence of the Philippines in 1946 by a series of IP laws.

Trademark law

The trademark law of 20 June 1947 (Republic Act No. 166) recognized trade and service marks as well as famous marks. A memorandum order issued on 20 November 1980 made it clear that non-owners of famous marks could not register them even if the marks had not been used before by the owners. However, trademark registration was optional. All applications (except those based on foreign registration) would have had to prove actual use. The Philippines had two registers, a principal and supplementary register for those already distinct enough and for those not so as yet, respectively. The term of protection was 20 years and was renewable depending on submission of affidavit of use or explanation of special circumstances that prevented use. Unfair competition law and the law against false trade description added to the protection provided by the trademark law.

In an attempt to bring its laws into line with TRIPS, the Philippines introduced an entire code of intellectual property in 1997. The Intellectual Property Code made substantive changes to the trademark law. It eliminated the prior use requirement for registration[91] as well as the Supplemental Register.[92] These changes in Philippine law only reproduce similar steps taken in other countries (such as Australia and the UK). The removal of the prior (actual) use requirement is in line with Article 15(3) of TRIPS which prohibits such a practice.

Other changes introduced by the Code are the reduction in term of protection to 10 years[93] and the period of tendering proof of use to be within three years from filing and affidavit of use within a year after the fifth anniversary.[94] The earlier requirement was to present affidavits on the fifth, tenth and fifteenth anniversaries. In addition, the law now allows a single application for multiple classes of registration[95] (again in line with the WIPO Trademark Law Treaty though the Philippines has yet to accede to that Treaty).

90 Jesus S.J. Sayoc, 'Protection of Intellectual Property in the Philippines', *Report*, ASEAN Law Association General Assembly 25–9 October 1982, Kuala Lumpur.

91 This is implied by Section 124.2 of the 1997 Intellectual Property Code.

92 Section 137.1, ibid.

93 Section 145, ibid.

94 Ibid.

95 Sections 124.3 and 128, ibid.

While the definition of 'mark' in Section 121 appears to be all encompassing, suggesting as it does that 'any visible sign' capable of distinguishing goods or services will cover 'colour' too, the registration of a mark consisting of 'colour alone' is however still an excluded subject-matter.[96] The only exception is where the colour would already have, through use, gained distinctiveness.[97] Clearly, the law will be subjected to further revision in this regard.

Copyright law

The copyright law (Act No. 3134) was replaced by the Presidential Decree No. 49, Decree on the Protection of Intellectual Property, which became effective from 1972. The law partially dispensed with the previous (apparently an imitation of the US) requirement of registration to claim copyright. The Decree made the registration of a work and deposition of two copies with the National Library conditions for any entitlement to recovery of damages,[98] leaving out other remedies for the copyright owner such as seeking injunction or criminal prosecution against infringers, delivering up and/or destruction of infringing articles.[99] The copyright law also made unlimited exceptions for private use of reproductions, translation and adaptation of works 'lawfully made accessible to the public'.[100] Similarly exempted were recitations and performances of such works for educational, religious and charitable purposes. No copyright subsisted in works produced for the government subject to the requirement of prior approval should any use of such works be for profit; the concerned government agency might also impose the payment of royalties, apparently where exploitation of such works was for profit.[101]

The Decree also recognized, apart from the general rights one finds in copyright law of many nations, *droit de suite* (subject to registration in the National Library),[102] moral rights[103] and the rights of performers, broadcasters and sound recorders, although the terms of protection would be limited to 25 years after such works were made.[104] A compulsory licence system for translations was in place if the original work had not been translated into the national or other languages in the Philippines within five years after publication.[105] It extended protection to

96 Section 123.1(l), ibid.
97 Section 132.2, ibid.
98 Section 26, Presidential Decree No. 49.
99 Section 28, ibid.
100 Section 10, ibid.
101 Section 9, ibid.
102 Sections 31–2, ibid.
103 Sections 34–40, ibid.
104 Section 55, ibid.
105 Section 14, ibid.

computer programs as well (having abandoned Philippine's earlier attempt[106] to introduce a *sui generis* system).

The 1997 Intellectual Property Code provides for protection of 'literary and artistic works' ('original works') as well as what it contrasts as 'derivative works'. The uncanny resemblance to Indonesian copyright law as regards the cited distinction and the difficulty that a long list of the 'works' presents to analysis, is immediately apparent. The 'works' attract copyright 'by the sole fact of their creation, irrespective of their mode or form of expression'.[107] Previous exclusions from copyright appear to have been kept as have been 'follow-up rights' and moral rights. The Code has also included a section for rights of performers and producers of sound recordings and broadcasts.

The copyright provisions of the Code have been extended to the Internet through the 2000 Electronic Commerce Act. Nonetheless, the Code has been criticized by the USTR as containing 'ambiguous provisions relating to the rights of copyright owners over broadcast, rebroadcast, cable retransmission, or satellite retransmission of their works, and burdensome restrictions affecting contracts to license software and other technology'.[108]

Patent law

The patent law of 20 June 1947 (Republic Act no. 165) established universal standards employed in the industrialized countries for inventions as well as industrial designs; it required foreign applications to be notarized and authenticated by a Philippine consul. The law also allowed protection for ornamental designs (design patents). A change was effected in 1953 to include utility models as protectable subject-matter for five years and renewable for a maximum of two periods of five years. The duration of a patent was 17 years while that for designs was the same as for utility models. On the other hand, a provision allowed the grant of a compulsory licence over an invention where it had not been worked to meet local demand adequately. Again, licensing of patents between foreign and domestic companies was required to have prior approval by the respective government body (Bureau of Patents, Trademarks and Technology Transfer) and registration.

The 1997 Intellectual Property Code defines and lists the criteria for patentability or exclusions, very much in line with other experiences elsewhere. It also specifies the usual conditions under which compulsory licences can be issued, the terms of protection for patents and utility models (respectively, 20 years from filing or a non-renewable seven years).

---

106 See, Gert Kolle, 'Computer Software Protection – Present Situation and Future Prospects', *Copyright* 13:70, March 1977, at 9

107 Section 172.2, note 91, above.

108 See, US Trade Representative (USTR), '2008 National Trade Estimate Report on Foreign Trade Barriers' at http://www.ustr.gov/reports/index.html.

Other IP rights

Both the 1947 Trademark Act and the 1997 Code contain identical provisions for 'unfair competition'. In both of them, the provision is linked to trademarks instead of all forms of IP. Essentially, the provision (Section 168 of the Code) outlaws any deceptive or other means 'contrary to good faith' in appropriating someone's good will or mark (whether registered or unregistered). It cites examples of unfair practices such as imitation of appearances of goods or their packaging. The consequences to a person in breach of the unfair competition rules are similar to those who infringe registered marks.[109]

The 1997 Code has not included any provisions for the protection of trade secrets (i.e. confidentiality, etc.). The general practice of protecting such secrets by placing an obligation on a contracting party will obviously continue, although the Philippines was expected to introduce a law by 2000. Protection of layout designs for integrated circuits has been covered by a law issued in 2001. Plant varieties have likewise been brought under a new law, the Philippine Plant Variety Protection Act of 2002.

Membership of IP conventions

The Philippines has a bilateral arrangement for the protection of copyright with the US (from 1948). It has also been a member of two of the major IP conventions (Berne in 1951, Paris since 1965). In recent years, it has joined the Patent Cooperation Treaty (in 2001) and both the WIPO Copyright Treaty and the WIPO Performances and Phonograms Treaty in 2002.

Intellectual Property in Singapore

The IP laws of Singapore depended very much on the parent laws in the UK for a long time, even after independence. In the area of patents, the local law (the Registration of Patents Act) merely facilitated the continued application of the UK patent law, although indirectly. Copyright protection was available in Singapore for a long time on the basis of the UK Copyright Act 1911, even while the UK itself adopted a new one in 1956. The Trademarks Act (Cap 332), first introduced as the Trademarks Ordinance No. 38 of 1938, closely followed and reproduced the 1938 UK Act. Changes have been effected in all these areas and the general direction has been, just as for the laws as a whole, towards a comprehensive legal framework.

109 Section 168.4, note 91, above.

Trademark law

The 1939 Trademarks Act defined a 'trade mark'[110] and the grounds for registrability in the same way as the previous UK Trademarks Act 1938;[111] the Singapore Act also adopted from the latter the characteristic division of the register in two parts.[112] The Act allowed registration of associated trademarks where the marks are identical or applied to the same goods (and therefore operate as series of trademarks).[113] Opposition to the registration of a trademark might be submitted to the Registrar whose decisions were subject to appeal to the regular courts.[114]

The assignment of marks (including associated marks) was permissible subject to registration of the user[115] and that there would be no trafficking in the mark,[116] although there was no requirement that there be a connection of the mark with the goodwill of the business.[117] The validity of marks registered on the A register would be conclusive after a period of seven years had passed;[118] on the other hand, the use of a mark in Singapore for not less than two years or registration in Part B in the UK might be sufficient grounds for an application to be registered in Part B.[119] A statutory declaration was expected to accompany such an application. The duration of registration was for seven years and renewable for period of 14 years. On the other hand, the lack of bona fide intention to use the mark or non-use of a mark for a continuous period of five years could entail cancellation of the mark.[120]

In the area of infringement, Section 70 made counterfeiting (nowhere defined in the Act) of any mark an offence with penalties of imprisonment and/or fine. The prosecution of counterfeiters by the police proceeded on the basis of Section 73 of the Trademarks Act. While, in general, the complainants themselves are expected to pursue and stop the infringers, such activities by the police authorities signalled a readiness to intervene when the scale of infringement became flagrant.

Various changes were effected on the Trademark Act 1939 after Singapore became independent in 1965. However, the most comprehensive reform was undertaken through the Trademarks Act 1998 which incorporated aspects of the respective laws of UK (1994) and Australia (1995). The 1998 Act extended the scope of trademarks by allowing three-dimensional shapes and colours. It also

110 Section 2, the Trade Marks Act 1939.
111 Sections 10–11 (for Part A); Sections 12–13 (for Part B), ibid.
112 Section 5, ibid.
113 Sections 26–7, ibid.
114 Section 19, ibid.
115 Sections 29–30 together with Section 43, ibid.
116 Section 30(6), ibid.
117 Section 42(1), ibid.
118 Section 48, ibid.
119 Section 12(1), ibid.
120 Section 40(1), ibid.

provided a special regime for well-known marks, retained the exhaustion of rights and abolished the division of the register into parts A and B. In addition, the law removed the concept of associated marks and replaced it with collective marks and the need to register licences. Border protection measures form part of the new law as well. Finally, application procedures were further streamlined such that a single application can include many classes of goods or services.

Further changes were introduced in 2004, through the Trademarks (Amendment) Act 2004, to implement the US–Singapore FTA. Thus a new category of 'well known marks' was created, separate from those recognized in the 1998 law to cater for those marks that are known among the public in Singapore.

As regards unregistered marks, the law of passing off continues to operate by virtue of a specific provision in the 1998 Act.

Copyright law

A Committee on Revision of Copyright Laws that was established to remove the anomaly of Singapore keeping the old UK Copyright Act 1911 while the UK itself had made subsequent changes decided to draft a completely new law rather than revise the old one. The draft law however followed the provisions of the Australian Copyright Act of 1968,[121] which was in turn based on the UK Copyright Act 1956. The fact that there was an international factor at play was suggested by *The Asian Wall Street Journal*,[122] which reported that a four-man delegation from the USA scrutinized the draft. Wright quotes the *Journal* as writing that the draft law emerged 'undoubtedly as a result of strong pressure which Singapore is under from American producers who are reportedly lobbying the United States government to deny Singapore [any preferential trade] … unless it improves its copyright protection'.[123] He adds further 'The pirate industry is a thriving part of the Singapore economy which the Government here seems to be reluctant to completely dismantle … The Government of Singapore therefore seems to be caught between the rock of Singaporean interests and the hard place of pressure from foreign private and government sources.'[124]

121 Ricketson referred to the Australian act as having been dubbed 'somewhat outdated even at the time it was passed'. See Staniforth Ricketson, *The Law of Intellectual Property*, Law Book Company: Sydney, 1984, at p. 50. Compare, however, George Wei's remarks that the Copyright Act 1987 'gives Singapore one of the most advanced systems of copyright protection known to common law countries'. George Wei, *The Law of Copyright in Singapore*, Singapore National Printers Ltd., 1989, at viii.

122 See *The Asian Wall Street Journal*, 6 August 1985 at 1 and 11 quoted in Shelley E. Wright, 'Copyright in Singapore: Some recent developments', *Malayan Law Journal* 1, 1 April 1986, at cviii–cxviii.

123 Ibid., at 26.

124 Ibid., at 29–30.

The Copyright Act 1987 repealed all previous laws with any full or partial coverage of copyright subject-matter. The Act covers computer programs (which are incidentally defined[125] in exactly the same manner as in the equivalent Malaysian law of the same year[126]) by assimilating them to literary works.[127] The incidence as well as duration of copyright in works and 'subject-matter other than works' (that is derivatives) are also treated similarly. The only exception was the lack of protection for performances.[128] The fair dealing exceptions involve the use of works so long as the purpose is for research or private study.[129] The use in either case is restricted to non-profit activities or to 'not more than a reasonable portion of the work' concerned; besides, corporate or commercial research are out of bounds. The Act also incorporates rules regarding the copying of works by libraries for archival purposes,[130] including preservation.[131] The copying of 'insubstantial' portions of works by educational institutes is similarly exempted.[132] The making of a larger portion and in multiple copies might be allowed, on payment of 'equitable remuneration', for purpose of conducting courses provided there are no commercial outlets at 'ordinary' commercial prices.[133] The Act goes towards meeting the needs of handicapped readers.[134] The grant of a compulsory licence for translations into the official languages of Singapore and publication thereof[135] as well as the reproduction of works unavailable in Singapore or not on sale for six months after first publication elsewhere[136] seems to be limited to instructional use or scholarship and research. The conditions for grant are similar to the Malaysian approach.

The nearest the Act came to recognizing moral rights was in its prohibition of false attribution of authorship.[137] The copyright in materials generated under the auspices of the government accrues to it[138] and, indeed, the government reserves the right to use any work on payment of corresponding royalties.[139] Finally, the Act also affirmed the principle of reciprocal protection for foreign nationals[140] as Singapore continued to remain outside the Berne Convention until 1998.

125 Section 7(1), Copyright Act 1987.
126 See Section 3, ibid. The definition has been reproduced, at note 68, above.
127 Section 7(1), note 125, above.
128 See Sections 82–6, ibid.
129 Section 35, ibid.
130 Sections 45–7, ibid.
131 Section 48, ibid.
132 Section 51, ibid.
133 Section 52, ibid.
134 Section 54, ibid.
135 Section 144, ibid.
136 Section 145, ibid.
137 Sections 188–93, ibid.
138 Section 197, ibid.
139 Section 198, ibid.
140 Section 184, ibid.

Further amendments of the Copyright Act 1987, introduced in 1998, related to the use of copyright material in the digital media, border enforcement measures and the recognition of rights of performers. Yet another wave of reforms was effected through the Copyright (Amendment) Act 2004 and Copyright (Amendment) Act 2005 by way of implementing the WIPO Copyright Treaty and the US–Singapore FTA (such as the extension of the copyright term).

Patent law

Until 1994, The Registration of Patents Act (Cap 271) allowed re-registration, within three years, of patents first issued in the UK or issued (from 1982) per the European Patent Convention by designating the UK as the country sought by the patentee. A locally issued Patent (Compulsory) Licensing Act provided a mechanism for the making of foreign patented inventions (largely for manufacturing and construction) available to local manufacturers where the patented invention failed to be worked or imported to satisfy existing demand. Applications for the grant of a compulsory licence would be made to the Registrar three years after grant of the patent in the UK.

Singapore broke loose from the patent law of the UK by issuing its own Patents Act 1994 (Cap 221). The independent patent law provides for general rules that are found in most patent laws elsewhere: the grounds for patentability, procedures for grant, dealings in patents, determination of infringement and remedies. Most notable is the absence of any reference in Section 13(2) to plant and animal varieties or microorganisms that are usually excluded in laws of many countries and still allowed under the TRIPS. Singapore appears therefore to have more than fully embraced the TRIPS formula of allowing patents 'in all fields of technology',[141] although a roundabout exclusion found its way in Section 16(2) where methods of treating humans and animals are declared not to be taken as capable of 'industrial application'. One wonders whether this was meant to improve upon the omission in Section 13(2) or to smuggle in the exception at the least detectable place! Yet, Section 13(3) exempts a 'product' (as opposed, therefore, to the 'method') from exclusion 'merely because it is invented for use in any such method'.

Special measures have been introduced in light of the Patent Cooperation Treaty (of which Singapore subsequently became a member) regarding applications which are linked to other corresponding international applications. The applicant in such a context may have to supply English translations of any relevant information[142] or file a copy of the research report produced abroad.[143] By contrast, Singapore residents are not allowed, at the pain of a fine and/or imprisonment, to apply directly for a patent with a foreign patent office unless an application has already

141 See Article 27(1), the TRIPS.

142 Section 29(4), the Patents Act 1994.

143 Section 29(5), ibid.

been placed at the national office for not less than two months.[144] Moreover, the application should not pertain to sensitive matters (defence, public safety).[145]

The term of protection for 20 years is in accord with what many nations have adopted in the last two decades. Unless court proceedings are taking place or the validity of the patent is not under attack, the Registrar may allow a patentee to amend his specifications even after grant. On the other hand, a patentee may be able to restore a lapsed patent provided he does so within 12 months after the lapse.[146]

The patentee has rights of licensing, assigning or mortgaging his patent provided the transaction is in writing and signed[147] as well as entered in the register of patents kept at the Registry.[148] Restrictive conditions inserted by the patentee in such transactions are outlawed, just as in European patent laws, for instance.[149] A similar requirement is imposed on patents which the owner wishes to place under the voluntary licensing scheme ('licence of right').[150] On the other hand, extensive rules were introduced in the 1994 Act to use compulsory licensing as a means of forcing the working of a patented subject-matter in Singapore.[151] Apart from the usual grounds for such licensing (non-working for three years after grant, inability to meet local demand or the high prices they are been offered for), the Patents Act 1994 listed broader economic consequences that might have flowed from the refusal of the patentee to grant a licence: not meeting the export demand; not adding to the efficiency in or even preventing the contribution to the working of another patent; and the establishment or development of commercial and industrial activities being unfairly prejudiced.[152] In addition, the Registrar could grant a licence on inventions relating to food, medicine or curative devices[153] without going through the stages that were necessary for a normal compulsory licence, already mentioned. Perhaps more curious was the provision allowing a compulsory licensee to import the patented product,[154] contrary to what might have seemed to be the inherent rationale behind compulsory licensing, namely the desire to encourage local working. It may be recalled that the Malaysian law has explicitly outlawed such an avenue in the use of a compulsory licence.[155] Nevertheless, even in Singapore, the use by the government or its departments,

144 Section 34, ibid.

145 Applications which might consist of information will be given separate treatment, per Section 33, ibid.

146 Section 39, ibid., read with Rule 53, the Patent Rules 1995.

147 Section 41, ibid.

148 Section 42, ibid.

149 Sections 51–2, ibid.

150 Section 53, ibid.

151 Sections 55–60, ibid.

152 Section 55, ibid.

153 Section 56, ibid.

154 Section 56(4), ibid.

155 See Section 52 of the Malaysian Patents Act 1983.

without the consent of the patentee, of inventions with implications for 'foreign defence purposes' and for public health is guaranteed under Sections 61–2 of the Act. This power might be greater in emergency conditions where all categories of inventions may be pooled to sustain the economic life, alleviate suffering and restore supplies.[156]

Exemptions from infringement are acts done privately and with no commercial consequence as well as experimental use.[157] The importation or use of patented matter placed on the market with the consent of the patentee is also excluded.[158] A concern that remains is the absence of opposition proceedings against a grant although a revocation proceeding can be initiated afterwards.[159] The possible grant of a patent irrespective of examination results to the contrary[160] may have to be changed to make the Act consistent with international practice.

The Patents Act 1994 was subjected to changes by the Patents (Amendment) Act 1995 largely, as the explanatory statement attached to the Bill introduced in Parliament indicated,[161] to bring the Act into line with Singapore's impending obligations under the TRIPS.[162] The major changes relate to a further extension of the patentable subject matter, a reining in of the compulsory licence system and government use of patented inventions. The exclusions from patentability in Section 13(2) have been removed completely together with the power given to the Minister concerned to vary the same range of exclusions (found in practically every national patent legislation across the globe) in accordance with the state of development in science and technology.[163]

156 Section 65, note 142, above.

157 Section 66(2) (a) and (b), ibid.

158 Section 66(2) (g), ibid.

159 Section 80, ibid.

160 Section 30(3), ibid. does not indicate that such a failure might lead to refusal; besides, all references in Section 30(2) to the receipt of examination reports carry no indication as what use they might be put to.

161 Bill No. 31/95, at 9.

162 It might be apposite to cite that the report for 1995 of the Office of the US Trade Representative (USTR) commented negatively on the new patent law in Singapore. It stated that 'the provisions of the law concerning compulsory licensing and government use are inconsistent with the TRIPS agreement, and in some respects, inferior to the provisions in Singapore's previous patent law'. See *1995 National Trade Estimate Report on Foreign Trade Barriers*, 277–9, at 278. The annual reports are now available at http://www.ustr.gov/reports/index.html.

163 Section 3, the Patents (Amendment) Act 1995. It may be interesting to see whether and how the Patents and Trademarks Office will refuse to accept any application for patents in discoveries, even literary works or schemes and presentation of information now that these have been unexplainably removed from the category of normal exclusions in patent law!

The resort to compulsory licensing has become restricted, by removing the old provisions[164] and instituting a new single provision[165] in their place that requires proof of insufficient supply of the patented invention in the local market or supply with unreasonable terms after the passage of three years from grant. The shift in the power to order a licence from the Registrar to the High Court adds to the narrowing down of any possibility of such a licence. Nevertheless, it should be noted that the major aim of such laws before the TRIPS sought to slice them beyond recognition was to promote indigenous working of inventions; thus the new-found concern for sufficiency of supply has effectively watered down the rationale for compulsory licensing so much that even importation can be categorized as working and therefore the chance of a licence being issued will be very remote indeed. This is not to say that the amendment in Singapore is anything spectacular; indeed it is a practice in line with the same kind of provision in the laws of the major industrial powers. Following the same pattern, the use of patented inventions by the government is now to be limited in a number of ways; use or sale of an invention for foreign defence purposes does not extend to the sale of integrated circuits;[166] the compulsory use of inventions in non-emergency conditions must be preceded by 'having first taken all reasonable steps to obtain the consent of the patentee to the use of the patented invention on reasonable commercial terms and conditions, and having failed to obtain such consent within a reasonable period of time'.[167] In any case, such use is conditional on the payment of remuneration.[168]

Other changes have been made to make application procedures as easy as possible. Hence, the requirement for an English translation of an application will be discretionary to the Registrar; amendments to an application are received until a research report has been completed. In addition, lapsed patents may be restored within 30 months as against the previous 12 months.[169] Further revisions have been prompted by the US–Singapore FTA through the Patents (Amendment) Act 2004 and Patents (Amendment) Rules 2004.

Other IP rights

The common laws of confidential information and trade secrets of the UK have been absorbed into Singapore law. The protection of designs was dependent for years on the UK Registered Designs (Protection) Act (Cap 339), which allowed re-registration on the basis of the UK Registered Designs Act 1949, in exactly the

164 Sections 55–60, note 142, above.

165 Section 55, ibid. Similarly Rules 76–80 of the Patent Rules 1995 were deleted by Rule 49 of the Patent (Amendment) Rules 1995.

166 Section 6, note 163, above; the new Section 61(2) (c), note 142, above.

167 Section 9, note 163, above; the new Section 65A(3), note 142, above.

168 Section 9, note 163, above; the new Section 65C, note 142, above.

169 Section 39, the Patents Act 1994 read with Rule 53, the Patent Rules 1995.

same way as the re-registration of patents under the old patent system. Singapore came up with an indigenous law, the Registered Designs Act 2000. The Act retains the basic requirements for registration of a design contained in prior law. The only changes are the requirements of worldwide novelty as against novelty locally and in the UK, and the withdrawal of 'eye appeal' from the definition of 'designs'.

Other laws newly introduced into Singapore, in keeping with the urge to make that country TRIPS-compliant, have been the Geographical Indications Act 1998, the Layout-Designs of Integrated Circuits Act 1999 and the Plant Varieties Protection Act 2004.

Membership of IP conventions

Singapore became a member of the Paris Convention and of the Patent Cooperation Treaty from 1995, the Berne Convention from 1998, and the WIPO Copyright Treaty and the WIPO Performances and Phonograms Treaty from 2005. It has also joined many other treaties, whether ratified or not.

Intellectual Property in Thailand

The Thai legal system was initially modelled on the common law but a switch was made to the civil law in 1924. Efforts were made from early on to make the indigenous law consistent with other legal systems. Thus an urge to make the law conform to indigenous requirements appears to have become a major characteristic of Thai law. This might partly explain the relatively long delay in enacting IP laws in Thailand as compared with other ASEAN emerging economies. The other main reason is the fact that Thailand was never a colony and therefore in a position to have had a system of laws made for, or imposed on, it.

Trademark law

Trademarks were protected under an old law (Trademark Act B.E. 2474) that dated back to 1931 but was amended in 1961. The law followed the UK trademark law (the Trademark Act 1905) and regulations issued to implement them in the UK. A significant provision of the Act set out a classification of goods (numbering 50) for the purpose of registration. The duration of protection for trademarks was 10 years; renewal was not subject to proof of use. Unfortunately, the Act did not include any actions that an owner might take against infringement of his rights. The only avenue was a resort to the Civil and Commercial Code or the Penal Code.

A new Trademark Act 1991 (in force from 1992) brought Thai law into line with TRIPS. Apart from the provision for protection of service marks, the definition of a mark includes combinations of colours, shape or configuration of objects. The

Act however left out whether or not prior use would be considered a prerequisite for registration.

Another law, the Trademark Act 2000, introduced changes relating to permissibility of having company names registered as trademarks, so long as they leave out their legal status (Co. Ltd or Limited); where applicants seek to register the whole lot, registration will be considered if presented in stylized form and is distinctive enough. Anther change is the extension of the range of items capable of registration – combinations of colour, shapes or forms of objects – very much in line with the current trend and the prescriptions of the Trademark Law Treaty. The amendment seeks to shorten the registration process and introduce additional grounds for cancellation of registration: where the mark lacks distinctiveness, its registration is forbidden, and where the registered mark is identical to, or confusingly similar to, another registered mark belonging to a third party. Stricter enforcement measures have also been proposed, enabling the pertinent authorities to enter and search premises and facilities, vehicles, seize evidence or property and arrest offenders, in certain circumstances, without a search warrant. Obstruction of the enforcement agencies may become a criminal offence and officers of legally established entities might face prison terms.

The Thai law of passing off is available for the protection of unregistered marks by virtue of statutory provision in Section 46, paragraph 2. Yet the term is undefined in the Act.

Copyright law

Copyright law was introduced in 1931 through the Act on Protection of Literary and Artistic Works, B.E. 2474. The Copyright Act, B.E. 2521 (1978), repealed and brought that first law up to date by defining what works are and by making changes in the extent of remedies for infringement. The only types of work left unprotected were performance rights.[170] Government generated works, save legislation, other forms of laws, decisions and reports,[171] entitled the department concerned to copyright unless a different agreement was signed with their employees.[172] The Act bestowed copyright automatically without any need to register the subject-matter of the rights. The term of protection was the usual life plus 50 years for original and 50 years for derivative works; the exception was 'work of applied art' which presumably covered artistic designs – the period of protection being 25 years.[173]

A key section of the Act was the fair use exception in Section 30: reproduction for research or education, for use by libraries, 'for one's own benefit', or for the

---

170 Section 4, Copyright Act, B.E. 2521.

171 Section 31, ibid.

172 Section 11, ibid.

173 Section 19, ibid.

benefit of the family, relatives or friends.[174] Use in educational institutions was supposed to be towards meeting needs and not for making profit or harming the copyright owner. The contradictoriness of the extended nature of the fair use exception in the law with the concept of copyright as a matter of principle was obvious in the objective of balancing between benefiting nearly everybody except commercial organizations and not harming the copyright owner! Other important exclusions from copyright protection (Section 32) were the set of laws, regulations and reports of the government departments as well as judgements and decisions. In addition, a time bar operated against an owner of copyright if that owner did not initiate action within three years after becoming aware of the infringement, or later than 10 years after such infringement.[175]

The state of copyright law became a source of conflict with the US which had a bilateral treaty with Thailand. Article V of the Treaty signed in 1966 provided for reciprocal protection of IP. Consequently, to forestall US retaliation, Thailand had to introduce changes in the law. A copyright bill, first placed before parliament in 1987 to repeal previous legislation, became law in 1994. The new Copyright Act defines (in Section 6) copyright subject matter in the same way as Indonesia and the Philippines by pointing to a list (eight categories). The Act covers computer software within the category of 'literature'. A separate chapter (Chapter 2) is devoted to the protection of the rights of performers.

The 1994 law expands the range of activities to be protected under copyright: sound recordings and performances (Section 44). It also provides for civil and criminal remedies for infringement (Sections 69–73). Still the previous exemptions from this have been kept in Section 32, although with a new caveat: that the use 'does not conflict with a normal exploitation of the copyright work by the owner of copyright and does not unreasonably prejudice the legitimate right of the owner of copyright'.

Patent law

Thailand did not provide legal protection to inventions and product designs until 1979. In that year, the Patents Act (BE 2522), which imitated the model law prepared by the WIPO for developing countries, was introduced. The standards for patentability of inventions and product designs adopted in the Act were, needless to say, universal ones. The Act provided protection for 15 years for inventions and seven years for product designs from the date of filing. Exclusions from patentability included beverages, agricultural machines, pharmaceutical products, animals and plants, including processes that might be used to produce them. Foreign patentees would have no protection unless they were granted a patent in Thailand; however Thailand had entered reciprocal arrangements with most of the

174 Section 30, ibid.
175 Section 29, ibid.

industrial nations by the early 1980s. Otherwise the only avenue left for protection of foreign patentees would be contract law.

The 1979 Act (Section 46) provided for compulsory licensing in situations where the patentee did not make the patent available to local producers (three years from grant) and the needs of the local economy were not met without legitimate reasons. Licensing was subject to the requirement (to be spelled out by the respective Ministry) that no condition, restriction or royalty be detrimental to the development of industry and commerce in Thailand. Royalties could not be paid for lapsed patents. Anti-competition laws (the Price-Fixing and Anti-Monopoly Act 1979) prohibited such activities where consumer interests might be harmed.

In 1992, a new Patent Act (No. 2 BE 2535) sought to amend the 1979 law and bring Thai law into line with the TRIPS. It changed the term of protection for patents and designs to 20 and 10 years, respectively. Although Section 9 of the Act maintained that micro-organisms, plant and animal varieties were exempted from patent protection (until these were removed in the 1999 revision), the other exceptions to patentability have also been narrowed down. Nevertheless, the grounds for exemption of certain acts from infringement appear to have changed very little. Thus acts done in the interests of education, experimentation or research are permissible. Furthermore, the Act requires applications for a patent to provide clear and exact details of the working of an invention.

A further amendment, Patent Act (No. 3) 1999 was passed in October 1998 and became effective from 27 September 1999. It made important changes in such areas as national treatment, priority filing, extension in the rights of the patentee and compulsory licensing. The first two were necessitated by the fact that Thailand remained outside of the Paris Convention, although it had signed TRIPS. The Act also extended the category of inventions that could be patented to drugs, food, beverages and life forms. As well, it established a petty patent system ('utility model') for inventions which fail under the patent criteria. Petty patents are valid for six years in the first instance and renewable for two sets of two years. Finally, Section 36 made it permissible for parallel importing to be undertaken in Thailand.

Other IP rights

A new law governing varieties of plants, the Plant Varieties Act, was issued in 1999. Similarly issued were the Protection of Layout Designs of Integrated Circuits Act of 2000 and the Trade Secrets Act 2000. The latter used to be protected under contract law. Again, the Protection of Geographical Indications Act of 2003.

Membership of IP conventions

Thailand became a member of the Berne Convention in 1931 although the Convention was put into the local law only in 1983 (through the Royal Decree Providing Conditions for the Protection of international Copyright, B.E. 2526).

After a rather long wait, it has also become a member of the Paris Convention on 28 August 2008. It is to be expected that accession to others will follow.

Chapter 3
Intellectual Property in China: A Review

Introduction

The problem of intellectual property (IP) enforcement in China has become a familiar story featured regularly in the news. Thus following his visit to China, the Assistant US Trade Representative Joseph Papovich reportedly stated, 'They've made some important changes to their laws ... and the enforcers are better trained and more sophisticated than they were. But the companies tell me the problem is still as severe as it was' in his visit of November 2000.[1] A US Congressman back from a trip to China stated, 'The Chinese steal intellectual property right and left'.[2] Later, Steven Pinkos, deputy director of the US Patents and Trademarks Office (USPTO) declared, in a Beijing seminar on the criminal justice system (funded by the US as part of efforts to combat IP piracy), that the USTPO's 'primary focus on the international front is on China'.[3] A commentator added, 'Widespread intellectual property rights violations continue to rank as probably the most important World Trade Organization (WTO) non-compliance issue that foreign investors and businesses raise about China'.[4]

In October 2005, Japan, the US and Switzerland individually initiated a process under the WTO rules demanding China account for the continued lack of enforcement between 2001 and 2004.[5] US Trade Representative Rob Portman explained, 'Our goal is to get detailed information that will help pinpoint exactly

1 [Anonymous] 'Piracy Remains a Problem in China, U.S. Says', *The Wall Street Journal*, 24 January 2002; available online from the Dow Jones Interactive; accessed 3 February 2002.

2 John Schmid, 'Two Cars and One View: U.S. Taken for a Ride', *The Milwaukee Journal Sentinel*, 25 January 2004, 1A; accessed through Factiva on 7 February 2004, After visting a General Motors plant in Shanghai, Congressman Sensenbrenner complained of the flagrant disregard of US IP as the reason behind the similarity of a domestically produced car to the GM model: 'If you didn't have the name tags on the car, you couldn't tell them apart'. Ibid.

3 William New, 'U.S. Official Cites Possible Chinese TRIPS Violations', *Intellectual Property Watch*, 18 February 2005; available at http://www.ip-watch.org.

4 Arjun Subrahmaryam, 'China and the WTO: Perspectives on a Chaning Environment', *China Law & Practice*, 21–6 February 2005, at 25.

5 Tove Iren S. Gerhardsen, 'US, Switzerland, Japan Launch New WTO Probe On China's IP Enforcement', *Intellectual Property Watch*, 26 October 2005; available at http://www.ip-watch.org.

where the enforcement system is breaking down so we can decide appropriate next steps'.[6]

In spite of the constant criticism of its IP enforcement, China stands out as the nation with the fastest transplantation of IP laws that evolved over hundreds of years in Europe and the Middle East. In a matter of a decade or so, starting from 1982, China virtually copied the entire spectrum of laws available in the statute books of most industrialized nations and promulgated them as its own. This was not necessarily because China never had any laws of its own before 1980; far from it.

During the pre-1979 period, China had laws on trademarks from 1904, patents from 1911 and copyright from 1910. After the overthrow of the Kuomintang in 1949, Soviet-style laws were introduced from 1950 onwards; that is, until the spate of new borrowings from the West following the 1979 US–China treaty. Although that treaty seems to have goaded the Chinese authorities into accepting the menu of Western IP laws of the time as part of China's legal landscape, there were far more fundamental reasons for the *volte-façe*. The immediate cause for the rush to modernize the IP system was the recognition of foreign technology and capital as keys to China's modernization and the view that IP could serve as a means of attracting the two. Clearly, neither the state of industrialization in China nor the role of private property in the 1980s created the urgency for the flood of new laws. The insignificant role of IP in the domestic economic context was evidenced by the fact that the state had the overwhelming share of economic power as recently as 1995.[7]

Parallel to the rush of new IP laws – trademarks in 1982, patents in 1984, copyright in 1991 – China snapped up membership of international treaties. China signed bilateral treaties with the US in 1979, 1992 and 1995. It has also joined the Treaty Establishing the WIPO (1980), the Paris Convention (1985), the Nice Agreement on Classification (1988), the Madrid Agreement on the International Registration of Marks (1989), the Berne Convention (1992), the Geneva Convention for Protection of Producers of Phonographs (1993) and the Patent Cooperation Treaty (1994) and the WIPO Copyright Treaty (2007). It has yet to accede to, among others, the Trademark Law Treaty and the Patent Law Treaty.

Despite the persistent efforts of the Chinese to imitate the laws of other countries and subscribe to every treaty available, China continues to be the most intensely criticized nation for not implementing those laws. The problem of IP enforcement in China has remained a recurrent theme for commentators and governments espousing the cause of foreign proprietors of IP.[8]

---

6 Ibid.

7 See A. Endeshaw, *Intellectual Property In China: The Roots of the Problem of Enforcement*, Acumen Publishing Company: Singapore, 1996, at 151–3.

8 See for example, Richard J. Ansson, Jr, 'International Intellectual Property Rights, the United States and the People's Republic of China', 1 *Temple International & Comparative Law Journal* 1, 1999; See National Intellectual Property Law Enforcement Coordination

This chapter aims to explore whether, with its rapid embrace of the entire gamut of IP laws found in most developed nations, partly in view of its desire to accede to the WTO, China has brought about any changes to reduce or even eliminate the persistent problem. The broad context for such an exploration is the role and significance of the Agreement on Trade-Related Aspects of Intellectual Property Rights (TRIPS) to members of the WTO, in particular to the developing countries (DCs). In the final analysis, the study of the problem of IP enforcement in China, post-WTO, merges with the increasing call for review of the 'costs and benefits' of the IP system (as championed by many DCs for decades and formulated by the 'Friends of Development', since 2004, into a 'Development Agenda'[9]) and for its revision, a subject examined in Chapter 12.

The chapter is organized in two sections. The first will summarize the main features that characterize China's imitation of IP laws found elsewhere. This includes the changes China had to make in its IP laws in preparation for joining the WTO. The second reviews the state of the problem of enforcement and the improvised mechanisms that have emerged in China to remedy the deficiency. It concludes that progress in IP protection in China will remain tied to internal or domestic developments and the rise of local forces that demand it.

The Evolution of the Chinese Intellectual Property System

It will not be possible, within the limited space available to us, to examine in detail the IP laws that China has accumulated in its statute books. Nor will that be necessary. This is because, one the one hand, there are abundant sources that expound the laws both for practitioners and academics.[10] On the other hand, the fact that the IP laws in China have been adaptations or imitations of those already in force in the EU and the US means that the available commentary in those countries will continue to be relevant to understanding their contents. Hence, we will only attempt to highlight here the main features in the evolution of Chinese IP laws. This will hopefully help us gain an understanding of their links with, or divergence from, TRIPS and other international developments in the IP field.

Council (NIPLECC), '2006 Report to the President and Congress on Coordination of Intellectual Property Enforcement and Protection'; available at www.commerce.gov.

9 WIPO, 'Proposal by Argentina and Brazil for the Establishment of a Development Agenda for WIPO', Geneva, 27 August 2004; WO/GA/31/11.

10 See Alan Gutterman and Robert Brown (eds), *Intellectual Property Laws of East Asia*, Sweet & Maxwell Asia: Malaysia, 1997; Raymond A. Mantle et al., *Intellectual Property Law of China*, Juris Publishing Inc., 1999; Mark A. Cohen et al. (eds), *Chinese Intellectual Property Law and Practice*, Kluwer Law International: London, 1999; Rebecca Ordish and Alan Adcock, *China Intellectual Property – Challenges and Solutions: An Essential Business Guide*, Wiley: Chichester, 2008.

The evolution of Chinese IP law, post-1979, can be classified into three phases. The first phase was that between 1979 and 1992, both dates representing the first and second time that China and the US signed bilateral treaties on IP. The period 1993–5 is the second phase in which China sought to respond to criticisms on the types and scopes of the IP laws enacted until then and, prompted by the 1992 treaty, to amend them through further imitations. It may be noted that China and the US signed a third IP treaty in 1995. The third phase stretches from 1996 to 2001, when China became a member of WTO.

Overall, Chinese law-making before 1995 was largely an exercise in unmitigated borrowing of similar laws from the major industrial powers. This was true of whatever form of IP law the Chinese authorities sought to introduce. The predominant concern before 1995 was to prove to Western proprietors of technology and potential investors that the IP laws in China had the same provisions as those in the West. The urge to create this impression of similarity of Chinese IP laws with those in the West was so paramount that China did not commission any special study beforehand into whether it should introduce any of the laws and what the scope and contents of those laws might be. The authorities' main concern during that period was to remove any noticeable gaps in the laws. Once the laws had been rushed through, the authorities sought to dispel any criticism that China did not have equivalent laws to those in the West by pointing to the similar, if not identical, concepts and rules adopted in the various IP laws. One official thus asserted that the promulgation of the Trademark Law and Patent Law had 'eliminated the concerns of foreign investors regarding the protection of industrial property rights in their economic cooperation and technical exchange with China'.[11]

The third phase is characterized by the shift in focus of (largely Western) criticism of Chinese IP laws from pointing out loopholes and gaps to that of pouring scorn on the level of enforcement. The 1995 treaty was the first attempt to persuade China to transform its array of laws, which seemed to the US to remain largely as 'law in the books', into 'law in the streets'. Other attempts have been made since then by the US and EU, often in the context of trade negotiations, to put pressure on China to improve its level of IP enforcement. However, regardless of Chinese claims to the contrary, success in that direction continues to elude all sides in the controversy and the contention that China has yet to achieve any marked change continues to reverberate not only in the news media but also in the relevant literature.

11 Wang Yaoting, Chairman of the China Council for the Promotion of Internaitonal Trade in his 'Message' on the launch of *China Patents & Trademarks*, Issue No. 1, April 1985, at 5.

The first phase (1979–92)

A critical feature of Chinese IP during the first phase was the absence of scrutiny by the Chinese authorities into the nature of the laws being considered for adoption and before any final decision was made. Issues of fundamental importance for the economic and technological development of a non-industrial country relating to patentablity (e.g. local versus worldwide novelty and workability) and the scope of 'exclusive rights' in trademark, copyright and similar laws do not appear to have been raised, let alone addressed, during the successive promulgation of the assortment of laws by the Chinese authorities. There are no records of policy considerations regarding any of these issues that the authorities engaged in or decided upon. The closest to an admission of such a lack of broader examination of the underlying issues was provided by another official who stated, 'In the course of drafting, we paid attention to the commonly accepted international practices'.[12] In other words, the concern, even emphasis, appeared to have been the similarity of the newly concocted laws to 'the commonly accepted international practices'. In short, any semblance of differences or detraction from those practices would probably have been considered unwise by the authorities. For instance, the drafting committee for patent law appeared to have engaged in some sort of discussion and even produced divergent views,[13] but the outcome did not reflect any serious challenge to the urge to absorb everything the West had to offer to China.

In copyright, one would have assumed that the long delay in promulgating a comprehensive law (in 1990) must have been preceded by scrutiny of the implications of further legal transplantation. Yet, the promulgation was not accompanied by any serious attempt to weigh the merits or otherwise of the new law. Some semblance of recognition of domestic needs for free flow of information and the availability of Western knowledge to enhance the 'modernization' process did figure in some of the articles of the 1991 law, but they appear to have been included rather more instinctively than as part of a pre-planned measure.

The deficiency of a systematic enquiry into the policy of adopting foreign IP laws as well as of the nature and scope of the rights created is corroborated by the fact that the promulgation process proceeded at a pace never before experienced by any other nation. The Chinese authorities have often referred to this as a remarkable achievement and even as defence for the dearth of enforcement. Inevitably, Chinese IP laws have nothing to distinguish them from the foreign sources they were patterned on in terms of content. To illustrate this, we will briefly survey the salient features of those laws.

To start with trademarks, the scope of protection under the 1982 law was defined in a rather woolly fashion, although it resembled most pre-TRIPS laws

12 Huang Kuny [Director of the China Patent Office], 'The PRC is Going to Put into Effect their Patent Law', *China Patents & Trademarks*, Issue No. 1, April 1985, at 13.

13 See, Zheng Chengsi with Michael D. Pendeleton, *Chinese Intellectual Property and Technology Transfer Law*, Sweet & Maxwell: London, 1987, at 53.

of other nations. The lack of recognition for shape, smell and the like was also in line with the same in most nations. Trademark registration and other practices (such as exclusion from registration) were again similar to laws of other countries. On the other hand, the 1982 law made the registration of trademarks compulsory for pharmaceutical products, although it was not mandatory for all (similarly to the treatment under TRIPS). Yet, an action in passing off was linked to registered marks only, hence indirectly making registration a *sine qua non* for the protection of all marks.

The 1984 patent law covered inventions, utility models and designs without any indication of why the three forms were incorporated into a single legal instrument. Although other countries have adopted such forms in respect of the different levels of technical innovations, the solution in China of stuffing them into one law was exceptional. It seemed that China preferred the midway, though unarticulated, approach of a fully-fledged patent law for major inventions (potentially from abroad) side by side with some form of a petty patent system (for the inevitably low levels of domestic innovations).

Having absorbed instinctively the primary rationale of patent law, namely the promotion of innovation in the domestic economy, it could not be unexpected for the 1984 law to have copied the general exceptions to patentability that were commonly available in most laws – before TRIPS. The 1984 law hence excluded plant and animal varieties while including micro-organisms (process and product). Thus genetically engineered animals and plant species were placed outside the scope of patentability. The 1984 law also excluded from patentability food, pharmaceuticals and substances obtained by means of chemical processes.

Otherwise, patent grant and other practices were so identical to those of other nations that further discussion seems hardly necessary. Rules that were adopted only in one country, such as the US, were occasionally injected into the law. Thus the requirement of disclosing the best mode of application of a product or process was spelled out (in rule 18 of the 1985 Implementing Regulations of the Patent Law).

In copyright law, the scope and nature of protection related to artistic, literary and 'scientific works' as well as related rights. Moral rights were also recognized. In a major departure from most laws of other countries, Chinese copyright law extended protection to folk arts, which were defined as those performed by talking or signing.

In an apparent attempt to rein in overbearing licensors, a copyright licence was limited to 10 years, although it could be renewed. An important exemption from copyright is the permission granted to translate from Chinese (Han) language to minority languages. Yet, such an exemption is restricted to materials originally created in that language. Obviously this was intended not to anger copyright holders of foreign materials.

For no apparent reason, the Chinese sought to introduce requirements of registration for software under the Regulations on the Protection of Computer Software of 1 October 1991. The Regulations nevertheless allowed certain exemptions that were unparalleled: (1) users could modify software to make it suitable to the actual working environment of their computer; (2) users could undertake limited reproductions for non-commercial purposes, e.g. classroom teaching, scientific research and performance of official duties required by state organs. Registration of software was not mandatory but legal redress was only available to those who registered.

The second phase (1993–5)

Subsequent to the 17 January 1992 US–China Memorandum of Understanding on the Protection of Intellectual Property, China undertook a revision of its laws. The 1993 amendment of the trademark law included service marks. The earlier law did not provide for criminal penalties, only injunction and compensation. After the 1993 revision, prison terms of a maximum seven years could be imposed on infringers in addition to injunction, fine and compensation Furthermore, the import or export of goods carrying infringing marks became a prohibited activity.

The revision of the patent law in 1992 led to changes in the terms of protection for patents and utility models as well as designs. They were extended from 15 and 5 (under the first law) to 20 and 10 years, respectively. The 1992 amendment also removed the working requirement in the earlier version.[14] The 1992 change included pharmaceutical products and processes as well as chemicals. Finally, it introduced compensation for infringement and allowed the use of injunctions.

Under the 1984 patent law, any infringement action was tied to knowledge of lack of authorization, otherwise the wrongdoer would be exempt from liability. Moreover, remedies did not include criminal prosecution. Guidelines were issues by the Supreme People's Procuratorate in 1992, whereby counterfeit sales exceeding a predetermined value of US$12,000 would lead to prosecution.

In copyright law, too, previous remedies of injunction, making open apologies, compensation, confiscation of illicit income and infringing articles and fines were modified. Stiffer measures such as prison terms of up to three years were announced by the Standing Committee of the National Congress in 1994.

Following US opposition, 'Measures for the Registration of Copyright in Computer Software' was issued in 1992 to remove the requirement of registration for US proprietors and to allow them to be exempt. This became available to non-US proprietors automatically when China became signatory to the Berne Convention in 1992.

Finally, China adopted the Unfair Competition Law in 1993. That law listed the type of 'unfair methods' considered unacceptable. It also specified remedies and penalties mainly in terms of compensating the 'damaged party'.

14 Article 51 imposed an obligation on the patentee 'to make the patented product, or to use the patented process, in China' or to license other people. This fell short of making any breach of such an obligation a basis for revocation of the patent.

The third phase (1996–2001)

The 1995 agreement between China and the US exerted more pressures on China to implement its laws and not merely to rest content with their existence on the statute books. Previous criticisms against China's inability to enforce its commitments were reduced to a series of measures that it was expected to introduce. China was also expected to report to the US on the measures taken and the results achieved.

After the 1995 agreement, only minor revisions were made on the IP laws as China had completed, by then, the imitation process in its eagerness to accede to the WTO. Of the few changes, one was the imposition of criminal liability where passing off another's patent is involved.

Well-known marks were also to be protected pursuant to the 1995 treaty. In March 1995, the trademark law was amended to allow the protection of collective and certification marks. A regulation was issued in August 1995[15] making Chinese import and export corporations accountable for checking the validity of trademarks that subcontractors in China use on their goods while fulfilling orders. This regulation was introduced because such corporations do not hold any stocks and infringing goods might not be seized from them while documents might be easily destroyed.

New rules on Trademark Review and Adjudication were issued on 2 November 1995 to deal with appeals against decisions of the trademark office. These appeals could be on opposition against registration, refusal for registration, assignment etc. The Trademark Review and Adjudication Board (TRAB) hears the appeal which must be made in writing and renders its decision by a majority vote of members, two-thirds of whom must be present. The appeal must be made in a prescribed form, within the specified time limit, upon payment of fees, and should provide facts and evidence.

Last minute changes were also made in 2001 just before China's accession to the WTO was finalized. The latest amendments involved patents (July 2001), copyright (October 2001) and trademarks (December 2001). The changes in the Patent Law extended the patentee's right by including offering for sale or marketing of patented matter. Moreover, judicial review of the decisions of the Patent Office was introduced; injunction (preliminary) was allowed; the rules for compulsory licensing were narrowed down; submission of foreign search reports before grant was removed; and revocation was substituted by the right to appeal (to Patent Re-Evaluation Board) against grant.

The reform of the Trademark Law related to extension of the scope of trademark protection to include three-dimensional marks and combinations of colours, recognition of collective and certification marks as well as well-known marks and geographical indications. Individual persons (citizens) were for the first time allowed to file an application for registration (Article 4). The law also introduced the simplification of the registration procedures provided by the Trademark Law

15 'Regulations Controlling Use of Trademarks in Foreign Trade'.

Treaty. An appeal to the courts was allowed in cases of trademark cancellation and validity decisions.

The latest changes in the Copyright Law sought to fill gaps in the protection of performances, broadcasts, rental rights, databases and the communication of copyright matter through the Internet. It also increased penalties for infringers, allowed interim injunction (upon depositing a sum of money), introduced changes to damage assessment such that if actual loss could not be assessed the court is given the power to award and opened the possibility of intervention by collection societies on behalf of members.

Subsequent to its entry into WTO, China has continued to promulgate, revise or annul laws in all manner of directions. Changes have also been effected at regional levels and by the diversity of state agencies operating at every level. While this might be a good thing, both for domestic and foreign businesses, the vast changes introduced in the laws has generated the problem of keeping up with them and, indeed, of finding them. The various levels of law-making authority have created somewhat of an anarchic situation which makes the task of those who practice law far more difficult. It is usually bigger law firms which can keep track of laws and make translations for in-house use. Furthermore, the sheer size of the country and the complexity of the administrative machinery mean that information flow (and transmission of law) may take time for such to reach the intended people and businesses. Add to this the differences between regions in laws and practices as well as policies which do not augur well for enforcement of the law.

The Problems of, and Mechanisms for, IP Enforcement

Up until China's entry into the WTO, the gap between the fast pace of enactment of Chinese IP law, partly prompted by the bilateral agreements with the US – after virtually every trade negotiation and the trip of a USTR official or other to China – and the low level of enforcement was a continuous source of bitter confrontation between the US and China. The EU had also expressed its dissatisfaction with the sate of IP enforcement in China, although not as vociferously or threateningly as the US. Nonetheless, the threat of sanctions and other measures against China for its pronounced failure to translate the promises and laws into reality sparked tremendous interest among students of IP and international trade. Yet beyond the heated discussions, often not as dispassionate as they might have appeared, the underlying issues in IP law-making and implementation were hardly addressed by the participants.

The demand for enforcing IP in China has been never-ending. This is not necessarily because the Chinese were doing nothing but because the expectation of the foreign proprietors was that China should provide an environment similar to practices in Western Europe or the US. At all times, the main response of the Chinese was to produce evidence of measures taken against piracy. Contrary to the general perception, however, there are cultural and philosophic hurdles to IP enforcement in China. It is now commonly accepted that the adoption of an IP system in China was in the context of 'a culture embedded with traditions completely antithetical to the patenting of inventions and to the granting of property rights in other forms of intellectual products'.[16] The implications of this, particularly for the implementation of the laws, are often ignored. However, commentators have indicated that the transformation of thousands of years of tradition will stand in the way and make enforcement a formidable, if not impossible, task for far longer than is realized.[17]

The foreign nature of nearly all the IP that China has promulgated has not made it easy for the general public as well as local businesses to embrace it as their own. The weakness or lack of legal infrastructure is another major factor that has contributed to the gravity of the problem of IP enforcement. China's huge size and the increasing decentralization of power to the autonomous regions, provinces and municipalities have made coordination of IP enforcement more difficult. Local interests that take advantage of the lack of a central authority and connive with IP 'pirates' have often been cited as major sources of the problem of IP enforcement in China. Added to this are undeveloped state of the legal and administrative system, and the absence of sufficient numbers of trained judges who can make impartial decisions.[18]

In addition, institutional means take root only gradually and could not be legislated into existence. China has striven to create the institutional basis for recognition and enforcement of IP. In the field of patents, the Patent Bureau was established in 1980, even before the law was promulgated. The National Bureau of Copyright (later called the National Copyright Administration) was similarly established in 1990. All of these were brought together in April 1998 as the State Intellectual Property Organization (SIPO) to administer and monitor enforcement of IP in China.

Moreover, there is also the State Administration for Industry and Commerce with powers to impose administrative sanctions, order cessation of infringement and compensation for losses. In addition, the Office of National Antipiracy and Pornography (NAPP) was established to assume control over coordination of copyright enforcement. The State Council's Working Conference on Intellectual Property Rights coordinates protection and enforcement of IP across the country. The police and customs authorities have also taken part in their respective areas of activity.

---

16 John R. Allison and Lianlian Lin 'The Evolution of Chinese Attitudes Toward Property Rights in Invention and Discovery', 20 *University of Pennsylvania Journal of International Economic Law* 735, Winter 1999.

17 Endeshaw, note 7, above; see, also Susan Tiefenbrun, 'Piracy of Intellectual Property in China and the Former Soviet Union and its Effects Upon International Trade: A Comparison', 46 *Buffalo Law Review* 1, Winter 1998.

18 Allison and Lin, note 16, above.

There have also been attempts to provide room for non-governmental organizations and associations of right holders to help in the generation of awareness in IP matters and enforcement. After the first copyright collection society, the Music Copyright Society of China, was established in February 1993, many others have emerged. Writers, dramatists, film distributors and publishers as well as software producers, among others, have set up their respective associations.

China has also learnt to use the news agencies to report routinely, often citing the Chinese news agency, Xinhua, that China had confiscated hundreds of thousands of pirated video and audio cassettes as well as compact and laser discs with infringing copyright content. Reports also routinely cite increases in the number of inspectors monitoring markets daily as well as the courts that have been established for the specific purpose of curbing IP infringement. The courts are also cited as having handled hundreds of cases. Overall, whether or not in an attempt to dampen the increasingly vociferous critique against China's performance and the call for measures against it, government media and officials in China have published reports of success and progress in the enforcement of IP.

Chinese attempts to explain away the dismal record in enforcement of the various agreements it concluded with the US or to demonstrate some progress in combating, for instance, the production of counterfeit CD-ROMs and their dissemination throughout Asia and Europe never succeeded in forestalling repeated US announcements of new sanctions against it or calls for the revocation of China's Most Favoured Nation (MFN) trading status with the US, and/or blocking of its entry into WTO. From the US point of view, all these were meant to be effective means of making China comply with treaty obligations in the IP field. Furthermore, a number of other issues have also been raised together with the enforcement of IP rights in China, such as the control of dissemination of military technology, the Taiwan–PRC relations, WTO membership of China, human rights and economic reforms in China. As a result, for years, the debate has raged in the US on whether *engaging or containing China* would be an appropriate policy for the US to adopt. The continuous swing in policy between the one and the other has exacerbated US–Chinese relations as a whole. Some of the leading policy makers in the US and abroad have grappled with the issue and proposed a compromise solution. Thus Kissinger advised, 'If hostility to China were to become a permanent aspect of US foreign policy, America will find no allies. Nationalism would accelerate throughout the region'.[19] According to him, 'A wise US policy will not seek premature confrontation; it will try to benefit from its biggest asset – that the US has fewer real quarrels with Asian nations than they have with each other, enabling it to act as balancer of the Asian equilibrium.'[20]

Senator Sam Nunn similarly disagreed about the imposing of sanctions against China for alleged sales of nuclear technology and human rights violations on purely economic grounds. 'Our friends in Europe and Japan would be most

19 *The Los Angeles Times*, 2 April 1996.

20 Ibid.

delighted to fill any Chinese need which might develop if we employ economic sanctions'.[21] The instance of Boeing's loss, in 1996, of a contract to build a new 100-seat jetliner to Airbus Industries of Europe was widely attributed to strains in US–Chinese relations at the time.[22]

Jeffrey E. Gartern, a former under-secretary of Commerce in the Clinton administration, advised gluing China to the US through trade. In an apparent reference to growing fears among US businesses that they are or will be losing to their European or Japanese competitors, he proposed a strategy to close ranks: 'Ask allies to help. Washington should marshal its allies to pressure China when necessary. Going mano a mano with Beijing, be it over intellectual property rights, human rights or arm sales, is increasingly ineffective. End self-defeating threats to stop trade. Congress should stop threatening to revoke trading privileges every time there are human rights violations.'[23]

Burton Levin, a former US diplomat added his voice to pillory those in the US whom he considered to have a picture of China as an 'evil incarnate, communist dictatorship at its worst'.[24] According to him, such people support Taiwan 'not recognising that communism died in China long before it did in the former Soviet Union'. He added, 'The Chinese cling to their secretive ways and tend to see conspiracy all around, particularly when the US is involved.'[25]

Conclusion

It is a matter of public record that Chinese promises to provide a transparent system of rules in exchange for gaining market access to the US (which has grown to 40 per cent in the last decade) have led to the flood of foreign IP laws. Writing in 1996, two commentators stated, 'China now boasts an array of intellectual property laws that rival those in the most developed countries.'[26] The repeated promises to wipe out piracy largely through the establishment and strengthening of the enforcement machinery that would search, seize or destroy pirated works of US-protected IP appeared to put all contentions and US–Chinese disputes to rest.

The reports of Chinese enforcement of their IP laws and obligations under the various agreements with the US have not, however, satisfied the US, nor the

21 Reuters, 23 February 1996.

22 *The Asia Wall Street Journal*, 20 May 1996, at 1 and 2.

23 [Opinion]. 'How to Accompany the Rise of a Might China', *The International Herald Tribune*, January 16, 1996.

24 Burton Levin, 'On Taiwan: Why Rock The Boat?', *International Herald Tribune*, 19 June 1995; available at http://www.iht.com/articles/1995/06/19/edburt.php; accessed 9 February 2009.

25 Ibid.

26 Jerome A. Cohen and Terence A. Dixon, 'Intellectual Property in China', *IPAsia* 24, March 1996, at 24.

other industrial powers. Indeed, the gravity of fakery and counterfeiting in China was not contested even by China itself,[27] until they found their feet and started to push counter-arguments. The pervasive nature of piracy has been demonstrated many times.[28] Thus, even prestigious cars produced by state automakers in China find their fake counterparts, made by cobbling together old parts and smuggled imports, on Chinese roads. Various tales have been spun of the availability of pirate copies at knockdown prices not very far from commercial establishments in Beijing and other main cities in plain sight of the police.

Despite Chinese attempts to placate Western IP interests by promulgating the latest forms or issuing reports of progress on the front of enforcement, repeated criticisms have been directed at its enforcement practices. A common line of argument has sought to ascribe to the Chinese authorities sheer lack of will to implement the laws. However, the lack of IP protection on the level that foreign proprietors expected was not always the same as lack of will by the authorities. The underlying problems of IP in China lie deeper than mere refusal by the authorities of the merits of implementing such laws.

Indeed, the principal inquiry into the problem of enforcement should have been directed at the fact that China still possesses administrative, cultural and competence problems. Many commentators have gradually come to recognize that these are more fundamental than the reference to the leadership's lethargy. The foreign proprietors who earlier perceived the problems in light of Western attitudes towards the law and its implementation have started to switch to the view that perhaps China needs to transform itself in that field too. Hence the idea of providing assistance to China in the realm of law enforcement and institutional building has started making headway.

It follows from this that reliance on the current enforcement machinery in China will not necessarily be the best means of protection for the time being. Apart from the fact that legal action in China has its limits, the framework for such action might not be readily available. Moreover, the inherently contradictory position of an emerging economy caught between asserting loyalty to international standards

27 According to one professor at Fudan University in China, 'China has experienced difficulty in providing effective enforcement of these new laws within a short period of time. Those difficulties have been the greatest in the area of protecting foreigners' copyrights. This is due to the short history of copyright law in China, the lack of Chinese officials with experience in the enforcement of copyright law, and the general ignorance of copyright law among many Chinese'. See Naigen Zhang, 'Intellectual Property Law Enforcement in China: Trade Issues, Policies and Practices', 8 *Fordham Intellectual Property, Media and Entertainment Law Journal* 63, Fall 1997; 13 March 2001.

28 For a discussion of state of piracy in China and further proof that it has become 'a massive, complex, and intractable problem', see Daniel C.K. Chow, 'Counterfeiting In The People's Republic Of China', 78 *Washington University Law Quarterly* 1 Spring, 2000; for a more current study, see Martin Dimitrov, *Piracy and the State The Politics of Intellectual Property Rights in China*, Cambridge University Press: Cambridge, September 2009.

not reflecting local interests and domestic social–economic realities that demand commitments to internal development needs pushes China's IP on an erratic course. It would seem that any progress in IP protection in China will remain tied to internal or domestic developments and the rise of local forces that demand it. By contrast, foreign IP proprietors could do better by helping create national awareness and speeding up the building up of an indigenous legal infrastructure.

Chapter 4
Harmonization of Intellectual Property Laws in ASEAN*

Introduction

The Association of South East Asian Nations (ASEAN) now groups together nine countries,[1] most of which have put in place intellectual property (IP) laws that were originally either inherited from the colonial past or adopted later as part of the urge to modernize. The ASEAN law-making process in the post-independence era was predicated, as a former Secretary General of the ASEAN Law Association wrote, on the need to 'provide guarantees for the safety of loans and investment capital' and the transfer of technology from abroad for national development, as well as to meet new requirements triggered by changing values resulting from advances in modernization.[2]

There is an additional contemporary factor that impels members of ASEAN to revise their IP laws: they are expected to streamline their laws with that of the main industrial nations in order to live up to their treaty obligations under the World Trade Organization (WTO) incorporating the Trade-Related Aspects of Intellectual Property Rights (TRIPS). Furthermore, while nearly all of ASEAN made changes in their pre-TRIPS laws and effected transition fully by 2000, there is a new desire to come up with an ASEAN perspective and, however surprising it might seem, a unified IP system for all of them. Although no fixed timetables have been drawn up, ASEAN leaders adopted, on 15 December 1995, the 'ASEAN Framework Agreement on Intellectual Property Co-operation', including the setting up of a regional patent and trademark office. That agreement was followed up on 10–12 April 1996 by another agreement reached in Thailand on a two-year action plan for IP cooperation. The action plan was hoped to lead to the establishment of a regional

* An earlier version of this chapter appeared, in the author's name, as 'Harmonization of ASEAN Intellectual Property: Issues and Prospects', 2(1) *The Journal of World Intellectual Property* 1–23, January 1999.

1 ASEAN currently comprises Brunei, Indonesia, Laos, Malaysia, Myanmar, The Philippines, Thailand, Singapore and Vietnam. Of these, Brunei joined in 1984; Vietnam became a member in 1995; Laos and Myanmar were admitted in 1997; Cambodia in 1999. The rest, six of them, were signatories of the treaty from 1967.

2 See Tunku Mohammad Radhie, 'Harmonization of Laws: Issues and Prospects in ASEAN Law, Technology and Development', 1(2) *ASEAN Law and Society Journal* 50–1, July–December 1986, at 52–3.

electronic information network, an IP database and a common system of protection for industrial designs, patents and copyright. Two expert groups were established at the same time to work on common patent and copyright systems, respectively.[3]

In the years after the onset of the 1997 Asian economic and financial crises, any talk of harmonization was confined to promoting the value of IP protection for, among other things, inter-ASEAN trade.[4] Otherwise, no further details have emerged so far as to how the framework adopted in December 1995 for an ASEAN-wide IP system would translate into reality. In November 2004, ASEAN again agreed on a six-year action plan, the 'ASEAN Intellectual Property Right Action Plan 2004–2010', to help them accelerate 'the pace and scope of IP asset creation and commercialization' as well as enhance its protection.[5] Achievements have, however, been recorded by the experts in coming up with common filing forms for trademarks while those for patents are still pending.[6]

This chapter seeks to examine the prospect for ASEAN of adopting a single regional IP system. First the international context against which such an effort should be assessed is formulated. Then the domestic context for harmonization is surveyed, namely the current comparative standings of the members of ASEAN in terms of economic interaction, the significance of, and divergences in, IP. Next, in view of these findings, it is investigated whether the expressed desire for an ASEAN-wide IP system might materialize. The chapter concludes that ASEAN will find it very hard to innovate in the form and substance of the IP they seek to adopt, and that the only 'safe' areas for any independent law-making by ASEAN will be in removing, totally or partially, the territorial bases of IP and in introducing a single administrative machinery for an ASEAN-wide system.

The International Context for Harmonization of Intellectual Property

Today, more than ever before, IP rights are recognized worldwide. As of 31 January 2009, the membership of the Paris and Berne Conventions stands at 173 and 164 nations, respectively.[7] It is only a small number of countries (among them Brunei, Laos and Myanmar from ASEAN) that remain without the full range of IP laws on their statute books.

---

3 World Intellectual Property Report, Vol. 10, No. 5, May 1996, at 127–8.

4 The Director of the ASEAN Free Trade Area Bureau was reported to have so stated at the ASEAN Intellectual Property Association conference in Kuala Lumpur, Malaysia, in May 1998: 'Weak IP legislation and lack of enforcement of IP laws would limit the growth of intra-ASEAN trade in high technology goods and retard the development of an indigenous research and development sector'. See, Vasantha Ganesan, 'Call to Protect Region's Intellectual Property', *Business Times* (Malaysia), 11 May 1998, at 18.

5 Available at http://www.aseansec.org/17071.htm.

6 See, http://www.aseansec.org/6412.htm; last viewed on 31 January 2009.

7 See 'WIPO Administered Treaties', at http://www.wipo.int/treaties.en.

Considering the growing interdependence of all countries in trade, the globalization of economic forces and processes in general and the rise of information as a major factor in the competitiveness of industries and countries, the increasing similarity of economic laws such as IP across nations should be expected. Indeed, the tendency towards a levelling of legal regimes is becoming more and more commonplace. The principal actors in the international economic and trade order, the multi-national corporations (MNCs), not only benefit from the creation of a single legal regime across national or state borders, but they also work towards extending it and making it permanent.[8] The MNCs would not operate or prosper without such a vital part of the infrastructure in any country as the legal system being available to them. Inevitably, one of the most critical benchmarks of any country's attractiveness as a haven for foreign investment and as a trading partner has long been the transparency of its legal system. Transparency has in turn been expressed in terms of the legal system's accessibility to foreigners (intent on doing business whether through foreign direct investment, FDI, or otherwise) and the availability of enforcement mechanisms in case legal rights have to be asserted.

The significance of intellectual property to national economies

Among the range of laws that impact on trade and commerce, IP has come to occupy a special place. Nevertheless, the significance of IP rights in single states has long been a subject of debate in many countries, whether industrially advanced or not. The economic and other ramifications of intangible information in general but particularly of those pertaining to technology have been studied from the 1960s. These studies were propelled by US anxiety about the decline of its market share in the world and its loss of world leadership in the economic and technological fields. The role of IP in the economic and commercial standing of the US as against its trading partners was also studied. One such study[9] concluded that there was no evidence to support or reject the view that IP was instrumental for the economic development of the US. It is unfortunate that more recent studies,[10] generally

---

8 See generally, Gunther Teubner, ed., *Global Law Without a State*, Dartmouth: Aldershot, 1997.

9 Fritz Machlup, *An Economic Review of the Patent System*, US Congress, Senate Committee on the Judiciary, Subcommittee on Patents, Trademarks and Copyrights, Study No. 15, Government Printing Office: Washington, DC, 1958. He later summarized his findings in 'Patents', in 11 *Encyclopaedia of the Social Sciences* 461 edited by D. Sills, 1968. He stated in that article: 'Present knowledge does not enable us to make numerical estimates of the total social costs and benefits of the patent system. Apodictic assertions about the "great" net benefit or net loss are without any foundation. Most of those who have made such assertions have not even considered the relative order of magnitude of the various items', ibid., at 470.

10 See for example, The President's Commission on Industrial Competitiveness, *Global Competition, the New Reality*, Washington, DC, 1985 which recommended strengthening IP rights internationally as 'the priority item on the nation's agenda', ibid.,

conducted for purposes of promoting US trade policy, have merely assumed the value of IP for US industries and provide no objective assessment along the lines attempted earlier.

Other countries followed up the earlier US inquiry by undertaking the same into their systems. The Canadian,[11] Australian[12] and British[13] IP systems were scrutinized to establish their significance. Except for the British study, which established with certainty that the pharmaceutical industry was the main beneficiary of the patent system, none of the others suggested that IP was indispensable for technological advances. The Canadian and Australian studies concluded identically: that both countries did not benefit as much from their respective systems anywhere near as much as foreigners (particularly MNCs) did. Yet, in both of these countries, the fact that IP was not useful to the national economies but operated in accelerating the technological and economic domination of the particular country by foreign MNCs was downplayed. No one dared suggest that IP should be abandoned. Astonishingly, despite the anomaly uncovered by the studies, the advice given to the two countries was to keep the IP system intact in order to maintain the status quo and not to create problems in their international relations.

The experiences of other countries with lower levels of industrialization and technical infrastructure could not be any different either. Almost all nations of Asia, Africa and Latin America have generally transplanted to themselves the types and quantum of IP rights recognized in the foremost industrial countries of the US, Britain and France.[14] Until the end of the Uruguay Round of GATT negotiations, practically every country had adopted a regime of IP laws, although the range of rights recognized and the efficacy of the laws (in particular, their enforcement) differed in many ways.

The impact of the TRIPS on national intellectual property systems

US persistence to level the IP regime on an international scale and raise standards across the board paid off when TRIPS was enshrined as part of the world trade

---

at 52. See also R. Michael Gadbaw and Timothy J. Richards (eds), *Intellectual Property Rights: Global Consensus, Global Conflict?*, Westview Press: Boulder, CO, 1988.

11 Economic Council of Canada, *Report on Intellectual and Industrial Property*, 1971, Ottawa.

12 T.D. Mandeville et al., *Economic Effects of the Australian Patent System: A Commissioned Report to the Industrial Property Advisory Committee*, Australian Government Publishing Service, Canberra, 1982.

13 Board of Trade, *The British Patent System, Report of the Committee to Examine the Patent System and Patent Law*, HMSO, London, 1970. See also C.T. Taylor and Z.A. Silberston, *The Economic Impact of the Patent System: A Study of the British Experience*, Cambridge University Press: Cambridge, 1973.

14 For a discussion of that process see generally, Assafa Endeshaw, *Intellectual Property Policy for Non-Industrial Countries*, Dartmouth: Aldershot, 1996, especially at 98–116.

regime agreed at Marrakesh, Morocco, in December 1993. Countries which could hardly keep up with the demands of the advanced industrial countries to bring down trade barriers have now the additional obligation of upgrading the IP regime in their respective jurisdictions. The Newly Industrializing Countries (NICs) that continue to knock on the doors of the OECD and stand at the edge of entry into the status of 'developed country' face sterner scrutiny and pressures to 'graduate' in the IP field too. This is no doubt part of the general thrust to compel them to finish graduating by meeting the spectrum of requirements that have expanded since the end of the Cold War by the inclusion of such species as human rights, the environment and trade unionization (the so-called 'social condition').

Signatories of the WTO must bridge any gaps between their existing IP laws and the requirements under TRIPS.[15] Failure to do so would amount to a breach of international trade rules. The WTO agreement has thus transformed IP issues which seemed previously to belong to the legal domain into trade issues. The juxtaposition of IP with 'other' trade issues has therefore had the effect of making IP an important instrument for international trade policy and practice.

It is to be recalled that all previous attempts to remove trade barriers throughout the world concentrated on quantitative or indirect measures that distort trade. The introduction of IP as an element in the creation of free trade in the entire world hence appears somewhat anomalous because IP is inherently prone to creating barriers rather than to removing them. IP is about protecting territory, dividing up markets and sealing walls between competitors. The recognition of this important characteristic of IP provided the impetus for the European Court of Justice's (ECJ) innovative approach of 'exhaustion of rights' in IP.[16]

However, notwithstanding increasing calls for an international competition law, TRIPS incorporates no equivalent principle that might be applied to the world, least of all in industrial countries. Neither is there any clear understanding among the proponents of sticking IP into the midst of trade issues as to how IP can operate to remove barriers or facilitate trade in any way. If anything, past practice among the industrialized countries continues unaffected by the introduction of TRIPS. In spite of the boost to the role of IP that TRIPS brought about, there has yet to be a major shift in thinking regarding how IP might be modified to remove the inherent barriers that continue to ensnare it so that world trade can ultimately become freer. Unfortunately, the basic issue of whether IP can serve WTO's *raison d'être* of opening up markets and extending them has yet to be grasped even before it can be tackled.

---

15 Article 72 of TRIPs makes it mandatory for members of WTO to adhere to the entire TRIPs. No exceptions are allowed. Still, some leeway has been given to countries in matters of enforcement. See Article 41(5), which leaves members to devise enforcement mechanisms without requiring them to allocate their resources in any specified way.

16 The Court so ruled for the fist time in the *Deutsche Grammophone* v. *Metro-SB-Grossmarkte* [1971] E.C.R. 487.

It is public knowledge that bilateral as well as multilateral IP agreements have helped the major industrial powers such as the US to open up markets for their industries and businesses but that has to be viewed against the exclusion from those markets, through the use of IP rights, of the industries of other less powerful nations. As things stand, major industries can be closed clubs for MNCs that possess distinct advantages in certain types of information. It is therefore doubtful if TRIPS will benefit other industries or countries when there is nothing they can do, under the present arrangement, to obtain that information legitimately in the open market and use it to establish themselves or cut their own corner. Consequently, if the use of IP is to avoid creating or maintaining barrier effects, as it has been so far, the way in which TRIPS was formulated needs to be re-examined from the perspective of free trade. In other words, if TRIPS is to have an impact not just on the export potential of the major industrial powers, but on that of all nations universally, it must allow for freer flow of information.

Indeed, information will have to be allowed to move across boundaries freely before one can talk about the rights of those who generate and process that information being protected against imitators and counterfeiters. The rights of those who possess legally protectable information will have to be weighed against the availability of that information freely throughout the world in order for that protection to be legitimate and economically sound. Free trade cannot have a meaning under conditions of monopoly of information in a world that is increasingly information-based and -driven.

The expansion in world trade and the creation of a fully barrier-free global market will require the dismantling of all forms of barriers whether through IP, the procurement policies of governments or in the creation or provision of services (communications and other infrastructure). In any case, global free trade in goods and services implies *free trade for all countries* and not the continuation of managed trade for some and borderless trading for others. It is most unfortunate that TRIPS has been deployed as a means of fostering the misconception that its implementation on a global scale will open up international trade for all.

The expanding scope of international intellectual property

It is common knowledge that the international IP regime is in a state of ferment. US unilateral moves to create new forms of IP that serve their need of safeguarding the lead they have attained in high technology have been followed by their major competitors, the EEC and Japan, albeit grudgingly. This has been evident in the extension of copyright protection to computer programs, the use of *sui-generis* legislation (such as the Semi-conductor Chip Protection Act of 1984) and the patenting of biotechnological innovations.[17] The linking up of IP issues to trade issues and the resort to the GATT machinery, instead of WIPO, to push through

17 This was first established by the landmark US case, *Diamond* v. *Chakrabarty* (1980) 100 S.Ct 2204.

the same US concerns (in the form of a 'universal system' of IP[18]) has precipitated reluctant EEC and Japanese acquiescence.

However, the EU (with Germany in the driving seat and as the more vocal mouthpiece) has emerged with a standpoint different from the US. Having completed its patent harmonization in the 1970s and being in the process of doing the same in other fields, the EU may yet have to confront fully the issue of a 'universal system' in the not too distant future. There is hardly any study that examines the alternatives available for the EU, Japan or the NICs in this direction. The Japanese seem to delight quietly at the prospect of the US initiatives being transformed into law with remarkable speed but in the apparent absence of any discord among the industrial and technology powers. Indeed, they might hope to assume the technological leadership widely believed to be slipping from the US.

In any case, ever since the TRIPS sought to update the dimensions of the then existing international agreements in IP (namely the Paris and Berne Conventions) and raise the minimum standards that had not been explicitly laid down in those conventions, the pressure to add to the scope and make implementation of IP the paramount task of the major nations has been mounting. A number of treaties signed before TRIPS await ratification. An example is the WIPO Treaty on Intellectual Property in Respect of Integrated Circuits (1989), signed by 19 nations (including China but none of them from ASEAN) and ratified only by Egypt (as at 31 January 2009); that Treaty seeks to protect, not just masks as in the 1984 US law relating to microchips, but lay-out designs.

There has also been a further 1989 protocol[19] to the Madrid Agreement to enable the UK, the US and other countries which stayed outside of the former to join. As of 31 January 2009, it has been adopted by 78 nations (including Singapore from ASEAN) and been deployed to serve as a further means of streamlining and simplifying the recognition of industrial property rights. Besides, more tightening of the procedural steps that national offices must adopt will make those offices more uniform and the rules they follow more universal.

As regards obtaining international protection for trademarks or patents through a single application in a national office, they have always been available. The Madrid Agreement Concerning the International Registration of Marks adopted in 1891 and the Patent Cooperation Treaty (adopted in 1970) have enabled applicants to initiate the registration process in their home country and at the same time designate the countries in which they seek additional protection. The processing of an international application is centralized in the Madrid Agreement at WIPO and in the PCT at the designated patent offices (numbering nine at the moment). The purpose

18 The latest proponent of a universal patent is US Commissioner of Patents and Trademarks, Bruce Lehman, who called for the establishment of a global patent office 'that takes advantage of technical advances' (*BNA Daily Report for Executives* 4 February 97; quoted by educause@educause.unc.edu).

19 Protocol Relating to the Madrid Agreement Concerning the International Registration of Marks.

of allowing a single application and multi-country designation is to ease the burden on applicants, although they could do this in accordance with the Paris Convention priority provision, that is country by country or piecemeal, as it were.

In the few years since TRIPS became an international yardstick to measure the compatibility of national and regional IP laws, other new treaties have been signed or ratified in a number of fields. Thus have emerged the WIPO Copyright Law Treaty of 1996, the Trademark Law Treaty (adopted on 27 October 1994) and the 1996 Treaty on Intellectual Property in Respect of Databases. Only 42 states have signed the Trademark Law Treaty and 69 states the Copyright Treaty, although both have entered into force. On the other hand, a few drafts are in the pipeline. The WIPO Patent Law Treaty (to supplement the Paris Convention and simplify procedures for grant), signed or ratified by 19 states, as at 31 January 2009, has also entered into force. On the other hand, the WIPO Draft Treaty on the Settlement of Disputes between States in the Field of Intellectual Property has yet to reach even that.

The supplements to the various treaties seek to extend the general scope of the specific IP forms already protected under the Paris, Berne or other Conventions or simplify the paths for recognition or enforcement of those rights. The importance of these new treaties, as far as ASEAN is concerned, is that many countries (contracting parties) have already incorporated the changes into their domestic laws. As a consequence, any harmonization will have to start not from where the ASEAN member states find themselves but from the positions that their trading partners, particularly those in the WTO, have reached.

In sum, ASEAN harmonization will have meaning only if a start is made by adopting the contents of, if not all, at least the major international IP treaties whether relating to substance or procedure as the foundation. It is inconceivable for ASEAN to claw back the advances and extensions in international IP and yet remain within the international trading framework of the WTO or other regional blocs.

The Comparative Standings of Member States of ASEAN

Were the member states of ASEAN only to contend with the international factors outlined in the previous section, their chosen task of forging a uniform, regional law and administrative structure would be relatively easy. However, the differences in economic standing of the members as well as the divergent levels in standards and complexity of IP laws among them suggest otherwise. Although it might be argued that the significance of IP laws for the national economies might not be far apart, it is difficult to maintain that ASEAN would transit to a single IP system on that account alone. Consequently, we will attempt to weigh the domestic factors separately in this section before considering below the overall importance of both the international and domestic factors for any progress towards realizing the projected harmonization of IP.

The level of economic interaction within ASEAN

The decision to form ASEAN in 1967 emanated from a desire to secure the region's peace and stability from threats of Soviet and Chinese expansionism and not to embark on integration, whether political or economic, as such. However, enough momentum had gathered by 1992 for a further decision to be made to form a free trade area, known as the ASEAN Free Trade Area (AFTA), by 2008. Nonetheless four of the member countries, Cambodia, Laos, Myanmar and Vietnam, will not join AFTA before 2012, owing to the apparent gap that continues to exist between them and the earlier members. As such, therefore, economic integration was not a rationale, or a precondition, for the proposed harmonization of IP in ASEAN, unlike in the EU.

Yet, the extent of intra-ASEAN trade and other forms of economic interaction as well as policies will have a bearing on the form, extent and speed of any harmonization, whenever that becomes a reality. For one thing, the five-yearly figures for intra-ASEAN trade during 1970–92 (Table 4.1) demonstrate that ASEAN interdependence on trade is very limited. Even the relatively higher figure of 25.1 per cent for 2006,[20] more than a decade later, does not counter this assessment.

Table 4.1 Intra-ASEAN trade 1970–1992 (percentage of total ASEAN trade)

1970	17.1%	**1980**	15.5%	**1990**	16.6%
1975	13.2%	**1985**	17.9%	**1992**	18.3%

Source: Naya and Iboshi in Chia Siow Yue (1994) at 57.

Regarding ASEAN policies towards Foreign Direct Investment (FDI) and transfer of technology (TOT), Toshihiko Kawagoe and Sueo Sekiguchi write that 'almost all countries regard FDI as an important instrument to develop their technology, promote industrialization, enhance employment, accelerate regional development, and to earn foreign currency'.[21] It is remarkable that the reliance on FDI includes the perception that technological advance will accompany it – something no one would have found credible at the height of the Group of 77's exploits during the 'North–South' confrontations at the United Nations Conference on Trade and Development (UNCTAD) in the 1970s and 1980s.[22]

20 See 'ASEAN Statistics: Intra- and Extra-ASEAN Trade', 2006: Table 18; available at http://www.aseansec.org/Stat/Table18.pdf.

21 Toshihiko Kawagoe and Sueo Sekiguchi (eds), *East Asian Economies: Transformation and Challenges*, Center for Asian and Pacific Studies, Sekei University: Tokyo; and Institute of Southeast Asian Studies: Singapore, 1995, at 110.

22 See, for instance, C.M. Correa, 'Transfer of Technology in Latin America: A Decade of Control', 15 *Journal of World Trade Law* 388 (1981).

Even considering that manufacturing in the ASEAN economies was 'facilitated by the massive inflows of foreign direct investment',[23] the share of manufactured goods in the total export of Indonesia, Malaysia, the Philippines, Thailand and Singapore was 36, 44, 52, 64 and 73 per cent respectively in 1990.[24] Besides the economic structures of Indonesia, Malaysia, Philippines and Thailand are 'more competitive than complementary … ASEAN economies are more complementary to the industrial countries (as well as to the Asian NIEs) than to each other. And each ASEAN country wants to protect its domestic industries from competition from neighbours'.[25] The overall consequence is that ASEAN countries, except Singapore, are 'not markets for each other's primary products. And they cannot supply each other's needs for technology and capital goods'.[26] Singapore's status as the largest trading nation within ASEAN is exemplified by the fact that it captures 47.09 per cent of intra-ASEAN trade in 1993; Malaysia comes a distant second with 25.98 per cent followed by Indonesia with 13.43 per cent.[27] The relevant figures for the three countries for 2006 were 28.6, 25.7 and 23.4 per cent, respectively.[28]

The disparity in levels of industrialization and the competitive standing of ASEAN economies inevitably translates into reluctance 'to share markets' but an urge to protect 'domestic industries from regional cooperation'.[29] The less developed of them tend to be more inward-looking and preoccupied with the basic development problems of unemployment, poverty and income inequality. They fear that premature competition for their industries will result in benefits biased in favour of the more developed members; the industrial competence of the latter will enable them to pre-empt the high value added industries and processes if industrial location is left to market forces under free trade.[30]

Under these circumstances, any IP harmonization will clash with some of the member states' policies of maintaining protection of local markets and industries. This is simply because harmonization of IP will have the inevitable effect of breaking down some of the barriers.

The significance of intellectual property for members of ASEAN

It must be stated up-front that the driving force of the changes in the municipal laws of the South East Asian nations in IP has not always been indigenous demand. Domestic commercial and industrial concerns have not been central to any of the

---

23 Chia Siow Yue, 'Progress and Issues in ASEAN Economic Integration', pp. 265–304, ibid., at 269.

24 Note 21, above, Table 6.3, at 182

25 Note 23, above, at 267–9.

26 Ibid., at 270.

27 Ibid., Table 9.3, at 273.

28 Note 20, above, ibid.

29 Note 23, above, ibid., at 282.

30 Ibid.

new changes that were wrought at various times in the past. Since the Second World War in particular, the growing importance of the region to US commercial and investment interests and the commitments of the US military could not but force a review of the legal climate in the region by way of fostering closer ties for the common cause. If IP laws figured at all, it was with a view to attracting foreign capital and technology. As one writer put it some time ago,

> While the five ASEAN countries have not at this point of time attained the same level of industrialization, it is nevertheless true to say that all five countries are in varying stages of industrialization. All five countries are equally anxious to attract foreign investment in order to promote and accelerate the economic development in their territories.[31]

The statistics available for the years 1990–95 (Table 4.2) bear out this role of foreign IP in ASEAN. First we take up the applications and grants for utility models recognized in four member nations: Indonesia, Malaysia, the Philippines and Vietnam. Of these, only Vietnam appeared to have consistent records and recognition of utility models. The comparative decline in non-resident applications and grant in utility models in Vietnam suggests that the opening up of its economy to outsiders has had an impact in the IP sphere too. In terms of absolute figures, the highest numbers of applications ('A') and grants ('G') for residents were recorded in the Philippines (456 and 170, respectively), while the respective numbers for the other nations were 27–64 and 8–42, respectively. Otherwise, the disparity in the available records prevents a more reliable analysis of the use of utility models in the respective member countries of ASEAN.

Table 4.2 Percentage of applications for and grants of utility models to residents 1990–95

	1990		**1991**		**1992**		**1993**		**1994**		**1995**	
	A	**G**	**A**	**G**	**A**	**G**	**A**	**G**	**A**	**G**	**A**	**G**
Indonesia									38	70		
Malaysia											35	–
Philippines			96	96								
Vietnam	100	100	98	98	97	96	66	90	58	64	41	33

Source: WIPO, *Industrial Property Statistics* (years 1990–1995), Geneva.

31 Chao Hick Tin, 'Protection of Intellectual Property', ASEAN Law Association 1982 General Assembly, *Report*, 25–9 October 1982, Kuala Lumpur.

The state of industrial designs differs to a certain extent both in the smaller number of nations that recognize them and involve themselves in their upkeep and in their importance to the economies of those nations. It is worthy of note that the figures for industrial designs are generally higher than those for utility models. The range for resident applications for industrial designs extends from 193 to 481 for Thailand and from 420 to 1018 for Vietnam. The relevant figure available for the Philippines is 410.

Table 4.3 Percentage of applications for and grants of designs to residents in 1990–95

	1990		1991		1992		1993		1994		1995	
	A	G	A	G	A	G	A	G	A	G	A	G
Philippines			75	43								
Thailand	31	24	44	21	41	39	47	51	50	21		
Vietnam			99	98	99	99	95	97	88	93	90	87

Source: WIPO, *Industrial Property Statistics* (years 1990–1995), Geneva.

It is easy to see from Table 4.3 that residents in Vietnam constituted the highest number of applicants and grantees of industrial design registration certificates. This might be explained by the fact that Vietnam then had yet to receive applications from the outside world. Nevertheless, one can discern a small but gradual decline in the numbers towards the later years. The respective figures for Thailand indicate that residents accounted for, on average, less than half of the applicants and grantees.

Table 4.4 Percentage of trade and service marks applied for and granted to residents in 1990–95

	1990		1991		1992		1993		1994		1995	
	A	G	A	G	A	G	A	G	A	G	A	G
Brunei	1	1	0.3	0	1.5	1	1.3	1				
Indonesia	87	82	85	63	81	80			66	73		
Laos			1	?			0	0	2	2	3	5
Malaysia			45	?	26	19	49	24			49	25
Philippine			51	34								
Thailand	55	58	58	49	54	54	59	56	56	55		
Vietnam	28	14	36	34	23	23	25	25	21	26	24	22

Source: WIPO, *Industrial Property Statistics* (years 1990–1995), Geneva.

The ratio of trade and service marks granted to residents in seven countries in ASEAN is indicated in Table 4.4. One notices immediately that there are no figures for Singapore. This is because the available figures are always given as a total of applications or grants for any specified year without dividing them up into the resident and non-resident portions. As a matter of interest, applications and grants in Singapore stood at 8791 and 7901 in 1990 and at 12,577 and 9324 for 1995, respectively.

The ranges of applications in the seven ASEAN members extend from the lowest figure of two (for Laos in 1993) and three (for Brunei in 1991) to the highest of 27,488 for Indonesia in 1992. The figures for Malaysia and Thailand were also comparatively as high as that for Indonesia. Table 4.4 shows that the respective percentages of resident applications and grants were either stable (in Brunei, Malaysia and Thailand) or on the decline (the rest of them) over the years. The figures in Brunei and Laos indicate also that local applicants or grantees were too few, not to say, negligible. On the other hand, most applications and grants in Indonesia were to residents while those in Thailand were a clear majority. It could be remarked in general that applications by and grants to non-residents were on the increase across the ASEAN region during the period in question. Some of the relatively less industrialized nations like Brunei, Laos and Vietnam appear to have indeed received relatively more non-resident applications than the rest. The figures for Vietnam reveal a hectic penetration of, or preparation for entry into, its market by non-residents.

Table 4.5 Percentage of trade and service marks applied for and granted to residents in 1997–2007

	1997		1999		2001		2003		2005		2007	
	A	G	A	G	A	G	A	G	A	G	A	G
Brunei	6.2											
Indonesia	?		?		67.6		77.9		75.2			
Laos	1.3	1.3	5.4	6.1	2.4	3.4	5.2	6.2				
Malaysia	40.8	29.9	36.8	26.4	39.3	22.7	46.9	24.9	47.3	32.2	47.5	46.6
Philippine	29.1	23.4	48.8	17.5	52.5	9.6	57.8	20.4	55.7	27.6		
Singapore			22.1	16.7	19.5	13.3	25.7	19.8	24	22.3	22.8	23.2
Thailand	47.8	44.3	60.6	46	64	57.4	70	63.6	66.6	67.4	60	59.9
Vietnam	21	18.9	36.5	22.3	35.3	36.2	60.5	54.6	62.4	53		

Source: WIPO, *Statistics Database*, December 2008 (http://www.wipo.int).

A look at the figures in Table 4.5 (which includes data Singapore has started supplying WIPO from 1998) provides even more evidence regarding the emerging picture in the area of trade and service marks. It is interesting to note that, among the emerging economies in ASEAN, Malaysia, Thailand and Indonesia continue to have a much higher figure of grants for residents than the Philippines and Singapore. Remarkably, the strongest economy among them, Singapore, appears to have the least number of grants for residents, suggesting that its success may have become a magnet for increased foreign applications. Indeed, until accurate data is available about the real 'national' (as opposed to that based on the venue of registered offices for corporations) standing of the 'resident' applicants and grantees, even the higher figures for the other three nations might not be totally accurate.

We will now take up patents, another good indicator of the level of interest that foreigners might have in an economy. Table 4.6 presents the figures for five ASEAN members. Singapore does not appear among them simply because of the nature of figures available (as referred to above in connection with trade and service marks). It might be noted nevertheless, by reference to the single year (1995) for which data is partially available, that the applications received in that year from residents in Singapore constituted less than 1 per cent. That figure does not of course make Singapore an exception. All the nations represented in the table display a similarly low ratio of local applicants and patentees. They range from as low a figure as 1 (for Vietnam in 1993) to the highest of 16 (for Thailand in the same year and in 1994) for applications. The relative figures for grantees or patentees are a low of 1 (Malaysia in 1993) and a high of 20 (for Thailand in 1993).

Table 4.6 Percentage of patents applied for and granted to residents in 1990–95

	1990		1991		1992		1993		1994		1995	
	A	G	A	G	A	G	A	G	A	G	A	G
Indonesia			4	?	2	?			?	7.5		
Malaysia		4.5	4	?	6	1	7	1	6	1	3	2
Philippine			8	5								
Thailand	4	2	4	8	3	5	16	20	16	9		
Vietnam	12	2	6	5	41	54	1	2	0	3	0	5

Source: WIPO, *Industrial Property Statistics* (years 1990–1995), Geneva.

The extraordinarily large figures for Vietnam in 1992 have no easy explanation, though the absolute figures they represent are not that significant (37 applications and 12 grants). The round figures for the rest of the nations in Table 4.6 will indicate the level of foreign interest in the respective nations. Thus the resident applications in Thailand jumped from 73 in 1990 to 634 in 1995, those in Malaysia from 106 in 1991 to 223 in 1994, in Indonesia from 54 in 1991 to 80 in 1992, in the Philippines 147 in 1991 and in Vietnam 7 in 1990 and 23 in 1995.

A perusal of developments between 1997 and 2007, presented in Table 4.7, indicates that, despite the lack of full data for Indonesia and Vietnam, patenting has picked up throughout ASEAN. Still, the trend of foreign penetration of the patent systems across ASEAN has continued with the exception of Singapore, which has seen a progressive increase in local patenting since 2003. That country's vigorous pursuit of research and development in biotechnology must help explain the distinct departure from previous years that the figures portray.

Table 4.7 Percentage of patents applied for and granted to residents in 1997–2007

	1997		**1999**		**2001**		**2003**		**2005**		**2007**	
	A	**G**	**A**	**G**	**A**	**G**	**A**	**G**	**A**	**G**	**A**	**G**
Indonesia	2		6.3		5.3		6.1		5.4			
Malaysia	2.8	6.6	3.7	5.4	4.6	1.2	7.4	2	8.3	1.5		
Philippine		2.7		0.8		0.9		0.6		0.9		
Singapore	4.5	0.6	5.3	1.1	6	2.4	7.9	4	6.6	7.4	7	6.3
Thailand	9.4	3	11.1	7.4	13.7	7.3	15.2	5.4	14.6	11.2		
Vietnam	2.4	0	3.2	2.7	4	?	6.8	?	9.2	?		

Source: WIPO, *Statistics Database*, December 2008 (http://www.wipo.int).

Overall, the general picture that emerges from the contrast between resident and non-resident applications and grants in IP rights in ASEAN is an absolute domination by non-residents. In spite of the relatively high figures for residents in Thailand and Indonesia with respect to trade and service marks, the overwhelming sway in IP rights by non-residents is very clear. Even in the case of Thailand and Indonesia, it would not be surprising if the resident applications were from foreign right holders doing business in the two nations.

Perhaps the picture painted here is not typical of ASEAN alone as many NICs too display the same characteristics. However, the reality of the situation is not matched by most official pronouncements (including those referring to the topic under discussion), which gloss over this aspect of ASEAN affairs or even create the impression that ASEAN are firmly in control.

Divergences in intellectual property among ASEAN

The diverse background in the origins and evolution of IP in the ASEAN member states was bound to find reflection in the divergent conceptions as to form and substance of IP. We have already traced the development of IP laws in the emerging economies of ASEAN in Chapter 2. We need here only mention a few heads of comparison across ASEAN.

First, we will look at the general picture. Most members of ASEAN do not provide the entire spectrum of IP protection. The Philippines has been in the lead for a very long time in the relatively broader range of IP rights it recognizes as compared with the other members of ASEAN. Indonesia, Malaysia, Singapore and Thailand have followed suit in filling the gaps by adding to the minimal IP rights or revising old ones from 1987 onwards. The rest of ASEAN (Brunei, Cambodia, Laos, Myanmar and Vietnam) are still in the process of either drafting new or adapting old IP legislation to bring themselves to the same levels as those in the leading pack. This process has been hastened by the advent of TRIPS and the newly assumed obligations of ASEAN states as signatories of WTO. One of the most recent examples is Indonesia, which introduced changes to its IP laws in 1997 only to replace them all in 2001–2: expansion of the scope of patentable subject-matter; recognition of well-known marks as well as service marks and geographic indications of origin; and protection of rental rights and rights in performances. It is to be noted that the Philippines, Thailand, Malaysia and Singapore have done the same or more in the couple of years before and after 2000.

The specific impact of TRIPS on each nation's pursuit to update national IP legislation will be beyond our scope. It would be sufficient for our purposes here to mention the general consequences of the thrust of TRIPS on ASEAN. Because of their obligations under the WTO and the concerns of the major industrial powers regarding the divergence in enforcement of IP rights and the threat of piracy in each nation, the respective ASEAN members' national IP laws have been subjected to constant criticism. More often than not, international pressures on ASEAN governments to modify or enforce their IP laws play a large part. The most direct of these pressures are exerted by the United States Office of Trade Representative (USTR) through its annual investigation into trade practices of trading partners of the US. Thus the Philippines was rapped by the USTR in an out-of-cycle review for allowing computer software 'decompilation', that is reverse-engineering.[32] The 1998 annual review of the USTR[33] repeated the same critique against the Philippines and stated alleged shortcomings against other ASEAN nations, notably Indonesia (that the recent amendments 'are not completely TRIPS-consistent'). The 2008 review has reiterated virtually the same disapproval of the state of IP in the Philippines; namely that it has 'generally failed to improve the prosecution and conviction of IPR violators. Print piracy and end-user piracy of business and entertainment software also are serious problems. The United States has urged the Philippines to further improve and sustain enforcement efforts and to take steps to enhance judicial capacity'.[34]

We will now turn to the general variations between the ASEAN members in each form of IP. With respect to patent laws, it might be recalled that those laws have not

32 The then USTR-designate, Barshevsky, so stated on 20 December, 1996; quoted by 11(2) World Intellectual Property Report, February 1997 at 52.

33 Available online at http://www.ustr.gov/reports/index.html.

34 See USTR, *2008 National Trade Estimate Report on Foreign Trade Barriers*, ibid.

been long in existence in the majority of ASEAN. Thus, Malaysia introduced one in 1983, Indonesia in 1989 and Singapore in 1995. Although standards of novelty and inventiveness have long been identical to those in the industrialized countries, there are divergences and gaps not only within each national legislation but also as between them. Whatever may be the rationale, the major points of divergence among ASEAN relate to the scope of patentable subject matter (most excluding micro-organisms, pharmaceutical products and the like) and the extent of resort to compulsory licensing (to compensate for lack of working or unavailability of patented product or process in the national economy). Both the scope of patents and the use of compulsory licensing have increasingly been narrowed down, in particular because of the ASEAN member states' obligation to make their laws TRIPS-consistent and the reforms they have had to undertake as a result.

Besides the variations in the scope of patentability and compulsory licensing, there are different approaches towards minor inventions and their terms of protection as well as that for patents. Thus Indonesia accords protection to small product improvements through a 'Simple Patent' (obviously a 'petty patent') for one time of five years. Vietnam, on the other hand, grants protection for 'Utility Solutions' for six years. By contrast, Malaysia recognizes 'Utility Innovations' for a period of five years but renewable for a further five. The Philippines recognizes design patents (which include utility models) and protects them for five years too, but with a possibility of renewals for two consecutive periods of five years.

In copyright, the major point of variation between most national legislation is the extent of recognition of rights – rights in performances being one of the chief gaps until the spate of TRIPS-inspired changes were introduced in recent years. Besides these, the boundaries and degree of fair use remain variegated. The need to make foreign works available to satisfy local demand and/or in local languages stands out as the main reason for this. While generous provisions in the national copyright laws which legitimized this practice in the past have been eroded gradually and somewhat restricted in recent years (the Philippines, Indonesia, Malaysia and Singapore being cases in point), the fact is that there is no single uniform practice across ASEAN, save the traditional fair use exceptions one finds in legislation in the UK or France, for instance.

In trademark law, gaps remain as to the scope of registrability of trade marks and service marks (the contentious issues of whether any colour, smell or shape could be protectable), the status of famous marks and what might be considered 'use of a mark' as a defence against removal for non-use. In terms of administration of trade or service marks, such provisions as that of the Trade Mark Law Treaty have yet to be discovered by all ASEAN legislators.

As regards other forms of laws, the situation is as follows. In the protection of industrial designs, most of ASEAN lacks any legal instruments or, at any rate, local laws. Thus, until a few years ago, both Singapore and Malaysia relied on prior registration in the UK according to UK registered design law before allowing any local re-registration. On the other hand, animal or plant varieties are not protected in all of ASEAN. The state of trade secrets or confidential information is still undecided for many or governed by non-statutory law in those with a common law heritage. Laws relating to integrated circuits and digital forms of creativity (multimedia) have yet to be thought of in most nations.

The overall state of divergence and incoherence in IP laws of ASEAN is exemplified by the attitude towards parallel importing. The general trend in ASEAN has been towards allowing parallel importing, although some countries have backtracked to prohibit it from time to time. This is often an indication of confusion between restrictions of imports on the basis of the rights of IP owners and the legitimate prohibition of imports of infringing copies. In any case, the concern for a more open and barrier-free ASEAN market has not been served by the conflicting positions on parallel imports.

The Prospects for Harmonization of ASEAN Intellectual Property

Arguments have surfaced from time to time in the past in member countries of ASEAN for a system of IP laws that reflect national needs and culture. Thus a former Registrar of Trademarks of Singapore[35] had counselled, at a WIPO-organized seminar in Singapore, that the establishment of a patent system should be assumed very carefully: 'Indeed much time and effort may be dissipated if the end result would be only to serve a mere handful of applications. As in all economies of scale one should evaluate both cost and effect and any new Patent processing system should be economically justifiable'.[36] To prove his point he produced the following figures[37] on the number of patent applications annually submitted in Singapore between 1975 and 1980: 499, 689, 533, 635, 864 and 603, respectively. Of these figures, the applications from Malaysia or Singapore did not go beyond a maximum of three for Singapore and six for Malaysia.

The Registrar recommended the adoption of a patent system incorporating 'the best features of the varied patent system in Japan, the United States and Europe' backed by an 'internationally recognized searching or examining authority'.[38] In the same breath, he suggested the adoption of a petty-patent system for Singapore,[39] an idea that was eventually adopted. It may be noted that the Registrar did not suggest the postponement or even abandonment of instituting a patent system for Singapore by reference to the fact that its value for the local economy was not borne out by the figures he himself provided.

35 Ang Koon Hian, 'The Existing Patent System in Singapore and its Contemplative Development – As Seen from the Viewpoint of the Registry', in *Seminar on Patent and Trademark Licensing Singapore*, 10–12 December 1980, WIPO, at 4–13.

36 Ibid., at 10.

37 Ibid., at 7–8.

38 Ibid., at 11.

39 Ibid., at 13.

One writer[40] went beyond the needs of single states and proposed the harmonization of industrial property for ASEAN through, among other things, inserting in the national laws of a provision stating that importation does not constitute working of a patented invention, a common standpoint regarding black lists in licensing agreements. Another commentator also called for 'enactment of legislation providing for registration of uniform protection of intellectual property rights especially in the field of trademarks, patents, and designs extending to the whole territory'.[41]

While maintaining that 'it would be almost impossible to create a uniform legal system'[42] for ASEAN, because of their 'varied socio-cultural and political background', Radhie advised harmonizing the laws in certain fields to facilitate 'cooperation in the economic, social and cultural fields as intended by the Bangkok Declaration of 1967'.[43] Yet, he suggested a step by step harmonization in such 'neutral' areas as trade and business that do 'not directly impinge upon the cultural sensitivities and legal consciousness of the member states'.[44]

The conflict of interests surrounding the making of IP laws by countries in the regions is further illustrated by the nature of the submissions to the Singapore Parliament during the drafting stage of the Copyright Act 1987.[45] Foreign interests were adamant that the proposed bill fell short of their requirements while local interests argued that it did not give them more leeway. Thus, among the foreign interests, the International Intellectual Property Alliance submitted that Singapore has totally failed to create a climate conducive to the creation, distribution and trade in products and services dependent on the protection of intellectual property. Because of its failure to protect intellectual property, it has been stigmatized with the reputation as one of the world's leading pirate nations and its role and reputation in the world has suffered accordingly. The Government's position has resulted in the United States copyright industries having suffered significant damage due to uncontrolled piracy and for many years Alliance members have sought to convince Singapore, to no avail, to remedy its woefully short-sighted policy.[46]

The Alliance suggested that there be minimum statutory fines and prison terms, the elimination of the distinction between secondary and primary infringement as well as the exception given to those who do not have knowledge that any article they may be dealing with is infringing. The Alliance further suggested the need for

---

40 Wurjati Martosewojo, 'Protection of Intellectual Property in Indonesia', ASEAN Law Association 1982 General Assembly, *Report*, 25–9 October 1982, Kuala Lumpur.

41 Wong Say Fong, 'Protection of Intellectual Property in Malaysia', ASEAN Law Association 1982 General Assembly, *Report*, 25–9 October 1982, Kuala Lumpur.

42 Note 2, above, at 52–3.

43 Ibid., at 53.

44 Ibid., at 54.

45 Report of the Select Committee on the Copyright Bill (Bill No. 8/86), Presented to Parliament on 22 December 1986.

46 Paper S.C. No. 19, ibid., at A116–A125.

clarification of cable programmes and performances as protectable subject matters as well as the limitation of fair-use provisions such as for education and home taping.

Among the local representatives of industries, the Singapore Chinese Chamber of Commerce and Industry was forthright about the necessity of Singapore adopting IP while noting that 'For the continued economic growth and development of Singapore, it is important that our local business community have access to intellectual properties [*sic*] especially in scientific and technical works, of the developed countries at costs which we can offord [*sic*]'.[47] It therefore suggested that the law make an exception for those who reproduce 'intellectual works, subject of copyright, for non-profit making purposes, e.g. promotional, charitable and educational'. It added that works copied for 'strictly personal use' should be exempted; so should reproduction of performances or for purposes of study and research 'in all fields of education'.[48] The Consumers' Association of Singapore, on its part, pleaded for changes in the bill that take into account the interests of the Singapore consumer, 'principally the student', and sought to extend the area of fair use for educational purposes and to legalize parallel imports.[49] The National University of Singapore Students' Union submitted similar views.[50]

We all know what became of the demands for provisions that took into account local or national development requirements. The residual concessions in the 1987 Act in Singapore or in the equivalent laws of the other countries of ASEAN (notably that of Indonesia, Malaysia and Thailand) have been removed systematically over time, particularly in the urge to come into line with those countries' commitments under TRIPS. Vietnam too entered into a 1997 bilateral arrangement with the US leading to the same ultimate effect. A mere glance at the rush of legislation adding to (Vietnam), amending or revising (the original five ASEAN) the IP laws will establish that any room for local initiative or improvisation has been virtually eliminated. It would seem that a new era has opened in the making of IP laws in the ASEAN region as much as elsewhere: that of complete and unquestioning acquiescence to the onward march of international IP laws.

This is not to say that the march is without any resistance. Thus intermittent calls for asserting local or national demands concerning forms and substance of IP as against the relentless advance of international IP have been expressed chiefly on behalf of Malaysia. At the inauguration of the ASEAN Intellectual Property Association, the Minister of Trade and Consumer Affairs of Malaysia, Datuk Abu Hassan Omar, reportedly stated it was 'time ASEAN countries formulated their own system on the use of trademarks and patents, that would still suit ASEAN's

47 Ibid., Paper S.C. No. 30, at A175–A179.

48 Ibid.

49 Ibid., Paper S.C. No. 15, at A87–A103.

50 Ibid., Paper No. 24, at A144–A147.

needs and expectations'.[51] He added that ASEAN should self-regulate and cooperate among themselves

> in setting up a system or systems compatible to the needs and culture of its member countries. We have to set our house in order and we have to lead and not follow all the time. Otherwise, others will come into the region to impose on us what they want done, which would be mainly beneficial to IP owners from outside the region.

It is difficult to understand how the Minister could envisage such a course of action without at the same time calling for a drastic revision of the existing laws accompanied by a withdrawal from current international treaties, such as the TRIPS. Nevertheless, we have no indication that the Malaysian proposal ever served as a basis for any radical transformation of the IP regime in ASEAN.

The obvious question for policy makers then is this: if international IP is advancing without any let up and ASEAN are bound, expected or pressurized to follow, should one even think of an ASEAN regional IP system? One can always deny or ignore the international developments in IP law-making and seek to carry on as if nothing has changed. Such a view is implicit in the ASEAN Framework Agreement on Intellectual Property Cooperation.

The Framework Agreement envisages creating 'closer cooperation' among the members in the making, administration and enforcement[52] of IP laws. The underlying objective of such a cooperation is stated as being to support the economic and technical advances in the region. Yet, the Framework cites at the same time the need to live up to TRIPS and the international obligations of the member states. It hardly requires pointing out that both TRIPS and the post-TRIPS extensions of, or additions to, international treaties are in the service of the strongest economies grouped in the OECD countries. Consequently, the ASEAN desire to create a patent and trademark system in conformity with the international IP regime but with a view to boosting the economic and technical advances in the region is rather baffling.

For one thing, it cannot be taken for granted that cooperation in making, administering and enforcing IP laws will automatically enhance the economic and technological positions of the members of ASEAN. Quite the contrary! Any possible benefits to be derived from such a cooperation will not necessarily go to ASEAN; indeed, the real beneficiaries will be those countries that made it their business to push for extension and implementation of IP laws throughout the world and succeeded in doing so.

---

51 Jeffrey Ramayah, 'ASEAN Needs Own Laws to "Protect IP Rights"', *The New Straits Times* [Malaysia], 12 February 1996; accessed from the Down Jones News/Retrieval [Online] on 4 May 1998.

52 Article 3, ASEAN Framework Agreement on Intellectual Property Cooperation.

On the other hand, the fast pace in the development of the international IP regime has already pre-empted, to a large extent, any national law-making, whether it be in the major industrial or the least industrial nations. The quick retreat and, eventually, total rout of the Andean Pact in the IP sphere was a consequence of that emerging reality in the early 1990s. Similarly, the desire for an ASEAN-wide IP system should be perceived more as an acquiescence to international developments than an attempt to blaze a new trail. As it is, many ASEAN members have acquired 'uniform' laws by virtue of their accession to the international conventions as well the amendments they had to put through as part of their international trade obligations (WTO-TRIPS).

Therefore, if one can make any sense of the projected harmonization, it should mean following closely and implementing the process set in train by TRIPS and the post-TRIPS arrangements. Just as other countries and blocs will gradually but surely be drawn into more and more 'harmonization', the ASEAN exercise of fashioning an exclusive IP system and dashing for some undefined uniformity will end up treading the beaten path.

Moreover, if the purpose of harmonization in ASEAN is to provide a level playing field for any possible IP-based industries that each member might have, that can be achieved just as well through accession to the existing international treaties. If, however, there is an imbalance or unequal relationship with the more powerful industrial nations that ASEAN needs to redress, then harmonization will only make it worse for them. If, as seems more likely and rational, the desire is for a more efficient administrative machinery that reduces waste and leads to a sharing of common resources such as trained personnel, that could be achieved even without harmonizing the substantive aspects of the members' IP laws.

In the final analysis, ASEAN leaders need to address the underlying policy issues frankly. It is not difficult to see that, at this stage, members of ASEAN would be engaged very much in gap filling. Apart from the disparities within the domestic IP laws of the members of ASEAN, indicated briefly above, a number of them have still not gained membership of the major international IP conventions. This cannot be a revelation. ASEAN comprises countries that have barely started the transition from laws of the colonial era (such as Brunei) as well as those which have embarked on forging a TRIPS-consistent regime.

Obviously, gap filling by members of ASEAN singly or as a region will eventually bring IP laws to the same level as international developments (the TRIPS arrangement included) necessitate. Whatever the content of those gap filling measures (substantive, procedural or administrative) might be, the approach will remain the same: however reluctant some members might be, they would have no option but to continue willy-nilly to operate within parameters developed in the more advanced countries (chiefly grouped in the OECD) and to fill any gaps in their IP laws as a matter of course by reference to those countries' IP systems. Any success ASEAN might achieve in forging a common IP system will depend on a clear understanding of this.

Conclusion

On the surface, it may appear to members of ASEAN that they should stop reacting to external pressures and start becoming proactive and issue their own laws independently of international factors and developments. In so far as the ASEAN members, at least the more advanced among them (that is, the five emerging economies), plan to leap into the league of the most industrialized in the world, there may seem to be no reason not to do that. At the very least, they may assume that they have the ability and power to decide whether or not to adjust their laws to meet international requirements at their discretion.

Yet, the sketch of international developments in IP undertaken above has demonstrated that no nation or group of nations can stay outside of them. The progress being made on all fronts, the unrelenting extensions in the substance of IP rights as well as the drive to 'universalize' their administration leave no one in doubt that any deviation will have only one consequence: to be left out of the global economy and trade. This is simply because IP issues have been submerged in trade issues and no one may be able to undo that. Clearly, ASEAN members cannot opt to remain within WTO but seek to work out their own regional IP system commensurate with the demands of their respective economies, cultures and export performance. In short, their options would appear to be to follow the lead of the major industries countries rather than set their own pace in IP at the world level.

Even where ASEAN 'choose' to harmonize what can only be their adoption of international standards, they have serious issues to consider. Given the divergence in IP laws among members of ASEAN, success in such a 'hamonization' might not be in the actual range or scope of rights they recognize as a basis for a regional IP system, but in the achievement of a common minimal framework for all.

If ASEAN can develop a framework to be deployed both in raising existing levels of IP within some but also in introducing new standards of IP law and enforcement in others, that will be a major success. The varying scopes and complexity in the range of IP laws in ASEAN mean that any harmonization will of necessity be a long, drawn-out affair. While the leading five members (the emerging economies) succeeded in making their laws TRIPS-consistent by the year 2000, the task of raising the lowest common denominator in IP among the remaining members of ASEAN will take more time. Hence harmonization of ASEAN intellectual property, in the sense generally understood, will be a matter for the future.

Chapter 5
Intellectual Property Law-Making in Developing Countries in the New Century*

Introduction

At the beginning of the new century, the plight of the developing countries (DCs) and emerging economies as well as the predicament of AIDS sufferers grabbed the attention of international public opinion. The controversy surrounding the availability or otherwise of cheap drugs for AIDS sufferers in DCs has provoked diverse attitudes (ranging from sympathy to the sufferers to anger against the drugs manufacturers). In the same measure, it rekindled interest in the role of intellectual property in general and that of the Agreement on Trade-Related Aspects of Intellectual Property Rights (TRIPS) in particular in the transformation, or otherwise, of the social and economic conditions of the DCs. In spite of the abundant material on the subject and the decade or so of scrutiny it has been subjected to, the new developments have called for a re-opening of debate on TRIPS, whether as to its rationale or ramifications.

It would have seemed, however, that, for all practical purposes, the standing of TRIPS in international IP and trade had been placed beyond contention and that any further rancour could serve only to let off steam or to engage in academic diatribe without any practical consequence. Yet, arguments are still being proffered to support or assail TRIPS. Besides the temptation to weigh the merits of those arguments, there is a need to examine the future of IP law-making beyond TRIPS, at least to gauge if there are any grounds for optimism on the part of DCs as well as the newly found forces that have embarked on championing their causes.

Nevertheless, this chapter stops short of rehearsing the arguments on the appropriateness or otherwise, to DCs, of adopting IP laws that have been developed in the advanced economies of Western Europe, North America and Japan. Various works abound on that very subject,[1] although much of the discussion in

---

* This chapter originally appeared in the author's name, as 'The Paradox of Intellectual Property Lawmaking in the New Millennium: Universal Templates as Terms of Surrender for non-Industrial Nations; Piracy as an Offshoot', 10(1) *Cardozo Journal of International and Comparative Law* 47–77, Spring 2002.

1 See, amongst others, Edith T. Penrose, *The Economics of the Internatinal Patent System*, Baltimore, MD: Johns Hopkins Press, 1951; Helge E. Grundmann, 'Foreign Patent Monopolies in Developing Countries: An Empirical Analysis', 12 *Journal of Development Studies* 186, 1976; A. Samuel Oddi, 'The International Patent System and Third World

recent years repeats earlier arguments under the guise of studying the impact or implementation of TRIPS.[2] By contrast, this chapter argues that the role of DCs in intellectual property law-making has vanished for the most part and that piracy in DCs is partly the flip side of the inability of DCs to craft IP laws in aid of their national economic and cultural pursuits and partly as an ideologically motivated label (hence a misnomer).

The chapter is arranged in four sections. The first sketches the nature of the new demands on the major economic powers and the pharmaceutical companies to alleviate the chronic problems of development in general and AIDS in particular. The second briefly surveys the prospect for developments in IP law-making beyond TRIPS and at the behest of the major industrial countries (ICs). The third maintains that IP law-making has come to a virtual end in DCs because the crucial issues that compel the adoption of national formulae to enhance economic and cultural progress are precisely those already blocked by TRIPS. The imposition on non-IC members of the WTO to adopt TRIPS, the latest by 2005, has effectively put paid to the role of DCs to intervene in their own interests and devise appropriate IP laws. The last section contends that, while piracy is a global problem, rampant even within the ICs themselves, the incidence of piracy in DCs could be better characterized as the main direct consequence of the forcible incorporation of incongruent or inappropriate IP laws into their statute books. The chapter concludes that there are no ways forward in IP law-making for DCs, that any movement to redress the in-built biases in the international IP system against the DCs should aim at introducing exceptions to TRIPS in the interest of national development, health, education and culture.

New Pressures to Reopen Debate on TRIPS

Two important developments in recent years have highlighted the importance, indeed urgency, of addressing the well-known issues affecting the developing nations: economic and technological stagnation, chronic foreign debt, poverty, hunger and disease. The first was the debacle of the December 1999 Seattle World Trade Organization (WTO) Ministerial Conference where protesters upstaged the event, forced its cancellation and pushed the plight of the poor countries high on the

---

Development: Reality or Myth?', *Duke Law Journal* 831, 1987; P.S. Sangal and Kishore Singh (eds), *Indian Patent Sytem and Paris Convention: Legal Perspectives*, Ashoka Printers: Delhi, 1987; and A. Endeshaw, *Intellectual Property Policy for Non-Industrial Countries*, Dartmouth: Aldershot, 1996.

2 A good example of this is Robert M. Sherwood, 'The TRIPS Agreement: Implications for Developing Countries', 37 *IDEA* 491, 1997. Sherwood purportedly undertook a study for the WIPO in 1996 on the indicated topic. However, the study merely rehashed the role of IP in ICs as being synonymous with its significance for DCs (the very problems under contention) and ended by explaining the TRIPS Agreement.

international agenda.[3] The glare of publicity that accompanied the Seattle protests and subsequent ones (including at Prague[4]) catapulted the problems afflicting the DCs into recurrent concerns of the various international organizations[5] and the major industrial powers, particularly the Group of 7 (G-7) countries. The barricades erected to keep away protesters from every global venue of discussions and deliberations on the world economy (including the most recent in Davos, Switzerland[6]) have only kept the issues alive and compelled participants at the diverse fora to express, at least, a measure of commitment towards resolving the underlying problems of debt and inequitable international relations that straddle DCs.

The second important development relates to the continuing tragedy of the devastating impact of AIDS/HIV on developing nations as a whole, but Africa in particular. The controversy surrounding the huge profits registered by the

3 See Christiane Oelrich, 'Chaos in Seattle as Violence Mars WTO talks', *Deutsche Presse-Agentur*, 1 December 1999; available online from the Dow Jones Interactive; accessed 2 March 2001. See also Ron Scherer, 'No Halting the Trade Juggernaut? Civil Unrest in Seattle adds Visibility to Environmental, Labor', *The Christian Science Monitor*, 2 December 1999; available online from the Dow Jones Interactive; accessed 2 March 2001. According to one commentator, on the anniversary of the event, 'groups pursuing such varied agendas as feminism, labor and ecology came together to oppose what they saw as an anti-democratic WTO that mainly served the interests of multinational corporations at the expense of Third World workers and the environment'. See Keir Graff, 'Is This Revolution For Real?', *The Chicago Tribune*, 2 February 2001, at C 10; available online from the Dow Jones Interactive; accessed 2 March 2001.

4 Michael Adler, 'Thousands of Protestors in Prague Streets against World Bank and IMF', *Agence France-Presse*, 24 September 2000; available online from the Dow Jones Interactive; accessed 2 March 2001. A leader of one of the groups was quoted as having said, 'We will fight on until the poorest countries are not forced to put the payment of debt to foreign creditors ahead of the lives of their children', ibid.

5 The heads of three international organizations declared, on the eve of the ill-fated Seattle Conference, 'We shall build on the strong collaboration between our three organizations to enhance the capacity of developing countries to use the new trade negotiations, and their membership in the WTO, to foster their economic and social development'. See 'Joint Statement by the Heads of the International Monetary Fund (IMF), the World Bank, and the World Trade Organization (WTO)', 30 November 1999; available at http://www.wto.org/wto/english/news_e/pres99_e/pr153_e.htm; accessed 26 March 2001. Later, the Director-General of the WTO, Mike Moore, spoke on 19 March 2001, in London, at the 'Ministerial Roundtable on Trade and Poverty in Least-Developed Countries' in favor of alleviating poverty and of the intention to focus on their problem at the forthcoming WTO Round of trade negotiations in Qatar in November. See 'Poor-Country Issues must be at Heart of new Round – Moore'; available at http://www.wto.org/wto/english/news_e/news_e.htm; accessed 26 March 2001.

6 Kate Millar, 'Opponents Defend Right to Protest against Prestigious Swiss Summit', *Agence France-Presse*, 26 January 2001; available online from the Dow Jones Interactive; accessed 2 March 2001.

British giant pharmaceutical company, Glaxo SmithKline,[7] and its attempts to stop the importation and local production of cheap generic drugs by many African countries in response to the AIDS/HIV pandemic[8] resuscitated issues of intellectual property (IP) long considered resolved. A general impression has emerged that the AIDS/HIV pandemic in Africa has reached such a level that entire nations may perish while the cure, though available, is locked away through systematic patenting or becomes unaffordable as a result of the pricing strategies of the major pharmaceutical companies. The apparent reluctance on the part of these companies to allow the production of generic drugs cheaply[9] and to make them affordable to sufferers and the local communities in Africa and elsewhere attracted lots of commentary and generated heated exchanges. An editorial in *The Guardian* (London) observed:

> The dreadful dimensions of this plague brutally expose the growing inequality of health provision across the globe. Aids is a death sentence in Africa, whilst in Britain a cocktail of drugs can manage the disease ... Right at the heart of it lies the issue of how access to essential medicines is now regulated and patented under the trade related intellectual property agreement (TRIPS) enforced by the World Trade Organization.[10]

Considerable sympathy continues to be expressed towards the victims of AIDS/HIV through widespread criticisms of the pharmaceutical companies even by institutions that uphold entrenched legal precepts of property as sacrosanct.[11] The number of Western aid agencies that have been calling for affordable drugs for the same sufferers has increased at the same time as their voices have become more strident.[12] However, the suggestion that lowering prices or allowing local

7 Gautam Naik, 'GlaxoSmithKline Posts 13% Rise in Profit – Firm to Strengthen Efforts to Offer Poorer Nations Discounted AIDS Drugs', The Wall Street Journal 22 February 2001 at A19; available online from the Dow Jones Interactive; accessed 27 February 2001.

8 [Editorial] 'Millions of Lives at Risk: Drug Companies must Temper their Power', *The Guardian* [London], 15 February 2001, no page; available online from the Dow Jones Interactive; accessed 27 February 2001.

9 Rachel Zimmerman and Jesse Pesta, 'Cipla AIDS-Drug Offer Changes Outlook', *The Wall Street Journal*, 8 February 2001, at B13. Zimmerman and Pesta comment, 'The sudden offer by an Indian drug manufacturer to sell lower-priced AIDS drugs in Africa has sent a jolt through the drug industry and the international AIDS community, but many questions remain about whether or how poor countries could take advantage of it', ibid.

10 *The Guardian*, note 8, above, ibid.

11 Ibid.

12 Donald G. McNeil Jr, 'Oxfam Joins Campaign to Cut Drug Prices for Poor Nations', *The New York Times*, 5, column 3, 13 February 2001; available online from the Dow Jones Interactive; accessed 27 February 2001. Oxfam reportedly accused the pharmaceutical companies and the 'rich nations' of '"waging an undeclared drugs war" against poor nations

production on license form the patentees will transform the reality underlying the AIDs pandemic borders on the absurd when viewed against the enormous social and economic ills that characterize the DCs in general today and have plagued them for far longer than the decade and a half of AIDs. One writer appropriately commented, 'For Glaxo to sacrifice its patents would not result in eradication of Aids. The problems of developing countries could not be solved simply by carpet-bombing Africa with Aids drugs. Food, education, infrastructure and the eradication of poverty are at least as important as medicine in ending the horror story'.[13]

On the level of policy, the debate has sparked off the question whether IP, as currently framed in TRIPS, should take precedence over human lives in DCs? The editorial of *The Guardian* mentioned above recognized the importance of the support for charitable causes that the pharmaceutical companies produce as a defence for their huge profits; however, it did not consider that support to be sufficient. It called for a shorter life for drug patents to meet 'the needs of desperately poor countries where millions will die' and warned the drug companies of an otherwise impending 'public relations disaster'.[14]

A Judge of the Court of Appeal of South Africa sought to extend the discussions on how best to alleviate the plight of AIDs sufferers into the general question of the significance of IP to ordinary people in DCs: 'Many of those living in the South reside in insulated communities cut off by a lack of infrastructure and education. They cannot benefit from IP. How can they understand the merit of its protection? ... If one does not have bread, why should one protect gourmet recipes?'[15]

At the opposite end of the spectrum stand the US and advocates of the strictest enforcement of IP irrespective of the social and economic circumstances of DCs, including those where most of the AIDS suffers reside. Far from backing down and recognizing the need to reconsider if the pandemic deserves a different treatment than that preordained by TRIPS, the US government has adopted the familiar aggressive stance – threatening many countries it views as being in violation of its law on drug patenting with one form of action or another.[16] According to *The Guardian*,

---

by keeping drug prices high and by using trade sanctions to protect the patent treaties that give companies 20-year monopolies on their drugs', ibid.

13 Patience Wheatcroft, 'Patent Need for Careful Thought', *The Times of London*, 17 February 2001, at 55; available online from the Dow Jones Interactive; accessed 27 February 2001.

14 Note 8, above, ibid.

15 L.T.C. Harms, 'Offering Cake for the South', 22(10) *European Intellectual Property Review* 451, October 2000, at 451 (discussing the need for finding solution for the widening gap between the rich North and the poor South).

16 See US Trade Representative (USTR), '2000 National Trade Estimate Report on Foreign Trade Barriers'; available at http://www.ustr.gov/html/2000_contents.html; accessed 16 March 2001.

> The reason for this aggression on the part of the US government is not difficult to discern. The pharmaceutical industry ... is a powerful operator within the Washington establishment. In just two years, members of the US pharmaceutical association spent a staggering $236m on lobbyists and a further $14m went to political parties. This is likely to get still worse under a Bush administration, which includes several members with close links to the drug companies.[17]

The debate has also triggered the question of national sovereignty in the use of resources and the adoption of the requisite policies to alleviate deep-seated social and economic predicaments. Moves by the pharmaceutical companies to take the South African[18] and other governments to court[19] for allowing the import and sale of generic anti-AIDS drugs, even with the knowledge that TRIPS recognizes the legitimacy of such measures in certain instances,[20] triggered angry protests and street demonstrations both in South Africa and elsewhere.[21]

Overall, the various sides in the continuing debate have only revived issues considered buried and done away with. Neither the Seattle or Prague events nor the AIDS phenomenon have provoked anything unheard of. The commanding role of the international financial institutions and the global trading regime vis-à-vis the DCs had been translated into unadulterated free trade and private enterprise principles by the end of the 1980s. Those principles have been imposed on DCs

---

17 Note 8, above, ibid.

18 A group of 40 drug companies filed a suit in February 1998 (heard for the first time on 5 March 2001 but postponed to 18 April 2001) at the Pretoria High Court asking the latter to declare the Medicines and Related Substances Act of 1997 unconstitutional. Signed into law by Nelson Mandela, the Act allows parallel importing of drugs 'from the cheapest sources available, regardless of whether the patent holders give their approval' and compulsory licensing. The apparent aim by the South African government was to provide affordable drugs for AIDS sufferers. See Helene Cooper, Rachel Zimmerman and Laurie McGinley, 'Patents Pending: AIDS Epidemic Traps Drug Firms in a Vise: Treatment vs. Profits – Suit in South Africa Seeks to Block Generic Copies; U.S. Reverses its Policy – Activists Warn Mr. Papovich', The Wall Street Journal, available online from the Dow Jones Interactive; accessed 2 March 2001, at A1.

19 Note 8, above, ibid.

20 See Articles 8(1), 30 and 31, TRIPS.

21 For the demonstrations in South Africa, see Cape Argus, 'South Africa; Campaigners Lay Protest At US Door', Africa News 6 March 2001; available online from the Dow Jones Interactive; accessed 26 March 2001. For demonstrations and campaigns elsewhere, see Gumisai Mutume, 'Health: Drug Companies' Lawsuit in Africa Under Attack', Washington: Inter Press Service, 12 March 2001; available online from the Dow Jones Interactive; accessed on 26 March 2001, describing the demonstrations outside the offices of the Pharmaceutical Research and Manufacturers of America (PhRMA) in Washington, USA demanding that the drug companies drop their lawsuit in South Africa. One of the activists was quoted as having said 'The pharmaceutical companies would like to call South Africa a criminal for extending access to cheap drugs to people with HIV, but we know who the real criminals are', ibid.

through voluntary acquiescence or forcibly as recipes purportedly to overcome the deadlock in the prospect for their development. Hence the manner in which DCs should revive their economies and achieve progress had been pronounced resolved or passé by the beginning of the 1990s.

Moreover, in spite of the understanding that had been reached, at least among development theorists,[22] on the contributory role of much of the transplanted law (including the IP system) in DCs to the continuing deterioration in their economic and social conditions, the DCs were compelled to incorporate TRIPS into their legal system. Consequently, it should have been apparent to all sides in the renewed debate that the roots of the AIDS pandemic lie buried deep in the economic and socio-political deprivation of the mass of people in the developing parts of the world. To that extent, any further discussion of the role of TRIPS must be either to confirm its irrelevance to DCs or that it has proved to be an obstacle for their daunting task of social-economic revival – as predicted by many, including this author.[23]

The Post-TRIPS Drive Towards More Universal Templates

It is widely recognized that the introduction of the TRIPS, as part of the General Agreement on Tariffs and Trade (GATT) replaced by the 1994 Agreement Establishing the World Trade Organization, was a watershed in the development of the IP system,[24] both on the international level and for law-making in single nations, particularly in those still languishing in economic doldrums – the DCs.

22 See, among others, R.B. Seidman, The State, Law and Development, Frances Pinter, 1978; D.M. Trubek and Marc Galanter, 'Scholars in Self-estrangement: Some Reflections on the Crisis in Law and Development Studies in the United States', *Wisconsin Law Review* 1062, 1974.

23 See Endeshaw (1996), note 1, above, at 85–6.

24 Vincent Chiappetta characterized TRIPS as 'a dramatic shift away from the traditional view that intellectual property law primarily serves the interests of national cultures, values, and politics. Grafted onto the General Agreement on Tariffs and Trade ('GATT') as part of that regime's conversion into the World Trade Organization ('WTO'), TRIPS moved radically beyond the highly deferential standard of non-discriminatory treatment to an actual harmonization of substantive intellectual property rights'. See Vincent Chiappetta, 'The Desirability of Agreeing to Disagree: The WTO, TRIPS, International IPR Exhaustion and a Few Other Things', 21 *Michigan Journal of International Law* 333, Spring 2000, at 334. Hicks and Holbein viewed TRIPS as constituting 'a landmark in the evolution of an international consensus on intellectual property protection and is the most significant advance in the international protection of intellectual property since the adoption of the Berne and Paris Conventions in the late 19th century'. See Laurinda L. Hicks and James R. Holbein, 'Convergence of National Intellectual Property Norms in International Trading Agreements', 12(5) *American University Journal of International Law and Policy* 769, 1997, at 783. Correa and Yusuf refer to it as 'the most far-reaching and comprehensive

The characterization of intellectual property law-making and enforcement as trade issues was a shrewd device which transposed the internal policies and legal formula concocted by the US in 1974[25] to the international area from 1984 onwards.[26] Increased pressures of industry lobbies on the US government 'to use its domestic law to assure protection in foreign markets'[27] as well as the necessity to find 'alternative methods to protect its intellectual property interests' abroad[28] that it had lost after its withdrawal from UNESCO in 1984, led to a gradual linking up of its efforts in international IP protection with the resort to trade measures where US interests are perceived to be at stake. The assessment made in a 1987 study by the United States International Trade Commission for the United States Trade Representative (USTR) on the supposed impact of the inadequacy of international IP protection as well as other 'barriers' on US foreign trade[29] supplied further ammunition for action. Gadbaw asserted that 'The United States economy has moved steadily into areas where the value of its products is tied to intellectual and artistic creativity. If these assets are as vulnerable to plunder as the slow-moving merchant ships of the 1700s were to the Barbary pirates, the United States' ability to trade with countries that harbour such pirates could be seriously hampered'.[30] William P. Alford also commented that, although academic interests in IP had barely taken off in the US until the 1970s,[31] the 'link between intellectual property and trade, especially concerning East Asia [was] … more than just rhetorical. Indeed, by the mid- to late 1980s, it had become an important element of our public policy'.[32]

No other industrialized nation had dared suggest such a formula in previous times in view of the complications that such an approach might engender in international relations and the risk of creating further rifts during the Cold War era

---

legal regime concluded in the era of intellectual property rights (IPRs)'; see, Carlos M. Correa and Abdulqawi A. Yusuf (eds), *Intellectual Property and International Trade: The TRIPS Agreement*, Kluwer Law International: London, 1998, at xvii.

25 Section 301 of the Trade and Tariff Act of 1974.

26 This was achieved through the Trade and Tariff Act of 1984, 98 Stat. 2948 (1984) and later the Omnibus Trade and Competitiveness Act of 1988, 19 U.S.C.A. 2411–20, both of which were amendments to the Trade and Tariff Act of 1974.

27 Terence P. Stewart (ed.), *The GATT Uruguay Round: A Negotiating History (1986–1992), Volume II: Commentary*, Kluwer Law and Taxation Publishers: London, 1993, at 2253–5.

28 Ibid., at 2255.

29 US International Trade Commission, Foreign Protection of Intellectual Property Rights and the Effect on US Industry and Trade, ITC Publication No. 2065, February 1988.

30 See R. Michael Gadbaw, 'Intellectual Property and International Trade: Merger or Marriage of Convenience?', 22(2) *V. and. J. Transnational Law* 223, 1989, at 232–3.

31 See W.P. Alford, 'How Theory Does – And Does Not – Matter: American Approaches To Intellectual Property Law In East Asia', 13 *UCLA Pacific Basin Law Journal* 8, Fall 1994, at 9.

32 Ibid., at 13.

between the Western ICs and the DCs. Such a move could definitely have backfired when in the 1970s and 1980s the DCs constituted a huge majority in the United Nations and were demanding a transformation of the international economic order[33] and, parallel with it, the international intellectual property system.[34] The reluctance of the EU to endorse fully the US push at the Uruguay Round[35] while the Japanese quietly acquiesced was hence a clear reflection of their appreciation of the delicate state of relations between the ICs and DCs at that juncture.

The resistance of many DCs during the course of the Uruguay Round negotiations to stem the tide towards establishing universal standards in IP mainly directed at them failed to produce any concessions along the lines of the reforms proposed in the 1960s and 1970s or even that nominally achieved through the 1967 Stockholm Protocol.[36] India,[37] Brazil[38] and Mexico[39] presented more pronounced and relatively articulate positions than most DCs but to no avail. Any semblance of concessions extracted from the ICs by virtue of the majority that the DCs commanded at the international gatherings was largely wiped out under TRIPS. To all intents and purposes, the passage of TRIPS represents a veritable reordering of international relations, tragically not in the way that DCs had sought for decades but in the opposite direction – further erosion in the standing of DCs and their capacity to influence decisions made in their name but against their vested interests. The reordering has, no doubt, become evident on a general level,

33 Declaration on the Establishment of a New International Economic Order, 1 May 1974, U.N. Doc. A/95559 (1974) reprinted in 13 I.L.M. 715 (1974).

34 The United Nations Conference on Trade and Development (UNCTAD) conducted a study into the requirements of DCs in the realm of technology which supported their demand for instituting compulsory licensing of patented technology. See 'The Role of the Patent System in the Transfer of Technology to Developing Countries', UN Doc. TD/B/C. 6/12, New York; UN, 1975. For an overview of the attempts of DCs to reform that system and their dismal failure see Endeshaw (1996), note 1, above, at 101–13.

35 See the 'Guidelines Proposed by the European Community for the Negotiations on Trade-Related Aspects of Intellectual Property Rights' of 20 November 1987, in F.K Beier and G. Schricker (eds), *GATT or WIPO? New Ways in the International Protection of Industrial Property*, VCH: Weinheim, 1989, at 202–10. See also the update of the same document on 7 July 1988, at 323–32. Germany in particular sought a compromise solution for both ICs and DCs without any mandatory standards being imposed on the latter, see ibid., at 37–8.

36 For an account of the disappointing experience of DCs in their attempt to revise the international conventions in their favour, see Endeshaw (1996), note 1, above, at 105–13.

37 India argued for the freedom of countries to formulate laws appropriate to themselves; the inclusion of more favorable treatment for DCs in IP. See Stewart, note 27, above, at 2271. India also proposed imposing a requirement of working on patents at the risk of lapse if that is not done; ibid. at 2286–7.

38 Brazil sought to inject a compulsory licensing for patents; ibid. at 2271.

39 Mexico generally argued against overprotection of IP for fear that it might prevent DCs from securing access to modern technology; ibid., at 2267.

not just in IP. The phrase 'New World Order'[40] indeed aptly signalled the dramatic reversals in the state of affairs on the international level.

Arguments offered to sustain the US position (in authoring the introduction of TRIPS into the international trading regime) work by way of fighting rearguard actions and are often framed in ideological terms such as the natural rights theory[41] and free trade.[42] In reality, the US demand for rigorous international protection emanated form its urge to forestall perceived US technological decline[43] as well as to reduce the growing trade deficit in the 1980s and 1990s.[44]

Post-TRIPS, intellectual property law-making has become rapid, almost a tidal wave, among all nations, big and small, industrial and developing. Once the prerogative embedded in the major international IP treaties allowing all nations to adopt or frame the type and scope of IP laws that suited them most was removed through TRIPS, it no longer seemed rational or desirable to maintain a national system of IP. Even Brazil, India and Mexico, which had vociferously resisted the introduction of TRIPS and the proposed link with the international trading system, had to cave in eventually. After all the criticisms and protestations against the abandonment of national principles and

---

40 Terence Hunt, 'Bush Asks Allies to Help Pay in Gulf, Says "New World Order" Could Result', *The Associated Press*, 30 August 1990; available online from the Dow Jones Interactive; accessed 26 March 2001.

41 For a critique of such a theory, see A. Samuel Oddi, 'TRIPS – Natural Rights and a "Polite Form of Economic Imperialism"', 29 *Vanderbilt Journal of Transnational Law* 415, May 1996.

42 Hicks and Holbein assert by reference to the North American Free Trade Agreement (NAFTA) and the Mercado Comun del Sur, that is Common Market of the Southern Cone (MERCOSUR), consisting of Argentina, Brazil, Paraguay and Uruguay: 'The protection of intellectual property rights in a free trade market is essential to allow the free circulation of goods among member nations. In order to create a free trade market, member states must harmonize different intellectual property regimes and base the integrated system upon common rules of protection and enforcement. This is a difficult process due to divergences between national intellectual property regimes within a free trade agreement's member countries'. See Hicks and Holbein, note 23, above, at 771. See also Leaffer, 'Inadequate protection of intellectual property undermines the goal of free trade because it leads to trade distortions. Absent sufficient protection, creators can no longer recover the cost of their investment in research and development, resulting in lower production, fewer trading opportunities, and higher costs to the consumer. As a result, intellectual property protection has become a major trade issue, and the GATT appears to offer a practical structure that promotes quicker and more effective protection for U.S. intellectual property than is provided by the existing international conventions'. See Marshall A. Leaffer, 'Protecting United States Intellectual Property Abroad: Toward a New Multilateralism', 76 *Iowa Law Review* 273 (1991), at 277.

43 See, the Report of the President's Commission on Industrial Competitiveness, Volume II, Washington, DC, 1985.

44 Alford states that 'intellectual property issues also came to prominence in our public life because of the link forged between them and the growth of our trade deficit during the mid-1980s'. See note 31, above, ibid., at 12.

their replacement by reciprocity died down, or proved ineffective, the fundamental question that lies at the core of national IP law, namely conformity with the socio-economic conditions of the nations that introduce or adopt it, seemed irrelevant. It was, and had to be, conveniently ignored by the major industrial nations once they got away with TRIPS, under the leadership of the US. Any further progress in the scope and nature of IP protection would only be on their terms. Simply put, once the propriety of forms or standards of IP and their enforcement became linked to compliance with economic and trade requirements expected of nations under the WTO, the dominant trading nations could seek further changes in the existing IP regime, at will, to suit their purposes. Thus, although TRIPS might be the minimum standard for all *trading* nations, that is members of WTO at the moment, the very fact that the major ICs can wield their standings in WTO to push ever higher standards means that, henceforth, a general adoption of the highest common denominator is likely to become the way forward for international IP.

Such a forward movement in the state and level of IP introduced in the major ICs (and consequently internationally) is inevitable when the entire pack of the major ICs decides so and provided that there is no open revolt by the DCs or a significant number among them, at any rate. The pecking order among the ICs (such as G-7, non-G-7; OECD members and non-members) forces those in the lower rungs to defer to those above them; most often, partly because of the force of tradition since Cold War times, the US can get its way or succeed in anything it proposes as long as its desires are not too far ahead and do not contradict the interests of its allies.

The quick embrace of amendments to copyright, patent and trademark treaties (through the device of Protocols drawn up by the WIPO) demonstrates the readiness of the major IC powers to get on with further consolidation of the IP regime. However, this time it is not about the minimum standards but the maximum expected in any new legal construct. The US position has been, not for the first time, to push on with setting not just international standards but universal ones.[45] Reichman accurately spotted increasing pressure to move IP to even higher standards, post-TRIPS, when he wrote

> higher international minimum standards that developed countries espouse in the course of harmonization exercises in other forums will add to the pressure on developing countries, on the grounds that emerging new standards make it necessary further to reduce trade-distorting intellectual property practices. These and other pressures concerning matters not yet covered by the TRIPS Agreement, especially *sui generis* modes of protecting new technologies likely to arise over time, could be exerted [against DCs as specified in TRIPS].[46]

45 See Endeshaw (1996), note 1, above.

46 J.H. Reichman, 'Universal Minimum Standards of Intellectual Property Protection under the TRIPS Component of the WTO Agreement', 29(2) *International Law* 345 Summer, 1995, at 383–4.

In the area of patents, US ongoing efforts to tip international IP in its favour find support in arguments directed at establishing universal standards, not just multilateral ones.[47] Thus Mossinghoff and Kuo assert that, owing to the ongoing transformation of the US economy to one based on information, 'the most critical task – and in many ways the most challenging – will be to establish a global or world patent system, one that will serve the needs of multinational research-based industries as well as small and independent inventors at a cost that will promote, not hinder, the development of inventions'.[48] Accordingly, they propose a 'World Patent System' that will remove the current costly, repetitive and redundant procedures for grant.[49] They call for the establishment of an international organization[50] replacing national patent offices and granting a 'single unitary patent respected in all of the member states'[51] and enforceable by a 'world patent court'.[52]

Japanese willingness to accept such a process was expressed in 1997 by a Commission set up to look into the future of IP in Japan in the new century.[53] The Commission stressed the necessity to develop 'Comprehensive IPR protection systems … that will be conducive to the intellectual creation and international harmonization' and remove the difficulty of ensuring 'adequate protection' of 'information' that 'border-less network technology' generates. The Report recommended 'international cooperation toward a global patent system'.[54]

The European Union, by contrast, has been slow to adopt any clear standpoint. As the author has argued elsewhere, 'Having just about completed its patent harmonization in the 70s and that of copyright and trademarks in the 80s and 90s, and still doing so in other fields, the EU would have been expected to confront fully the issue of a "universal system"; but to this date, that course seems to have eluded it'.[55]

The new (Doha) round of WTO negotiations, launched in Qatar in November 2001, was expected to consider IP issues within the framework of TRIPS. For one thing, TRIPS includes a provision for review of its contents.[56] Secondly, TRIPS has its own 'built-in agenda' in the sense that there are issues that await

---

47 See Gerlad J. Mossinghoff and Vivian S. Kuo, 'World Patent System circa 20XX A.D.', *Intellectual Property Review* 1999, 1999, pp. 3–42.

48 Ibid., at 4.

49 Ibid.

50 Ibid., at 21.

51 Ibid.

52 Ibid., at 27.

53 See the Report of the Commission on Intellectual Property Rights in the Twenty-first Century, 'Toward the Era of Intellectual Creation, Challenges For Breakthrough', 7 April 1997; available at http://www.jpo-miti.go.jp/tousie/21cene.htm; accessed 28 February 2001.

54 Ibid.

55 See Endeshaw (1996), note 45, above, at 269.

56 Article 27(3) concerning the protection of plant varieties.

further resolution and need to be considered.[57] The major ICs (EU, Japan and the US) have already expressed their respective proposals regarding geographical indications for the forthcoming negotiations ('TRIPS-plus').[58] Ironically, the US did not express any need to add to the agenda merely seeking the WTO to oversee that transitional provisions have been met.[59] In the end, nothing happened at the Doha meeting in terms of reconsidering, let alone revising, TRIPS.

Needless to say, the inevitable resistance of DCs would again have to be broken for any forward movement in IP beyond TRIPS. The DCs expressed misgivings about engaging fully in the Doha Round of negotiations without any redress for past injustices they claim to have been committed against them in previous Rounds.[60] One commentator has advised the 'highly industrialized Members of the WTO – led by the United States' to extend, through multilateral institutions, concessions to DCs in terms of creating 'an environment that promotes the transfer of knowledge and technology in ways that are productive for both industrialized and developing countries' so that 'all WTO Members will emerge as winners'.[61] In the event, as will be discussed in Chapter 6, the major industrial nations did not show any signs of being prepared to dole out such a generous dispensation to DCs at the Doha Round. Moreover, judging by the cumulative effects of the sway of the major ICs on the DCs, not just in economic and technological terms but also in the legal sphere, the future holds no major surprises for DCs, particularly from any benevolent ICs.

Intellectual Property Law-Making Beyond TRIPS: The Role of DCs

The extant literature on the nature, forms and impact of IP does not distinguish between the roles of DCs and ICs in IP law-making. It tends to jumble them together as if the state of economic and technological development of nations matters little to the forms and scope of IP law they adopt. All nations are hence perceived as having to subscribe to universal standards irrespective of any diversity they may have. However, the role of DCs as regards IP law-making is completely different from that of the major ICs. In recent years, the DCs have repeatedly stated their

57 Such are Articles 23(4) and 24 (1) concerning geographical indications of origin; Article 64(2) and (3) on recommendations for use or further discontinuation of the 'non-violation' provision of WTO as a form of dispute resolution.

58 They have submitted them to the TRIPS Council at various dates. See WTO NEWS: 'TRIPS Council 17 February 1999' at http://www.wto.org/wto/english/news_e/news99_e/; accessed 22 March 2001.

59 See Frederick M. Abbott, 'TRIPS in Seattle: The Not-So-Surprising Failure and the Future of the TRIPS Agenda', 14 *Berkeley Journal of International Law* 165, 2000, at 168.

60 See 'Poor-country issues must be at heart of new Round – Moore', at note 5, above.

61 See Abbott, note 60, above, at 179.

basic concerns and arguments about the lack of congruence between the formulae adopted in TRIPS, on the one hand, and their domestic economic and cultural requirements, on the other. Commentators have also argued along the same lines for more than a decade now. Hanns Ulrich, for instance, wrote

> It is not difficult to imagine that pressure rather than persuasion will be the driving force for making developing countries accept [TRIPS]. Even if they are accepted, is there any hope that laws which have been pressed upon these countries really will be applied by domestic authorities with any degree of effectiveness? The danger is that [TRIPS] will either remain a dead letter or else become a source of permanent dispute.
>
> The real question, however, is not whether [TRIPS] will be accepted and actually applied, however reluctantly, by many countries, but why industrialised countries propose standards of intellectual property protection in developing countries which are virtually identical to their own domestic standards.[62]

Hamilton has cast TRIPS in the same vein as attempting 'to remake international copyright law in the image of Western copyright law. If TRIPS is successful across the breathtaking sweep of signatory countries, it will be one of the most effective vehicles of Western imperialism in history'.[63] Evelyn Su has also stated, 'the TRIPS Agreement limits the available range of trade and industrial policy options available to developing countries'.[64]

Other writers refer to the allowances in TRIPS, extended to DCs, not to implement their obligations under it for a transitional period of up to 10 years (if not more on a showing of particular difficulties or delay) as well as the provision for suspension of their obligations under certain circumstances. Thus Reichman declares that certain provisions of TRIPS (namely Articles 7, 8, 31 and 40) 'arm developing and least-developed countries with legal grounds for maintaining a considerable degree of domestic control over intellectual property policies in a post-TRIPS environment, including the imposition of compulsory licenses'.[65]

There is no doubt that, on the face of it, TRIPS allows members to adopt 'measures necessary to protect public health and nutrition, and to promote the public interest in sectors of vital importance to their socio-economic and

---

62 See Hanns Ulirch, 'GATT: Industrial Property Protection, Fair Trade and Development', in Beier and Schricker, note 35, above, at 148.

63 Marci A. Hamilton, 'The TRIPS Agreement: Imperialistic, Outdated, and Overprotective', 29 *Vanderbilt Journal of Transnational Law* 613, May 1996, at 614.

64 Evelyn Su, 'The Winners And The Losers: The Agreement on Trade-Related Aspects of Intellectual Property Rights and its Effects on Developing Countries', 23 *Houston Journal of International Law* 169, Fall 2000, at 202.

65 See Reichman, note 47, above, at 357–8.

technological development'.[66] In addition, the allowance for devising 'appropriate measures … to prevent the abuse of intellectual property rights or the resort to practices which unreasonably restrain trade or adversely affect the international transfer of technology'[67] may sound a broad concession in the interest of DCs. Add to this the seeming extension to members, in Articles 30 and 31 of TRIPS, to resort to compulsory licensing by way of some derogation from grant of exclusive rights (including for emergency purposes[68]). However, as long as the basic yardstick employed to measure compliance with TRIPS remains, not coherence in intellectual property policy, national treatment or its efficacy in the DCs, but the specific economic and trade requirements of the major ICs, the value of these apparent concessions to DCs will ever be theoretical. Moreover, all these allowances are tied to the requirement of consistency with the entire agreement, that is, serving to protect the interests of IC rights holders above all.

Indeed, it would appear more likely that the interpretation of any permissible deviations from the main prescriptions of TRIPS, as envisaged in Article 8, will be to herald further changes upwards, in other words to deepen the extent and scope of IP protection at the behest of the foremost industrial nations, nothing less. It would hence be naive to think that the decisive blow dealt to the attempt of the DCs to revise the IP conventions prior to TRIPS could be circumvented through tongue-twisting interpretation of clauses in the very same agreement! It suffices to mention that the sale of imported products is now treated (under TRIPS) as satisfying the requirement of local 'working'.[69] Yet this type of provision used to be a bone of contentions among many countries (including the industrialized ones) in the past century and more. In light of this, one can only wonder how anybody could argue that the 'short and medium-term social costs' of DCs adhering to TRIPS will be 'offset by the prospects of enhanced market access, of technical co-operation to implement the TRIPS Agreement, and of relief from unilateral trade sanctions in future discussions of intellectual property protection'.[70] The tautological nature of the proposition requires no argument – DCs will benefit if they quietly accede to laws handed to them on a platter; if they are good, perhaps there will be some food on the platter too!

Ironically, the same writer has provided suggestions for reforming TRIPS.[71] He counsels that 'What the developing countries need for the immediate future is not strong, nineteenth-century-type patent protection, but rather, more appropriate intellectual property regimes to stimulate investment in new technologies and in various forms of subpatentable innovation that lie within their limited technological

66 Article 8(1), TRIPS.

67 Article 8(2), TRIPS.

68 Article 31 (b), TRIPS.

69 Article 28(1) (a) read with Article 6, TRIPS.

70 See Reichman, note 47, above, at 382–3.

71 J.H. Reichman, 'Compliance with the TRIPS Agreement: Introduction to a Scholarly Debate', 29 *Vanderbilt Journal of Transnational Law* 363, May 1996.

reach'.[72] He suggests accordingly that the DCs adopt a 'general purpose innovation law built on modified liability principles' so as to be able to 'arguably accelerate their catch-up time notwithstanding their obligations to recognize foreign patents under the TRIPS Agreement'.[73] It is incredible that one could suggest sticking to, or even promoting, TRIPS for the purpose of accelerating development through an appropriate innovation law! Was that not precisely what TRIPS targeted to kill – removing any room for local innovations, defined according to the rules expressing specific economic and technological requirements, and subjecting all and sundry to the same standards world-wide?

In spite of the lingering desire, on the part of DCs, to have laws scrutinized in their respective national legislatures, their unfavourable standing in the international economic and trading regime vis-à-vis the industrial powers dictates that they pass IP laws handed down, or 'recommended', to them by those powers without much debate or even change of language or style. The fear of losing access to the lucrative export markets of the US and Europe or the threat of withdrawal of credit facilities from international institutions – where both the US and EU almost certainly have a representation if not a controlling say – makes sure that the ruling elites of most DCs act swiftly to rush to accept and put into law every demand and whim of these ICs. The evidence is so overwhelming that to cite examples will be superfluous. One needs to refer to the case of South East Asian nations to illustrate the magnitude of the constant twists and turns in their IP laws in the face of unceasing US demands for change.[74] In the case of Taiwan, Andy Y. Sun acknowledges that 'the United States is no doubt the single most influential player in shaping Taiwan's IP policy and reform'.[75] Sun adds that the economic linkage of Taiwan with the US and the fact that it 'depends heavily on the health of the American economy … gives the USTR much needed ammunition and strong leverage in its bilateral trade negotiations with Taiwan'.[76]

Unfortunately for DCs, the story does not end there. If economic or cultural life could be reordered by a mere pronouncement of some rule or other, then the task of DCs would be very easy. Yet, as development theorists have discovered,[77] more law has not been synonymous with, or led to, more development. The existence of

72 Ibid., at 372.

73 Ibid.

74 For a detailed account see, Elizabeth Upoff, Intellectual Property and US Relations With Indonesia, Malaysia, Singapore, And Thailand, Southeast Asia Program, Cornell University, 1991. For a more recent comment on the fate of IP in Indonesia and the fact that its enforcement has belied the success of any push for more law, see Darko Djaic, 'Why does the Enforcement of Indonesia's Intellectual Property Laws continue to be a Problem?', 22(10) *European Intellectual Property Review* 454, October 2000.

75 Andy Y. Sun, 'From Pirate King to Jungle King: Transformation of Taiwan's Intellectual Property Protection', Occasional Papers/Reprints in *Contemporary Asian Studies*, No. 1997 (143), School of Law, University of Maryland, at 5.

76 Ibid., at 6–7.

77 Note 22, above.

more or less IP law on the statute books of nations cannot be taken as a yardstick for judging their advance or backwardness. The fact of the matter is that any nation, industrialized or not, can introduce, virtually overnight, any amount of IP law it chooses to but that would not necessarily change its economic backwardness. In recent years, the confrontations of China with the US on trade and piracy did not subside just because China was discovered to have had one of the most modern IP laws.[78] Indeed, quite the reverse! The rush of laws in China has possibly made the tasks of academic lawyers and policy makers more enjoyable, engaged as they would be in discovering and resolving perceived or likely legal problems – all be it theoretically – and working out the trappings of institutional change.

Shorn of the economic and cultural roots that it is, or is supposed to be, based on and evolve around, IP is a set of rules of indeterminate value except to those that the rules happen to serve because they codify the latter's national needs. It is therefore not coincidental that IP laws in place in DCs will serve ICs, whether as an intended consequence or not. We have already referred to various writers[79] who have advanced the general view, for more than 50 years, that IP needs to be congruent to each nation's economic and technological circumstance and not to any abstract standards[80] (usually coded standpoints or requirements of the leading industrial nations).

Counter to these arguments, scores of writers[81] in the US and Europe continue to propagate the erroneous perception that forms of IP and the problems of piracy are not subject to time or other general factors (economic, technological and cultural conditions). This perception pervades standard IP text-books, even WIPO publications.[82] Pick up any of these writings and you will see a discussion beyond the concrete, an outpouring of rules and policies that do not tie in with the specific

78 For an extended discussion of the China-US conflict on IP, see generally Assafa Endeshaw, *Intellectual Property in China: The Roots of the Problem of Enforcement*, Acumen Publishing Company: Singapore, 1996.

79 See note 1, above.

80 See for instance, Sherwood who asserts, 'it is now well understood that the introduction of new technology into an economy accounts for a great portion of the economic growth of that economy and produces a very high social rate of return. It can also be noted that in countries without effective intellectual property protection, that high social rate of return is sacrificed in favor of a high private rate of return for a few'. See Robert M. Sherwood, *Intellectual Property and Economic Development*, 1990, Westview Press: Boulder, CO, at 7.

81 Ibid.. See also F.K. Beier, 'The Significance of the Patent System for Technical, Economic and Social Progress', 11(5) *IIC* 569, 1980; Anthony D'Amato and Doris Estelle Long (eds), *International Intellectual Property Law*, Kluwer Law International: London, 1997.

82 See, for instance, World Intellectual Property Organization (ed.), *Introduction to Intellectual Property: Theory and Practice*, Kluwer Law International: London, 1997.

conditions of countries. Perhaps this had to do with the misfortune of IP being in the suffocating care of lawyers and not economists.[83]

Often, the above-mentioned types of commentators seek to present the proposition for congruence as opting for weaker forms of protection, free access to foreign IP or the imposition of minimal restriction.[84] One also often hears the typically reductionist view that, because of 'the increasing interdependence of virtually all economies', countries like China must imitate what the major ICs possess, such as 'well-developed patent systems' – 'to be a true participant in the global economy'.[85] Indeed, proponents of such views have elevated their prescriptions to the level of ideology, often couched with a vague hint that retaliatory action will follow against DCs that may seek to tread a different path in IP law-making than that ordained for them by ICs, such as through TRIPS. Thus Hansen wrote, rather triumphantly, that the 'The WTO, or TRIPS, regime provides mechanisms for both the United States and the European Union to enforce provisions that increase protection in newly industrialized and developing nations. If these mechanisms fail, there is little doubt that bilateral trade restraints will be used'.[86] He adds that, though the US and EU will resolve their areas of disagreement in IP through 'reciprocity provisions', there can be no 'doubt that coercion will continue to be used against newly industrialized and developing nations when broad levels of protection are at stake'.[87]

Whether DCs will continue to receive and quietly legislate on IP at the behest, and in line with the demands, of the major ICs is certainly a matter to be decided in practice. DCs have resisted the adoption of TRIPS and it may be expected that they will continue to find appropriate formulas to meet their respective national requirements whether through or outside of TRIPS. It is also conceivable that, heartened by the recent waves of sympathy to their cause, DCs will mount concerted efforts to inject a fundamental revision of TRIPS. As Abbot rightly observes, 'They will continue to resist changes to their IPRs laws, and when they do make changes, they will be slow to enforce them in favor of foreign enterprises. To the extent that the TRIPS Agreement may adversely affect the economic interests of

83 See Grundmann, note 1, above.

84 Thus Leaffer asserts rather sharply that 'In Third World countries, the piracy of intellectual property is justified by an ideology of development. Ready access to intellectual property is viewed as important to development, whereas the enforcement of intellectual property law is considered a burden on development'. See Leaffer, note 42, above, at 282.

85 John R. Allison and Lianlian Lin 'The Evolution of Chinese Attitudes Toward Property Rights in Invention and Discovery', 20 *University of Pennsylvania Journal of International Economic Law* 735, Winter, 1999, at 737.

86 Hugh C. Hansen, 'International Copyright: An Unorthodox Analysis', 29 *Vanderbilt Journal of Transnational Law* 579, May 1996, at 592–3.

87 Ibid., at 593.

developing countries, passive resistance of this type may under present financial circumstances be the most likely counter mechanism'.[88]

The extent to which DCs may succeed in challenging, if not reversing TRIPS will entirely depend on whether they can muster enough forces, including countries such as China, India and Brazil, which have invaluable experience and assets to back up their demands. It will be recalled that in its confrontation with the US, over enforcement of IP, China skilfully used the scramble for its market among its trading partners to offset or defer (indefinitely as it happened) the threat of sanctions.[89]

Piracy as 'Crime', Retribution for 'Sin' or as a Self-Serving Tag

Regardless of the politically motivated[90] spread of IP across countries and the acquiescence of most DCs to the onward rush of legal formula concocted by the major ICs, the issue of whether the IP law in any such country promotes or impedes that country's industrial progress, on the one hand, or thwarts piracy, on the other, has remained contentious. Indeed, against the backdrop of the avalanche of IP laws of many nations, especially DCs, persistent doubts have surfaced if 'piracy' has been totally uprooted since TRIPS. Sodipo[91] claims that, despite the ever strengthening of the national and international IP systems, piracy has not been

88 Frederick M. Abbott, 'Symposium On Global Competition And Public Policy in an Era of Technological Integration: The New Global Technology Regime: The WTO TRIPS Agreement And Global Economic Development', 72 *Chicago-Kent Law Review* 385, 1996, at 399.

89 Thus Lara refers to 'the allure of the Chinese market' as impeding 'the U.S. from using strong-arm tactics to protect American films'. See Gerardo Lara, 'The Piracy of American Films in China: Why The U.S. Art Form is not Protected By Copyright Laws in the People's Republic of China', 2 *UCLA Journal of International Law and Foreign Affairs* 343, Fall 1997/Winter 1998 at 354.

90 One US government study noted that 'There are no simple solutions to the political issues raised by intellectual property rights. Although US economic interests would most likely be served better by strict enforcement of intellectual property protections in other nations, political relations may also be a consideration'. See US Congress, Office of Technology Assessment, *Intellectual Property Rights in an Age of ElectroDCs and Information*, Robert E. Krieger Publishing Company, Malabar, Florida, 1987, at 230. Gadbaw and Richards observed, from their study of IP in seven countries, that 'Theoretical arguments alone … have not provided a sufficient incentive for developing countries to undertake intellectual property rights reform. Only when the potential loss of their economic benefits is introduced into the equation have governments of the nations studied concluded that it is in their interest to reform their intellectual property protection regimes'. See R. Michael Gadbaw and Timothy J. Richards (eds), *Intellectual Property Rights: Global Consensus, Global Conflict*? Westview Press: Boulder, CO, 1988, at 21.

91 See Bankole Sodipo, *Piracy and Counterfeiting: GATT, TRIPS and Developing Countries*, Kluwer Law International: London, 1997.

reversed to a significant extent. He therefore proposed to add to the IP legal regime to make it more effective.[92] At the same time, he suggested, somewhat naively, that the key to better protection of IP of the major industrial powers would be 'not external trade pressure' but the development of 'local talents' in DCs and their commercialization.[93] This flies not only in the face of reality, in that all nations are responsible for their own advances – and ICs would definitely not be involved in developing 'local talent' for DCs and generate competitors for themselves – but shifts the problem in IP to that in economics.

On the other hand, the perception that IP is a good thing in itself and capable only of providing a positive outcome for all nations, provided one cultivates local talent, ignores the running thread through more than 500 years of IP legal development, namely that a specific level of industrial progress prompts the creation of corresponding IP legal constructs and their enforcement rather than the other way round.[94] Indeed most justification for IP is *post facto* rationalization.[95] As a consequence, showering DCs with the latest IP constructs from the ICs will in no way lead to their industrialization or the 'creation of local talent'. Sure enough, legal transition (in IP) may be effected separately from industrial and commercial processes (indeed, it only requires copying the established laws in the major ICs), but if the law is not to remain a fig-leaf (or Quixotic substitute for modernization and industrialization) and permanently detached from those processes, it should be linked to, and reflect, requirements in them. It is no wonder that Sodipo's foray into the justification of the IP system and the problem of piracy descended into a defence of the relevance of IP in the abstract ('will to fight'[96]), in a vacuum, and as a mere echo of the repeated call of major ICs to stamp out piracy.

Inquiries into the justification for IP are complicated by the fact that a great deal of confusion surrounds the use of the term 'piracy'. Scherer traces the ascendancy of the term in recent years to a public relations campaign on behalf of multinational pharmaceutical companies to make it 'the accepted term to describe the imitation of drug or software products in nations with permissive intellectual property laws, even though "knock-off" production was quite legal under accepted international conventions'.[97] Oddi[98] lays the blame for the loose use of the term on proponents of the natural property rights theory who seek to portray such rights as having universal reach. He refers to them as proposing, in relation to patents, that '"theft", and "pirating" and "infringement" occur any time an invention patented anywhere

92 Ibid., at p. 4

93 Ibid., at 26.

94 See Endeshaw (1996), note 1, above, at 53–87.

95 Ibid., at 87–93.

96 See Sodipo, note 92, above, at 4; see also Sherwood, note 81, above, ibid.

97 F.M. Scherer, 'Taking Stock: The Law and Economics Of Intellectual Property Rights: The Pharmaceutical Industry and World Intellectual Property Standards', 53 *Vanderbilt Law Review* 2245, November 2000, at 2248.

98 See Oddi, note 41, above.

in the world is copied anywhere else in the world, including in countries where that invention was not patented or even not patentable because of that country's positive law'.[99] He affirms that imitating an invention that is public domain in any country 'is neither theft nor piracy nor even infringement in the legal sense'.[100]

However, if one were to adhere to the natural property rights theory and extend universality to IP, various nations would be adjudged 'guilty' of the practice of maintaining standards of IP law that best suited their economies or level of technological innovations. Talking of major 'pirates' throughout the ages, Belgium was such a 'pirate' in the eighteenth century[101] (thus triggering the French-initiated drive for international copyright protection),[102] the US in the nineteenth century,[103] and Russia in the late nineteenth and twentieth centuries.[104] A 1986 study for the US Congress admitted that the US was a 'pirate': 'When the United States was still a relatively young and developing country … it refused to respect international intellectual property rights on the grounds that it was freely entitled to foreign works to further its social and economic development'.[105] Other counties have had the same experience in one industry or another; thus Switzerland did not grant product patents until 1977 and Italy could engage in 'knock-off' production until 1978, when the Supreme Court declared it unconstitutional.[106]

The alleged problem of piracy affecting major ICs today therefore suffers from a fundamental lack of understanding of what it constitutes. Most often, piracy is perceived to be a manifestation of lack of IP protection or enforcement. Indeed, both are treated as being identical. Yet, while any nation's decision whether or not to introduce its own laws must be a measure of its sovereignty and its choice to adopt one specific form or another should be considered legitimate, the current (dominant) thinking among policy makers and academic lawyers in US and Europe disavows that.

Typically, the characterization of non-enforcement as 'piracy' overlooks the possibility, even reality, of incongruity of IP to the degree of industrial development in the 'pirate nations'. Where the nation allegedly infringing foreign IP has instituted laws congruent to its economic and technological circumstances and implements them, it is difficult to see what legal principles or standards can be deployed to persist in calling that nation a pirate. Yet, condemnations of this type

---

99 Ibid., at 432.

100 Ibid., at 432–3.

101 See Endeshaw (1996), note 1, above, ibid., at 70.

102 It is to be recalled that France unilaterally granted protection to foreign works in 1810. Id.

103 Ibid., at 71–2.

104 Ibid., at 71.

105 See US Congress, note 90, above, at 228.

106 See Scherer, note 97, above, at 2250.

are numberless.[107] Promoters (not to say 'ideologues') of the universal value of IP developed and adopted in the current major ICs invariably suggest that a stronger IP system and more effective enforcement are to the benefit of all nations. Often the gaps between the existence or lack of IP, on the one hand, and the absence of enforcement, on the other, are treated in an identical fashion.[108] According to this approach, nations that may have put in place their preferred form of IP law are decried as almost having no law! This may be true in the sense that their laws do not resemble or provide the same scope or breadth of rights as those in the major ICs (or the US, as the most frequent advocate of, to use Hamilton's term, 'imperialistic' TRIPS[109]). Similarly, nations that possess a modicum of IP laws and seem to be comfortable with the enforcement levels of those laws are portrayed as having not only inadequate IP protection but also as pirates without any concern for the enforcement of foreign IP.

Moreover, the references to alleged harmful effects of adopting laws and practices suitable to DCs themselves but not necessarily to ICs (such as impact on local creators, on transfer of foreign technology or even investment),[110] is not compared against the likely benefits of laws and practices that are in tune with the social and economic circumstances of those nations. In any case, who is to say that DCs cannot understand, nor discern, what is in their best interest? Have they not heard enough of the paternalistic and arrogant dispensation of unsolicited advise from quarters who express disgust at 'development'[111] as an objective of the DCs?

An embodiment of the flawed thinking which equates lack of enforcement of foreign IP rights to lack of IP protection in general or inability to enforce them in DCs is none other than the *National Trade Estimate Report on Foreign Trade Barriers*[112] of the USTR released on an annual basis. The USTR routinely monitors the supposed violations of its IP, whether or not by reference to international treaties to which the targeted nations may be party and, hence, may presumably justify the US to take a measure of those countries' performances. The results are published each year and, depending on the perceived degree of violations, the various culprits are placed on warning lists, stretching from the most to the least serious, with obvious implication for retaliatory actions by the US (from imposing imminent sanctions to periodic review to see if such may be necessary and the like).

---

107 Leaffer, for instance, castigates non-IC approaches of seeking IP laws congruent to their needs while ignoring IP laws of other countries as equivalent to justifying piracy 'by an ideology of development'. See Leaffer, note 42, above, at 282.

108 Ibid.

109 See Hamilton, note 64, above, ibid.

110 See Leaffer, note 42, above, at 282.

111 Ibid., at 282.

112 The reports are available at http://www.ustr.gov/html. For the latest report, see note 16, above, ibid.

There are broad implications of the USTR's stance to flog the legal system and performance of other nations, particularly the hapless DCs, and force them into action to enhance the chances of success of US international trade goals. Firstly, the determination by any nation of the degree of violation of rights that its citizens enjoy, not in the jurisdiction over which it has deserved authority, but across the oceans and global landscape is unprecedented in human history. Secondly, the summary ruling against nations that have or have not transgressed US intellectual property imparts the presumption that it is immaterial to the US whether such a finding has any legitimate basis. As it is, the reports do not divulge in any way if the assessment takes into consideration domestic consistency in terms of legislating or implementing IP. Thirdly, there are no channels of appeal where alleged offenders may be able to rectify any mistaken assessment. Indeed, contrary to general principles of criminal law where alleged offenders are never proven guilty until such has been determined in a court of law, the USTR routinely issues its damning judgment over nations across the world, even those (EU and Japan, possibly also China) against whom such judgments are merely rhetorical.

If the list of supposedly violating countries in the annual reports of the USTR serves anything at all, it is to provide illuminating proof as the barometer of US consternation, on the one hand, and the degree of technological development attained in those nations, on the other. Clearly, leaving aside the squabble within the ICs, any measure of progress in the domestic IP requirements of DCs would not necessarily be in the service of the US economy but of those nations. On the other hand, if at all the violation of US intellectual property is in the area of patents, the DCs must have attained a level of technological prowess to have been able to copy them.

Contrary to the prevalent thinking which simplistically equates lack of IP protection to piracy, there is a growing understanding that a variety of factors impede the enforcement of foreign IP in DCs, not necessarily because the latter are unwilling but owing to the impossibility of doing so. These factors are often discounted by advocates of the universality of IP who see enforcement to be an overriding task of DCs, subject to no exceptions or excuses for any laxity. One well-known factor that facilitates piracy is the advancement of technologies; this is more pronounced in the case of copyright materials[113] but extends to all forms of information.[114]

Institutional factors also account for inability to enforce foreign IP. Most DCs do not have the judicial apparatus that is a prerequisite for adequate enforcement of civil laws in general, let alone IP. One good example is China, which, owing to persistent pressure put on it by the US, established special courts. However, the

113 See Lara, note 90, above, at 359–60.

114 See Fred H. Cate, 'Symposium: Introduction: Sovereignty and the Globalization of Intellectual Property', 6 *Indiana Journal of Global Legal Studies* 1, Fall, 1998, at 2 (describing how technological advances have lead to obsolescence of traditional forms of protection).

record of those courts has not been startling, to say the least. For one thing, access to the IP courts is not easy. As Jenckes commented, 'In order to obtain evidence, the injured party must investigate on its own and then convince the court and the police to conduct a raid on the pirate factory'.[115] He adds that the Chinese courts have been slow in pursuing claims and the resulting awards, if any, are small, that the judges, apart from their susceptibility to bribery, lack legal training.[116]

The influence of history and culture on law-making and efficacy of its implementation is another factor. In the case of China, the influence of Confucianism and other attitudinal and cultural factors have been cited often and are gradually gaining acceptance as causes for the absence of proprietary perception among the Chinese populace.[117] Moreover, the fact that legitimate products are generally not available to non-IC consumers at affordable prices means that pirates are left to enjoy a lucrative market to which they supply cheaper products.[118] Reference has also been made to the fact that DCs 'face formidable cost in enforcing the TRIPS Agreement'.[119] Finally, the growing (nationalistic) perception among DCs[120] that they are being coerced into implementing IP laws modelled on foreign IP and therefore meant to protect foreign interests against an unwilling and resentful population contributes to incipient defiance of those interests.

Among the appropriate solutions suggested for such problems are promoting awareness in the entire population, training judges, lobbying governments and making the non-IC industries aware of the benefits of protecting IP.[121] In the case of China, Peter Yu has suggested (to the US) a comprehensive approach of treating it equitably and fairly, so as to coax it into enforcing IP gradually.[122]

---

115 Kenyon S. Jenckes, 'Protection of Foreign Copyrights in China: The Intellectual Property Courts and Alternative Avenues of Protection', *Southern California Interdisciplinary Law Journal* 55, 1997, at 561.

116 Ibid.

117 See William P. Alford, *To Steal a Book is an Elegant Offense: Intellectual Property Law in Chinese Civilization*, Stanford University Press: Stanford, California, 1995; see also Endeshaw (1996), note 79, above, at 105–8; Allison and Lin, note 85, above, at 742–5.

118 Eric M. Griffin, 'Stop Relying on Uncle Sam! – A Proactive Approach to Copyright Protection in the People's Republic of China', 6 *Texas Intellectual Property Law Journal* 169, 1998, at 195.

119 See Evelyn Su, note 65, above, at 217.

120 Thus Djaic refers to the perception among Indonesian officials that 'protecting foreign intellectual property is contrary to Indonesia's self-interest'. See Djaic, note 35, above, at 465.

121 See Griffin, note 119, above, ibid.

122 Peter K. Yu, 'From Pirates to Partners: Protecting Intellectual Property in China in the Twenty First Century', 50 *American University Law Review* 131, 2001.

Conclusion

There is no doubt that TRIPS heralded a major shift in intellectual property by establishing unprecedented levels of protection to be enforced worldwide. However, the fact that such a shift took shape by reference largely to the needs of the US economy (and to a lesser extent that of the other major ICs) has left many significant questions unanswered. Principally, the materialization of adopted IP laws into an effective framework for all trading nations is not a certainty.

Firstly, the incorporation of TRIPS into the international trade regime sealed the fate of developing nations by robbing them of the opportunity to decide by themselves what forms of law would best suit their national aspirations. The creation, instead, of certain formulae as the minimum standards for all nations together with the possibility of further changes, in pursuit of the policies and requirements of the major ICs, virtually erects 'universal templates' for intellectual property law-making. Under these circumstances, the task of DCs would ever remain tailing and mimicking the laws already in place or produced from time to time by the major ICs

The reverse effect of this denial, to DCs, of their sovereign right to engage in law-making as they see fit is to push them to adopt a position of indifference, at best, or resentment as regards the enforcement of foreign IP. The perceived lack of legitimacy and fairness in forcing DCs to subscribe to IP laws that significantly ignore their plight, in particular their need to set up legal forms and structures that are congruent to the state of their economy and technology, will make the enforcement of foreign IP in those countries an uphill struggle. While legislative changes in DCs can be undertaken (forcibly pushed through) virtually at the stroke of a pen, enforcement of such adopted laws will ever remain contentious, if not impossible. The simple truth is that DCs will be made (or expected) to become instrumental for the implementation of the very laws that they never chose to introduce or, left to themselves, would opt to repeal.

It should therefore be easy to understand how counter-movements may assert themselves against perceived illegitimacy and plain old-fashioned colonialism. Piracy may surface as a backlash or retribution against 'ephemeral property rights of foreigners'.[123] Indeed as Harms put it, 'Because one does not appreciate its worth, one loses one's respect for the property of others'.[124] Then again, certain segments of the society develop a taste in systematic plunder of foreign IP. Thus the lucrative income that local businesses or other interested groups (such as the army, other government agencies and officials) in China reap was attributed to this. As Tiefenbrun observed, 'Pirating in China is too profitable a business, and if stopped, may even detract from the growth of the booming Chinese economy. Chinese citizens stand to lose money

123 See Harms, note 15, above, at 451.

124 Ibid.

and jobs if their government were to enforce and comply with its agreements with the United States regarding copyright and trade'.[125]

In the final analysis, the forcible adoption of IP laws, alien to the social–economic circumstances of countries, by dint of either economic necessity (the debt burden, continued access to credit facilities, securing an export market), ignorance or wilful neglect may be beneficial to the major ICs. However, as the paltry response to the AIDS epidemic (by the pharmaceutical companies on the one hand and the governments of the major ICs on the other) has demonstrated, the consequences of resolving the underlying issues of IP law-making in favour of the mighty and powerful forces could be lethal to DCs. The current impasse may yet lead to a slow death of whole nations or populations.

As the Doha Round of WTO progresses, the chimera of fast-track spread of universal IP templates increasingly being devised by the major industrial powers will continue to confound the inherent incapability of DCs to enforce foreign IP. Instead of characterizing the phenomenon appropriately and recognizing the right of DCs to formulate their own laws in the manner they choose to, the prevalent temptation on the part of the major ICs will be to ideologize the entirety of the problem in terms of natural property rights, free-riding and the rest and to castigate 'late-comers' to development as pirates. Unless the major ICs realize that this approach will turn the overwhelming majority of the world population against the notion of intellectual property as such (thereby turning it into a 'casualty of the crossfire'[126]) and voluntarily initiate moves to accommodate the needs of the DCs in TRIPS and any further changes to that treaty in the future, the conflicts with DCs will never abate. Unless a reassessment is made by the ICs of the grim reality of economic and technological decay in DCs and subject TRIPS to a serious correction, any persistence to subdue them by foisting the latest form of IP law on their reality will remain illusory and end up as endless denunciation of theft and piracy. For neither the introduction of TRIPS nor making its enforcement mechanisms even more watertight (so that 'piracy' can be brought under control) will change the persistence of the gap between the foreign-initiated or imposed IP law and the grim realty in DCs, we referred to – no doubt a variation of the dichotomy of 'law in the books' and 'law in the streets'![127]

125 Susan Tiefenbrun, 'Piracy of Intellectual Property in China and the Former Soviet Union and its Effects Upon International Trade: A Comparison', 46 *Buffalo Law Review* 1, Winter 1998, at 37.

126 See Harms, note 15, above, at 453.

127 See Trubek and Galanter, note 22, above.

Chapter 6
Asian Perspectives on Post-TRIPs Issues in Intellectual Property*

Introduction

Just like the non-industrial[1] or developing countries (DCs) in other parts of the world, Asian DCs, including the emerging economies, have slavishly imitated the intellectual property (IP) system entrenched in, or newly introduced by, the major industrial nations. Their continuous transplantation of IP laws, often modelled on those of the European Union or the US, picked up speed in the 1980s and 1990s as they sought to attract foreign technology and investment,[2] on the one hand, and to placate criticisms directed at their foreign trade or domestic policies,[3] on the other.

The most dramatic development in the transplantation process followed the long-standing, particularly US, calls for the creation of uniform *substantive* rules cutting across differing cultural and economic conditions[4] and the conclusion of

---

* An earlier version of this chapter appeared, in the author's name, as 'Asian Perspectives on Post-TRIPs Issues in Intellectual Property', 8(2) *The Journal of World Intellectual Property* 211–35, March 2005.

1 The author takes 'non-industrial countries' to mean countries that have yet to achieve industrialization fully or, at any rate, as a dominant sector of their economies. The economic basis of such countries is agriculture or mining (such as minerals and oil) and thus engage in the production of raw or primary materials; they are usually unable to process those materials themselves because they lack the technology and capital to do so.

2 Alan Gutterman and Robert Brown, *Intellectual Property Laws of East Asia*, Sweet & Maxwell: Hong Kong, 1997, at 18.

3 Jane Innes and Tim Turpin thus write of Australia, China, Indonesia, Korea, the Philippines and Thailand, 'the state of IPR legislation has been driven by international forces and demands for regulatory change'. See Jane Innes and Tim Turpin, *Intellectual Property Legislation and Innovation in Asia-Pacific Economies: Case Studies of Intellectual Property Law in Australia, China, Indonesia, Korea, the Philippines and Thailand*, Hybrid: Ormond, Vic., 1999, at 8.

4 The pursuit of universal laws in IP has been noted in many studies. See, for instance, David Sarnoff, 'A World Patent System, Kettering Award Address to the Tenth Annual Public Conference', 10 *IDEA* 143, 1966; Report of the President's Commission on the Patent System, To Promote the Progress of … Useful Arts: In an Age of Exploding Technology, Washington, DC, 1966; Gerlad J. Mossinghoff and Vivian S. Kuo, 'World Patent System Circa 20XX, A.D.', *Intellectual Property Law Review* 1999, 3–42.

the Agreement on Trade-Related Aspects of Intellectual Property Rights (TRIPs) at the Uruguay Round of GATT in 1994 (and the founding of the World Trade Organization, WTO). Consequently, the forms and scope of IP that DCs were forced to embrace increased. In particular, the conscious linkage of IP issues with trade issues and the administration of TRIPs by the WTO, instead of the World Intellectual Property Organization (WIPO) as well as the fear of persistent threats of trade sanctions (chiefly by the US) compelled the DCs not only to adopt the further expansion of IP but also to strive to enforce the same.

By 2000, practically all nations on the globe with a sizable industrial and commercial sector in their economies had made adjustments to their IP laws to bring them into line with TRIPs. Meanwhile, the scope and type of IP rights have continued to expand in all kinds of directions. Terms of copyright protection were lengthened both in Europe and the US; patents have been extended to management methods and software;[5] the electronic medium and digitization have spawned a new form of IP, domain names, at the same time as helping proprietors lock in previously accepted margins of free use as private domains.[6] All in all, IP has been expanding by leaps and bounds and encroaching on areas and activities (such as free speech,[7] human rights, innovation) previously considered sacrosanct or, at any rate, legitimate.

A principal consequence of this development is that certain sectors of the major industrial countries have started to question whether the unrelenting expansion of IP might not be throttling innovation and competition.[8] Furthermore, a rising demand for cheaper medicines to combat epidemics has expressed itself through grief and

---

5 The United States Patent and Trademark Office has liberally issued patents for new methods of doing business on the Internet by treating them essentially as 'processes'. The US Court of Appeals for the Federal Circuit has endorsed the practice in *State Street Bank & Trust Co.* v. *Signature Financial Group, Inc.* 149 F 3d 1368 (Fed. Cir., 1998).

6 The protection, under the sui generis mechanism, of databases regardless of the (non-) copyrightable merit of the material they hold and against the legitimate interests of others who might seek to use the material freely in effect hands to the proprietors a blank cheque. In particular, material that would have remained in the public domain had it not been for its inclusion in a database opens an unearned revenue stream for such proprietors of databases.

7 *The US Digital Millennium Copyright Act* (DMCA) of 1998 has been cited by federal authorities as supporting their action against the release, by individual researchers, of software codes (such as encryption) protecting digital devices, e,g. DVDs, while those who released them sought protection under the First Amendment of the US Constitution.

8 See, amongst others, Peter Drahos with John Braithwaite, *Information Feudalism: Who Owns the Knowledge Economy?* Earthscan: London, 2002; Lawrence Lessig, *The Future of Ideas: The Fate of the Commons in a Connected World*, Random House: New York, 2001; and Christopher May, *A Global Political Economy of Intellectual Property Rights: The New Enclosures?* Routledge: New York, 2000 and Debora J. Halbert, *Intellectual Property in the Information Age: The Politics of Expanding Ownership Rights*, Quorum: Westport, CT, 1999.

public outcry across the world against the big pharmaceutical companies and the TRIPs, altogether exerting huge pressure towards loosening the stranglehold on all DCs. Resurgent demands for protection of traditional or indigenous knowledge as well as solutions to environmental problems also reflect deep-seated needs for change in the international IP system in favour of such countries.

The lot of Asian DCs, including the emerging or 'Tiger' economies, has been to continue to imitate and copy foreign IP laws and practices regardless of whether the latter had adverse ramifications to their economies or cultures. Asian DCs are still grappling with how to accommodate or assimilate the latest additions to rules and mechanisms of IP protection in EU and the US.[9] The constant fear of sanctions, possible loss of investment or technology flows into their economies as well as lack of understanding of the international processes at work and the implication of introducing more IP leave them prone to such a path of perennial acquiescence to developments in the major industrial nations.

Yet, sooner or later, Asian DCs would have to respond to the potentially harmful trend of overarching IP, just as some sectors in the developed countries have begun, or proposed, to do. This chapter will examine attitudes of Asian DCs towards the diverse issues that have sprung up since TRIPs with a view to establishing whether there might be any discernible signs of an Asian response to further extension of IP. To that end, it starts off with a summary of the contributions, or otherwise, of Asian DCs during the preparation for the Doha Ministerial. It then reviews the participation of Asian DCs in the post-Doha debate on IP issues, especially on whether they could reshape TRIPs to suit their current requirements. Next it briefly looks at the stance of Asian nations on the potential role of IP at the failed Cancun Ministerial. The chapter concludes that Asian DCs are bogged down in a confrontation with the developed countries on a number of fronts in current international trade negotiations and that their stakes in IP appear to have been smothered under the weight of the multiplicity of issues.

Asian Contributions to the Post-TRIPs Debate Preceding Doha

The implementation of TRIPs by all members of the WTO is subject to the review of the TRIPs Council[10] every two years.[11] Moreover, the Council has been entrusted

9 For a review of attitudes towards the so-called WIPO treaties, see Assafa Endeshaw, 'The Asian Approach in Responding to Developments in Intellectual Property', in *Asian Communications Handbook 2001*, A. Goonasekera and L.C. Wah (eds), *Asian Media Information and Communication Centre and Schools of Communication Studies*, Nanyang Technological University, 2001, at 269–77.

10 TRIPs, Article 68.

11 TRIPs, Article 71.

with handling the unresolved issues in TRIPs – the so-called 'built-in agenda'[12] – and making proposals for 'modification or amendment' of the same Agreement.[13] To that effect, it has reviewed the performance of member states, including those from Asia. It has also examined some of the TRIPs provisions that have become contentious, the 'built-in agenda' in respect of geographical indications and 'non-violation' disputes. Still it has not yet proposed any 'modifications' or 'amendment' as arguably allowed under Article 71 of TRIPs.

Just as those from other continents, Asian nations made various representations to the TRIPs Council to influence the outcome of negotiations and planned Ministerial conferences. India thus sought to 'initiate discussions on issues' relating to transfer of technology, the relationship between the UN Convention on Biological Diversity (CBD) and that of TRIPs and the protection of geographical indications other than wines and spirits.[14] It proposed a vaguely defined form of intervention to ensure that the objectives of TRIPs to promote transfer of technology could be realized. It also recommended inserting a provision in TRIPs (requiring 'a clear mention of the biological source material and the country of origin') to make it purportedly compatible with the CBD.[15] As regards the protection of goods other than wines and spirits, it suggested extending such to 'products of export interest like basmati rice, Darjeeling tea, alphonso mangoes, Kohlapuri slippers in the case of India' as well as to other nations' goods.[16]

Indonesia, Malaysia and Pakistan and three other DCs outside of Asia iterated their views with respect to the application of the non-violation remedy as specified under Article XXIII of GATT 1994.[17] They asserted that the introduction of 'the non-violation remedy in intellectual property may constrain Member's abilities' to

---

12 Such are in Article 24.1 (entering into negotiations for increasing the protection of individual geographical indications); Article 24.2 (on reviews of the application of the TRIPs provisions for geographical indications); Article 23.4 (on undertaking negotiations for establishing a multilateral system of notification and registration of geographical indications for wines); Article 27.3(b) (the review, after four years from entry into force of TRIPs, of members' measures to protect plant varieties and any exclusion from patentability they might make); Article 64.3 (establishing modalities for non-IP complaints five years from entry into force of the WTO Agreement); Article 71.1 (review of implementation of TRIPs by developing nations, post-2000).

13 TRIPs, Article 71 (1).

14 WTO, General Council, 'Preparations for the 1999 Ministerial Conference, Proposals on IPR Issues', Communication from India, WT/GC/W/147, 18 February 1999. This document was later circulated as WTO, TRIPs Council, 'Communication from India', IP/C/W/195, 12 July 2000.

15 Ibid.

16 Ibid.

17 WTO, TRIPs Council, 'Non-Violation Nullification or Impairment Under the Agreement on Trade Related Aspects of Intellectual Property Rights (TRIPs)', Proposal from Cuba, the Dominican Republic, Egypt, Indonesia, Malaysia and Pakistan, IP/C/W/141, 29 April 1999.

devise or implement measures appropriate for their development.[18] They therefore proposed further extension of the five year suspension of that remedy 'until the complexity of the implications of such a remedy in the area of intellectual property is better understood and the possible scope and modalities are adequately addressed'.[19]

India again submitted, on 2 July 1999, a separate document[20] that restated its standpoint on the protection of geographic indications of goods other than wines and spirits. That same document was circulated later without any change.[21] India also declared its position on the revision of Article 27.3(b) of TRIPs.[22] It maintained that the review should cover the scope and forms of exclusions from patentability of life forms; the effectiveness of the protection for micro-organisms and non-biological and microbiological processes as well as the appropriateness of *sui generis* systems for the protection of plant varieties.

India characterized the concept of rights in IP as being confined to 'formal systems of knowledge only'. As far as it was concerned, failure to recognize 'informal systems' embedded in tradition 'can have severe adverse consequences on mankind, some say even leading to our extinction'.[23] It therefore proposed to exclude patents as a whole, but if such was unrealizable, to deny it for traditional knowledge or at least to make any grant subject to disclosure of source, prior consent of communities as well as a proof of a benefit sharing arrangement being in place.

Concerning micro-organisms, India affirmed that the distinction between discovery and invention be maintained and that only inventions satisfying the usual criteria become patented. As regards the patentablity of micro-organisms, it proposed that man-made, genetically engineered varieties meeting the criteria should be granted such. It reasoned that 'unless there is human intervention involved and unless they fall in the category of micro-organisms', biological material cannot qualify as invention and, in any case, 'it should be left to national policy to decide what are patentable micro-organisms'.[24]

India judged that the exclusion from protection under Article 27.2 of TRIPs could be used in national laws as a basis to allay 'many of the fears arising out of possible adverse consequences of patenting of micro-organisms'.[25] It believed that

18 Ibid.

19 Ibid.

20 WTO, General Council, 'Preparations for the 1999 Ministerial Conference, Proposals Regarding the TRIPS Agreement in terms of Paragraph 9(a)(i) of the Geneva Ministerial Declaration', Communication from India, WT/GC/W/225, 2 July 1999.

21 WTO, TRIPs Council, 'Communication from India', Documents IP/C/W/196, 12 July 2000.

22 WTO, TRIPs Council, 'Review of the Provisions of Article 27.3(b)', Communication from India, IP/C/W/161, 3 November 1999.

23 Ibid.

24 Ibid.

25 Ibid.

the requirements under Article 27.3(b) for instituting protection for plant varieties provided a 'wide latitude' to member states to work out a system appropriate to their objectives. Citing the existence of various models (such as the UPOV Convention and the biological diversity laws), India asserted that countries could develop systems acceptable to themselves. It further contended that the CBD and farmers' rights do not constitute a dilution of TRIPs. India affirmed, in conclusion, that

> developing countries like India cannot accept any further strengthening of the protection provided to life forms at present. Developing country laws in this area are still being developed. It may take some more time for developing countries to acquire experience on the level of protection necessary and desirable as well as the exceptions and balances necessary for ethical, social and economic needs of their peoples. Perhaps it may be beneficial to wait till such experience is acquired before debating the extent of protection of intellectual property rights in this area. In fact, it may be ideal to exclude patent protection for life forms from all national laws until such time. Until then, it may also not be advisable for the WTO community to assess the implementation of obligations in this area.[26]

Meanwhile, the Philippines presented a 'Proposal for a Declaration on Developing Countries' to the General Council of the WTO on 24 November 1999.[27] The Proposal essentially called for an assessment of the impact of WTO-linked obligations on DCs to establish whether they had benefited from them and the institution of preferential treatment in their favour (longer transition periods, flexibility in implementation or even exemption from obligations).

India then presented its proposals for resolving IP issues in traditional knowledge and biodiversity.[28] It referred to the difficulty of challenging, in foreign countries, patent applications on an invention based on biological material. It asserted that 'the time, effort, and money involved in getting individual patents examined and revoked in foreign patent offices is prohibitive. Hence, an internationally accepted solution to such bio-piracy is necessary'.[29] It further pointed out that only an international mechanism that harmonizes TRIPs with CBD, recognizes the rights of indigenous communities on their traditional knowledge and introduces a mode of sharing of benefits from its exploitation would resolve the problem of 'bio-piracy'. It argued that established forms of IP essentially directed at individual property rights do not protect indigenous knowledge, which is collective in nature, accumulates over

26 Ibid.

27 WTO, General Council, Preparations for the 1999 Ministerial Conference, Proposal for a Declaration on Developing Countries, Communication from the Philippines, WT/GC/W/393, 25 November 1999.

28 WTO, TRIPs Council, 'Protection of Biodiversity and Traditional Knowledge – The Indian Experience', Submission by India, IP/C/W/198, 14 July 2000.

29 Ibid.

time and may be in existence among different communities simultaneously. India added its voice to the need for documenting traditional knowledge, maintaining a digital library and the like, at least for defensive purposes, as well as extending help to traditional communities to realize the value of their resources.[30]

Again, India, Pakistan and Sri Lanka submitted a paper together with other DCs[31] outside Asia pertaining to the possible extension of protection, in view of negotiations under Article 24.1 of TRIPs, for geographical indications to products other than wines and spirits. They argued that there is 'no systematic or logical explanation for the distinction' in Section 3, Part II of TRIPs between the general protection for geographical indications as a whole (in Article 22) and the special protection extended to wines and spirits (in Article 23). They asserted that the 'distinction ignores that geographical indications for categories of goods other than wines and spirits are equally important for trade'.[32] Consequently, they contended that the issue of extension is 'an integral part of the built-in agenda' of TRIPs.[33]

Subsequently, India, Pakistan and Sri Lanka, along with the other nations mentioned as well as new ones who joined them, sought to reinforce their proposal for extending protection for geographical indications to products other than wines and spirits.[34] They amplified their arguments about the insufficiency of the level of protection provided by Article 22 of TRIPs and demonstrated the unjustified nature of providing two different levels of protection and the necessity of creating one uniform level of protection.[35]

Along with the same mix of nations and new members who joined them, India, Pakistan and Sri Lanka reiterated their views again,[36] this time in response to a reaction to their proposals by a group of other nations.[37] The latter had raised the implications of such an extension in terms of potential costs to WTO members, effects on consumers and on trade. The group of countries, consisting of India, Pakistan and Sri Lanka, among others, maintained that the extension would not

30 Ibid.

31 WTO, TRIPs Council, 'Communication From Bulgaria, The Czech Republic, Egypt, Iceland, India, Kenya, Liechtenstein, Pakistan, Slovenia, Sri Lanka, Switzerland and Turkey', Document IP/C/W/204/Rev. 1, 2 October 2000.

32 Ibid.

33 Ibid.

34 WTO, TRIPs Council, 'Proposal From Bulgaria, Cuba, The Czech Republic, Egypt, Iceland, India, Jamaica, Kenya, Liechtenstein, Mauritius, Nigeria, Pakistan, Slovenia, Sri Lanka, Switzerland, Turkey and Venezuela', Document IP/C/W/247/Rev. 1, 17 May 2001.

35 Ibid.

36 WTO, TRIPs Council, 'Communication From Bulgaria, Cuba, The Czech Republic, Georgia, Hungary, Iceland, India, Kenya, The Kyrgyz Republic, Liechtenstein, Moldova, Nigeria, Pakistan, Slovenia, Sri Lanka, Switzerland and Turkey', Document IP/C/W/308, 17 September 2001.

37 WTO, TRIPs Council, 'Communication From Argentina, Australia, Canada, Chile, Guatemala, New Zealand, Paraguay and the United States', IP/C/W/289, 29 June 2001.

necessitate establishing 'any new mechanism or scheme of protection'[38] as the protection already available for wines and spirits could also serve the additional products. They argued that extending protection to other products under Article 23 has the advantage of removing the need to prove any misleading of the public or unfair competition as currently required under Article 22. The benefit of this would be to expedite the process of enforcement as 'the authorities would simply have to examine whether the product actually originates from the place indicated by the geographical indication' instead of having 'to establish time-consuming and costly legal proof' under Article 22.[39] According to them, this would do away with the 'uncertainty and lack of transparency' in applying the evidentiary requirements of Article 22.[40] They concluded that the extension would bring about 'a reduction of the workload of judicial and administrative authorities' and 'more than offset any costs that might be incurred by extension.'[41]

With reference to the issue of costs to consumers, because of the presumable 'need to re-name and re-label products as well as by the disappearance of terms customarily used to identify products', they argued that the prohibition of the false use of geographical indications only helps consumers to ascertain the true origin as well as qualities and reputation of a product.[42] They pointed out that those indications exempted in Article 24 of the TRIPs will not have to be re-labelled and the market will remain open to them. Indeed, they equated the prohibition of the use of untrue geographical indications to the avoidance of free-riding on the reputation of others and the preservation of the true geographical indications from becoming generic.[43] Furthermore, they insisted that the supposed negative implications on trade that such a change might bring about could just as well be ascribed to other forms of IP too.

In the area of the impact of TRIPs on public health, medicines and the like, a representation was made by the Africa Group, certain countries from South America as well as India, Indonesia, Pakistan, the Philippines, Sri Lanka and Thailand.[44] They called for 'a common understanding that confirms the right of governments to ensure access to medications at affordable prices and to make use of the provisions in the Agreement whenever the scope or exercise of IPRs result in barriers to access to medicines'.[45] They read Article 7 as clearly establishing

38 WTO, TRIPs Council, note 36, above.

39 Ibid.

40 Ibid.

41 Ibid.

42 Ibid.

43 Ibid.

44 WTO, TRIPs Council, 'Submission by the African Group, Barbados, Bolivia, Brazil, Cuba, Dominican Republic, Ecuador, Honduras, India, Indonesia, Jamaica, Pakistan, Paraguay, Philippines, Peru, Sri Lanka, Thailand and Venezuela', IP/C/W/296, 29 June 2001.

45 Ibid.

that 'the protection and enforcement of intellectual property rights do not exist in a vacuum. They are supposed to benefit society as a whole and do not aim at the mere protection of private rights'.[46] In their view, TRIPs cannot stand in the way of implementing health policies through technological innovation and transfer, among other things.[47]

They also asserted the rights of members (pursuant to Article 8.2) 'to take measures to prevent the abuse of intellectual property rights by right holders or the resort to practices which unreasonably restrain trade or adversely affect the international transfer of technology'.[48] They cited the examples of charging 'excessively high prices' for drugs or not offering them in sufficient quantities, thus preventing 'adequate access to medications by the general public'.[49] They also referred to the members' right, pursuant to TRIPs, to deploy exhaustion principles as well as compulsory licences to increase access to medicines.[50]

As part of a group of DCs, Bangladesh, India, Indonesia, Pakistan, the Philippines, Sri Lanka and Thailand submitted a draft declaration to the TRIPs Council regarding the recognition of certain principles in the implementation of TRIPs in the area of public health and nutrition: the exhaustion of IP rights, compulsory licensing, the rights of marketing generic medicines and similar products and disclosure of patent information for such purpose.[51]

Japan, on the other hand, explained its position[52] more in support of upholding the status quo that the other industrial powers also seek to maintain than revising it, as the Asian DCs were calling for. Japan thus maintained that the issue of permissible limits of patentability as linked with development is 'only a small fraction' of several issues that impact on the latter. It asserted that the most efficient manner of transfer of technology would be through the market because most technologies protected under IP belong to the private sector. Thus DCs seeking such a transfer would have to institute appropriate IP as the lack of it would have adverse consequences. With respect to the patentability of life forms, Japan declared that genes or microorganisms could be patentable so long as the patent claims specify their structure or parameters. It added that their mere existence in nature should not categorize them as being in the public domain.

---

46 Ibid.

47 Ibid.

48 Ibid.

49 Ibid.

50 Ibid.

51 WTO, General Council, 'Proposal by the African Group, Bangladesh, Barbados, Bolivia, Brazil, Cuba, Dominican Republic, Ecuador, Haiti, Honduras, India, Indonesia, Jamaica, Pakistan, Paraguay, Philippines, Peru, Sri Lanka, Thailand and Venezuela', WT/GC/W/450, 4 October 2001.

52 WTO, TRIPs Council, 'Review of the Provisions of Article 27.3(B) – Japan's View', Communication from Japan, IP/C/W/236, 11 December 2000.

In relation to ethical issues of patenting life forms, Japan stressed, citing Article 27.2 in support, that member countries can set limits, even total prohibition, on the use of patents rather than prohibiting them outright. On the issue of consistency between the TRIPS and the CBD, Japan expressed the view that they are 'mutually non-exclusive' as they had 'totally different objectives'.[53] According to Japan, the CBD and TRIPs 'can be implemented in a non-conflicting manner'.[54]

As for the proposal to require applicants for grant of patents to disclose the origin of the biological and traditional resources for the claimed invention, Japan contended that it would be outside the scope of the CBD as that treaty allows members to introduce measures they prefer. Moreover, according to Japan, disclosure is required to enable the person skilled in the art to determine patentability and not to facilitate control of access or exploitation. In Japan's view, therefore, the step would amount to imposing an additional obligation on members.

Japan expressed opposition to re-writing TRIPs because it perceived the provisions as striking 'a balance between rights and obligations of inventors/ applicants and third parties, which is the result of the long-term negotiation of the Uruguay Round'.[55] To Japan, the proposed introduction of a disclosure requirement 'could be unreasonably burdensome to patent applicants, and thereby upset the present balance'.[56] Even if such were to be allowed for biological resources, it would represent a discriminatory procedure imposed on one invention alone in disregard of Article 27.1 of TRIPs.[57]

In the area of benefit sharing, Japan expressed the view that the introduction of this new requirement in TRIPs as part of the review of Article 27.3(b) would be 'beyond the obligations of the CBD'. Moreover, instituting a monetary benefit sharing scheme requiring patentees to pay royalty to the holders of biological materials would be unworkable as various inventions might result from the same resource and the returns are dependent on a number of factors besides the resource itself. While recognizing that proprietors of resources should be compensated, Japan recommended that, '[f]or the sake of balanced benefits of holders of biological resources and inventors/patentees', payment issues be resolved by the concerned parties alone.[58]

Japan's view of the call for protection of traditional knowledge and farmers' rights is not firm yet. Japan sought to leave it open for further discussion on whether a new, *sui generis* system would be necessary to protect traditional knowledge. It asserted that 'Discussion on traditional knowledge should not pre-empt the establishment of new intellectual property systems for the protection

53 Ibid.
54 Ibid.
55 Ibid.
56 Ibid.
57 Ibid.
58 Ibid.

of traditional knowledge'.[59] Japan nevertheless agreed that documentation of traditional knowledge could serve patent examiners and avoid grants on prior art.

There were also discernible divergences within the ASEAN[60] members of the WTO before the Doha conference. At the various meetings of the TRIPs Council, the Philippines, Malaysia and the Philippines and Thailand appeared to espouse the same positions as regards the nature and scope of the review of TRIPs Art. 27(3) while Singapore was closer to the positions of the EU and US.[61] The former group, though not often acting in unison, sought to extend the review to broader policy issues, instead of confining it to implementation as Singapore and the major powers preferred. Thailand and Malaysia indeed sought to extend it to an explicit recognition of the right of states to control or use genetic resources, farmers rights and the protection of plant varieties.[62]

The demand for extension of rights in the manner suggested by Thailand and Malaysia, and agreed to by the Philippines, as well as the search for broader interpretation of Article 27(3) in light of its impact on economic and social welfare, did not win the sympathy of Singapore, which warned against a lowering of IP standards. Instead, it proposed continuation of the status quo as a minimum.

Overall, by the eve of the Doha conference, Asian nations had put forward diverging views and proposals relating to the implications of reviewing the scope of patents under Article 27(3) of TRIPs and the extension of protection to geographic indications other than wines and spirits. The range of views and elements of disparity in their respective positions suggest that Asian nations were still divided at the fundamental level in whether they desired a revamp of the international IP system as a whole. India emerged during that period as the leader of the whole pack of Asian, if not all, DCs by pushing for a reform of the international IP system across a spectrum of issues. Its views were more articulate and comprehensive in the area of biodiversity and protection of traditional knowledge. It is noticeable that East Asian nations (China, Taiwan, South Korea and Hong Kong) were remarkably silent as regards the same issues. Singapore had begun to emerge as a champion of the status quo very much in tune with Japan (and the US), which expressed diametrically opposed views to those of Asian DCs.

Nonetheless, Asian DCs contributed to the major outcomes of the Doha conference, namely the 'Declaration on the TRIPs agreement and public health', as well as the instruction given to the TRIPS Council to examine 'the relationship between the TRIPS Agreement and the Convention on Biological Diversity,

---

59 Ibid.

60 The ASEAN (Association of South East Asian Nations) comprises Brunei, Cambodia, Indonesia, Laos, Malaysia, Myanmar, the Philippines, Singapore, Thailand and Vietnam.

61 For a review of the contrasting positions, see Christoph Antons, Michael Blakeney and Christopher Heath (eds), *Intellectual Property Harmonisation Within ASEAN and APEC*, Kluwer Law International: London, 2004, 139–58.

62 Ibid.

the protection of traditional knowledge and folklore, and other relevant new developments raised by members pursuant to Article 71.1'.[63]

Asian Views on Intellectual Property Issues During the Post-Doha Period

At the conclusion of the WTO Ministerial conference at Doha (November 2001), the WTO was mandated to negotiate accords among the members on further trade liberalization (in agriculture, services, market access) and implementation of previous agreements by 1 January 2005. That did not materialize as the range of trade liberalization issues that needed to be addressed were eclipsed by rancour among the major industrial nations and the resistance of DCs on questions that affect the latter's economic development and trade. One of the agreements pending implementation is the multilateral system of notification and registration of geographical indications for wines and spirits vigorously pursued by European nations but opposed by the US and the Cairns Group (representing agricultural exporting nations, including Indonesia, Malaysia, Philippines and Thailand from Asia). The members of Mercusor (Southern Common Market) – Argentina, Brazil, Paraguay and Uruguay – have also threatened to block any progress in the post-Doha negotiations if trade liberalization in agriculture was stalled by the EU and other nations.[64] The EU indeed froze any reforms in its common agricultural policy (CAP) until 2007[65] and the likelihood of any significant changes in its positions in the future remain uncertain.

In the area of TRIPs, the Doha Development Agenda[66] had not singled out any specific directions for change. That was surprising, particularly in view of Asian and other DCs' continued interest in some form of equitable intervention on their behalf. Still, Asian DCs did not refrain from legislating to meet their outstanding obligations. Thus on 14 May 2002, India passed an amendment to the 1970 patent law allowing extension of duration of process patents from seven to 20 years. The five emerging economies of ASEAN introduced diverse changes in their IP laws, as outlined in Chapter 2. There was no let up on that front in China either, as pointed out in Chapter 3. Taiwan established an 'integrated enforcement task force (IETF)'. South Korea joined the Trademark Law Treaty on 25 February 2003. The list of new legislation goes on and on.

In contrast to the general and silent acquiescence of most Asian DCs to treaty obligations in IP, the Indian stance highlighted the kind of issues that underlie

63 Paragraph 19, the DOHA WTO Ministerial Declaration 2001 adopted on 20 November 2001, WT/MIN(01)/DEC/1.

64 Gustavo Capdevila, 'Trade: MERCOSUR Threatens to Block WTO Liberalisation Talks', Inter Press Service: Geneva, 1 November 2002.

65 Ibid.

66 This is another name for the Ministerial Declaration of 20 November 2001; see, note 63, above.

the continuing debate. Owing to domestic opposition, the Indian government remained hesitant to introduce product patents for drugs, pursuant to its obligations under TRIPs. Yet the government expressed readiness to table a bill to amend the patent law in 2002.[67] The Confederation of Indian Industry (CII) welcomed the passage of the Patents (Second Amendment) bill 1999 hailing its capacity to 'safeguard national security and protect varied interests of the nation including public health',[68] although it pointed out that 'the government may still need to clarify provisions in terms of compulsory licence norms and exclusive marketing rights (EMRs)'.[69]

Nonetheless, multinational pharmaceuticals directed criticism against the amendment. The Indian Drug Manufacturers Association, which openly opposed the demand for data exclusivity of multinational pharmaceuticals, retorted: 'to say that Indian law is weak or not TRIPs compliant is an insult of the Parliament which has gone through it very carefully before passing it'. [70] It asserted that the demand was 'in violation of the spirit of Doha declaration, which reaffirmed the right of WTO members to use all flexibility to meet health emergencies and urgencies'.[71] The Association defended the amendment as fully TRIPs-compliant and declared that to push for further changes was to go beyond the existing requirements and inject TRIPs-plus demands. It contended, 'The phrase "data exclusivity" does not figure in the TRIPS agreement, this is a phrase which appears in US Food and Drug Administration regulations'.[72]

During the 2003 Non-Alignment Movement (NAM) meeting in Kuala Lumpur, the Indian Minister for Investment, Information Technology and Communications, expressed strongly the need to have the DCs rally around their own interests: At the NAM Business Forum, he argued that members 'must pool their resources to remedy the imbalances in the World Trade Organization (WTO), particularly in ensuring their developed counterparts do not dilute their commitments made at the WTO Doha Ministerial meeting in November 2001'.[73] He noted the lack of advances since the Doha meeting in the implementation of commitments of WTO members. He cited the example of the protection erected by the major industrial nations for their pharmaceutical sector so as to block out competition from DCs. He advised that 'NAM should seriously consider establishing a research group to

---

67 'Indian Cabinet Okays Amendment Bill On Product Patents', *Asia Pulse*, New Delhi, 28 February 2002.

68 'Indian Chamber Hails Passing Of Insurance Amendment Bill', *Asia Pulse*, New Delhi, 16 May 2002.

69 Ibid.

70 'Indian Drug Manufacturers Ciriticize Multinationals', *Asia Pulse*, New Delhi, 16 January 2003.

71 Ibid.

72 Ibid.

73 'Help Remedy Imbalances at WTO, Nam Business Forum Told', *Malaysia General News*, Petaling Jaya, 23 February 2003.

counter such inadequacies, which in the process could insulate developing societies from fly-by-night advisers from the west, especially in the area of Intellectual Property Rights (IPR)' and the international capital market.[74]

He called upon NAM countries 'to present a unified and common stand especially in the WTO negotiations as well as in global economic issues to ensure a sense of fair play for all, especially developing countries which have all this while been subjected to unfair trade and investment policies pushed through by developed countries'.[75] In the meantime, the Indian government came up with fresh views by proposing a '"development coalition" of bio-diversity rich countries to evolve an internationally agreed instrument to recognize national level systems for the protection of traditional knowledge'.[76]

By contrast, China has become non-committal in its positions; this is discernible in the language used by its officials. It refrains from openly expressing anything of substance. It merely states generalities and platitudes about meeting the 'reasonable demands' of DCs and 'new international rules' for all. For instance, a vice-minister of Foreign Trade and Economic Cooperation (MOFTEC) and former China WTO chief negotiator suggested that 'the WTO should provide technical assistance to developing countries, help them understand the procedures and content of rule-making and enhance their capacity to participate in the new round of negotiations'.[77] The call for technical assistance and increased awareness is a far cry from what the DCs themselves have been demanding – a fundamental transformation of the status quo.

As regards China's role, the minister iterated that 'China should work to make the World Trade Organization (WTO) a truly fair and efficient trade body at the Doha Round of trade negotiations … The WTO should balance the interests of developed countries and those of developing countries in laying down new international trade policies'.[78] At the same time, he reportedly asserted 'the Uruguay Round of WTO negotiations, presided over by developed countries, passed many rules that are detrimental to the economic development of developing countries'.[79] The Chinese Minister of Foreign Trade and Economic Cooperation, Shi Guangsheng, similarly stated, after a meeting with his EU counterpart, that 'The talks agenda set at the Doha meeting should not be changed or weakened', adding that the 'reasonable requests from developing countries needed to be considered.'[80] It is not clear what China is proposing to do – overthrow the status quo and replace it or continue

74 Ibid.

75 Ibid.

76 'India Proposes Coalition for Protection of Knowledge', *Asia Pulse*, New Delhi, 5 April 2002.

77 Meng Yan, 'Call for WTO to change', *Business Daily Update*, 24 May 2002.

78 Ibid.

79 Ibid.

80 'China, EU to Boost Coordination in New Round of Trade Talks', *Xinhua, Beijing*, 17 October 2002.

to work on improving it bit by bit? It seems that the Chinese Ministers had the latter in mind. Moreover, while prophesizing about a rosy future, they ignored the cumulative manner in which the laws have been introduced and reinforced to date and their inherent bias against non-Western countries in general and DCs in particular.

The position of the US did not change in any significant way after Doha. Except for the muted approach it assumed during the confrontations with the DCs afflicted with the HIV/AIDS pandemic and the persistent plea to make an exception for the sufferers and roll back the powers of patentees, the US remained unapologetic. In the 2001 Annual Report and 2002 Trade Agenda, the US Trade Representative, Zoellick, stated, 'America's trade agenda needs to be aligned securely with the values of our society'.[81] While expressing the view that maintaining that the TRIPs 'contains flexibilities for developing nations to obtain access to critical medicines to help address public health emergencies, such as HIV/AIDS, tuberculosis, and malaria', he asserted that the use of such flexibilities 'must be compatible with the crucial protection of intellectual property'.[82] In other words, back to square one. Yet, the mounting pressure exerted on the US and EU to allow DCs, regardless of whether they had drug manufacturing facilities, to produce or import them by overriding the relevant patents without fear of sanctions or other measures, achieved the expected outcome – a subject we will turn to presently.

The issue of bypassing patents in national emergency or for public health

It is to be recalled that the Doha Ministerial had agreed that countries could resort to compulsory licence for domestic use of patented drugs.[83] The question remained whether countries such as India, which exported generic drugs, or those without domestic manufacturing capacity could do the same. Moreover, DCs and non-governmental organizations like Oxfam, Medicins Sans Frontiers and Third World Network have continued their campaign to treat trade in medicines under human rights values rather than those of the market. They have extended their critique of the limitations of TRIPs to the negative impacts of other agreements such as those on Technical Barriers to Trade, Sanitary and Phytosanitary Measures, and Trade

81 Federal Information and News Dispatch Inc., State Department, 'Zoellick Reiterates Trade Negotiating Authority Push; Cites Multilateral, Regional, Bilateral Goals in 2002', 19 March 2002.

82 Ibid.

83 Paragraph 6 of the Doha Ministerial Declaration 2001 partly reads, 'We recognize that under WTO rules no country should be prevented from taking measures for the protection of human, animal or plant life or health, or of the environment at the levels it considers appropriate, subject to the requirement that they are not applied in a manner which would constitute a means of arbitrary or unjustifiable discrimination between countries where the same conditions prevail, or a disguised restriction on international trade, and are otherwise in accordance with the provisions of the WTO Agreements'.

in Services. They feared that liberalization of services could lead to market-based provision of education, health and water with devastating implications for most of these. The European Union, US, the African Group and other DCs had presented their proposals to the TRIPs Council, which was grappling with a formula to please all before the end of 2002, as mandated by the Doha Declaration.

Among the DCs that presented their proposals for possible solutions to the implementation of paragraph 6 of the Doha Declaration on the TRIPS Agreement and Public Health[84] were China, India, Indonesia, Pakistan, Sri Lanka and Thailand. These countries exhorted the TRIPS Council to 'refrain from considering narrow, burdensome, or ineffective solutions that would ultimately defeat the very purpose of the solution under Paragraph 6'.[85] They cited cases where manufacturing facilities may not exist, the patent law does not protect drugs or economies of scale may not be found as possible factors that the Council will have to ignore to arrive at a judicious solution.

The persistent fear of the developed industrial nations (such as US and Switzerland) with pharmaceutical MNCs was that cheap drugs despatched to or produced in DCs might eventually find their way back to other markets, including those in Europe and North America. Additional issues were the types of medicines that would be placed under compulsory licence, and whether parallel imports could be allowed. The US had sought to limit the list to 15-odd diseases.

Among the Asian DCs, India was, as usual, most alert about the issues. Its pharmaceutical companies 'expressed apprehensions that the Government of India would not be able to withstand the pressure from the US and other developed countries' to define the mode of implementation of the Doha Declaration on TRIPs and Public Health.[86] The Indian Pharmaceutical Alliance (IPA) pressed the government 'not to accede to the US' view' of requiring a licence from both the importer and exporter because it saw such a process 'would be both time-consuming and costly, with both the exporter and the importer having to pay royalty to the patentee'.[87] The IPA also argued against the importer's responsibility for trade diversion while expressing the suspicion that the leading pharmaceutical companies were undercutting their opportunity to export medicines to non-IC countries ravaged by AIDS and other diseases by creating alliances with some of the latter.[88]

84 'Paragraph 6 of the Ministerial Declaration on the TRIPs Agreement and Public Health', Communications to the Council of TRIPs from the Permanent Mission of Brazil on behalf of Bolivia, Cuba, China, the Dominican Republic, Ecuador, India, Indonesia, Pakistan, Peru, Sri Lanka, Thailand and Venezuela (IP/C/W/355), 24 June 2002.

85 Ibid., at paragraph 14.

86 '"Government Must not Bow to US View on TRIPs", WTO to Review Pharma Policy for Poor Nations (Say Major Pharmaceutical Companies of India)', *India Business Insight*, 24 September 2002.

87 Ibid.

88 Ibid.

The Philippines took centre stage when it opposed EU proposals to tighten the procedures for compulsory licence under discussion even after the deadline to finalize such by the end of 2002 had passed. The EU proposal required the involvement of the World Health Organization (WHO) as well as making importing countries take measures to prevent trade diversion.[89] The EU had proposed a list of 22 diseases for which DCs could issue compulsory licences. The EU also proposed that poor countries be able to address other public health problems they face as long as the WHO determined whether the problem was serious enough to warrant such.[90] The Philippines Trade and Industry Secretary objected to the EU proposal on the basis that it 'detracts from the flexibility granted by the TRIPs Declaration allowing countries to determine on their own what constitute public health problems, without need of confirmation or advice by any other country of international organization'.[91]

Oxfam International declared support for the position taken by the Trade and Industry Secretary of the Philippines 'despite the pressure you are undoubtedly under'.[92] In return, the Secretary asked Oxfam to 'help mitigate the pressure made to bear upon us by urging other developing countries to follow our lead in remaining firm on the foregoing issues'.[93] He also criticized the US suggestion as seeking to restrict the 'broad and comprehensive scope enunciated in paragraph 1 [of the Doha Ministerial Declaration] under the guise of a classificatory definition'.[94]

Eventually, the US declared a moratorium on its use of WTO measures against nations that might resort to compulsory licensing for drugs. The European Union followed the US in declaring to the same effect 'as a purely stop-gap, temporary measure'.[95] In return, the other nations had to accept the notification requirements.

The zigzags in submissions of proposals, the contentious views among the protagonists and the failure to meet the deadline for reaching agreement on medicines and patents bred anxiety among WTO officials. Carlos Perez del Castillo, chairman of the WTO General Council, thus stated that the problem had developed into 'a banner issue due to its humanitarian characteristics', among

89 'WTO-EU-Medicines-Expert: WHO Expert Rejects Listing Diseases in WTO Medicines Talks', *Agence France-Presse*, 9 January 2003.

90 'Developing Countries should have Greater Access to Drugs: Philippines', *Agence France Presse* [Manila], 31 January 2003.

91 'Philippines Disagrees With EU's WTO Drug Agreement Proposal', *Asia Pulse* [Manila], 21 January 2003.

92 'Philippines Gets Support From Oxfam on Parallel Drug Imports', *Asia Pulse* [Manila], 6 February 2003.

93 Ibid.

94 Ibid.

95 Ibid.

DCs, and that, if there was no progress, 'I doubt that the countries of Africa and the rest of the developing world are going to accept compromises on other matters'.[96]

The actions of the US (in deference to its pharmaceutical companies who feared that allowing import of generic drugs by DCs would lead India and Brazil to flood the market with their own cheap drugs) to block the commonly agreed 16 December 2002 text was later overcome by the MNCs' own fear that the lack of agreement might open them up to further attacks at the Cancun Conference. The drugs industry had apparently informed the WTO of 'its willingness to resolve the matter prior to the Cancun ministerial conference'.[97] The SARS (Severe Acute Respiratory Syndrome) scare in Asia also contributed to the view that limiting the compulsory licence right to certain type of diseases would be unworkable.[98]

The deal struck on 30 August 2003 (known as the 'Perez Motta text', after the former Chairman of the TRIPs Council) was a compromise between the EU and US, on the one hand, agreeing not to assert their IP rights against generic drug manufacturing and import by DCs and other WTO members who pledged not to abuse the facility by importing generic medicines for commercial or industrial purposes or diverting such back to the industrial nation's markets. Twenty-three industrial countries[99] also pledged not to resort to such a measure while another group of developing countries[100] declared to desist from such a measure except in a national emergency.

The waiver introduced in favour of DCs was expected to become, by July 2004, an amendment to Article 31(f) of TRIPs, which otherwise restricts products made under compulsory licence to remain 'predominantly for the supply of the domestic market'. The amendment was only approved by WTO members on 6 December 20005, yet it is awaiting ratification by two-thirds of the WTO members, who were supposed to have done this by 1 December 2007. An extension has been allowed by the General Council of WTO to finalize acceptance by 31 December 2009.[101]

In terms of its substance, the waiver is not absolute. It has a number of preconditions and intricate procedures that the eligible importing member should comply with. Moreover, the measure can be deployed 'only in the case of a national emergency or other circumstances of extreme urgency or in cases of public non-

96 Gustavo Capdevila, 'Trade: Health Problems Afflict WTO on Way to Cancun', *Inter Press Service*, Geneva, 11 July 2003.

97 Ibid.

98 Ibid.

99 These are Australia, Austria, Belgium, Canada, Denmark, Finland, France, Germany, Greece, Iceland, Ireland, Italy, Japan, Luxembourg, Netherlands, New Zealand, Norway, Portugal, Spain, Sweden, Switzerland, the UK and the US.

100 Turkey, Slovenia, Estonia, Lithuania, Latvia, Hungary, Slovakia, Czech Republic, Poland, Malta, Cyprus, Israel, Korea, Singapore, Hong Kong China, Mexico, Chinese Taipei, Kuwait, Macao China, Qatar and United Arab Emirates.

101 WTO, 'Amendment of the TRIPS Agreement – Extension of the Period for the Acceptance by Members of the Protocol Amending the TRIPS Agreement', 21 December 2007; available at http://docsonline.wto.org.

commercial use'.[102] Clearly, the needs of a country to provide adequate health services and medicines do not form part of the grant.

Neither are the requirements and procedures any easier for the exporters. The issue of the compulsory licence by an exporting Member is subject to certain conditions: volume and specific labelling or marking of the licensed products and posting of information on the web before shipment. The exporting Member must also notify the Council for TRIPs of the grant of the licence and provide information about the licensee. Neither is the grant of a compulsory licence free. 'Adequate remuneration' must be paid in the exporting Member. The waiver extends to regional blocs to which the eligible importing member belongs if the blocs 'share the health problem in question'.[103]

Clear winners in the saga were Indian drugs manufacturers. It was apparent that the tug of war between the EU and US who sought to block imports of cheap drugs by the DCs but allow manufacture only, on the one hand, and the rest of the DCs who had no manufacturing capacity and would therefore need to import them from elsewhere, on the other, would end in benefiting India and similar countries. Thus 'India's pharma industry breathed a sigh of relief'[104] when US proposals were rejected during the final hours of the negotiations on the compulsory licence issue. A member of the Organization of Pharmaceutical Producers of India (OPPI) declared, 'If the deal had gone through, it would have imposed subtle, but very tricky conditions on poor generic drug manufacturing countries effectively tying us up in knots. We are relieved that some two dozen WTO members rejected the proposal'.[105]

India saw the benefit of the moratorium on patents for emergency health as a windfall.[106] Indian manufacturers of generic drugs were hoping to cash in on the allowances extended to DCs to import cheap drugs not only for HIV/AIDS but also for other diseases such as TB and malaria.

Issues of safeguarding and exploiting indigenous or traditional knowledge

Many nations had presented their views at various times to address the problem of safeguarding and exploiting indigenous or traditional knowledge as well as the

102 Decision of the WTO General Council of 30 August 2003, 'Implementation of paragraph 6 of the Doha Declaration on the TRIPS Agreement and public health', WT/L/540, 1 September 2003, paragraph 1.

103 Ibid., paragraph 6.

104 'India's Pharma Industry Breathes Sigh of Relief as WTO Drugs Pact Collapses', *Agence France Presse*, 29 August 2003. Available online from Factiva.

105 'Oxfam Urges Africa to Unite Ahead of WTO Meeting', *Agence France Presse* [Nairobi], 29 August 2003.

106 'US Windfall Awaits Indian Pharma Companies (Expected to Benefit from Specific Steps to be Taken by US to Liberalise Sales of Generic Drugs)', *India Business Insight*, 31 August 2003.

creation of consistency between TRIPs and the CBD. Essentially, the submissions called for the amendment of TRIPs to allow members to demand from an applicant for a patent on biological materials or traditional knowledge the disclosure of the source and country of origin of the same and to provide evidence of prior informed consent as well as of fair and equitable benefit sharing (as required under the CBD). The attempt culminated in the recognition given by the Doha Ministerial Declaration[107] to the need to conduct negotiation to resolve the matter.

A group including China, India, Pakistan and Thailand from Asia thus made a submission to the TRIPs Council in June 2002.[108] It argued that TRIPs needed to be modified to make it consistent with the objectives of the CBD. In particular, it sought for TRIPs to include provisions outlawing biopiracy, requiring prior informed consent from the owners of the biological resources as preconditions for grants of IP, and mechanisms of enforcing claims for fair and equitable sharing of benefits by source countries.

The group of nations contended that the establishment of 'an internationally accepted solution' would constitute a saving of valuable resources by avoiding expensive patent revocation proceedings in diverse jurisdictions. The group viewed that approach to be more beneficial to DCs because they 'do not have the resources to follow each and every patent issued outside their territories on the use of their resources'.[109] It also called upon going beyond the 'defensive protection for traditional communities from misappropriation of their knowledge' to instituting 'an international framework' capable of achieving those objectives 'at the national and regional levels'.[110]

Another group of Latin American nations as well as India and Thailand submitted their proposals to the TRIPs Council, which circulated the same at its meeting of 4–5 June 2003.[111] The submission sought to achieve similar objectives of consistency between TRIPs and the CBD by amending the former. Moreover, the group contended that the disclosure of the source and the country of origin as well as provision of evidence of consent and benefit would help prevent 'biopiracy and misappropriation and ... the issue of "bad patents"'.[112] It noted that, in the absence of such an amendment, legal recourse on an international level would

107 Adopted on 14 November 2001.

108 WTO, Council for TRIPs, 'The Relationship Between the TRIPs Agreement and the Convention on Biological Diversity and the Protection of Traditional Knowledge' (communication from Brazil, on behalf of China, Cuba, Dominican Republic, Ecuador, India, Pakistan, Peru, Thailand, Venezuela, Zambia and Zimbabwe), IP/C/W/356, 24 June 2002.

109 Ibid.

110 Ibid.

111 WTO, Council for TRIPs, 'The Relationship between the TRIPS Agreement and the Convention on Biological Diversity and the Protection of Traditional Knowledge', Submission by India on behalf of Bolivia, Brazil, Cuba, Dominican Republic, Ecuador, India, Peru, Thailand and Venezuela IP/C/W/403, 24 June 2003.

112 Ibid.

remain 'complicated and expensive, and may not be economically feasible for many aggrieved countries ... Placing the onus on a patent applicant to disclose the basis of its claims is a step that can pre-empt any misuse of patent laws and thereby prevent misappropriation of knowledge and resources'.[113]

The submission then addressed arguments that such requirements amount to violation of the principle of non-discrimination between fields of technology or impose unnecessary burden on applicants.[114] It contended that the use of different procedures dependent on the 'field of technology' is the norm and hence the argument is unsupportable. Secondly, it countered that provision of information or evidence by the patent applicant makes sense because such information is readily available with that applicant. It then pointed to the limitation of using only available databases for determination of rights as not all information would possibly be deposited in them. Finally, it rejected the contractual route or the resort to purely national measures suggested by some (Japan, amongst others) as being sufficient to protect resources, although it admitted that some have already used both, more as an additional means. It therefore pointed to the only solution as being to amend the TRIPs so that it can be applied in a harmonious way with CBD and both complement each other.

Geographical indications

The negotiation for extension, as envisaged in Paragraph 18 the Doha Ministerial Declaration, of the protection available through TRIPs to wines and spirits (and largely confined to a few European and other nations) to other countries and products has not been easy. For one thing, a group of countries including the US[115] has opposed the EU and other countries' proposal[116] to recognize other geographic indications such as Darjeeling tea, Indian saris, Turkish carpets and Jasmine rice. The argument against extension has focused on costs to WTO members if such a change were effected. Interestingly, Asian countries have not adopted a uniform position. Thus, the Philippines and Taiwan have joined the US, while Pakistan, Sri Lanka and Thailand supported the EU proposals.

---

113 Ibid.

114 WTO, TRIPs Council, 'Communication From the United States', IP/C/W/257, 13 June 2001.

115 Australia, Canada, Guatemala, New Zealand, Paraguay, the Philippines and the US (document IP/C/W/360), and a subsequent communication from Argentina, Australia, Canada, Chile, Chinese Taipei, the Dominican Republic, El Salvador, Guatemala, New Zealand, Paraguay, the Philippines and the US (IP/C/W/386). Still another, Argentina, Australia, Canada, Chile, Chinese Taipei, Colombia, the Dominican Republic, Ecuador, El Salvador, Guatemala, Honduras, New Zealand, Panama and the US (IP/C/W/395).

116 Bulgaria, Cuba, Cyprus, the Czech Republic, the European Communities and their member States, Georgia, Hungary, Iceland, India, Kenya, Liechtenstein, Malta, Mauritius, Pakistan, Romania, Slovakia, Sri Lanka, Switzerland, Thailand and Turkey (IP/C/W/353).

Asian Nations and Intellectual Property at the Cancun Ministerial Conference

In the run-up to the Cancun conference, 10–14 September 2003, many DCs expressed their positions chiefly in terms of the removal of subsidies for agriculture and other barriers to trade. Only a minority among them seemed to think that TRIPs deserved to continue to be scrutinized or that the negotiations at Cancun should include them. Thus Indonesia welcomed the agreement on compulsory licensing for health but sought to go beyond issues of market access and agriculture. It urged that 'a higher level of protection should also be given to other products which are now only given to wine and spirits under geographical indication. We wish that this protection be extended to traditional knowledge such as batik Solo, jamu, Toraja coffee, basmati rice, and many others'.[117]

The Philippines was unconcerned whether the 'new round of talks at the World Trade Organization' convened or not.[118] The Trade and Industry Secretary Manuel A. Roxas II stated plainly, 'We will not be unhappy if there was no new WTO round at all', apparently in line with 'President Gloria Macapagal Arroyo's policy change to go slow on trade commitments'.[119] The Philippines Trade and Industry Secretary remained steadfast in his position of ensuring the country's sovereign right to determine its public health needs. He stated, 'Our country should be allowed to avail of the agreement's foreseen benefits, including our objective of lowering prices of essential medicines for the poor.'[120] The view was echoed by various civil society groups such as the 'Stop the New Round! Coalition' bringing together many smaller organizations that 'warned that further liberalizing trade without any safety nets would only leave local industries in peril'.[121]

By contrast, the Thai Prime Minister manifested the common illusion that the WTO was meant to benefit both developed and developing countries equally. He stated this optimism in his visit to the Philippines by expressing his hope that the meeting 'be more balanced between developed and developing countries'.[122] He said the 'ultimate goal' of the Cancun talks should be 'how the developing world can develop under WTO'. He also called on developed countries to open their markets further to poorer countries, saying this would help both sides.[123]

---

117 Ministerial Conference, Fifth Session, Cancun, 10–14 September 2003 Statement by H.E. Mrs Rini M.S. Soewandi Minister of Industry and Trade of Indonesia, World Trade Organization, WT/MIN(03)/ST/7, 10 September 2003.

118 Iris Cecilia C. Gonzales, 'RP Says no New WTO Round not a Cause of Great Concern', *BusinessWorld* [Philippines], 9 April 2003.

119 Ibid.

120 'Cheaper Drugs Get WTO Nod', *Manila Standard*, 8 October 2003.

121 Ibid.

122 Iris Cecilia C. Gonzales and Karen L. Lema 'Philippines: Thai PM Sees "Little" Hope of Concessions for Poor Countries in WTO', *Global News Wire*, 9 September 2003.

123 Ibid.

Surprisingly, Indian Prime Minister Atal Behari Vajpayee declared at an India-ASEAN trade meeting that 'the contentious issue of TRIPS … and public health' had been resolved.[124] Malaysia saw the objective of the fifth WTO ministerial meeting at Cancun in terms of ensuring 'greater market access for its products and for an equitable multilateral trading system to evolve'.[125] According to Rafidah Aziz, the Malaysian Minister of International Trade and Industry, the push for liberalization of the services sector by the EU and US, among others, must be tempered by 'due regard for the domestic needs, situation and environment' of DCs as the latter 'do not have the capacity to open up while others do not even have a services sector to speak of'.[126]

In the speeches that the Asian countries' representatives made at the opening of the Cancun conference, they iterated diverse positions. Thus a Thai minister pointed to the disparity among the WTO members and the huge reliance of DCs on agriculture and therefore the need to involve everyone in the negotiations rather than allowing 'only some members' to dictate them, 'while others are left on the sideline and forced to accept the outcome'.[127]

The Singapore position was to try to speed up negotiations lest 'those who oppose liberalization and prefer protection' in the domestic politics of every country benefited from the failure.[128] The Minister projected a future where danger lurked for everyone if progress towards further trade liberalization was not achieved. In particular, he contended that nations might otherwise work on 'alternative arrangements' such as economic blocs that parcel out the world trading system.[129]

As regards the topical agenda of the conference, namely elimination of subsidies in agriculture, the Philippines argued for the provision of special and differential treatment for DCs in view of their requirement of 'pursuing rural development and food security'.[130] The delegation of Papua New Guinea stated identical views on removal of subsidies in agriculture.[131] Myanmar added that

124 Biman Mukherji, 'Indian PM fires potshot at rich nations ahead of WTO summit', *Agence France Presse*, New Delhi, 4 September 2003.

125 'M'sia to Seek More Market Access at Cancun WTO Meeting Next Week', *Malaysia Economic News*, Kuala Lumpur, 5 September 2003.

126 Hardev Kaur, 'Ensuring Fair Play at Cancun', *New Straits Times – Management Times*, 8 September 2003.

127 Statement by H.E. Dr Adisai Bodharamik, Minister of Commerce, World Trade Organization, WT/MIN(03)/ST/16, 10 September 2003 (03–4750).

128 Ministerial Conference, Fifth Session, Cancun, 10–14 September 2003, Statement by H.E. Mr George Yeo Minister for Trade and Industry of Singapore, World Trade Organization, WT/MIN(03)/ST/1, 10 September 2003.

129 Ibid.

130 Ministerial Conference, Fifth Session, Cancun, 10–14 September 2003, Statement by the Honourable Manuel Roxas, Secretary of Trade and Industry, World Trade Organization, WT/MIN(03)/ST/63, 10 September 2003.

131 Ministerial Conference, Fifth Session, Cancun, 10–14 September 2003, Statement by the Honourable Allan Savenat Mesak Marat, Deputy Prime Minister and

> harmful practices such as economic coercive measures, trade sanctions, linkage to trade preferences, development aids or debt relief initiatives being used by some major developed countries are contrary to the multilateral trade rules that negatively affect the socio-economic lives of the people and also slow down the development process. We strongly believe that developing countries have the right to choose the path of development in accordance with their national priorities and objectives.[132]

India provided an extended argument:

> Given the differences in levels of development and the ability of countries to assume obligations, it is imperative to ensure that equal rules do not apply to unequal players. With very few exceptions, today's developed countries in the past practised and benefited from the same protection they now seek to deny to developing countries. Anyone can dismantle all protection after growing wealthier and powerful. The multilateral trading system has to acknowledge that developing countries cannot afford to travel at the same speed as developed countries to achieve gains. Therefore, obligations to be undertaken by the developing countries should not arise out of coercion. Rather, they should have a feeling that these obligations are in their interest and that they are in a position to accept and implement them.[133]

The G-20 Group of DCs,[134] which started apparently informally in the course of preparations for the Cancun ministerial meeting in Geneva, has started to make its mark. It tabled a framework proposal highlighting the group's concerns and making agriculture the central issue for the Cancun (WTO) ministerial conference. Its emergence or activities has not, however, elicited a favourable response from the EU and the US.

According to one commentator, 'Brazil and other G-22 countries could transform the WTO from a vehicle aimed at negotiating trade disputes into a forum in which a politically energized South would be launching attacks against

---

Minister for Trade and Industry, World Trade Organization, WT/MIN(03)/ST/72/Rev. 1, 14 September 2003.

132 Ministerial Conference, Fifth Session, Cancun, 10–14 September 2003, Statement by H.E. Brigadier General Pyi Sone, Minister for Commerce of Myanmar, World Trade Organization, WT/MIN(03)/ST/105, 12 September 2003.

133 Ministerial Conference, Fifth Session, Cancun, 10–14 September 2003 Statement by H.E. Mr Arun Jaitley Minister of Commerce and Industry and Law and Justice, World Trade Organization, WT/MIN(03)/ST/12, 10 September 2003.

134 They comprise Argentina, Bolivia, Brazil, Chile, China, Costa Rica, Cuba, Ecuador, Egypt, El Salvador, Guatemala, India, Mexico, Nigeria, Pakistan, Paraguay, Philippines, South Africa, Thailand and Venezuela. Note that the numbers have not been constant.

the North, and especially on the United States'.[135] Predictably, the US has started 'to co-opt some of the developing economies in Latin America, Asia and Africa, by offering them separate trade deals with the US'.[136] In the meantime, the G-20 Group (among whom figure China, Thailand, Philippines and Indonesia) has been pushing a post-Cancun agenda largely as 'an essential and recognized interlocutor in the agricultural negotiations'.[137]

In the aftermath of the failure of the Cancun meeting, Rafidah Aziz, the Malaysian Minister of International Trade and Industry, commented that, while the industrial powers were 'reluctant to undertake reforms in agriculture', they are 'seeking to turn WTO into an all-purpose supranational organization by introducing global rules on new issues like investment, competition policy, government procurement and trade facilitation'.[138] She argued that such moves would trample on

> the sovereign rights of governments to determine domestic policies to achieve particular development goals. No responsible government can be expected to undertake such commitments that can deny its people the legitimate rights to exercise policy options in the pursuit of development, particularly when these same policy options had been exercised by the proponents of the 'new issues' at the earlier stages of their development. The rush to negotiate multilateral rules and disciplines in these areas, without clear and thorough understanding of the ramifications and manifestations, can impinge upon and undermine those sovereign rights.[139]

One must note, nevertheless, that the Minister did not view the concessions already given under TRIPs as forming part of the same problems the DCs continue to face.

In any event, it is surprising that almost all the Asian nations were prepared to shelve IP issues altogether. Even when some acerbic arguments were made against the international trade regime and the domineering positions of the major industrial powers, it was confined to the liberalization of the services sector and agricultural subsidy issues and not extended to the international trading system as a whole and to TRIPs in particular. The fact that calls for special preferences have been made in the context of agriculture without any references to other industries or fields of activities such as innovative work, R&D and the like, suggests either morbid fear of retaliatory measures or utter ignorance of the links that subsist among all of them.

---

135 Leon Hadar, 'World Trade – Back to the North vs South split?' *The Business Times* [Singapore], 5 November 2003.

136 Ibid.

137 See the group's webpage at http://www.g-20.mre.gov.br/history.asp.

138 Datuk Seri Rafidah Aziz, 'Cancun Conference: The Malaysian Perspective', *Business Times* [Malaysia], 3 November 2003, at 2.

139 Ibid.

Conclusion

Up until 1995, the only enthusiastic champions of IP in Asia were Japan and British Hong Kong. By 2000, almost all Asian DCs had updated their IP laws to make them TRIPs-compliant, as expected under that Agreement. No sooner had they done so than the so-called WIPO treaties were pushed through by the major industrial nations. Predictably, Asian DCs had to imitate and transplant the contents of those treaties.[140]

As the discussion in this chapter has showed, Asian DCs take positions on developments in IP in a largely reactive manner. Thus before the Doha WTO Conference recognized the urgency of the need of DCs for cheaper drugs and affirmed their right to resort to extraordinary measures, none of them embarked on such a measure. (Thailand had asserted its right at some stage, in response to popular demands, but caved in to US criticism and latent fear of retaliation.) Neither during the course of the debate before Doha nor afterwards did they ever identify what needs to be changed in the patent system. Clearly, after the advances that the industrial powers achieved through TRIPs in 1994, none of them would accept any retreats. Yet, Asian DCs could not muster the arguments, leave alone the strength, to achieve that.

Indeed, during the period under consideration, Asian DCs seem to have been taken in by the perception that the more pressing concern for cheaper medicines had been addressed fully through the Doha Declaration. Although anecdotal evidence suggests that all DCs ignore or shelve IP on the statute books if it does not serve their purposes, more empirical study is required to account for the lack of serious arguments for the revision of TRIPs as they seem to desire in their pronouncements vis-à-vis various issues.

It is not coincidental, therefore, that Asian Non-IC attitudes and policies towards the further expansion of IP across the world is still incipient. Any attempt to assess future prospects in that direction and the likelihood, or otherwise, of the emergence of a common position among them is a moot point. If at all Asian DCs have managed to throw up issues and standpoints, they remain limited to such disjointed aspects as biodiversity, compulsory licensing and extension of protection to geographic indications to cultural or other artefacts in Asia. Even then, one notes the tendency towards inward-looking measures such as asserting indigenous cultural or other values in opposition to, for instance, high-technology products they continue to acquire from abroad.

The obvious lack of a unified perspective across Asian states prevents the emergence of articulate positions on major IP issues that could command broader appeal among governments, civil society, the professional groups and consumers. One has only to see the virtual walkover of the USTR in negotiations with Asian (and other) DCs on free trade agreements, as will be discussed in Chapter 9, to

140 The manner in which they reacted to them and their habitual acquiescence has been reviewed in Endeshaw, note 9, above.

understand the paucity of a policy-based grasp of the implications of overarching IP to Asian DCs and beyond. That the latter are being dragged into such FTAs one by one – regardless of the common knowledge that they cannot possibly be ready for TRIPs-plus provisions, while their IP largely remains on the statute books and hence not yet fully enforced – underlines both the futility of the exercise on the part of the US and the state of despondency among the target nations.

Chapter 7
A Comparative Review of Intellectual Property in East Asia and Africa

Introduction

The role of intellectual property (IP) law in Asia has attracted a lot of attention in the last 10 years, partly because of the euphoric references to the 'tiger economies', the 'Asian Miracle' and the 'Asian Century', although such references have become rather restrained since the 1997 crisis. By comparison, Africa continues to grab the attention of the world largely on account of the numerous conflicts and human and ecological disasters that have plagued it for decades. The disparity between Asia and Africa, both in terms of past achievements and future prospects, is thus generally considered to be so apparent and unquestionable that a comparison of the respective roles of IP in Asia and Africa might not seem plausible.

However, there are a few common features shared by Asia and Africa. Both of them are vast continents with a multiplicity of nations, histories and cultures. The respective nations find themselves within an extended range of divergent economic, social and technological environments. Their laws have largely originated from, or been heavily influenced by, foreign or colonial traditions.[1] The equation of 'modernization' to 'Westernization' has propelled their legal developments in the direction of imitations, copying and full-scale transplants of further Western legal forms, institutions and jurisprudence.[2]

In the realm of IP too, despite the specific differences in the way that the laws may have evolved in each nation, the general patterns are broadly alike. A growing

---

1 Andrew Harding, amongst many others, recounts how legal pluralism emerged in South East Asia. According to him, custom or tradition was supplanted by waves of colonial or foreign imports culminating in the post-1945 movement to imitate more Western 'economic-development law and democratic constitutions' (typified by Malaysia and Singapore). He contends that, post-1990, 'globalization' has been 'driving much of legal development and transplantation in South East Asia in the field of international business and commercial law, for example relating to foreign investment and intellectual property'. See, Andrew Harding, 'Global Doctrines and Local Knowledge: Law in South East Asia', *International and Comparative Law Quarterly*, January 2002; available online through Westlaw, UK.

2 In the period 1960–95, the pace of legal change in 'formal law' was apparently 'piecemeal rather than comprehensive' for Japan, India, South Korea, Taiwan and Malaysia. See, Katharina Pistor, Philip A. Wellons et al., *The Role of Law and Legal Institutions in Asian Economic Development 1960–95*, Oxford University Press: New York, 1998, at 4.

body of literature has recounted how and at what stage the IP laws have been changing in each nation and, sometimes, across them. The primary purpose and, indeed, the pressure for the prevalence of such an approach has been the need of both foreign businesses and legal practitioners for guidance and a quick reference for action. Even then, the interests of foreign businesses and governments in all countries has not been identical; nor has the IP literature been oblivious to the level and state of development of countries.

It is symptomatic of the dissimilarity in the relevance of IP to the economies and societies of Asia and Africa (the vast majority) that the more economically successful command the attention of researchers and writers, foreign businesses and governments. Countries such as Bangladesh, Brunei, Cambodia, Mongolia, Myanmar, North Korea, Laos, Papua New Guinea and Sri Lanka from Asia and all but a tiny few (possibly four: South Africa, Egypt, Nigeria and Ghana) from Africa hardly ever get any attention at all. This is not to say that government officials or advisors of all kinds, including the World Intellectual Property Organization (WIPO), dissuade these countries from delving into the complexities of IP law. On the contrary, the haste with which all countries have been pushed to adopt laws compatible with the Agreement on Trade-Related Aspects of Intellectual Property Rights (TRIPs) and thereby rush towards universal rules and standards becomes evident when one looks at the explosion in the number of countries that joined the WIPO and the major IP treaties in the space of the last 10 years.[3]

On the other hand, the formation of regional groupings, whether economic, trade-related or aiming to bring about legal harmonization, has prompted a reductionist approach in the study of IP. Thus, works aspiring to deal with Asian or African IP law as a whole or on a regional basis (such as in the so-called English-speaking or Francophone Africa, in the Association of South-East Asian Nations –ASEAN – or the Asia–Pacific Economic Cooperation – APEC) or in individual countries provide a panoramic view of the IP systems in their areas of concern;[4] invariably, they fail to examine the interconnections, similarities or divergences among the respective systems on the one hand and the significance of those laws to their respective social–economic bases on the other. Works by indigenous writers have started to trickle but their focus is still on the provision of immediate information to practitioners and businesses as well as on spelling out where the respective IP law stands in all kinds of contexts (such as famous marks and brands, the Internet, biotechnology and the like), especially in view of the constant threats and pressures from the US for stronger enforcement and extension of rights.

3 The membership status on 31 January 2009 of the Paris Convention for the Protection of Industrial Property and the Berne Convention for the Protection of Literary and Artistic Works was 173 and 164, respectively. See http://www.wipo.int/treaties/en/index.html.

4 See, for instance, Alan Gutterman and Robert Brown, *Intellectual Property Laws of East Asia*, Sweet & Maxwell: Hong Kong, 1997; and Christopher Heath (ed.), *Intellectual Property Law in Asia*, Kluwer Law International: London, 2004.

Moreover, particularly since TRIPs, research in IP of developing countries tends to be obsessed with finding gaps in the current laws by reference to the treaty obligations that the respective states may have assumed.[5]

The upshot of all this is that policy issues that influence or even determine the role of IP in the social and economic environment are generally ignored or treated as being of marginal importance. The lack of empirical studies that back or disprove the significance of the IP legal system to the specific nations (in particular to their cultural and social progress) of Asia and Africa remains largely unaddressed to this day. As Harding saw it, perhaps the deficiency has a wider dimension:

> It is indeed one of the puzzles of legal scholarship that in the main streams of comparative law and also law-and-development, virtually no account has been taken of the South-East Asian legal experience, even though some excellent and highly relevant work on the region has been done. The depressingly small number of scholars in the field of law in South East Asia have in truth trodden a somewhat lonely path. Why, for example, has the relationship between law and economic development, and of course economic crisis too, in South East Asia been ignored by scholars, when ordinary South East Asian people taking to the streets to protest at corruption, mismanagement and abuse, understand its importance only too well? Can useful lessons not be drawn? The region presents an ideal laboratory in which … global doctrine and local knowledge are and always have been, partners locked in a dizzying embrace. The region has an abundance of legal traditions, practically all of them having been 'received' or 'transplanted' in one sense or another, and encompassing all of the world's major legal world-views and systems.[6]

This chapter seeks to establish a theoretical framework to fill that gap by examining the significance of IP in Asia, in particular its role in the 'Asian miracle', in comparison with developments in Africa. To that end, it starts of the discussion by summarizing the law-making process in IP across the two geographic spaces. It then addresses the role of IP in the economic miracles of Asia. Finally, it tackles the issue of whether the role of the IP system in the 'Asian Miracles' can throw up any lessons for Africa.

---

5 An example is D.W. Ruhukwa, Intellectual Property Rights & the Legal Implications for Zimbabwe of the Agreement on Trade-related Aspects of Intellectual Property Rights (TRIPS) arising from the Conclusion of the Uruguay Round of Multilateral Trade Negotiations, 1997 (Report presented to the University of London, Institute of Advanced Legal Studies/Nuffield Fellowship Program, 1997).

6 See, Harding, note 1 above, ibid.

Intellectual Property Law-Making in East Asia and Africa

Asian nations have on the whole adopted the latest IP laws through copying, imitation or sheer compulsion. Yet, the implementation of the laws remains weak or utterly deficient. The principal arguments adduced to explain these refer to the absence of political good will, scarcity of resources allocated for enforcement and a malevolent desire by non-industrial nations to pirate foreign technologies.[7] Thus Leaffer asserted,

> In Third World countries, the piracy of intellectual property is justified by an ideology of development. Ready access to intellectual property is viewed as important to development, whereas the enforcement of intellectual property law is considered a burden on development. Thus, developing countries resist allocating scarce government resources to the enforcement of intellectual property rights. As with the importation of capital, the importation of intellectual property often is viewed as a tool to dominate and exploit the economic potential of the importing countries. Paying for imports or making royalty payments imposed economic burdens and foster's a negative balance of trade.[8]

Contrary to such arguments, many writers maintain that the principal reason for lack of, or weak, enforcement of IP is the disconnect between the IP laws and the social, cultural and economic conditions of those nations.[9] Upon the creation of the link between membership of the World Trade Organization (WTO), comprising the vast majority of nations across the globe, and the mandatory adoption of minimal uniform IP laws (enshrined in TRIPs) since 1995, the disregard for the congruence of IP laws with the internal conditions of the developing countries was cast in steel. In other words, the disconnect was effectively sanctioned as a rule of public international law.

---

7 See, for instance, Robert M. Sherwood, *Intellectual Property and Economic Development*, Westview Press: Boulder, CO, 1990; Marshall A. Leaffer, 'Protecting United States Intellectual Property Abroad: Toward a New Multilateralism', 76 *Iowa Law Review* 273, 1991.

8 See Leaffer, ibid., at 282.

9 See Edith T. Penrose, *The Economics of the International Patent System*, John Hopkins Press: Baltimore, MD, 1951; Helge E. Grundmann, 'Foreign Patent Monopolies in Developing Countries: An Empirical Analysis', 12 *Journal of Development Studies* 186 (1976); A. Samuel Oddi, 'The International Patent System and Third World Development: Reality or Myth?', 1987 *Duke Law Journal* 831 (1987); P.S. Sangal and Kishore Singh (eds), *Indian Patent System and Paris Convention: Legal Perspectives*, Ashoka: Delhi, 1987; A. Endeshaw, *Intellectual Property Policy for Non-Industrial Countries*, Dartmouth: Aldershot, 1996; and Keith E. Maskus and Jerome H. Reichman, 'The Globalisation of Private Knowledge Goods and the Privatisation of Global Public Goods', 7 *Journal of International Economic Law* 279, June 2004.

Furthermore, the formulation of the desires of the industrial powers to secure protection of their IP in all lands through the TRIPs virtually turned other nations (especially the non-industrial ones) into surrogates of those powers.[10] Regardless of whether those nations had need for any form of IP protection at the local level or understood the implications of accepting limitless obligations for their development aspirations, they were forced to adopt all the standards and measures that the industrial powers had established for their advanced economies. It was known to all sides that the changes in the international IP system were made at the behest of the industrial powers and that the non-industrial nations had to play along for fear of repercussions to the so-called aid budget the same powers dangled before them as well as the ruse of gaining better trade access for their agricultural produce to the protected markets of the EU and North America.

Inevitably, all nations (whether in Asia or Africa) have had to contend with the disconnect between their social and economic circumstances and the barrage of imported IP laws and further amendments subsequent to their accession to TRIPs. Much of the literature on IP in these two areas of the world, indeed in Latin America as well, has concentrated on the saga of what changes had to be made and what the likely institutional, financial and practical impact on them might be. Typically, the main content of the legal literature appearing in the West (books or journals) has been to outline the gaps that needed to be addressed and to reassure non-industrial nations that, with more IP, their chances of economic transformation would increase.[11] Some writers appeared intent on portraying IP as a magical instrument for overcoming the economic backwardness of countries.[12] At any rate, there seems to be a universal consensus not to dissuade those nations from having second thoughts about acceding to the TRIPs or the WTO. Neither have any alternative paths outside of the framework of these treaties been suggested.

A number of false arguments have also been repeated ad infinitum: that more investments followed better protection of IP;[13] that lack of IP protection led to

10 One should note that even the EU has been the target of constant US threats and criticism as regards its IP laws and practices. The EU has been placed on the 'watch list' complied by the US, alongside the developing countries for as many years as the list was published. See http://www.ustr.gov.

11 Thus Maskus asserts, 'as developing countries strengthen their IPRs, accompanying market liberalization provides a more affirmative path to economic growth'. See Keith E. Maskus, *Intellectual Property Rights in the Global Economy, Institute for International Economics*, Washington, DC, 2000, at 169.

12 See, Sherwood, note 7, above.

13 While presenting his 2001 Annual Report, the US Trade Representative, Zoellick, stated, 'the local protection of intellectual property rights establishes the foundation for an attractive investment climate for industries of the future. Indeed, as developing countries have implemented the intellectual property protections in TRIPs, they have begun to benefit from increased technology transfer and investment – two key factors in long-term economic growth'. See Federal Information and News Dispatch Inc., State Department, 'Zoellick

flight of skilled persons and talent to industrial nations;[14] that pirates eroded the taxation base of the economies and perpetrated loss of jobs.[15] The putative economic role of IP in the domestic context, namely its encouragement of the generation and deployment of valuable creative works for the transformation of the society, is portrayed as not relevant, much less paramount. Indeed, any attempt to formulate IP laws in consonance with the internal requirements of developing nations is viewed paradoxically as a barrier against local potentials for economic development. The argument goes that the 'weaker' the standards of IP protection in non-industrial countries, the less their chances of promoting innovativeness and increasing the stocks of creative works would be.[16] All of these arguments only serve to camouflage the long-established fact that IP has served as an instrument of the industrial powers to hang on to the markets of the late-comer nations.

Then there are those who contend that IP merely represents a formal recognition of immutable, pre-existing natural rights without any policy or economic rationale to underscore it, or define its scope and characteristics.[17] It does not seem odd to these people that the law-making process in much of Africa and East Asia has taken the form of unadulterated copying and pasting of anything happening in the IP field in Europe or the US. Neither do they regard it as unusual that the training of personnel to operate the IP system is steeped in the natural law tradition and that such staff would not be made to acquire skills other than the manipulation of black letter law and hence remain unable to appreciate the time and space context of IP law. Thus as far as this (as it happens, dominant) perspective is concerned, IP laws across all nations should remain similar, if not identical. It is not without reason that the typical IP textbook is a list of the legal rules that have found optimal form in the Western tradition and therefore reflect solutions to problems the industrial nations have long passed through. To the question whether nations need to examine their circumstances and choose to adopt, reject or formulate their own forms of IP, the dominant frame of thinking would reply that such a move would only create a weak form of IP protection benefiting no one (sic!).

Reiterates Trade Negotiating Authority Push; Cites multilateral, regional, bilateral goals in 2002', 19 March 2002.

14 Thus Janet Reno, the former Attorney General of the US, asserted, 'For developing nations, the stakes [of theft of IP] are higher still [than the US]. Countries that fail to protect intellectual property will witness the exodus of their best talent, a loss of jobs and tax revenues, a nutrient environment for official corruption and an increase in crimes financed by intellectual property theft.' See Janet Reno, 'The Threat of Digital Theft: Intellectual Property Theft is Faster, Costlier and more Dangerous than Ever', 25 December 2000; available at http://www.usdoj.gov/criminal/cybercrime/AGdigitaltheft.htm.

15 Ibid.

16 See, Sherwood, note 7, above, at 159–78 ('The Myth of Weak Protection').

17 These are the advocates of the 'property rights theory'. In effect, they propound that IP has universal reach and is not subject to time or space contexts. See, for instance, Justin Hughes, 'The Philosophy of Intellectual Property', 77 *Georgetown Law Journal* 287, 1988.

Ultimately, the necessity for, and forms of, the IP system are portrayed as being dependent on the good faith of the power holders in Asia, Africa or elsewhere. In other words, those who do not uphold standards and measures adopted in the major ICs or enforce them to the extent demanded are perceived to possess no political will, as if law-making is a snap decision and enforcement a matter of convenience. This is contradicted by experience in both East Asia and Africa. On the one hand, IP enforcement remains blocked by social and cultural conditions that do not sit easily with property in mere ideas, useful artefacts or ways of doing things. Entire communities would find themselves at odds with a system that is so alien to their way of life; therefore, characterizing their reactions as being 'theft' or 'piracy' would merely amuse them.

On the other hand, at the state level, the instrumentality of law has still to make headway in many East Asian and African countries. The role of law in general as the organizing principle of government by force of circumstances (and not by choice of an electorate) underpins everyday life. The view therefore that IP should occupy a privileged position in terms of getting acceptance and being implemented ignores the peripheral role of all laws in such societies. Even where laws have begun to make a dent in the social and economic life, the institutional trappings necessary to implement IP are largely non-existent in the vast majority of states.

The Role of Intellectual Property in the Asian Economic 'Miracles'

The 'economic miracles' in Asia have attracted a great deal of examination and study, leading to an abundant literature. Central to the discourse has been whether there were discernible features of the 'miracles', and if so, whether they could be transposed to other countries, such as Africa? Development theorists found in the 'Asian miracle' cogent proof of their particular strands of thinking (neo-classical, dependency, for instance). Thus the neo-liberalists contended that the fast pace of economic development was testimony to the virtues of the operations of the free market economy buttressed by the rule of law and clearly defined property rights.[18]

However, the hierarchical structure of society and the state reflected in and reinforced by Confucianism and other forms of thinking, together with the designs of the US (supported by its European allies and Japan) to contain the perceived threat of the expansion of communism, broadly underscored and defined the path of change for the societies of East Asia.[19] The rise of dictatorial regimes that found favour and support from the US and its allies became the lever with which local commerce and the export trade could grow together with inflows of foreign capital and technology. The interventionst character of the state and

18 See R.P. Appelbaum and J. Henderson, *States and Development in the Asian Pacific Rim*, Sage Publications: London, 1992.

19 Ibid.

its spearheading of economic projects and plans was typically common across Asia.[20] As Gillespie noted, industrial growth in such states 'has been attributed not to neo-liberal institutions (the rule of law, independent courts and free markets) but to authoritarian states relying on bureaucratic power implemented formally through licensing-gateways, and informally through politically insulated state and quasi-state institutions'.[21] He adds further that, in comparison with factors such as marketing methods, culture and ideology, 'there is little doubt that universal legal norms played a relatively minor role in East Asian economic and social development'.[22]

It has been argued above that the role of IP in Asia and Africa as a whole represented a disconnect with the economic and social circumstances of those continents. A good guide of the significance of IP is the state of patenting activities in Asian and African nations throughout the last century. Statistics supplied by the WIPO[23] incontrovertibly proves that the economically backward nations have relatively fewer patents to show for their espousal of the IP system. The gradual picking up in the speed of patenting in 'emerging markets' of East Asia is more a demonstration of growing appreciation of the value of the markets for foreign multinationals and therefore of the perceived need to register rights in them than the growth in the IP portfolio of local businesses and other entities. This does not, however, overshadow the exceptional deployment of IP by Japan for many decades and the fast pace of changes, in recent years, in Singapore, South Korea and Taiwan (as shown in Table 7.1). Although the absence of data on Taiwan in the official statistics of the WIPO makes it difficult to judge accurately the state of patenting activity in Taiwan, one would notice the higher rate of increase in such activity by comparison, for instance, to Singapore.

It is not impossible to understand that in nations that have not yet achieved capabilities of processing their agricultural produce, minerals and fisheries, the need to foster creativity is peripheral in importance. All the available evidence points to a link between, at very least, the rise of a mercantile/manufacturing class in a few centres (which grew into towns) and the emergence of concerted efforts to foster a level of creativity and then to concoct forms of protection, mainly administrative and penal in character. The protection of manufacturing and commercial interests assumed specific forms of legal development at various

20 For an interesting account of how consecutive dictatorships headed by military men 'applied military thinking to economic development' and brought about the 'Korean miracle', see generally Robert P. Kearney, *The Warrior Worker: The Challenge of the Korean Way of Working*, Henry Holt: New York, 1991.

21 John Gillespie, 'Law and Development "in the Market Place"', in *Law, Capitalism and Power in Asia: The Rule of Law and Legal Institutions*, K. Jayasuriya (ed.), Routledge: London, 1999, at 123.

22 Ibid.

23 A good source is the WIPO Industrial Property Statistics available at http://www.wipo.int/ipstats/en.

stages of the industrial progress of nations. The issue of state-sponsored licences to recognize for a particular person or a group of people the exclusive use of forms of creativity for specified times and geographic space developed from the eighteenth century onwards into what was appropriately labelled 'intellectual property'.

Table 7.1 Patenting by residents in the leading East Asian 'Tiger Economies'

Countries	**Taiwan***		**Singapore**		**South Korea**	
Number of patents	**Granted to residents**	**Granted totally**	**Granted to residents**	**Granted totally**	**Granted to residents**	**Granted totally**
1980	?	6,256	1	548	186	1,632
1990	?	19,623	?	1,238	2,554	7,762
2000	3,834	31,096	110	5,090	22,943	34,956
2002	5,683	44,101	243	7,583	30,175	45,298

Note: The figures include patents for inventions, utility models and designs.
Source: WIPO, Statistics Database, December 2008 (http://www.wipo.int); * Intellectual Property Office, Ministry of Economic Affairs, Republic of China; http://www.tipo.gov.tw/eng/statistics/patent.pdf.

The fact of the matter is that most of Asia and Africa have not transited to an industrial society nor autonomously generated *comprehensive* legal systems for promoting creativity. This prompted their wholesale importation of such systems either during colonization or through the unwitting embrace of legal modernization (the cases in point being Ethiopia, Japan and Thailand). Even then, the transplant had no internal causes; neither did such a transplant take root in the local economy or culture. The apparent dichotomy between law in the books and law in the streets (or action) that lay at the heart of IP in Asia and Africa was inherent to the process of grafting foreign economic law on nations that could not measure up to the level of technological or commercial activity that bred them. The long story of most Asian and African nations struggling to keep up with the tempo of legislative development in the West without at the same time enjoying the benefit of their toil, indeed unfailingly suffering from the constant critique of the foreign powers who saw no progress in the implementation of the laws they forced onto those nations, has yet to be written.

Indeed, the abundant literature on Africa and Asia still dwells on the necessity of keeping faith with the same laws and practices inherited from the colonial powers as well as adopting the latest twists and turns in the laws and practices of the metropolitan powers, whether or not compelled to do so. The urge to keep imitating and following the trails of the metropolitan countries is partly fuelled by the mystique that the flow of investment to DCs is dependent on the level and enforcement of IP. Thus Chinese IP was formulated and placed on the statute books virtually overnight; the ASEAN nations, South Korea and Taiwan rushed through amendments to their laws or newly received forms of IP by reference to the same misconception.[24]

In Asia, three stages can be discerned in the 'development' of the IP legal system. The first stage represented complete ignorance and, hence, an unsuspecting embrace of IP, that is to say, without in any way trying to examine if it was relevant at all. The second stage was characterized by disregard of what might happen if they did not act on the international obligations foisted on them. Interestingly, an official Taiwan government document reportedly admitted

> The R.O.C. government has viewed imitation as a necessary process in the evolution of human civilization and believed that commercial counterfeiting is an inevitable phenomenon in most developing countries. Local officials were cognisant of the negative aspects of counterfeiting although they made little effort to accommodate overseas interests or enhance domestic enforcement efforts when such aspects were seen to be outweighed by the positive developments of the industrial base.[25]

The consequence of such a stance not just in Taiwan but in similar other countries was that foreign nations started pouncing on them and coercing them to copy and copy until they conformed fully with their presumed obligations. Currently, at most three latecomer East Asian nations, Singapore, South Korea and Taiwan, are transiting (graduating) to a third stage of benefiting from the IP system as understood and practised in Europe and the US. Korea may be considered to have already joined the leading pack of industrial countries (obviously including Japan from Asia) that see in IP a means of transforming their competitiveness in international trade. In Africa, nearly all nations (with the possible exception of South Africa) are still at the second stage.

The developments in the role of IP in Korea are instructive in a number of respects. To start with, as Ki-Su Lee wrote, 'In all fairness, it has to be said that until the mid-1980s, protection of intellectual property did neither receive widespread understanding nor support. This attitude gradually changed not least thanks to intensive lobbying and pressure by the United States'[26] and the conclusion of a bilateral agreement, 'Understanding on intellectual property rights' in 1986. The general perception in South Korea was that it needed to have access to foreign

24 See, Gutterman and Brown, note 4, above, at 18.

25 Robert Wade, *Governing the Market: Economic Theory and the Role of Government in East Asian Industrialisation*, Princeton University Press: Princeton, NJ, 2000; quoted in Nagesh Kumar, 'Intellectual Property Rights, Technology and Economic Development: Experiences of Asian Countries', Research and Information System for Non-aligned and Other Developing Countries, RIS DP no. 25-2002, May 2002, at 23.

26 See KI-Su Lee, 'General Introduction', in Christopher Heath (ed.), *Intellectual Property Law in Korea*, Kluwer Law International: London, 2003, pp. 1–4, at 2.

technology to expedite faster national economic development as, otherwise, South Korea 'by itself was unable to produce sufficient and adequate technology to accomplish its goals'.[27] The incentives extended by the government through the Foreign Capital Inducement Act from 1966 to attract foreign technology related to taxes and other financial benefits, including the guarantee of profit and royalty remittances.[28] At the same time, the government sought to protect local licensees 'from exploitation by foreign licensors'[29] by curbing 'restrictive and unfair trade practices' of foreign technology transferors though the Antimonopoly Act; these measures made the latter 'unhappy' because they felt they were 'negotiating the terms of an agreement effectively with the Korean government as a *de facto* third party'.[30]

In short, contrary to what the advocates of the untrammelled adoption and imitation of all forms of IP by developing nations maintain, South Korea did not resort to a wholesale importation of foreign IP laws in order to encourage inflow of foreign technology. The thought of doing so emerged only much later. Initially, the government determined that 'strict protection against acts of unfair competition would cause Korea to lose commercial power, and that Korean undertakings susceptible to development would not be able to compete with foreign enterprises by fair means'.[31]

The comparative experience of Taiwan could be summarized as a long and continuous attempt to satisfy foreign demands as regards its IP laws and their implementation.[32] The harder Taiwan tried to impress foreign multinationals and governments, especially the US, by rushing through all forms of new IP laws, the more difficult it became for Taiwan to put an end to the barrages of criticisms levelled against it. The USTR's report for 2003 thus stated, in reference to Taiwan, 'Official raids are hampered by lack of expertise and poor interagency coordination; resulting penalties are neither timely nor strong enough to deter infringement. The lax protection of IPR, including lack of enforcement against piracy and trademark counterfeiting in Taiwan therefore remains a serious concern for the U.S. Government.'[33] The government therefore took the unusual step of openly rejecting the dismissal of its efforts over previous decades to respond to criticisms of its IP system and remedy them.[34] This did not dissuade the US from

---

27 See Byung-il Kim, 'Licensing and Technology Transfer', in Heath, ibid., at 177.

28 Ibid.

29 Ibid., at 178.

30 Ibid.

31 Ibid.

32 Paul C.B. Liu, 'U.S. Industry's Influence on Intellectual Property Negotiations and Special 301 Actions', 13 *UCLA Pacific Basin Law Journal* 87, Fall, 1994.

33 See [USTR], 2003 National Trade Estimate Report on Foreign Trade Barriers; available at http://www.ustr.gov/reports/nte/2003/index.htm.

34 See 'Taiwan Expresses Regret over being Placed on US Counterfeiting List', *Agence France Presse*, 2 May 2003. Available online from Factiva.

placing Taiwan on the 'Special 301 Priority Watch List' in April 2004 and then, after a review in January 2005, on the 'Watch List'.

Just as in the other two East Asian Tigers, Singapore did not initially hurry to absorb every imaginable IP formula adopted in the US (its major trading partner and source of foreign direct investment) or elsewhere on the pretext of 'modernization' or industrialization. This stance continued until the late 1980s. As a result, it enjoyed the same notoriety as the other 'problem nations', that is 'those countries in which intellectual property laws do not confer an adequate level of protection'[35] – no doubt from the US point of view.

The Singapore government started to take notice of the importance of IP, at least for foreign proprietors, after repeated pressure from the US and Europe. Even as late as 1997, the local representative of the International Federation of the Phonographic Industry (IFPI) reportedly expressed the view that 'Singapore ranked among the highest in the level of music piracy in the region, alongside China, India and Pakistan'.[36] According to an official of the Singapore Phonogram and Videogram Association (SPVA), 'One of the reasons for the increase in piracy level may be the perception that the Government and intellectual property rights owners are not enforcing the law'.[37] Apparently, in July 1997,

> a petition signed by record companies, retailers, composers and artistes was sent to the Prime Minister to appeal for government action against piracy … [However] when there was no response, they followed up with several letters accompanied by pirated CDs, as well as proposals to improve legislation, streamline enforcement procedures and bringing copyright laws up to date.[38]

Receiving no response from the government, SPVA went to the extent of promising various levels of rewards to informants of individual or wholesale suppliers, even factories, of pirated CDs. The same official of the SPVA stated, 'Pirates no longer operate in secret. They're everywhere – in housing estates, at MRT [train] stations, at weekend *pasar malams* [literally, night markets]. This makes people think they're legitimate.'[39]

In the wake of the government's official stance, in 1999, that it had met all the WTO requirements arising from TRIPs 'a year ahead of the deadline' and taken 'a multi-agency approach involving the police, customs and various publishing associations' – leading to the conduct of numerous raids, educational campaigns

35 See Leaffer, note 7, above, at 274, footnote 5.

36 Koh Boon Pin, 'Report Music Pirates and Get Paid', *The Straits Times* [Singapore], 16 October 1997, at 38.

37 Ibid.

38 Ibid.

39 Ibid.

and the like[40] – the International Intellectual Property Alliance insisted that Singapore 'stumbled badly in its response to the new epidemic of digital piracy' and called upon the USTR to keep it on the 'Watch' list as it had been since 1995.[41] The Alliance reportedly demanded '"sustained, intensive police enforcement" rather than quarterly or bi-monthly raids on just two sites – Sim Lim Square and Bugis Street'.[42] The latter were always considered notorious for the availability of pirate copies of both hardware and software.

Still, the Singapore government contended that it was doing enough. Thus, in reply to a reader's letter in *The Straits Times* complaining that the government was turning a blind eye to piracy, an official of the Ministry of Trade and Industry stated, 'the police have consistently taken action against piracy, especially where there is evidence of large-scale operations'.[43] It added, 'independent reputable institutions have also rated Singapore's IPR regime highly … Realistically, we cannot hope to totally wipe out piracy – the problem persists even in developed countries such as the US'.[44] It needs to be pointed out that the alleged culprits in Singapore were not just corner shops, individual peddlers of imported pirate copies or even small and medium enterprises (SMEs) but major companies. One such culprit was listed on the Singapore Stock Exchange[45] while another was a major French hypermarket.[46]

---

40 Geraldine Yeo, 'No Let-up in Anti-piracy Fight', *The Straits Times* [Singapore], 24 March 1999, at 31.

41 'Alliance Claims Rising Piracy', *The Straits Times* [Singapore], 24 March 1999, at 31.

42 Ibid.

43 Sim Soo Kheng, 'The Government is Fighting Piracy on all Fronts', *The Straits Times* [Forum] [Singapore], 18 January 2000, at 65.

44 Ibid. As if to reinforce its declaration of strenuous efforts at curbing piracy, more raids were made two days later! See, Sharon Vasoo, 'Blitz on Pirates of Sim Lim Square', *The Straits Times* [Singapore], 21 January 2000, at 66.

45 Jean Chia and Chang Ai-Lien, 'Listed Company Raided for "Software Piracy"', *The Straits Times* [Singapore], 14 August 1997, at 1. (Reporting on the 15 h raid and seizure of documents, at the behest of the Singapore Business Alliance, of SM Summit Holdings, on suspicion of making and selling counterfeit CD-ROMs. Subsequent to the raid, BSA filed claims at the High Court on behalf of three software companies – Adobe Systems, Autodesk and Microsoft – but the claims were dismissed in October 1997. Their appeal was again dismissed in February 1998. SM Summit had counter-sued BSA and the three companies on the failure of the latter's claims. Nevertheless, all sides settled the whole matter out of court. See David Boey, 'Summit, BSA Reach "Negotiated settlement"', *Business Times*, Singapore, 9 June 2001. Available online from Factiva.)

46 Debbie Goh, 'Counterfeit Jeans meet a Fiery End', *The Straits Times* [Singapore], 20 October 1999, at 48. (Reporting on the discovery of 2500 pairs of Levi's 501 imitation jeans made in Mexico but imported and distributed by Carrefour. The latter claimed that it purchased them from 'a reputable overseas supplier. Therefore it had reason to believe that the jeans were genuine'. Ibid. In the event, Carrefour settled with the authorized distributors while the fake jeans were incinerated.)

All in all, the Singapore approach appears to presume that promotions and publicity will transform the importance of IP in the economy and 'turn Singapore into a compelling Intellectual Property Hub'; 'as a choice location for the conduct of IP business in the region'.[47] As in other areas of activity that Singapore chooses to become a leader in (note the overused word, 'hub'), the apparent hope is that a mere change of tack will do the trick. Thus, the otherwise purely regulatory organization, the Intellectual Property Office of Singapore (IPOS), sought to transform itself directly into a service provider, earning revenue in competition with the private sector. Yet, while theoretically Singapore could possibly partake of the provision of services in the IP sector, it would be a gross misunderstanding to presume that mere efficiency and a superior technical infrastructure[48] alone suffice as a precondition for attracting foreign customers. The bungled efforts at making the '.sg' country domain name a trademark owned by a subsidiary of a government department, the Info-Comm Development Authority of Singapore,[49] suggests that the constant glorification of IP as facilitating the minting of money was unfortunately taken literally.[50] In reality, as the leading industrial nations have

47 See, 'Speech by Assoc. Prof Ho Peng Kee Senior Minister of State for Law and Home Affairs', at the launch of the 'Intellectual Property – Creation, Exploitation and Protection Programme' on 8 November 2002 at Orchard Hotel Singapore; available at http://www.ipos.gov.sg/main/newsroom/speeches/speeches_081102.html.

48 Alethea Lim, 'Special Court to Settle Intellectual Property Disputes', *The Straits Times* [Singapore], 20 September 2002, at H4. (Reporting that the government appointed economic review committee believes that the establishment of an IP court will 'advance Singapore's ambition to be a premier world centre for resolving commercial disputes'. It also alludes to the establishment of an 'IP Academy' to spearhead training efforts and work towards the same objective.) It might be noted that IE Singapore (a government department) is also engaged in helping local businesses establish their brands. See Soh Wen Lin, 'Osim's Name Alone is Worth $203m', *The Straits Times* [Singapore], 12 March 2003, at 4.

49 'Withdrawn: .sg Trademark Application', *The Computer Times* [Singapore], 19 March 2003, at CT6. The Singapore Network Information Centre (Sgnic) official had explained that such a measure was proposed to '"protect its unique identity" and use of ".sg" as the national registry for .sg domain names'. However, in spite of the assurances that nothing would affect users, service providers and others had expressed unease at the attempt to grab a vital lifeline of the Internet in Singapore. See Eileen Yu, 'Govt wants to Trademark ".sg"', *The Computer Times* [Straits Times], 8 January 2003. It is apparent that the widespread opposition presented in the media culminated in the withdrawal though no such admission was made.

50 A commentator enquired about the change in stance: 'How did three years go by without a single person from the Government's army of top-notch policy planners raising the alarm to say a trademark isn't needed after all? More than a thousand days passed. Did no one care to check that countries including the United Kingdom had already decreed that .uk cannot be made a trademark? Instead, it took a lawyer to raise the flag. He had alerted Computer Times after seeing the notice for opposition posted by IPOS – a standard legal procedure inviting anyone to oppose a trademark application before it is approved. If IPOS had awarded the trademark to Sgnic, and it had come to ICANN's attention, the international

long discovered, becoming a net exporter of ideas requires a lot more than good wishes and publicity stunts.

Lessons African Nations Might Learn from Intellectual Property in East Asia

The experiences of the three East Asian nations (South Korea, Taiwan and Singapore), discussed above, demonstrate that the adoption of IP laws was not, until recently, in response to internal demands. As the respective figures for patenting activities in the three countries (Table 7.1) show, the protection of local inventions was not a paramount concern for governments for much of the period under review as the level of domestic creativity remained low. It would therefore not seem worthwhile to suggest that African nations could derive lessons from the East Asian 'Tigers'. This is principally because the few East Asian nations that are currently seeking to join the ranks of the industrial economies in IP terms have converted to such an approach only very recently. Their conversion was predicated upon their industrial and commercial achievements,[51] in particular on the success of their export trade with the US, and on their perception that further advances will only be possible through sustained scientific and technological progress supported by an IP system. Hence their belated embrace of a full-fledged IP system, and not just as a token of subservience to foreign business interests and compliance with the wishes of their trading partners and governments in the West, has been part of a strategic review of what the future might hold for their economies.

This is exemplified by the dramatic steps taken by Singapore to embark on harmonization of its IP laws with that of the US, pursuant to the 2003 free trade agreement it concluded with the latter. These moves would have been unthinkable barely a few years ago and the fact that they have been made points to a determination to beat its East Asian competitors and other industrial nations not just in the export trade, as in the past, but in the generation of new technologies and knowledge on the global scale henceforward.[52] These aims are evident in the

---

registry would most likely have enforced a retraction. That could have potentially given Singapore another source of embarrassment to have to withdraw its trademark registration'. Eileen Yu, 'Consult the People', *The Computer Times*, 19 March 2003; available at http://computertimes.asia1.com.sg.

51 See Maskus, note 11, above, at 93, regarding the strengthening of the IP system in South Korea and Taiwan.

52 Thus reasoned the then Prime Minister Goh Chok Tong in his speech at a rally in 2001, 'Our current problem is the consequence of being a small, open economy, highly dependent on external trade and foreign investment. When the US and other major economies were growing, we caught the strong winds and surged ahead. Now that the winds have died, our growth has slowed to almost a standstill. We do not have a large domestic market to go against changes in the wind in the external environment. We just have to cope with them. What the Government can do, however, is to make sure that the economy stays competitive over the long term, and soften the impact of downturns on businesses and workers through

huge investments being ploughed into biotechnology research and development in Singapore and the recognition of the necessity of being at the forefront of the 'fourth industrial revolution'[53] in order to remain competitive and become part of the leading industrial nations.

Thus there may be no clear IP lessons that the East Asian economies might supply to African latecomers. Firstly, the latter are still bogged down in a catch-up game of transition from agriculture and the extractive industries to manufacturing. By all accounts, IP was not relevant even for the East Asians that have since transformed their economies and now seek to join the leading industrial nations. Secondly, the internal demands for a patent system in Africa appear to be rather feeble. This is borne out by the data for arguably the leading economies in Africa, as shown in Table 7.2. Despite, their incompleteness, the available data reveal not only the low level of domestic patenting activities but also the relatively slow increase in foreign patent grants. One would readily recognize, therefore, that, with the possible exception of South Africa, all of the countries mentioned remain at the second stage of IP law-making we identified above as characteristic of East Asian nations in the post-war years.

Table 7.2 Patenting by residents in selected African countries

	Egypt		Ghana		Kenya		Nigeria		South Africa	
	R*	T**	R	T	R	T	R	T	R	T
1980	10	327	0	17	?	?	?	?	?	5390
1990	20	306	0	45	0	38	10	170	?	5465
2000	53	453	?	64	2	117	?	?	?	?
2002	117	757	?	?	?	?	?	?	?	?

Note: R* stands for 'Patents Granted to Residents'; T** for 'Total of Patents Granted'.
Source: WIPO, *Statistics Database*, December 2008 (http://www.wipo.int).

Inevitably, the current state of IP law and its implementation has made African nations susceptible to external criticisms and pressures for change. The 2004 review by the USTR of slightly less than a quarter of all African countries (namely Angola, Cote d'Ivoire, Cameroon, Egypt, Ghana, Kenya, Morocco, Nigeria and the Southern African Customs Union) dealt with, among other things, the perceived

cost-cutting measures and rebates'. See, Singapore Government Press Release, 'Prime Minister Goh Chok Tong's National Day Rally 2001 Speech at the University Cultural Centre, National University Of Singapore On Sunday, 19 August 2001', *New Singapore*; available at http://www.gov.sg/nd/ND01.htm.

53 These were stated as being 'IT, life sciences, and other knowledge-based activities'. Ibid.

deficiencies in the respective IP systems. For instance, as regards Egypt, the USTR asserted: 'Counterfeiting and piracy adversely impact most of the intellectual property industries in Eygpt, including motion pictures (in video cassette format), sound recordings, books and other printed matter, textile designs, and computer software'.[54] In relation to Kenya, it stated

> Violation of copyrights, especially on music and films, is pervasive, and enforcement remains sporadic at best … merchants are still free to peddle pirated versions of Kenyan and international works without fear of arrest or prosecution. Pirated materials and counterfeit goods produced in other countries are readily available in all major towns in the country.[55]

Overall, the USTR was intent on pushing the African nations to improve their IP systems, not with a view to increasing the stock of creative works available to their economy and culture, but principally to prevent losses to US industry exports. Only in one instance (Nigeria) did the annual report point to the 'government's lack of institutional capacity'.[56] The fact that the laws as enacted may have no, or little, relevance to the internal conditions of the African countries under review did not appear to have influenced its findings. Consequently, just as the East Asian Tigers before, African nations today will continue to be subjected to severe reproaches from external sources and governments.

Indeed, the 2008 USTR Report[57] picks up a few countries for reprimand. Of Kenya it commented that 'Pirated and counterfeit products in Kenya, mostly imported from South Asia and East Asia, present a major impediment to U.S. business interests in the country.'[58] Regarding Nigeria, it asserted 'piracy is rampant … Patent and trademark enforcement remains weak, and judicial procedures are slow and reportedly subject to corruption'.[59] Similarly, it chided Angola's IP system as being 'currently weak due to a lack of enforcement capacity'.[60] The criticism of Cameroon follows the same pattern: 'IPR enforcement is problematic due to corruption within enforcement agencies, the lack of resources dedicated to IPR enforcement and a general lack of awareness of IPRs'.[61] Cote d'Ivoire and Ghana receive chastisement too.

---

54 See [USTR], 2004 National Trade Estimate Report on Foreign Trade Barriers; available at http://www.ustr.gov.

55 Ibid.

56 Ibid.

57 USTR, 2008 National Trade Estimate Report on Foreign Trade Barriers; available at http://www.ustr.gov/Document_Library.

58 Ibid.

59 Ibid.

60 Ibid.

61 Ibid.

Ultimately, the path of conformity and acquiescence to foreign demands by African countries will not lead to a durable conversion by them to the IP system. As examination of the experiences in East Asia has demonstrated, only the feasibility of a transition to an industrial economy and the adoption of appropriate strategies towards its realization will make the IP system a worthwhile tool or counterpart of such a transition. In that sense, there may be only one broad lesson that East Asian countries provide African nations: the prospects of the IP system in African countries hinge on the resolution of their problems of development as a whole and the possibility of their industrial transformation.

Conclusion

The dominant view in the role of IP, as expounded by the property rights theory, does not recognize IP policy in general and law-making in particular to have to be congruent to the local circumstances of specific nations. It holds all nations to be equally capable of legislating and implementing the same set of laws and policies. It maintains that any review of the state of IP in any nation would not take stock of the internal economic and social conditions but would measure the gap between the achievements in one nation as against others. As a result, the standards of the leading industrial countries become the benchmarks for all countries and any perceived gaps are derided as shortfalls and therefore redeemable through further legislation and enforcement.

The experiences of the East Asian Tigers belie this effectively reductionist view. Initially, they imitated Western IP laws and placed them in their statute books, believing them to be trappings of modernization and industrialization. However, on the one hand, there were limited internal demands for their implementation. The main pressure was external (foreign businesses and governments). On the other hand, the East Asian Tigers (notably South Korea and Taiwan) realized soon enough that the strictest enforcement of IP on their statute books would lead to deprivation of foreign technologies to their domestic businesses. These account for their reluctance to stamp out alleged piracy and widespread imitations of foreign works. There appears to have been a realization that they needed to postpone any such actions for as long as possible.

Still, the Asian Tigers did not and, as matter of fact, could not confront the foreign powers (especially the US) as regards the manner of implementation of IP laws. In view of the importance of the volume of their exports, particularly to the US, and the fact that their development strategy banked on export-led growth, they had to acquiesce to any criticism and even legislate to the satisfaction of their foreign trading partners. Yet, the state of IP implementation in these countries has remained problematic until very recently. The three Asian Tigers have made rapid progress in their IP legislation and, to a limited extent, in their enforcement, parallel to the speed in their pace of industrialization and the growth in their share of the world market. Thus the state of IP in the three East Asian Tigers today is linked to their perceived stakes in the future. The enthusiasm shown, for instance, by South Korea and Singapore is more a reflection of a determination to join the ranks of the leading technology exporting nations than of a capability to do so right away.

There are therefore no direct lessons that African nations might derive from the East Asian Tigers. The speculative nature of the current stance of the leading East Asian Tigers cannot persuade African nations that their conversion to a full-scale IP system will transform their economies overnight. Neither are the alleged weaknesses in their IP system merely traceable to the lack of political good will or the desire to unfairly exploit foreign technology. Indeed, there is no evidence that African nations have realized the strategic significance of the exploitation of foreign technology as East Asians have done from the 1960s. Except in the context of the AIDS pandemic and the extensions of geographical indications to products other than wines and spirits,[62] African nations have not even participated in the smooth talk about the deficiencies of TRIPs as applied to developing countries; neither have they added their voices to calls for more reasonableness on the part of the developed countries in the future.[63]

62 WTO, TRIPs Council, 'Communication From Bulgaria, The Czech Republic, Egypt, Iceland, India, Kenya, Liechtenstein, Pakistan, Slovenia, Sri Lanka, Switzerland and Turkey', Document IP/C/W/204/Rev. 1, 2 October 2000.

63 See Peter Drahos and Ruth Mayne (eds), *Global Intellectual Property Rights: Knowledge, Access and Development*, Palgrave Macmillan: Basingstoke, 2002.

PART II
The Backlash Against Further Extension of Intellectual Property

Chapter 8
Intellectual Property Enforcement in Asia*

Introduction

In recent decades, Asian nations have raced against each other in enacting the latest intellectual property (IP) laws borrowed from the West on the assumption that the laws would function in the same manner as in the West. However, the Asian nations' dismal record of implementation of IP laws has become apparent and has turned into a source of dispute with their trading partners, chiefly the US, the European Union (EU) and Japan.

The fundamental reason for the impasse in enforcement of IP in Asia, as elsewhere in the developing world, lies in the huge economic and technological gap between them and the industrial nations. Historically, the need for international protection of IP grew out of the desire of a few Western European states in the early nineteenth century to stop imitations of creative products of their citizens beyond national borders. The first form of such protection was therefore an attempt to suppress, within national borders, illegitimate products affecting businesses operating beyond those borders. The major concern of countries that became parties to IP treaties (whether bilateral, earlier on, or multilateral, from the 1880s onwards) was not however about providing the same level of protection among treaty-members, but extending any available measure or form of protection to non-nationals. The recognition and extent of international protection ultimately hinged on the assimilation of non-national goods to those produced within the national borders.

The forms and scope of international IP protection changed dramatically with the introduction of the Agreement on Trade-Related Aspects of Intellectual Property Rights (TRIPS). What TRIPS did was to provide a level of cross-border protection that may or may not have been existing previously within the national setting. In other words, TRIPS substituted a structure and mode of protection that never considered the necessity of linking with or extending national IP forms and scopes as a pre-condition. In short, TRIPS became instrumental in planting a veritable disconnect between the IP laws of TRIPS and their social and economic conditions. It did not proceed from the nation-state's willingness or determination to have forms of protection adequate for its needs (with the discretion of not introducing any that it did not deem necessary), but regardless of such needs.

---

* An earlier version of this chapter has appeared in the author's name as, 'Intellectual Property Enforcement in Asia: A Reality Check', 13(3) *International Journal of Law and Information Technology* 378–412, 2005.

The pressure on developing countries (DCs) to legislate on a par with the major industrial nations (disguised as compliance with DCs requirements), lest they be treated as outlaws and pirates or the like, burdened them with an obligation unheard of in international law – that nations must be willing to take on board legal standards and measures even if the latter might be detrimental to their own domestic interests. The obligation to adopt standards and measures consonant with the requirements of the major industrial states but not necessarily with those of the DCs was not only a major blow to the pursuit of development in DCs but also a deadweight they have to carry forever.

The circumstances in which most developing nations were forced to forego their domestic interests and accede to treaty obligations without being given corresponding minimal benefits deserving of sovereign contracting parties lies at the bottom of the disconnect in the protection of IP internationally. The denial of the prerogative of developing nations as purportedly full sovereigns in international law to demand or foster mutually beneficial arrangements in IP protection has generated the disconnect and fuelled the continuity of so-called piracy across the developing world.

This chapter attempts to examine whether and how Asian nations have succeeded in managing the disconnect. It starts with a survey of the common misperceptions about the role of IP. It then attempts a brief appraisal of the conflicting interests and forces that condition the level, or lack, of IP law-making and enforcement in Asia. This is followed by a brief look at the external pressure on Asian DCs in both IP law-making and enforcement. Then the signs of change in IP enforcement in Asia are traced. The chapter concludes that, despite some emerging signs of change in attitudes and levels of IP enforcement, the very same issues will remain at the forefront of IP in Asia and as a major source of dispute with the US and, to a lesser extent, the EU and Japan. It stresses that progress will continue to elude all parties, whether Asian or foreign.

Common Misconceptions about the Role of Intellectual Property

A chorus of voices from IP experts, 'fly by night'[1] government advisors and consultants of all types asserts, and repeats *ad nauseam*, that more IP would lead to more investment and faster economic development. Thus, in explaining the 2001 Annual Report and 2002 Trade Agenda, the US Trade Representative, Zoellick, stated, 'the local protection of intellectual property rights establishes the foundation for an attractive investment climate for industries of the future. Indeed, as developing

1 A characterization by the Indian Minister for Investment, Information Technology and Communications at a speech he made at the 'NAM Business Forum' during the Non-Alignment Movement (NAM) meeting in Kuala Lumpur last year. See, 'Help Remedy Imbalances at WTO, NAM Business Forum Told', *Malaysia General News*, Petaling Jaya [Malaysia], 23 February 2003. Available online from Lexis-Nexis.

countries have implemented the intellectual property protections in DCs, they have begun to benefit from increased technology transfer and investment – two key factors in long-term economic growth'.[2] However, there is mounting evidence that belies those assertions. For one thing, more law has never led to more progress. The volume of IP law in any developing nation has never been a barometer for the attraction of investment or faster pace of development. One can glance at the statistics annually supplied by the World Intellectual Property Organization (WIPO) to notice the absence of any positive link between the volume of patents and trademarks in the registries of DCs and the state of economic advance (measured by gross domestic product, GDP) during the past four decades.

Transplanted IP has in effect become an albatross around the necks of the DCs, a stranglehold over their economies and cultures. Left to themselves, most DCs would simply have either ignored such imposed IP by relegating it to the statute books or even repealed it altogether. However, that avenue has long been shut to them both when most of the current DCs were colonies of the European nations (and had alien laws, including IP, extended to them) or afterwards, through the mistaken notion that modernization of laws implied copying all foreign laws verbatim and placing them on the statute books. Any open reluctance to implement the IP laws has had ominous consequences. As an Indonesian Minister of Justice and Human Rights admitted, 'Being on their [US] priority watch list, Indonesia risks facing punitive measures from the US, such as export bans, embargo and other penalties'.[3]

Another theory holds that the lack of protection of IP will drive out talented people from DCs and lead to decline in jobs and tax revenues as well as rise in crime financed by organized pirates of IP.[4] It is also alleged that such crimes will

---

2 Federal Information and News Dispatch Inc., State Department, 'Zoellick Reiterates Trade Negotiating Authority Push; Cites Multilateral, Regional, Bilateral Goals in 2002', 19 March 2002. More recently, the Assistant Secretary of Commerce William Lash warned the Philippines that it 'would not be able to attract more investments and become more globally competitive if it fails to crack down on counterfeiters, particularly those selling and exporting pirated disc and VCDs'. See 'US Loses Millions to Piracy in Philippines', *Agence France Presse*, 2 February 2004. Available online from Factiva.

3 Sari P. Setiogi, 'Government has Finalised Regulation on Optical Disks', *The Jakarta Post*, 6 February 2004, at 13. Available online from Factiva.

4 Janet Reno, the former Attorney General of the US, commented on the rise of 'economic espionage' targeting 'U.S. firms, with high-tech companies the most frequent targets' before adding: 'For developing nations, the stakes are higher still. Countries that fail to protect intellectual property will witness the exodus of their best talent, a loss of jobs and tax revenues, a nutrient environment for official corruption and an increase in crimes financed by intellectual property theft.' See Janet Reno, 'The Threat of Digital Theft: Intellectual Property Theft is Faster, Costlier and more Dangerous than Ever', 25 December 2000; available at http://www.usdoj.gov/criminal/cybercrime/AGdigitaltheft.htm. The Chairman of the Indonesian Intellectual Property Society similarly asserted that the loss of profits by Indonesian companies translated into lost investment, jobs and taxes.

lead to tax evasion and money laundering.[5] It is ironical that most of the outcry against piracy emanates from the major industrial nations who have a dominant share of the IP portfolio globally as well as in all of Asia.[6] Often, amidst the hysterical proportion of the charges of piracy thrown around indiscriminately, the critics fail to recognize that it is foreign IP that Asian countries (for that matter all DCs) are alleged not to have protected. Contrary to the allegations, the loss of earnings does not necessarily affect those countries, whether the businesses or the government treasury. The domestic economy in such nations gains in absolute terms when foreign IP is imitated, particularly when it is not accompanied by the outflow of payment. The creation of a local market, more jobs and the satisfaction of consumer demand through the supply of cheap commodities is attractive to governments since it does not cost them a cent. Was that not the reason why American 'pirates' of British works of literature refused to protect or pay for those works before 1891 (the Copyright Amendment Act)? As a general rule, the borrowed (even pirated) ideas serve as a basis for the emergence of a national industry (with possible technological capability) for the production of books, art and other types of goods.

While, therefore, it may be true that local creative works will suffer if imitation gets out of hand, and no government in all recorded history has allowed that to happen for long, it remains a fact that where those works are in short supply, foreign works become natural targets for exploitation and learning. The new value created by local imitators, even counterfeiters, fills the coffers of businesses that might eventually set up workshops and laboratories to come up with brand new innovations.

Still another widespread misconception is the view that IP is universal. The huge attention that IP has gained from the world press – itself a reflection of the fast rise in its importance to the world economy, particularly to countries and multinationals which have huge arsenals of valuable portfolios – has given a cloak of universality to IP rights. While the mechanisms of recognition of rights, registration and enforcement still remain within the control and purview of national authorities, the choice of proprietors in gaining those rights in countries they prefer to target leaves out a lot of other countries. The irony of this is that, where potential proprietors make a choice of which countries to target in registering their rights – and this is the case for nearly all forms of IP except copyright – the countries left

See, Novan Iman Santosa, 'Antipiracy Campaign Launched', *The Jakarta Post*, 9 March 2003. Available online from Factiva.

5 See Reno, note 4, above, ibid.

6 The Economist Intelligence Unit puts it thus: 'Overall, China's technology base remains limited and the capital infrastructure needed to produce advanced, high-tech goods largely absent. And while more and more high-tech goods are made in China, almost all the value is being captured by foreign companies … While foreigners own virtually all the intellectual property and most of the high-tech manufacturing capacity in China, piracy will remain an issue.' See, The Economist Intelligence Unit – Ebusiness forum, 'The Economist: The Allure of Low Technology in China', No. 324, 16 January 2004. Available online from Factiva.

out are not duty bound to enforce any of their putative rights. Simply put, if the patentees choose to leave out states as potential markets for their products, they cannot later demand protection from those states.

Most of the disputes in relation to adaptation or imitation of technology revolve around the scope and significance of patents. In principle, the identity of the patent holder or the place where such a patent is obtained should not make any difference because the patent so obtained is no less legitimate or more valuable than any by reference to the personality of the applicant or the country of application. Yet, applications for patents are generally made in countries with the market potential for the relevant goods or services. Inventors typically choose to apply in those countries where the goods or services that result from application of their inventions could be sold or supplied profitably. Thus, it is no wonder that the major industrial powers are battlefields for accumulation of patents. A quick look at any patent statistics reveals that Japan, the US, Germany, France and the UK stand out (in that order) as the major nations where applications hail from. They are also invariably the most intensely sought after countries for applications. Other industrial countries (ICs) too receive attention but patent applications to them are made selectively since the deployment of the patent in any specific country may not be profitable. In such instances, the patentee gets to produce the goods in a country secured by the patent and exports those goods to all other countries, regardless of whether a similar patent was obtained there.

The fate of DCs in this stampede of the industrial nations to register their patents, trademarks and other works so as to block any potential competition is to allow closure of their spaces, to become total backyards and, in the words of Penrose, turn into colonies. In theory, they could have turned away any request for registration or protection on the ground that it would not be commensurate with their domestic demands or requirements. However, after the accession of nearly all countries to the Paris Convention for the Protection of Industrial Property, DCs cannot discriminate between nationals and non-nationals or based on the identity of the applicants or rights holders. By extending the scope of the Paris Convention, DCs have fortified the rights of patent holders and included an obligation on countries to enforce them at the pain of losing trading privileges with other countries belonging to the World Trade Organization (WTO). Nevertheless, if imitations occur in countries where no IP recognition was sought or acquired by the purported owners, it is because they chose to run that risk. It has least of all to do with the violation of the universality of IP.

In the area of trademark registration, bona fide use, or the intention to do so, is the basis for registration. Where a mark is not intended or used for anything, the right to expunge it is recognized across national trademark registration systems. In theory, therefore, DCs can expunge trademarks that have been placed on their registers without any goods or services accompanying them at the point of registration or within a short period afterwards. However, advocates of the absolute rights of trademark registrants in Western industrial nations do not see this. Worse still, they hardly recognize that trademarks need to earn protection under national law. Thus so-called famous marks are portrayed as deserving of unconditional protection regardless of whether those marks were earlier regulated in the host nations or are now prepared to pay the accrued fees to the respective state where they seek to gain protection.

The global reach of today's TV, movies and commercials has given rise to awareness of brands across nations even without the goods or services to which they are supposed to attach becoming available or accessible to ultimate users. Were fame to be a basis for recognition in national law, it would create the anomaly that trademark law never contemplated – that the symbols, labels and coined words should be protected regardless of the underlying objective of link to the goods or services.

It is interesting to note that some of the advanced countries' courts have been able to see through the subterfuge of absolute rights and their unlimited expansion and have started to bring proprietors back to their senses. A case in point is that of the Norwegian Court of Appeal which rejected the locking in, through encryption, of legitimately and freely usable matter as being subject to copyright.[7]

A further misconception is the treatment of IP as a merely legal phenomenon. IP continues to be camouflaged as a purely legal affair and national policies in DCs rarely look at it as a means of economic and technological transformation or otherwise. The law-making or revision process is largely the province of legislators or government departments that prepare legal drafts. Policy papers or drafts of laws are seldom disseminated to let the public, business organizations and scholars state their views and reactions. Representations are rarely made or expected before legislators issue any laws. The only circumstances where laws are discussed, complaints aired, suggestions or improvements offered or opposition declared are through the press. News media in Thailand, Malaysia and the Philippines, among others, regularly serve as conduits of discussion and grievances.

Finally, we turn to the recurrent charge against DCs that have not lived up to the expectations of the major industrial powers in terms of IP enforcement, namely that they lack the political will. This is repeated so often and expressed in any context where enforcement of IP is discussed that it has become a cliché.[8] Its

---

7 A seven-judge panel of the Norwegian appeals court unanimously agreed with a lower court's ruling that a certain Jon Johansen who had devised a programme that could crack the encryption for DVDs and then posted it on the Internet for others to use had not violated that country's copyright laws. Circumventing copyright protection devices for personal use is apparently acceptable to Norway. The prosecutors dropped their plan for further appeal to Norway's supreme court. See 'Anti-piracy Forces Lose Appeal', *The San Diego Union–Tribune*, 23 December 2003, at 1,7, C-3; available online from Factiva.

8 'Taiwan Should Stay on U.S. IPR List: Expert', *The China Post*, 7 February 2004 (reporting on the speech of Eric Smith, President of the International Intellectual Property Alliance (IIPA), testifying before the US–China Economic and Security Review Commission). (Available online from Factiva.) Smith iterated that 'ultimately, effective protection of intellectual property is a 'political will issue. If you want to do it, it's not that hard'. Ibid.

only significance seems to be to reduce the problem of IP enforcement to that of morality and ethics.

The Conflicting Demands on Intellectual Property in Asia

In examining the broad context for IP in Asia, one should focus on general issues of social and economic development, the building up of technological capability and legal policy. We shall look at each of these factors briefly. The unrelenting pressures of the US to keep DCs in particular behind its global strategy for IP will be taken up in the following section.

The social and cultural factors

Asian countries differ widely in their social and economic characteristics as well as histories and cultures. Asia has been subjected to the diverse influences of religious (Islam, Buddhism, Taoism and Christianity) and social movements, within single states and regionally, as well as the brunt of different colonial powers (Dutch, British, Portuguese, French and others). Their legal systems consequently reflect such variance and complexity.[9]

On the other hand, Asian attitudes towards the concept of intellectual property appear to coalesce. Imitation or copying from works of other people is not generally viewed as illegitimate or, even, questionable. According to one commentator,

> in Asian cultures, inventions are freely disclosed, copying is a high form of flattery, and the individual is subservient to the community … Not only is the substantive law of private intellectual property rights alien to Asian society, but so is the concept of enforcing statutes through private litigation … The essence of litigation is that one party wins and the other loses. Since Asian societies value harmony most highly … [l]itigation and courts of law represent a failure of the community and a reflection of disharmony. Therefore court adjudication has never been a method of resolving commercial disputes in Asia.[10]

Reports of the widespread practice of buying cheap pirated products across Asia indicate that the cultural influences just referred to still have a grip on the societies. An Indonesian official at the Ministry of Justice and Human Rights conceded, 'Since the original DVDs and VCDs are still expensive, they would predictably

---

9 C. Antons, 'Legal Culture and History of Law in Asia', in Christopher Heath (ed.), *Intellectual Property Law in Asia*, Kluwer Law International: London, 2003, at 13–35.

10 Arthur Wineburg, 'Jurisprudence in Asia: Enforcing Intellectual Property Rights', 5 *University of Baltimore Intellectual Property Law Journal* 25, Fall, 1996/Spring, 1997. Available online from Lexis-Nexis.

buy pirated ones'.[11] A survey of the public attitudes towards buying pirated CDs in Singapore found that an overwhelming majority had engaged in such activity at one time or another.[12] It was also found that a majority 'favoured buying pirated CDs with only one in 10 saying that people with no morals buy them'.[13] The persistence of such a habit has been ascribed partly to the ineffectiveness of the educational campaign mounted in Singapore over the last few years,[14] but one must not lose sight of the underlying cause of the habit.

Apart from Japan where piracy does not seem to be a major problem domestically, the cultural factor in rejecting notions of property in ideas has been arguably in retreat. In South Korea, Ilhyung Lee thus writes, 'Although Confucian attitudes still influence Korean thinking and appear at the margins in the Korean copyright setting, many of the Confucian traditions are outdated or of historical interest, and economic interests play a more determinative role'.[15] Kyu Ho Youm argues similarly,[16] 'Copyright is no longer an empty phrase in South Korea. Indeed, it has now emerged as a fertile ground for litigation. The metamorphosis of copyright from a largely ignored legal notion to a hotly debated concept in and out of court over a 10-year period since 1987 epitomizes how Korea is on the move to a vibrant sociocultural and economic body politic.' In relation to the rights of performers in south Korea, Chung Hwan Choi notes the that 'the remarkable expansion of the entertainment industry and the public recognition of its importance' has led to an increased recognition of their status.[17]

The economic context

Asian DCs face the same dilemmas that the quest for development in general throws up in all DCs. Essentially, the development of DCs must be conceived within the context of a global economy whereby a few ICs occupy a dominant role while most of Africa, Asia and Latin America remain stagnant or even suffer from precipitous decline. The evolution of the international division of labour that has set in over the centuries, both during colonialism and afterwards, has transformed

11 Sari P. Setiogi, 'Government has Finalised Regulation on Optical Disks', *The Jakarta Post*, 6 February 2004, at 13. Available online from Factiva.

12 Braema Mathi, 'Singaporeans do not Fight Shy of Pirated CDs', *The Straits Times* [Singapore], 22 October 1999, at 38.

13 Ibid.

14 Ibid.

15 Ilhyung Lee, 'Culturally-Based Copyright Systems?: The U.S. And Korea In Conflict', *Washington University Law Quarterly* 1103, Winter 2001. Available online from Lexis-Nexis.

16 Kyu Ho Youm, 'Copyright Law in the Republic of Korea', 17 *UCLA Pacific Basin Law Journal* 276, Fall 1999/Spring 2000. Available online from Lexis-Nexis.

17 Chung Hwan Choi, 'Protection of Artists' Rights Under the Korean Copyright Law', 12 *Pacific Rim Law and Policy Journal* 179, January 2003. Available online from Lexis-Nexis.

the ICs of Europe and North America into producers of processed or secondary goods while the DCs have remained permanent importers of those goods and have paid for them through export of raw materials of one type or another.

The status of DCs as agricultural nations or producers of unprocessed or primary goods has inevitably resulted in unequal exchanges with the industrial nations and led to a permanent transfer of values from the DCs to the industrial nations, although, in recent decades, the multi-national corporations (MNCs) [18] have begun relocating traditional labour-intensive industries like textiles, garments and shoes to parts of Africa, Asia and Latin America (the so-called newly industrializing countries, or NICs). As the experiences of the Asian NICs, Mexico and Argentina during their crises periods in recent years have shown, the industrialization processes in those countries were totally dependent on, or extensions of, the same processes in the major industrial nations. The apparent inability of DCs to break out of the cycle of primary production, poverty and all forms of social ills as well as dependency on industrial nations for capital and technology generation testifies to the enduring impact of the entrenched international division of labour. DCs would therefore have to find the path for autonomous development and break out of the continuing dependency as well as social and economic decline.

Above all, Asian DCs would need to generate the requisite resources internally and externally. The mobilization of the potential domestic resources (whether human, financial, natural or environmental) must be reinforced by policies and measures to decrease transfer of wealth and values to the ICs. It is only with the accumulation and preservation of an economic surplus and its effective deployment that DCs can take advantage of foreign investment and technology to build a better future. Such a path of development in turn calls for casting the role of IP differently from that in ICs.

Building technological capability

A major area DCs need to engage in to achieve autonomous development is the building up of technological capability. The *World Science Report 1998* (issued by UNESCO) disclosed that 94 per cent of the global R&D expenditure as well as 95 per cent of scientific papers originated from the developed countries.[19] As

18 Roughly speaking, 'multi-national companies' (MNCs) are those companies registered and operating in as many countries as they can. They have such huge resources at their command that they spread their networks of manufacturing and/or services across the world. In recent decades, some of the bigger MNCs have been referred to as 'global companies' because, with the onset of the information and communications technologies (ICT), their operations run on a 24/7 basis and virtually never stop.

19 Referred to in Jane Innes and Tim Turpin, *Intellectual Property Legislation and Innovation in Asia–Pacific Economies: Case Studies of Intellectual Property Law in Australia, China, Indonesia, Korea, the Philippines and Thailand*, Hybrid: Ormond, Vic., 1999, at 8.

Table 8.1 shows, Asian DCs for whom data were available have sought to build some capability to make better use of foreign investment and domestic resources. The figures for Japan serve to highlight the immense gap that persists between that country and Asian NICs and DCs.

Table 8.1 R&D expenditures in selected Asian countries

Country	Year	R&D expenditure as % of GNP	Researcher per million inhabitants
China	1996	0.61	454
	1997	0.68	473
	1998	0.70	387
	1999	0.83	420
	2000	1.00	545
India	1994	0.73	149
	1996	1.23	157
Japan	1996	2.77	4909
	1997	2.83	4962
	1998	2.94	5160
	1999	2.94	5196
	2000	2.98	5095
Korea	1996	2.60	2199
	1997	2.69	2245
	1998	2.55	2005
	1999	2.45	2160
	2000	2.68	2319
Malaysia	1996	0.22	92
	1998	0.40	160
Singapore	1996	1.39	2,699
	1997	1.50	2,832
	1998	1.81	2,991
	1999	1.90	3,215
	2000	1.88	4,110
Thailand	1996	0.12	–
	1997	0.10	74

Source: UNESCO Institute for Statistics: Selected R&D Indicators (http://www.uis.unesco.org).

The dearth of R&D resources committed for the generation or adaptation of technology is reflected in the trickle of patents that are registered by nationals in Asian DCs (see Table 8.2). As a matter of fact, there are only a handful of patents that originate from within the DCs. If at all some of these countries are considered worthy of receiving patent applications by foreign inventors, most of the patents granted belong to inventors – residents of the ICs. Statistics for over 100 years have shown that the vast majority of patents granted in DCs originate from the ICs; again, most of these do not lead to the production or supply of goods or services in those countries. Hence, the patents registered in DCs by inventors from industrial nations are means of securing the market for those inventors' goods or services.

Certainly, the fact that an increasingly greater share of patents granted in DCs belong to MNCs implies that the exploitation of those patents has become part of their overall global strategies not only in the production and distribution of goods and services but also in the generation and acquisition of inventions and other technologies. In some instances, MNCs have a larger capital structure and size than the GDP of even the big industrial nations;[20] consequently, the possibility for the DCs to achieve the working of patents that find themselves on their national registers remains remote. That objective was on the top of their agenda in all international fora and to this day remains the single most serious defect in their national patent systems.

Even when DCs attempt to generate creative works internally, the overall conditions are not always conducive. In the Philippines, for instance, inventions and innovations face diverse difficulties. After citing some inventions that Filipino inventors had made, including awards they obtained at various competitions, a commentator pointed to certain problems: 'Despite their creativeness and resourcefulness, however, Filipino inventors can't seem to find a niche in Philippine society. Too many problems hound them … lack of protection from multinational companies, lack of funds, inaccessibility of tax incentives to backyard inventors, and lack of support from the government.'[21]

The writer also referred to government inaction in providing funding set aside by law. The large number of inventors' associations (24 to be exact) was also viewed as a source of 'feuding'. In addition, an inventor of a 'green charcoal stove' which could replace '"cancer causing" LPG stoves', recounted 'how he had to go through two decades of court proceedings to fend off attempts by multinational pest control companies and the Philippine Fertilizer Pesticide Authority to disprove his inventions'.[22] The inventor claimed that the MNCs felt so 'threatened' by his

20 Compare the number of patents of Asian DCs, in Table 8.2, with that of the major MNCs in 2000: IBM, 2922; NEC, 2034; Canon, 1897; Samsung Electronics, 1442; Lucent, 1415. See Barbara Darrow, 'IBM Leads Patent Pack – Again', *TechWeb News*, 10 January 2001. Available at http://www.techweb.com/wire/story/TWB20010110S0008. The figure in 2008 for IBM jumped to 4186, and that for Samsung Electronics to 3515. See Reuters, 'IBM Tops All Others in 2008 Patent Race', 14 January 2009; available at http://www.pcmag.com/article2/0,2817,2338944,00.asp#.

21 Tessa R. Salazar, 'Filipino Inventors Lack Gov't Support', *Philippine Daily Inquirer*, 15 November 2003. Available online from Factiva.

22 Ibid.

inventions that 'They worked hard so that I would not be able to sell my inventions in my own country'.[23]

Table 8.2 Patent grants to residents and non-residents in Asian countries, 1995–2001

Nations	Year	Patents granted to		Total
		Residents	Non-residents	
China	2001	5,395	10,901	16,296
	1999	3,097	4,540	7,637
	1997	1,532	1,962	3,494
	1995	1,530	1,863	3,393
India	2001*	234	78,288	78,522
	1999	633	1,527	2,160
	1997*			10,155
	1995	415	1,198	1,613
Indonesia	2001*		77,407	77,407
	1999*		42,503	42,503
	1997*		4,517	4,517
	1995	–	–	–
Malaysia	1997	52	734	786
	1995	29	1,724	1,753
Philippines	2001*		13,598	13,598
	1999	5	643	648
	1997	25	891	916
	1995	–	–	–
Republic of Korea	2001	21,833	12,842	34,675
	1999	43,314	19,321	62,635
	1997	14,497	10,082	24,579
	1995	6,575	5,937	12,512
Singapore	2001*		79,026	79,026
	1999	48	4,362	4,410
	1997*		9,506	9,506
	1995			1,968
Vietnam	2001		76,542	76,542
	1999	13	477	490
	1997		111	111
	1995	3	53	56

Note: * Patents applied for, no data for grants.
Source: WIPO Industrial Property Statistics, Geneva.

23 Ibid.

In Malaysia, IP is apparently still viewed as a means of countering lawsuits. According to industry leaders, there is a lack of an 'R&D culture' among Malaysian businesses.[24] The same industry leaders added, 'They do a little bit of development and, if at all they think of IP, it's only to protect their goods and products and not to capitalize on it'.[25]

The role of legal policy and specific forms of IP

Another major factor for autonomous development is the adoption by DCs of appropriate legal policy and specific forms of IP. Various studies have demonstrated that legal policy for DCs has to reflect the divergence and peculiarity of those countries from the developed or industrialized ones in terms of both their interests and their socio-economic standing.[26] It has been argued that IP law-making in DCs should of necessity go beyond mere gap filling or modifications of existing premises of laws in the major industrial nations and pursue a conception and structure at variance with them. In so far as DCs have to adopt economic and technological policies that help overcome the plague of underdevelopment and other problems that continue to throttle their future prospects, the IP laws they introduce must serve the same purposes.

Attempts by DCs to assert their sovereign right to legislate in IP matters in a manner that suited their social and economic circumstances have often been dubbed as seeking weaker forms of IP.[27] IP Laws which do not meet the requirements of the major industrial nations *within DCs* have been derided as deficient and eventually become a pretext for issuing threats or imposing trade sanctions against such nations. The US in particular has set up a governmental watchdog (the US Trade Representative Office, USTR) that monitors, amongst others, IP developments across the world and berates countries that it views as failing to legislate or implement IP laws to the satisfaction of US companies. The formal establishment of a government agency scrutinizing the private (civil) law

---

24 Annie Freeda Cruez, 'Creating Wealth Out of Intellectual Property', *New Straits Times*, 8 January 2004, at 13 (reporting the views of two business leaders during a press interview). Available online from Factiva.

25 Ibid.

26 See, e.g., Edith T. Penrose, *The Economics of the International Patent System*, John Hopkins Press: Baltimore, MD, 1951; Helge E. Grundmann, 'Foreign Patent Monopolies in Developing Countries: An Empirical Analysis', 12 *Journal of Development Studies* 186, 1976; A. Samuel Oddi, 'The International Patent System and Third World Development: Reality or Myth?', 1987 *Duke Law Journal* 831, 1987; P.S. Sangal and Kishore Singh (eds), *Indian Patent System and Paris Convention: Legal Perspectives*, Ashoka: Delhi, 1987; A. Endeshaw, *Intellectual Property Policy for Non-Industrial Countries*, Dartmouth: Aldershot, 1996.

27 Robert M. Sherwood *Intellectual Property and Economic Development*, Westview Press: Boulder, CO, 1990, at 159–78 (an entire chapter on 'The Myth of Weak Protection').

of other nations proves beyond doubt the intent of putting persistent pressure on those nations. The USTR has always had a goal more in tune with US national needs than those of the target countries. Taiwan serves as a good example of how IP law-making can be thwarted through such monitoring in favour of external (industrial power) interests rather than the indigenous economy or technological change.[28]

While the status of Japan as one of the foremost IP-intensive nations is well known, among Asian NICs and DCs only South Korea and Singapore appear to be edging towards the positions of the big ICs. Singapore has recently become more vocal in upholding IP without question and attempting to bolster it. More recent government statements and activities in the area of IP reflect a desire to strengthen all institutional and legal mechanisms. The Singapore government's keen sense of impending needs of transforming the economy yet further, in particular by investing in biotechnology, has apparently served to stock the desire for a tighter IP regime.

External Pressures on Asian IP Law-Making and Enforcement

The US, EU and, to a lesser extent, Japan, criticize the records of IP law-making and enforcement in Asian nations. The EU approach has noticeably been to persuade Asian nations and other DCs gently[29] – in keeping with its position during the Uruguay Round.[30] Japan occasionally seeks action in direct negotiations,[31] but it

---

28 See, generally, Paul C.B. Liu, 'U.S. Industry's Influence on Intellectual Property Negotiations and Special 301 Actions', 13 *UCLA Pacific Basin Law Journal* 87, Fall 1994.

29 Thus the European Commission recently conducted a survey (of its delegations abroad, rights holders and businesses) on enforcement issues 'with the objective of assessing in a detailed manner the current situation in third countries and identifying the most problematic intellectual property areas and countries'. See [European Commission] 'Survey on Enforcement of Intellectual Property Rights in Third Countries, July 2003'; available at http://europa.eu.int/comm/trade/issues/sectoral/intell_property/survey_en.htm. It is interesting that the survey was described as 'a diagnostic allowing DG Trade, and the Commission services to act more efficiently and to develop a clear strategy to tackle the growing problems caused by violations of IPR and by the deficient enforcement of such rights in third countries.' Ibid. In other words, the EC was not planning to dish out instructions to other nations or threaten to take action.

30 See generally, F.K. Beier and G. Schricker (eds), *GATT or WIPO? New Ways in the International Protection of Industrial Property*, VCH: Weinheim, 1989.

31 [Ministry of Economy, Trade and Industry, Japan] *The Report of the Task Force on Industrial Competitiveness and Intellectual Property Policy*, 5 June 2002 (available at http://www.jpo.go.jp) states that 'Japan has been approaching countries and regions where counterfeit infringement is grave by asking them to improve the situation. Japan has helped developing countries to enrich their intellectual property systems by such means

is still gradually coming out of its usual reticence. From 1992, Japan has been issuing its own annual assessment of the performance of its trading partners in their trade-related activities,[32] although it does not pronounce any threats of action against them for any alleged failure to enforce their laws.

By contrast, the US maintains an increasingly belligerent tone in its approach towards the records of its trading partners in IP law-making and enforcement. A number of Asian nations have thus been annually put on the infamous watch list published by the USTR. *The 2003 National Trade Estimate Report on Foreign Trade Barriers* rebuked a number of Asian countries for a wide array of omissions and deficiencies.

China was the only Asian nation mentioned under Section 306 of the Trade Act of 1974 and therefore subject to monitoring by the USTR for possible trade sanctions. The Report reiterated that, since joining the WTO in December 2001, China had shown 'improvements' in its IP protection but that 'significant concerns' remained in the area of enforcement. It referred, amongst others, to 'violations of IPR' as being 'still rampant', the 'lack of training and weak punishments', the absence of 'national treatment with regard to their well-known marks'.[33] It urged China to

> dedicate more resources to enforcement, and undertake more frequent, unannounced police raids in pursuit of IPR infringers; increase coordination between the various national and local authorities charged with IPR enforcement; ensure that China's officials take a serious and consistent approach to sentencing, including setting and enforcing deterrent levels of fines; and reduce the high thresholds for criminal prosecutions that, in practice, prevent effective

---

as cooperation in training for intellectual property-related human resources'. Ibid., at 5–6. As regards China, the Report specified that the Japanese government took 'actions toward the Chinese government such as presenting specific cases of damages and requesting crackdowns as well as requesting the strengthening of export regulations based on Japanese experience'. Ibid., at 36. Japanese industry groups such as automobile manufacturers have sent delegations to China to present their grievances to the government and request their counterparts to crackdown on infringements. Ibid.

32 In publicizing the 2003 Report. Japan's Ministry of Economy, Trade and Industry stated 'the biggest problem that Asian countries have in common to be that of intellectual property right infringement from the production and distribution of pirated copies, counterfeits and other illicit goods'. See, Ministry of Economy, Trade and Industry, *2003 Report on the WTO Consistency of Trade Policies by Major Trading Partners*, 28 March, 2003; available at http://www.meti.go.jp/english/report/. After naming China, Taiwan and Korea as 'the three largest offenders', it added, 'the region does not have sufficiently effective enforcement procedures for exercising rights and eliminating infringement, though countries are in the process of enhancing their legal systems for the protection of intellectual property'. Ibid.

33 See [USTR], *2003 National Trade Estimate Report on Foreign Trade Barriers*; available at http://www.ustr.gov/reports/nte/2003/index.htm.

> application of China's criminal law to IPR violators; provide adequate training for patent and trademark examiners and IP enforcement agents; and ensure that criminal action can be taken against exports of pirated or counterfeit product.[34]

All in all, the patronizing advice given by the US was about putting pressure on China to devote more resources for the enforcement of US businesses' claim to have priority status in China. It might be observed that none of the exhortations referred to, or linked with, internal domestic Chinese demands for any improvement in IP protection.

Apart from China, the 2003 USTR Report placed India, Indonesia, the Philippines and Taiwan on its 'Priority Watch List'. It also categorized Korea, Malaysia, Thailand and Vietnam on its 'Watch List'. We will look at the alleged 'crimes' of each country presently.

As against India, the Report judged its IP to be 'weak'. Even India's patent law amendments in May 2002 did not elicit any compliments. Indeed, the Report pointed to 'a major problem', namely 'India's export of counterfeit goods to the Middle East, southern Africa and Europe'.[35] It might be noted that, just as in China, Indian businesses have not demanded improvements in IP protection on the scale that the US put forward. In fact, if any improvements have been called for in recent years, they were only in favour of the fledgling software industry.

In regard to Indonesia, the US again announced that 'overall protection of intellectual property rights remains weak'.[36] It cited 'long delays' in prosecuting infringers, absence of 'sentencing guidelines with deterrent penalties' before pointing to the necessity for Indonesia of implementing an 'action plan' that the US had provided Indonesia with in May 2002.[37] All this was couched with the warning that Indonesia should not jeopardize its interests under 'the Trade and Investment Framework Agreement' with the US – indirectly, therefore, threatening to withdraw those facilities from Indonesia if it did not comply with the 'recommendations' set out in the 'action plan'.[38]

The Philippines was castigated similarly for having 'become a "safe haven" for organized piracy and counterfeiting as neighbouring economies improve their IPR enforcement'.[39] The Report referred to the 'IPR action plan' that the US Government provided to the Philippines in August 2002 'with specific recommendations on judicial, legislative/regulatory, and enforcement issues'.[40] It then directed the Philippines 'to pass the optical media bill, criminally prosecute IPR violators, expedite pending IPR cases, establish deterrent penalties for IPR

34 Ibid.
35 Ibid.
36 Ibid.
37 Ibid.
38 Ibid.
39 Ibid.
40 Ibid.

violators, and implement the WIPO digital treaties'.[41] The overbearing nature of the US approach towards the Philippines is so stark that comment would hardly be necessary. One wonders where all this will end.

Concerning Taiwan, the report stated, 'Official raids are hampered by lack of expertise and poor interagency coordination; resulting penalties are neither timely nor strong enough to deter infringement. The lax protection of IPR, including lack of enforcement against piracy and trademark counterfeiting in Taiwan therefore remains a serious concern for the U.S. Government'.[42] No doubt, the Taiwanese government was justified in taking offence at the summary fashion of the US critique dismissing everything that Taiwan has been doing throughout the last two decades as practically inconsequential.[43]

In relation to South Korea, the review threatened to put that country on the Watch List or move it upwards to the Priority Watch List if it failed to fulfil US directions on drafting laws and submitting them to the National Assembly, in a number of areas: transmission of sound recordings and granting powers to the relevant authority for film distributions 'to stop film piracy'.[44]

The Report praised Malaysia for actively seeking to stamp out pirated products through the Optical Disk Act of 2000 (in force since September 2001) but did not spare it the usual diatribe this time against piracy of electronic media and content as well as 'trademark counterfeiting'.[45] It alleged that 'the products of sophisticated Malaysian pirates are marketed worldwide … Prosecution is a weak link in the enforcement chain, and the judicial process remains slow'.[46]

With regards to Thailand, the USTR pronounced its dissatisfaction with the state of enforcement and urged Thailand 'to continue to strengthen its IPR regime'. It declared its plan to provide that country 'with specific recommendations on judicial, legislative/regulatory, and enforcement issues'.[47] The report admonished Vietnam for the weakness of IP enforcement and exhorted it 'to build upon its strong public commitment to IPR protection by effectively implementing and enforcing its new laws and regulations to reduce the pervasive piracy and counterfeiting that continue to exist'.[48]

The latest, 2008 USTR Report[49] reiterates in more emphatic terms its critique of the IP system and implementation in Asia. Of China, it commented that 'Since

41 Ibid.

42 Ibid.

43 See 'Taiwan Expresses Regret over Being Placed on US Counterfeiting List', *Agence France Presse*, 2 May 2003. Available online from Factiva.

44 See, note 33, above, ibid.

45 Ibid.

46 Ibid

47 Ibid.

48 Ibid.

49 USTR, *2008 National Trade Estimate Report on Foreign Trade Barriers*; available at http://www.ustr.gov/reports.

its accession to the WTO, China has overhauled its legal regime and put in place a comprehensive set of laws and regulations aimed at protecting the IPR of domestic and foreign entities in China'. Yet, it asserted 'Several weaknesses in all aspects of China's enforcement system – criminal, civil, and administrative – contribute to China's poor IPR enforcement record'. As a consequence, the United States filed two IP-related WTO disputes in April 2007 which were decided in its favour.[50] Thailand was berated in similar terms: 'Widespread counterfeiting and piracy continue to plague IPR owners in Thailand. The lack of sustained and coordinated enforcement, and, in particular, the lack of prosecution, remains a substantial problem.'[51] The Philippines did not fare well either: 'While the Philippines has made progress in combating optical media piracy through passage of the 2004 Optical Media Act (OMA), it has generally failed to improve the prosecution and conviction of IPR violators'.[52] Neither did Indonesia fare any better, although it was portrayed as showing improvements but still lacking in its laws as well as enforcement. Consequently, 'The United States will continue to raise concern about the range of IPR issues with Indonesia and work with it to help strengthen its IPR regime'.[53]

The critique levelled at South Korea was limited to inadequacy of the law and practice which has allegedly resulted in the proliferation in that country of 'unauthorized reproductions of copyrighted material'.[54] That against Taiwan referred to the same concerns and more: 'the availability of counterfeit pharmaceuticals … Internet infringement, illegal textbook copying on university campuses, and inadequate protection for the packaging, configuration, and outward appearance of products (trade dress)'.[55]

As an exception to its usual predictable stance, the USTR pointed to the fact that, in 2007, 'the Malaysian government continued to make progress in IPR enforcement', although still indirectly chiding it for letting US corporations suffer 'significant losses due to the manufacture and sale of counterfeit trademarked products in Malaysia'.[56] The highest praise was, however, reserved for Singapore: 'Singapore has developed one of the strongest IPR regimes in Asia'.[57]

Overall, it seems that a new period has emerged in IP law-making with the US not just waiting for things to happen at the DCs' end but intervening directly and making specific demands on governments to pass legislation and execute it. In effect, the overhauling of the legal regime and continuous monitoring of government enforcement is more and more in the hands of local representatives

50 Ibid.
51 Ibid.
52 Ibid.
53 Ibid.
54 Ibid.
55 Ibid.
56 Ibid.
57 Ibid.

of the US government. Nothing would appear to be beyond their scrutiny, advice or instructions.

The tone that the US has adopted in its approach towards Asian nations portrays a readiness to unceremoniously command every country to do its bidding. This is exemplified by the recurrent issue of 'action plans,' which are virtually orders that have to be complied with by supposedly sovereign nation states and their governments. Clearly, whether it is IP law-making in South Korea, the Philippines or Indonesia, each and every one is subject to the scrutiny, approval and directions of the US. Viewed against the fundamental fact that the US has become a major common destination for their exports, the Asian nations' vulnerability and total acquiescence becomes understandable. That each of them has to maintain smooth relations with the US in order to keep the latter's market open to their goods and to attract investments for their local economies must speak volumes for their perennial accommodation of US demands on them as regards IP legislation and enforcement, amongst others.[58]

It also explains why the language of the USTR Annual Report has increasingly become strident. The US projects an image of a self-appointed mentor, a superior authority or ruler over a subordinate hierarchy of nations. It blatantly expresses US interests in, and plans it has prepared for, specific countries that it selects for pressure. The more the US screams and fumes, the more it betrays the determination of a superpower to push others around for its narrow interests. Indeed, the more US criticism of other nations and their activities appears confined to unilateral expectations and interests, the more local people and businesses will see the IP system as an instrument of US MNCs and not necessarily amenable to benefiting all.

The upshot of this growing perception of the US stance on international enforcement of IP is that it might trigger anti-US sentiments on a wider scale and reinforce disregard for IP generally or even lead to campaigns singling out US interests and goods or services. For instance, the linkage of opposition to US policies in the Middle East with sidelining of its business interests in the region such as franchise chains and other outfits as well as the establishment of domestic rival brands (to displace the likes of Coca Cola or Pepsi Cola) has within it a threat more insidious to the US than potent forms of IP infringement by individuals.[59]

58 It has been reported that 'The U.S. is perennially the largest foreign investor in Thailand, with U.S. foreign direct investment in Thailand totaling over $7 billion in 2001'. See, 'US and Thailand Sign Bilateral TIFA', *Thai Press Reports*, 31 October 2002. Available online from Factiva.

59 According to one (not necessarily objective) commentator, 'since the anti-terrorism war was launched, people in the Middle East have become increasingly disgusted with US products. Before the United States started war against Iraq, US exports to the Middle East region dropped by 25 percent–40 percent. McDonald's declared that it would close 175 branches in 10 Muslim countries, Coca Cola's sales volume also began to go down.' See 'Price paid for victory of "hard strength"', *People's Daily Online*, 13 February 2004. Available online from Factiva.

Groups of people, even nations, switching off from US goods could have calamitous consequences for US corporations and its overall economy.[60]

Lately, the US has found a new weapon for pressing its demands for further extension of IP (constituting the so-called DCs-plus formula) and enforcement on other countries.[61] It has begun exploiting the willingness, or desire, of some of the Asian nations to conclude a free trade area agreement (FTA) with itself rather than wait endlessly for the unpredictable outcomes of the trade negotiations under the WTO. Singapore took the plunge earlier than most and entangled itself with all the carefully structured expansive scopes of IP protection and of effecting higher standards for their enforcement.[62] Other countries are still studying the concessions given by Singapore but seem resigned to the latter's stance, which has been portrayed as a model for others to follow.[63]

In the case of Thailand, the US has expressed the precondition of improvement in IP enforcement as a first step for any progress towards the conclusion of an FTA.[64] For its part, Thailand promised to pass legislation to control illegal disc production such that all CDs will carry print codes of manufacturers and machines to enable tracing of those illegally made.[65] Thailand has also sought to co-operate with Vietnam and China on, respectively, suppressing IP violations and introducing measures to control shipments of illegitimate products.[66]

---

60 For instance, at the end of workshop organized at one Nigerian university, a declaration was issued: 'In order to reduce the strength with which the U.S.A. uses to coerce us we call on all Nigerian Muslims to boycott U.S.A. and Israeli goods and services as much as possible'. A list of US brands then followed. See, Workshop on Middle East Crisis and the American Global Agenda Organised by the Abubakar Sadiq Research Centre Held at Bayero University, Kano on 13/07/2002; available at http://www.gamji.com/NEWS1501.htm.

61 President Bush called it 'the first of its kind between the United States and an Asian Pacific country'. See The White House, Office of the Press Secretary 'President Signed U.S.–Singapore Free Trade Agreement', 6 May 2003. Available at http://www.whitehouse.gov/news/releases/2003/05/20030506-11.html.

62 In an interview with the local press, a vice-president of the US Borland Software Corporation commented on the Singapore–US FTA, 'We heard Singapore was going the path of the FTA with US, with the most stringent IP protection of any Asian country. That was attractive to us … It will be the gold standard. There will be a domino effect in raising IP standards and opening up foreign markets'. See, 'Increased Intellectual Property Protection a Draw for Business', *Straits Times* [Singapore], 5 December 2003. (Available online from Factiva.) He added, 'Even as software companies lose billions each year to piracy, FTAs are a good platform for them to play a part in changing IP laws in other countries'. Ibid.

63 The Singapore Prime Minister thus stated in his speech at the signing of the agreement in Washington: 'The U.S.–Singapore FTA can be a model for other FTAs under President Bush's Enterprise for ASEAN Initiative, or EAI'. See note 52, above, ibid.

64 Phusadee Arunmas, 'Intellectual Property – US – More stringent action on piracy or no FTA talks', *Bangkok Post*, 21 January 2004 at 3. Available online from Factiva.

65 Ibid.

66 Ibid.

Immediate Factors Impacting on IP Enforcement

It is always easy for governments in the US and the EU to sound alarm bells of further rise in piracy levels in Asia or elsewhere and press the latter to do more. However, amidst the furore over laxity of Asian DCs, the lack of IP enforcement and the like, the multiplicity of *immediate* factors that have a bearing on the problems is scarcely examined. One needs to study those factors if one is prepared to get a good picture of what DCs face on a daily basis. In the absence of any serious discussion of these issues, the underlying rationale for the reluctance of DCs to fully commit to the cause of foreign companies will remain unknown.

The economics of enforcement

One of the major factors that continue to be ignored is the economics of IP enforcement. This is an area for IP owners to focus upon if they wish to understand the dynamics of the problem and overcome it effectively. Broadly speaking, the cost of enforcement of IP is borne by local governments and taxpayers who have nothing to do with foreign IP holders or receive no commensurate revenue from them.

The fact that foreign IP owners and governments that back them do not contribute directly to law enforcement, public education, development of infrastructure and procedures or human capacity building in the specific field of IP in the host DCs is rarely touched upon in studies. These involve both sunk costs and recurrent expenses that rise exponentially with the intensity and extent of IP enforcement. Yet, in many DCs, the deployment of significant resources for such a task is never possible. Foreign IP owners from distant lands do not elicit any sympathy, let alone the diversion of funds that might otherwise be used for educational or social programmes.

If it is any comfort to such IP owners, taxes are never levied on foreign IP whether at the point of entry into DCs or on distribution or other use later. The general taxes levied on importers and distributors do not target the IP content and the consequent invisible income that the major MNCs reap day in and day out. Even when DCs are provided with aid and technical assistance by the ICs, such acts are portrayed as charitable and beneficial to the recipients. The fact of the matter, however, is that the absence of any assistance does not have any immediate negative repercussions on the DCs themselves.

Merely laying the blame on DCs and their weak machinery of enforcement has been so overplayed (on top of the residual use of sanctions, denial of aid or loans from international sources) that progress in IP enforcement on behalf of major IP holders (Western MNCs) is destined to remain ever weak and trailing behind huge expectations. This explains why, increasingly, the task of enforcement is being organized, managed and paid for by agencies independent of state bodies. The educational tools for raising awareness, the creation of a knowledgeable workforce, the laying down of adequate infrastructure, all these and more would appear to be the preferred directions of investment for foreign IP holders (and the governments that back them) rather than applying pressure on national governments of DCs to inject more law or to set aside resources to implement IP.

It must be public knowledge by now that most DCs cannot afford to pay even normal infrastructure development costs. Education, roads, health and policing (keeping the peace) take such a huge chunk of the annual state budget (even without considering the toll of external debt repayments) that it would be idealistic to expect them to protect foreign IP interests. Nine times out of 10, the choices available to them are the same regardless of the rewards they might reap or the punishments they might face for any success or default in enforcement.

Otherwise, current vociferous demands for enforcement of IP rights parallel nineteenth-century schemes of protecting foreign nationals living in colonies or semi-colonies. Invariably, those nationals were cushioned from local courts/law and, in all dispute settlement proceedings where one or both parties were foreigners (metropolitans), the local courts ('customs') were unconditionally ignored or prohibited from asserting jurisdiction. Where the 'barbarian' state in question was nominally independent, a treaty with the various powers stipulated that the nationals of the great powers (or Europeans) would be handed over to their consulates or emissaries to be tried under 'civilized' laws and legal systems.

Today that same process continues in operation in the shape of respect for foreign IP, although the implementation is left to local courts. The pressure on local courts of the current DCs is accordingly to act as if they were similar to the courts of the big industrialized powers in passing judgment on the latter's citizens' issues, rights and claims. The use of local courts in DCs and the legal system as a whole to thrash out issues affecting developed country affairs is a backhanded service to the industrial powers. It is a subsidy extended to those powers by countries and peoples who have other priorities and urgent tasks to accomplish. At the very least one would have thought that IP holders in major ICs would pay for the compliment, but such never really happens.

A good example is the USTR's persistent pressure on Asian nations such as China to pour more resources into enforcement. Such a demand is plainly an argument for more subsidy that the Chinese economy should extend towards US proprietors without any equivalent value being offered to China or Chinese businesses. The elemental basis for IP protection by national governments, namely the provision of protection for value generated in the local economy, is thereby ignored.

Pricing issues

Another major contributor to the difficulty of IP enforcement in Asia is still the relatively higher price of IP-protected goods than, by all accounts, particularly low-income consumers can afford.[67] Even when the goods are made within Asia, they are expensively marketed as if they were imported from Western Europe or North America. Marketers therefore play into the hands of copycats, counterfeiters or 'pirates' by making access to branded goods difficult to wide sections of the public. In short, the growing popularity of branded goods and the readiness of the younger generation especially to acquire them have not been met by a corresponding lowering of prices or the use of distinguishing marks or quality indicators.[68]

Many Asian DCs have espoused the idea of cutting prices of IP-dependent goods. Thus, shortly after Thailand was placed on a 'priority watch list', the Commerce Ministry of Thailand attempted to encourage local music businesses to cut prices on their CDs to make them more competitive against illegally produced ones.[69] In Singapore, one of the recommendations made by researchers of consumer habits was for a reduction in prices of the genuine products to help curb pirated versions.[70]

The recording industry in Malaysia appealed personally to the former Prime Minister, Mahathir Mohamad, to help them stop the crippling impact of piracy on local music sales. They reportedly pleaded with him that 'the local music industry would be crippled in a few years if new launches by stars ... continue to suffer limp sales'.[71] Mahathir's response was a suggestion to amend the law so that end-users will be made to pay more for buying pirated copies. The irony of the Malaysian situation is that 'Malaysia has some of the toughest copyright

67 One commentator points out that the non-recognition of patents for drugs by India has been 'the most significant price-restraining factor' and that prices have remained low. See S. Venu, 'The IPR Effect on Drug Prices', *Business Line* (The Hindu), 28 October 2002. (Available online from Factiva.) The writer projects, by reference to studies, 'as Indian patents are introduced in the coming decade, prices are likely to be substantially higher on newly patented drugs than they would otherwise have been'. Ibid.

68 One commentator wrote, 'I'm not ashamed to say that I used to rely on pirated software when I was in school, since that was the only way to get it ... I needed the tools for my assignments and may allowance definitely wasn't enough to pay for original software ... my pockets weren't deep enough to act "ethically"'. See Eileen Yu, 'Opinion: Overpriced Software makes users Unwilling "Thieves"', *Computer Times* [Singapore], 27 November 2002 at CT64. The writer added, 'It is overly optimistic of anyone to assume that someone would choose to pay [the market price of the original] so the money would got to a developer that sits in a remote laboratory in a remote part of Silicon Valley'. Ibid. The writer concluded that 'the most effective way to battle piracy is to bring down the prices further'. Ibid.

69 'Commerce Ministry wants Price of CDs cut', *Business Daily* [Thailand], 6 May 2003. Available online from Factiva.

70 Braema Mathi, note 12, above, ibid.

71 Brendan Pereira, 'Piracy Woes: Malaysia's Entertainment Industry is Calling for Tougher Action against Copyright Infringement', *The Straits Times* [Singapore], March 2003, at A7.

legislation in the world and raids are conducted almost daily'.[72] According to the same commentator, 'A backlog of court cases, difficulty in compiling evidence and a question of priorities for government prosecutors and law enforcement agencies have all conspired to keep copyright pirates away from the courtroom'.[73]

The Malaysian Government sought to intervene and tackle the problem of piracy in a unique way. At first, its effort was confined to the persuasion of publishers to reduce their prices voluntarily.[74] When that failed, it threatened to use its Price Control Act to force music, movie and software publishers to lower their prices.[75] The US attempted to prevent such a measure by sending an official to talk to the Malaysians, but did not succeed. As usual, the US raised the problems that Malaysia could face in developing its software industry as well as in attracting foreign investment.[76] The Malaysian government eventually set out a price ceiling for locally produced VCDs and CDs only and enforced it from 1 January 2004 with the proviso that the prices would be reviewed in a year.[77]

It would seem that the message is getting to some of the big players. Microsoft has taken on board the suggestion for reducing the price of software by agreeing to supply the Thai government a 'low-cost version of its Windows operating system' for the Thai language to be used in customized PCs.[78] Microsoft's move has been viewed partly as a response to the competition from Linux-based operating systems embraced in many Asian countries and an attempt to address persistent calls for flexibility in price and to offer software in local languages instead of in English only.[79]

As a matter of fact, one of the responses that Asian DCs have thought up is the resort to public domain information or non-proprietary software such as open source. One commentator referred to industry sources 'who believe that enterprise software piracy can be further reduced by increasing the uptake of open source software', thereby legitimizing their activities and helping them avoid heavy fines

72 Ibid.

73 Ibid.

74 Sheridan Mahavera. 'Muhyiddin Criticises Industry Players', *New Straits Times* (Malaysia), 7 July 2003, at 4 (reporting on the statement of the Domestic Trade and Consumer Affairs Minister regarding the proposed price control and the failure of the industry to heed the government's voluntary price reduction to stave off piracy). Available online from Factiva.

75 The minister argued thus: 'This is a problem of the industry's mindset. That is why the Government has to step in this way. They underestimated the problem of piracy and they don't understand the Malaysian mentality'. Ibid.

76 Reme Ahmad, 'KL Spurns US Warning on CD price-fixing', *The Straits Times* [Singapore], 9 July 2003. Available online from Factiva.

77 'Government Fixes Rm14 as New VCD Price', *Bernama Daily Malaysian National News*, 17 September 2003. Available online from Factiva.

78 Matthew Broersma, 'Microsoft Offers cut-rate Windows', *CNet.News.com*, 9 February 2004.

79 Ibid.

or licence fees.[80] The proposal has been taken seriously in some countries. A case in point is Vietnam, which made it government policy to replace Microsoft's software with shareware. An official of Vietnam's Ministry of Science and Technology reportedly stated, 'We are trying, step by step, to eliminate Microsoft'.[81] The apparent plan is to have the public sector adopt open-source software within a year and pre-install the same in locally produced computers.[82]

This trend links with the pressure building up over the years to open up proprietary information for wider sections of the world and at no charge. The readiness of certain sectors to do so has only whetted the appetite of even broader groups of people – music lovers, students, researchers, sports fans, amongst others. Thus it is not surprising that a Hong Kong survey on the illegal downloading of online music found nearly half of the respondents had done so at least once. A director of the research company commented 'Downloading illegally is not a niche activity anymore, it's a mainstream activity ... We are seeing a situation where young people are growing up expecting to be able to get their digital products for free off the Internet – they now see music procurement as something that is done for free'.[83]

Conflicting interests of foreign businesses

Greed by foreign companies (whether or not multinationals) has contributed to the lack of progress in IP enforcement. Hence, although the state of IP in India has been presented as deficient in many respects, it does not seem that the allegedly high levels of IP piracy, 'poor enforcement', 'corruption, lack of resources and training for law enforcement officials and an overburdened court system'[84] have stopped any interest in the Indian market. Indeed, according to the same report, 'British, US and German firms have had the most success making revenue-producing agreements with Indian companies. Many foreign companies involved in India use a combination of exporting, licensing and direct investment'.[85]

In response to foreign proprietors' unwillingness to invest in India for fear of losing proprietary technology, the Indian government had to make changes in an earlier law that required 26 per cent of their equity to be handed over to Indians within three to five years. From August 1999, 100 per cent foreign-owned

80 Foo Eu Jin, 'Open Source Way to Combat Piracy', New *Straits Times–Management Times* [Malaysia], 15 December 2003. Available online from LexisNexis Academic.

81 Eddie Lee, 'Taking the Mickey out of Innovation', *Straits Times*, 20 January 2004. Available online from Factiva.

82 Ibid.

83 'Hong Kong a World Leader in Illegal Downloading – Survey', *Agence France Presse*, 15 January 2004. Available online from Factiva.

84 'India: Licensing and Intellectual Property', *Economist Intelligence Unit – ViewsWire*, Number 301, 6 January 2004. Available online from Factiva.

85 Ibid.

companies could operate without divesting their equity to locals.[86] The ultimate effect of this is not only the loosening of the pressure on India but also the creation of foreign enclaves with vested interests to ward off any future disapproval against India.

The same greed has become evident among foreign companies seeking to undercut legitimate businesses that compete against them through piracy and counterfeiting. Although most of the blame is levelled at DCs for not stopping the production or export of illicit goods, the question of who could ascertain the illegality and what kind of competence there might be in DCs often complicates the problem. One must realize that the magnitude of the problem has also to do with investors and importers from ICs who do not shun making money in manufacturing or distributing pirated stuff. There has also been a report of the admission to enforcement officers from the Ministry of Domestic Trade and Consumer Affairs of 'several foreign-owned companies' in Malaysia during raids that they had 'been using pirated computer softwares and promised to replace them with genuine ones'.[87]

Another example of the same trend is the appointment of Thai companies which were previously suspected of piracy as agents and business partners of five major music and movie makers – Sony, EMI, Universal, BMG and Time Warner.[88] One of the blacklisted Thai companies was at one time caught in possession of 'three unlicensed disc-pressing machines, [but] they claimed the devices were really being used to inject milk into bottles'.[89] Five of them were later declared 'clean' by the Thai government, and eventually clinched the deals mentioned. Their fortunes improved apparently because the MNCs were 'Faced with mounting losses from Internet file-swapping and rampant low-grade piracy that has rendered local markets in the developing world all but lost'.[90] Nevertheless, the debate on the potential risk that the MNCs could be exposed to if the Thai businesses reverted to their old ways remained open.

Still, the conflicting interests of foreign businesses and the cross purposes manifested in their attitudes towards the value, or, even, enforceability of IP contributes to the problem. The contradictory messages that non-IC governments receive no doubt play into the hands of profiteers and organized 'pirates'. Thus while the American video rental chain Blockbuster, a subsidiary of Viacom, decided not to enter the Chinese market, ostensibly because of the high level of

86 Ibid

87 'Foreign firms admit they use pirated software', *Straits Times* [Singapore], 26 September 2001. Available online from Factiva.

88 Shawn W. Crispin, 'Innovation', *Far Eastern Economic Review*, 8 January 2004, at 30.

89 Ibid.

90 Ibid.

piracy,[91] Time Warner Brothers agreed to open cinemas there.[92] According to the news report, 'Many other film houses see the sector as full of potential, but just as equally held back by onerous regulation requirements, mounting intellectual property piracy and high start-up costs'.[93]

Signs of Change in the State of IP Enforcement in Asia

A number of events and developments relating to IP enforcement in recent years suggest that changes are afoot throughout Asia. We will outline these presently.

Attitudes of, and measures taken by, governments

As demonstrated already in the discussion of US pressures on Asian countries, the latter have often had to bend over backwards to meet the demands of foreign IP owners and the governments that push their cause. The various Asian governments have had their particular approaches and immediate triggers for their responses.

In the case of Malaysia, its pursuit of getting every form of legal measure onto the statute books owes in recent years to the need to attract investment for the Multimedia Super Corridor (MSC). The persistent criticism of the alleged level of piracy has therefore been a headache for the government. As one minister commented, in the wake of renewed calls to toughen the laws once again, the perception that 'Malaysia was lax about enforcing intellectual property rights and that the country was a haven for copyright piracy' should be changed.[94] He argued that such a perception would have 'serious implications for the Malaysian economy' and 'compromise the government's policy' on building up the MSC.[95]

At a later stage, a Deputy Minister of Domestic Trade and Consumer Affairs iterated at a workshop that 'Malaysia has already been able to reduce its piracy rate by 10 points to 60 percent since 1995'.[96] He then projected further reduction in the piracy rate. Still, the only means of achieving the desirable goal that he referred to was his 'expressed hope that more emphasis would be given to educational programmes by the industry to tackle the problem on a long term basis'.[97]

91 Ien Cheng, 'Blockbuster Drops Expansion Plan in China', *Financial Times*, 30 January 2004. Available online from Factiva.

92 'Time Warner, Wanda Group to open 30 Cinemas in China over next 3–4 yrs – Xinhua', *AFX Asia*, 19 January 2004. Available online from Factiva.

93 Ibid.

94 'KL Plans Tougher Laws on Copyright', *The Straits Times* [Singapore], 19 March 1999, at 35.

95 Ibid.

96 'M'sia Stands to Gain US$200 Mln if Piracy is Reduced' (Malaysian National News Agency) *Malaysia Economic News*, Kuala Lumpur, 2 Decrmber 2003. Available online from Factiva.

97 Ibid.

The state of IP enforcement in Singapore has not been vastly different from the rest of Asia. However, in recent years, the Singapore government has demonstrated a capability to make sudden changes – the police have started to intervene directly in response to requests for searches, arrests of pirates or stoppage of infringing activities. This is quite a departure from previous times where they looked on while private complainants rummaged through alleged culprits' business premises to collect evidence of infringing activities. Now, even the popular night bazaars (*pasar malam*) for cheap software and CDs that used to be ignored in the past seem no longer off-limits to the police and the IP associations that conduct occasional raids.[98]

One stated reason for the apparent change of tack is, as elsewhere in Asia, the perception that IP enforcement will make Singapore 'more attractive to foreign investors'.[99] Another is the newly found enthusiasm for exploiting innovations through the re-established intellectual property office of Singapore (IPOS).[100] Pursuant to its projected additional role of marketing innovations, its director general reportedly stated on the launch of IPOS, 'We want to be an equivalent of the stock exchange, where we trade ideas instead of shares'.[101] The promise was taken up by IPOS and the Singapore Chinese Chamber of Commerce and Industry in devising a programme (named, the Intellectual Property – Creation, Exploitation and Protection Programme (IP-CEP) to educate and support local companies through talks, free phone advice, clinics and websites.[102]

Furthermore, the willingness to embrace more extended rights under the US–Singapore FTA seems to have been partly caused by Singapore's perception that it is, or will be, moving fast into the latest technologies. Again, the director-general of IPOS reportedly declared, 'an enhanced IP regime will strengthen IP protection particularly for Singapore's specialty industries like biotechnology, pharmaceuticals, IT development and infocomm'.[103]

On the whole, one can discern a tendency towards the appreciation by the two Asian NICs (South Korea and Singapore) that IP could become more important in future and that they need to take serious steps before it is too late. Ironically, some

---

98 'Police Target Night Market in Pirated Goods Raid', *The Straits Times* [Singapore], 8 July 2002, at H5.

99 Chong Chee Kin, 'S'pore's Anti-piracy Efforts Win Global Recognition', *The Straits Times* [Singapore], 14 July 2000, at 4 (quoting a TDB official reacting to the news of WTO's acceptance of the compliance of Singapore's IP regime to TRIPs).

100 Leslie Koh, 'New Stat [statutory] Board to Help Market Inventions', *The Straits Times* [Singapore], 3 April 2001, at H5.

101 Ibid.

102 'Drive to Make Firms IP-savvy and Mint Money', *The Straits Times* [Singapore], 9 November 2002, at H9.

103 Amit Roy Choudhury, 'S'pore Stands to Gain US$1b by Reining in Piracy', *The Business Times* [Singapore], 20 May 2003 (reporting on a study of the International Data Corporation (IDC) for the Business Software Alliance (BSA) and the benefits to Singapore in terms of new jobs created and revenues). Available online from Factiva.

of the Chinese leaders are beginning to realize that as globalization progresses the role of IP will be 'getting more and more important'.[104] Lin Binghui, vice-director of the State Intellectual Property Office, reportedly remarked, 'To some extent, the competition among the world's economies will be decided by the grabbing of IPR'.[105] A deputy director of the Trademark Office of the State Administration for Industry and Commerce added 'With the dramatic development of science and technology and the globalization of the world economy, intensified IPR protection will prevail for a comparatively long time in this century'.[106] He contended therefore that China would need to do more 'to compete with developed countries'.[107]

The reactions of artistes, inventors and local businesses

Across Asia, sections of the local business community have started asserting their IP rights and pressing their respective governments for appropriate action against infringement and piracy. Thus, demonstrations in Hong Kong led by local artistes, film makers and others protested against rising copyright piracy costing loss of revenue as well as jobs.[108] Organized by the 'Anti-Piracy Alliance', representing the film, theatre, music, software and broadcasting industries, the event was backed by the total closure of all the 73 cinemas in Hong Kong and stoppage of all music transmissions on radio channels for the day. As well as appealing to the public to refrain from purchasing pirated copies, they presented a petition to the government to act swiftly.[109]

A demonstration of nearly 100 Asian pop stars and their 5,000 supporters similarly took place in Taipei to plead with the government to stop rampant piracy which they alleged was 'sentencing music and movie to death'.[110] Cinemas and video arcades closed while radio stations stopped playing music for the day. The government's response was to tender an apology to the protesters and promise to set up 'a special task force to combat piracy'.[111]

In Singapore, governmental agencies such as the Trade and Development Board (TDB), renamed 'IE Singapore' from 2002, cooperated with associations representing motion picture, music and software to launch public education programmes. They developed posters bearing the words, 'Stop Piracy! Be Original,

---

104 Zeng Qingkai, 'IPR Protection Noted at Fair', *China Daily*, 10 September 2002 (reporting on a seminar in Xiamen during the Sixth China International Fair for Investment and Trade). Available online from Factiva.

105 Ibid.

106 Ibid.

107 Ibid.

108 'Hong Kong Stars March against Piracy', *The Straits Times* [Singapore], 18 March 1999, at 1.

109 Ibid.

110 Lawrence Chung, 'Gunning for the Music Pirates', *The Straits Times* [Singapore], 5 April 2002 at A1.

111 Ibid.

Buy Original', which were distributed in schools, libraries and community centres. They also co-opted the services of radio stations and celebrities to drive the point home that 'pirated products will hurt [the public] eventually'.[112]

The clear lesson one might draw from these episodes is that, in order to improve the conditions under which foreign works are protected, local inventors, artistes and businesses must feel that they have a stake and begin to assert themselves. Often, local inventors or innovators may not be in a position to assert their rights. Consequently, if at all they desire to have lasting impacts, foreign interests need to merge with and become allies of local businesses.

In the past, any proposals for forming joint ventures, technology transfer arrangements and the like between foreign entities and local businesses were viewed as charitable gestures towards DCs. However, it seems that the working formula in the foreign businesses' quest to wipe out illegitimate imitations of their works is the creation of a combined activity with local businesses in each nation such that the latter view their association as more than cosmetic and deserving of further strengthening. When such circumstances materialize, the local businesses will naturally tend to demand adequate protection for their achievements and, simultaneously, that of their partners.

A case in point is India, where local automakers linked with US partners to benefit from joint R&D and the resulting IP.[113] In the specific agreement, it was specified that 'The US company will get ownership of all the patents that TCS registers in the auto field and TCS will get ownership of all the intellectual properties that are outside the US company's area of operation'.[114] Incentives for India to minimize 'piracy' or enforce its IP have also taken the shape of US businesses such as Cisco Systems, GE, Intel, IBM and Texas Instruments generating IP within India itself through their local subsidiaries.[115] Further evidence is supplied by the R&D activities of the US-based HelloSoft company to generate technology related to the Internet and telecommunications such as third-generation wireless (3G) at Hyderabad.[116]

In China, local businesses have challenged the legitimacy of foreign brands and sought to use IP to stop any inroads into their market. For instance, Coca-Cola faced a trademark infringement lawsuit by a Chinese domestic drinks producer

112 Lim Seng Jin, 'Anti-piracy Drive Targets Buyers', *The Straits Times* [Singapore], 9 December 1998, at 3.

113 'TCS in Talks With US Auto Major on R and D (both companies to jointly conduct R and D and to share intellectual property rights of R and D outcome)', *Business Standard* [India], 19 January 2004, at 1 (reporting on negotiations between Tata Consultancy Services (TCS) and unnamed US automakers). Available online from Factiva.

114 Ibid.

115 'India: The Big Idea Hub of Patents (large amount of intellectual property is being created for US companies in India)', *Times of India* (New Delhi), 4 January 2004, at 1. Available online from Factiva.

116 'HelloSoft To Ramp Up India Headcount, Build Intellectual Property In 3G', *Financial Express*, 29 December 2003. Available online from Lexis-Nexis.

(a Shanghai-based company) for using a name (the Chinese character for 'Ku') similar to its own. Apparently Coca-Cola used the name 'Qoo' (or 'Ku Er' in Chinese characters) while the plaintiff used 'Ku Hai' and the characters for 'Er' and 'Hai' both mean 'children', thus creating the alleged confusion. Similarly, Nike had to respond to a copyright violation allegation by a certain online cartoonist for using a 'Stickman' cartoon figure in advertising.[117] Both disputes were settled out of court. Coca Cola had also to settle a claim in October 2003 for the alleged wrongful use of the photograph of a Chinese basketball star playing in the US for marketing its drinks in Shanghai, his hometown.[118]

In Honk Kong, a 'No Fakes Campaign' has been jointly conducted by the Intellectual Property Department of the government and the Hong Kong General Chamber of Commerce since 1998. Retail shops that pledge not to deal in counterfeit goods display logos that indicate such. They are assisted by their own trade organizations in monitoring the campaign.[119] The Hong Kong General Chamber of Commerce has also developed a 'code of ethics' on protection of IP to serve as 'broad guidelines' for businesses in their operations. The code counsels businesses against using illegitimate software or equipment in the workplace and to limit their copying to a reasonable portion of others' works. Businesses are also duty bound to educate their employees on the contents of the code.[120]

There has been increasing concern in Thailand that 'some famous goods are being exploited by other nationalities'.[121] A complaint was thus made to government officials by Thai restaurants in the US that the word 'Phad Thai' (Thai fried noodles) was used by foreign companies. They, therefore, sought 'protection to ensure that the authentic Thai cuisine would not be "stolen"'.[122] An official asserted that 'Phad Thai had a unique recipe and cooking technique handed down for generations. As Thailand cannot prohibit other countries from producing fried noodles, the government has to promote typical Thai cuisine including Phad Thai worldwide.'[123]

In a similar development, Thailand sought to stop a UK company's trademark application for a modified form of the 'tuk tuk', a slang for the popular three-

117 Amit Chanda, 'Copyright Cases Involving American Commercial Icons Highlight Chinese Intellectual Property Issues', *WMRC Daily Analysis*, 9 January 2004. Available online from Factiva.

118 Ibid.

119 See http://www.info.gov.hk/ipd/eng/information/studyaids/pub_ed_in_hk_c.htm.

120 Hong Kong General Chamber of Commerce, 'Press Release: Chamber Develops Code of Ethics on IPR Protection', 21 June 2000; available at http://www.chamber.org.hk/info/press_release/2000/000621.asp.

121 Somporn Thapanachai, 'Intellectual Property – Famous Thai Names Need Protection', *Bangkok Post*, 20 December 2001, at 1. Available online from Factiva.

122 Ibid.

123 Ibid.

wheeled scooter used as taxi, to be sold in Europe.[124] The feeling was that the 'tuk tuk' was a 'Thai symbol' and, hence, everything needed to be done to revoke the registration in the UK.[125] A Deputy Commerce Minister contended that this must have come about because 'Thai inventors of the Tuk Tuk vehicles have never sought to register a trade mark for their products ... making the vehicles vulnerable for foreigners to copy and patent the locally-invented products and brand names as their own'.[126] Nonetheless, the government expressed its determination to prevent the use of the word by companies in other countries (including the US).[127] An official of the Commerce Ministry stated, 'We see the registrations as an attempt to prevent someone else, especially Thai companies, to get into the markets. Therefore, we have to make some moves to protect opportunities for our product.'[128] In any case, the government did not succeed in removing the registration in the UK because the name 'Tuk Tuk' is generic.

Thailand has lately begun to chase after foreign counterfeiters and trademark violators of Thai silk, cosmetic products carrying local brands, music CDs by Thai artistes as well as Sriracha chilli sauce, noodles and jasmine rice.[129] However, the cost of international enforcement has been a problem for Thai IP owners. An official of the Department of Intellectual Property cited at least 20 countries, among them the United States, China and Vietnam where IP was violated and consequently hinted that the Department might post officials abroad to monitor such activities.

Private means of enforcement

Private mechanisms of enforcement are growing across Asia; private investigators and detectives are helping complainants collect evidence and keep track of illegitimate activities. Such investigators in turn create networks of informers and key contacts to tip them off about major organized pirating activities. Access to infringing materials and premises is often dependent on cultivating links with officials through gifts and other underhanded means. Incidentally, private investigators do not seem to be too worried about the long-term implications, for host countries, of the use of secret incentives and gifts to informers and officials.

---

124 'Thais Fight to Keep Tuk-Tuk Trademark', *The Straits Times* [Singapore], 4 January 2002 at A6.

125 Ibid.

126 'Government urges Thai Firms to Register Trade Marks', *Business Day* [Thailand], 7 January 2002. Available online from Factiva.

127 'Thai Government to Safeguard "Tuk-Tuk" Name Worldwide', *Associated Press Newswires* [Bangkok, Thailand], 13 February 2002. Available online from Factiva.

128 Ibid.

129 Edward Tang, 'Trademark Violation – Thais now on Receiving End', *The Straits Times* [Singapore], 20 July 2002, at 6.

A frequent means of raising public awareness and therefore of enforcing rights in Singapore has taken the shape of compelling alleged perpetrators to take up newspaper advertising pages to confess to their use of unauthorized materials and express unreserved apologies to the right-holders. Full-page advertising by such perpetrators has become common in the local press. One of the persistent themes of such full-page ads is the admission that the alleged victims own specified rights, though no further legal action would probably be taken against the alleged perpetrators. The educational value of the apologies as well as the noose that the perpetrators hang around their necks in view of any future relapse in their activities are undoubted benefits of this approach.

The persistence of the problem of piracy in Malaysia has also led to similar self-help moves. Out of desperation, one of the distributors of home videos 'decided to stop depending on the police or enforcement officers from government agencies. It has set up "enforcement" teams in every state in Malaysia'.[130]

The establishment of societies for the collection of fees and royalties from institutional users has gained ground, for example, in Singapore, Hong Kong and Japan. In Singapore, book publishers and local authors have set up the Copyright Licensing and Administration Society (Class).[131]

More use of the judicial system

There has been a noticeable increase in the use of the legal system, such as in China, particularly to highlight the importance of the victim company's clout and to shame infringers. Thus after conducting a raid on 21 Shenzhen shops dealing in counterfeit items of Tiffany jewellery and confiscating more than 800 counterfeit items with the help of 50 officers from the State Administration for Industry and Commerce (SAIC), a partner of the law firm Baker & McKenzie, acting on behalf of Tiffany, declared 'We are happy because the operation has sent a clear message to those shop owners selling counterfeit items that we would act. The number of items seized is not that important'.[132]

However, the use of the courts by foreign businesses (such as in the auto industry) in China has at times backfired. The courts helped local businesses to ward off lawsuits from foreign proprietors by finding for the locals.[133] Toyota Motor Corporation thus lost to a Zhejiang-based Geely Group (a local carmaker)

130 Brendan Pereira, 'Piracy Woes: Malaysia's Entertainment Industry is Calling for Tougher Action against Copyright Infringement', *The Straits Times* [Singapore], March 2003, at A7.

131 'Authors Team up to Collect Copyright Dues', *The Straits Times* [Singapore], 28 January 2000, at 71.

132 Kelvin Wong, 'Officers go Lightly on "Tiffany" sellers', *South China Morning Post*, 19 November 2003. Available online from Factiva.

133 Arun Sudhaman, 'Brand IDs Under Attack in China', *Media*, 12 December 2003. Available online from Factiva.

in its claim that the latter had used a logo similar to its own, although Toyota had apparently registered its logo earlier than the local carmaker.[134] However, this has not deterred foreign companies from using the same route. Thus Nissan Beijing, General Motors and Honda have initiated legal action against local manufacturers, respectively for infringement of designs, copyright and trademarks. According to a lawyer with Baker & McKenzie, 'foreign companies feel they have no alternative but to test the waters in Chinese courts. Failing to take action is an invitation to more infringements.'[135] Moreover, such actions have a deterrence value in that Chinese companies would have to consider the 'risk of embarrassment through court proceedings'.[136] In any case, there is arguably a shift in attitudes towards litigation. 'In previous years, foreign companies often hesitated to confront PRC imitators, but it is now clear that this confrontation should be initiated as early as possible, in order to deter investment in the imitation brand'.[137]

Regional assistance in enforcement

ASEAN efforts to streamline the administrative and enforcement aspects of IP are widely known. There are two other major regional bodies that work towards the same objectives. The EC-ASEAN Intellectual Property Rights Co-operation Programme (ECAP II) seeks to aid in the protection and enforcement of IP among participating ASEAN countries by providing European expertise on the same processes. Ultimately the programme aims 'to strengthen the mutual trade and investment flows' between EU and Asian countries (which is incidentally the third largest export destination for the former).[138]

Similarly the Asia–Pacific Economic Cooperation (APEC) has lent its support to the enforcement effort by adopting 'the Comprehensive Strategy on IPR in APEC',[139] which sets out general guidelines for effective protection and enforcement of IP and coordination of the activities of member states. Specific forms of guidance are expected to be worked out.

Conclusion

The driving forces in the development and evolution of IP laws in Asian DCs are still external pressure and threats of sanctions. Both the US and EU conduct reviews

134 Ibid.

135 Ibid.

136 Ibid.

137 Ibid.

138 See http://www.ecap-project.org/ecap/site/en/.

139 'Comprehensive Strategy on IPR Protection in APEC', submitted by Japan at the XVII Intellectual Property Experts' Group Meeting, Vancouver, Canada, 8–9 July 2003, 2003/IPEG/024.

of the level and enforcement records of Asian DCs followed by instructions on what and how to change specific legal and practical situations. Thus shortly after the threat of the US became public, in 2003, the Philippines passed the Optical Media Act to punish illegal manufacture, imitation or sale of recordable media and reorganized the Videogram Regulatory Board as the Optical Media Board.[140]

There are signs of increasing weariness of Asian DCs that the US is not appreciative of what they have done to protect US IP in their respective countries. The Director of the Taiwanese Intellectual Property Office Tsai Lien-shen thus contended that the recently revised Copyright Law had 'effectively halted illegal commercial piracy at home' and that 'it is no longer easy to purchase copied CDs, DVDs and VCDs at night markets across the country'.[141] He asserted that the evidence of decrease in value of pirated material caught by US Customs over previous years proved their claims of much improvement, justifying taking Taiwan off the USTR annual list.[142]

At the 2003 WTO biennial review of US trade policies and measures, Taiwan's representatives submitted a written report which called upon the US 'to recognise its efforts in protecting intellectual property rights (IPR) and its achievements in cracking down on commercial piracy'.[143] The Taiwan mission reportedly stated that placing Taiwan on the 'priority watch list', 'has an adverse impact on Taiwan's international image. It urged the United States to exercise prudence before claiming that other countries' alleged discriminatory or unreasonable trade practices have caused damage to US commercial interests'.[144]

South Korea reacted similarly on discovering the latest placement of that country on the 'priority watch list'. The Ministry of Foreign Affairs and Trade 'expressed regret over the US lack of appreciation over Seoul's progress in protecting intellectual property rights (IPRs), especially against music, recording and film piracy'.[145] An unnamed official of the Ministry of Culture and Tourism also reportedly called the latest US action 'unconvincing' because, according to him, IP protection of 'music records and movies in Korea have improved over the past few years'.[146] Others speculated that the US action may have been in retaliation for the South Korean ban of US beef imports because of the fear of the mad cow disease.[147]

---

140 'Philippine House Ratifies Anti-Piracy Bill', *Asia Pulse*, 29 January 2004. Available online from Factiva.

141 Flor Wang, 'Taiwan Efforts "noticeable" in cracking down on IPR violations', Central News Agency (Taipei), 13 January 2004. Available online from Factiva.

142 Ibid.

143 'US Urged to Recognise Taiwan's Efforts in IPR Protection', *Asia Pulse* [Geneva], 15 January 2004. Available online from Factiva.

144 Ibid.

145 'Seoul Suspects US Motives for Retaliatory Step', *Korea Times*, 10 January 2004. Available online from Factiva.

146 Ibid.

147 Ibid.

The growing resentment against the charge of piracy levelled at Asian nations has not led to any concerted attempt to redefine the nature of the dispute that continues to simmer between those nations and the US. Asian nations could, at least, impress upon their critics the existence of palpable factors that contribute to the lack of progress in IP enforcement. In particular, they could help them appreciate the depth of hostility towards, or irrelevance of, the notion of property in ideas that the general public in Asia feels should be shared.

It must also be noted that the rapidly increasing efforts of local artistes, inventors and businesses to gain recognition and protection for their works from Asian states have the potential to transform the IP landscape. Foreign IP holders could accelerate such a development by supporting it instead of permanently yelling at Asian nations for the well-established lack or inadequacy of protection. Ultimately, if foreign IP holders seek to attain the same objectives as the budding artistes and innovators in most of Asia, there is no better alternative than linking up with them in all possible ways and working together. There is very little that the probable establishment of an 'IP Attaché' at US legations around the world, in keeping with the much recent practice of setting up an FBI branch everywhere, can do.

Chapter 9

The Economics of Intellectual Property Enforcement in Asia: Who Should Pick Up the Bills?

Introduction

The role of the intellectual property (IP) system in national economies and cultures has been studied for many decades now. Attempts to measure its impact have not, however, been successful. Most of the attempts have concentrated on the patent system. The view seemed to be that the value of a patent system to an economy could be measured in terms of the returns that recognition made possible for innovators and inventors. It is a matter of historical record that Abraham Lincoln exalted the status of that system in 1859 with these words: 'The Patent System added the fuel of interest to the fire of genius'. However, nearly a hundred years later, doubts were expressed as to whether it had made positive contributions to the US economy.[1] Similarly, in the 1970s and 1980s, these views were reinforced by other studies in Canada,[2] Australia[3] and the UK.[4]

Studies of the impact of the intellectual property system on national economies and cultures have since become more cautious, although voices and interests allied to or linked with Western IP owners continue to exalt its value both to Western as well as non-Western societies and economies[5] without distinction. In the UK, the

1 F. Machlup, *An Economic Review of the Patent System*, Study No. 15 of Commission on Judiciary, Subcommittee on Patents, Trademarks, and Copyrights, 85th Congress, 2d Session, 1958.

2 Economic Council of Canada, *Report on Intellectual and Industrial Property*, 1971.

3 Mandeville, T. et al., *Economic Effects of the Australian Patent System* [A commissioned report for the Australian Industrial Property Advisory Committee], 1982.

4 C.T. Taylor and Z.A. Silberston, *The Economic Impact of the Patent System: A Study of the British Experience*, Cambridge University Press: Cambridge, 1973.

5 For instance, a study conducted on Egypt (by two Egyptian academics) enthusiastically and unreservedly endorsed the post-TRIPS regime. See, Mohamed Abou El Farag Balat and Mohamed Hossam Loutfi, 'The TRIPS Agreement and Developing Countries: A Legal Analysis of the Impact of the New Intellectual Property Rights Law on the Pharmaceutical Industry in Egypt' [2004] 2 *Web Journal of Current Legal Issues* 1. (Available at http://webjcli.ncl.ac.uk/2004/issue2/balat2.html#Heading370; accessed 31 March 2007.)

most recent Gower Report (issued on 6 December 2006)[6] leant firmly towards a wholesale endorsement of the IP system.[7] Another study of the role of copyright for the US economy[8] has done the same.

By contrast, Western IP owners routinely rage against 'counterfeiting' and 'piracy', often with the latter as the general tag, as the ultimate causes of the erosion of the value of the IP system. The IP literature often portrays the emerging economies or newly industrializing countries (NICs), that is, countries seeking to catch up with the advance of the industrial nations and on the verge of doing so, as the main culprits in this regard. Yet, this is a simplistic formulation of the problem of enforcement of IP in general as well as in NICs.

This chapter aims to explore the nature of the problems of 'counterfeiting' and 'piracy' in general in order to determine whether or not responsibility for its occurrence as well as eradication lies entirely with NICs, as Western IP owners and their loyal commentators and experts would seek to have us believe. The chapter thus first briefly outlines the nature of the problems of 'counterfeiting' and 'piracy'. It then discusses the role of non-IP issues in the problem of enforcement. Finally, it tries to tackle the issue of who must pay the bills for enforcement of IP. The chapter concludes that the constant pressure brought to bear on NICs and other nations might soon reach a point of no return where the IP system in those nations could collapse unless the industrial powers recognize the imminent danger and start to work towards an appropriate response, chiefly a financial settlement within those nations as regards fee structures for protection of foreign IP.

'Counterfeiting' and 'piracy'

A major concern for the industrial nations, in particular the US, remains the purported 'counterfeiting' and/or 'piracy' of their goods and technology in NICs. Although conceptual and practical distinctions remain between the two, the extant literature is more and more tending to jumble them together under the latter term. Daily news reports have also opted to use the latter term, apparently in consonance with the IP owners' predilection to portray any alleged acts as a moral outrage and not susceptible to determination of whether transgressions of the law may have occurred. Still, this chapter looks at the two separately before examining the combined effects on the problem of enforcement.

---

6 Available online at http://www.hm-treasury.gov.uk/media/583/91/pbr06_gowers_report_755.pdf; accessed 31 March 2007.

7 The Report concludes thus: 'The Review has shown that while in many regards the UK IP system works well, there are a number of areas where it could perform even better. The Review has made a number of recommendations to improve the framework for innovation.' Ibid., at 119.

8 See, Stephen E. Siwek, *Engines of Growth: Economic Contributions of the U.S. Intellectual Property Industries* [November 2005] (commissioned study for NBC Universal); available at http://nbcumv.com/corporate/Engines_of_Growth.pdf.

Counterfeiting

Counterfeiting is defined as 'affixing false or deceptive trademarks to products in order to make them superficially indistinguishable from their brand name counterparts'.[9] It is apparently undertaken with the intent to make the copy virtually indistinguishable from the original. It could thus be equated to the theft of reputation through deception. Although economic losses are suffered by the victim, hazards to health and crops have also been known to occur through the use of counterfeit insecticides, for instance. Thus, in Kenya, the coffee crop for 1979–1980 was devastated owing to defective fertilizers.[10]

There is no doubt that those who undertake counterfeiting systematically and on a large scale reap enormous benefits from their efforts. The contribution to the national economy may be such that countries that forbid it by law may be tempted to turn a blind eye to the goings on.[11] As Prebluda adds,

> Apparently, in most developing nations, counterfeiting is an inevitable phenomenon, which is endemic to a particular stage of development. For example, Japan was, notorious for producing counterfeit goods during the 1950s. At that time, the Japanese government permitted the copying of foreign goods, because counterfeiting aided Japanese industry striving to catch up with the Western world.[12]

It goes without saying that a solution to the persistence of counterfeiting in NICs must, apart from other things, take into account their economic, legal and cultural circumstances. Often, counterfeiting is a function of the impact of the demonstration effect on millions of would-be consumers of well-established brands as well as the non-affordability of the genuine goods to those masses. In addition, the relevant national authorities might not always be equipped to detect it when it occurs. There are also legal issues that pose difficulties to those authorities. Where the imitation of a mark is not accompanied by imitation of the total image of a merchandise, should enforcement agencies treat this as either? In addition, the difficulty of meeting the requirement of proof of intention in criminal proceedings

---

9 Quoted in Diane E. Prebluda, 'Countering International Trade in Counterfeit Goods', 12(2) *Brooklyn Journal of International Law* 339–67, March 1986, at note 1. TRIPS consists of a note by way of clarifying the operations of customs authorities under Article 51: '"counterfeit trademark goods" shall mean any goods, including packaging, bearing without authorization a trademark which is identical to the trademark validly registered in respect of such goods, or which cannot be distinguished in its essential aspects from such a trademark, and which thereby infringes the rights of the owner of the trademark in question under the law of the country of importation'.

10 Prebluda, note 9, above, ibid., at 341.

11 Ibid., at 342.

12 Ibid., at 342.

may inhibit any success in stamping it out. Where proof has become available, should the counterfeiters be compelled to disclose the entire chain of suppliers under the penalty of further imprisonment or fine for refusal?

Piracy

'Piracy' is not a term that has been defined appropriately or found a place within intellectual property law. The Agreement on Trade-Related Aspects of Intellectual Property Rights (TRIPS) surreptitiously introduced the term by way of defining the phrase in the text of Article 51.

> 'pirated copyright goods' shall mean any goods which are copies made without the consent of the right holder or person duly authorized by the right holder in the country of production and which are made directly or indirectly from an article where the making of that copy would have constituted an infringement of a copyright or a related right under the law of the country of importation.

Note that the term was used in TRIPS merely as an equivalent to infringement and nothing more. Yet, the World Trade Organization has sought to erect a wall between infringement and 'piracy' through its interpretation of the TRIPS.

> The [TRIPS] Agreement makes a distinction between infringing activity in general, in respect of which civil judicial procedures and remedies must be available, and counterfeiting and piracy – the more blatant and egregious forms of infringing activity – in respect of which additional procedures and remedies must also be provided, namely border measures and criminal procedures. For this purpose, counterfeit goods are in essence defined as goods involving slavish copying of trademarks, and pirated goods as goods which violate a reproduction right under copyright or a related right.[13]

Indeed, some have sought to use it as blanket term covering all forms of infringement as well as use of foreign works that may not have obtained appropriate legal protection in a host country. The Free Software Foundation contends, 'Publishers often refer to prohibited copying as "piracy". In this way, they imply that illegal copying is ethically equivalent to attacking ships on the high seas, kidnapping and murdering the people on them.'[14]

Streams of statistics are compiled and fed into the daily press and the Internet to drive home the point that 'counterfeiting' and 'piracy' are not insignificant or infrequent. All the figures tend to suggest that IP owners everywhere are in

---

13 See, 'TRIPS: IPRs Enforcement' at http://www.wto.org/english/thewto_e/whatis_e/eol/e/wto07/wto7_29.htm#note2; accessed 31 March 2007.

14 See, 'Some Confusing or Loaded Words and Phrases that are Worth Avoiding', http://www.gnu.org/philosophy/words-to-avoid.html; accessed 31 March 2007.

a perilous situation.[15] Nevertheless, the statistics provided by the agencies representing the Western IP owners on the extent of piracy may not be totally reliable. In the first place, the statistics are conjectural. For instance, instances of piracy are calculated on the probable use of software on machines other than those for which the software is purportedly purchased. An official of the Business Software Alliance (BSA) reportedly contended that 'The main source of software piracy remains businesses buying one copy of software legally and then installing it over several computers'.[16] According to this view, the estimated global software piracy rate in 2001 was 40 per cent. The BSA claimed that the rate had come down allegedly due to the educational activities it mounted.[17]

The statistics produced by all kinds of organizations have not gone unnoticed, principally by Western governments. Mounting external pressure on Asian and African nations, as on other nations elsewhere, has built up as annual reports of culprits and pirate nations have taken shape and proliferated. The tirades against the culprits extend to threats of retaliatory action, particularly by the US and more and more by the EU and Japan. The US has moved to issue 'recommendations' for governments in Asia and elsewhere to put into practice. These consist of an appraisal of the laws and practices in each country and directives as to what needs to be done by the respective country if that country seeks to remain on friendly terms or continue to trade with the US.

Lately, the US has put its weight behind a slew of measures that have yet to find acceptance among its own peers (the EU) and pushed them onto the statute books of other nations. The first victim of such an exercise in Asia was Singapore, which had to accept 'TRIPS plus' formulae in exchange for trade privileges and a guarantee for its security under the US umbrella within a strife-prone region.

The Role of Non-IP Issues

The problem of IP enforcement is generally viewed as independent of other issues that bedevil nations and societies struggling to feed their population, provide essential services and create an environment that facilitates and promotes economic advance and the general well-being. The fact of the matter, however, is that IP issues in the latter group of nations figure as peripheral to other more important, or even urgent, issues they face on a daily basis: building and maintaining an adequate infrastructure for communications, transportation and administration;

15 Thus the International Intellectual Property Alliance estimated for 2005–6 that the US copyright industries would lose US$5.2 billion in the Asia Pacific alone with China accounting for the US$2.2 billion. See http://www.iipa.com/statistics.html; accessed 31 March 2007.

16 See, 'Study: Software Officials Says Piracy Declined Last Year', *Dow Jones International News*, 2 June 2003. Available online from Factiva.

17 Ibid.

extending public education to all corners of the nation; combating diseases, some of which assume epidemic proportions; the provision of clean water and electricity – the list can go on and on.

In the end, any lapse in the enforcement of IP merges with the general problem of the establishment of the rule of law, of the recognition of civil rights and their implementation in practice. In societies where civil rights have yet to become part of the body politic, it should not make one wonder why IP enforcement is deficient, for the role of law has yet to become central to business and social life in most parts of Asia. The persistent call, therefore, for enforcement of IP in those nations should never lose sight of the fact that IP is an aspect of those civil rights which do not find themselves at the centre of business and social life. One thus wonders why, for instance, the US does not issue watch lists and the like on the basis of its annual human rights abuse reports and the well-known lack of democratic governance in the large number of Non-ICs and NICs?

Who Should Pick up the Bills?

To state the obvious, the enforcement of IP (through more training of personnel, regular raids, prosecutions and border controls, amongst others) demands deployment of resources. Yet these resources are critically lacking in most of Asia and Africa. The persistent call therefore for more deployment of such resources by the developing nations is an urge to allocate resources meant for other purposes such as health and education.

The competing demands on the public purse in Asian and African nations are such that expending any amount on the enforcement of IP of foreign origin would appear to be unjustified. Thus in Malaysia, the public prosecution of IP infringers had to give way to that of illegal immigrants.[18] This is not simply because of the non-availability of sufficient funds, but also the lack of trained prosecutors and appropriately staffed judicial bodies as well as the priority of domestic issues over and above largely foreign-based concerns.

In effect, this is an attempt to force such nations to subsidise the economies of the industrial nations since the dominant share of the stock of IP in such nations belongs to businesses and entities in the industrial world. While developing nations have no option but to acquiesce to such pressures, at least nominally, the swell of mass opinion is gradually to resent them. In the long run, these resentments could fuel boycotts of US goods and services. It is often forgotten that the soft power that the US has amassed is dependent on a perception of fair play in its international affairs. No sooner than this perception changes to that of a US wielding its power irrationally and as a bully, than the mass appeal of its goods and services could collapse. In the end, therefore, US intransigence and its whip of permanent pressure

18 [Institute of Development Studies, University of Sussex] 'Intellectual Property Rights', Trade & Investment Background Briefing No. 6, no date.

raised and meted out against the developing nations might backfire. Signs of a retaliatory boycott of US goods and services have already appeared.[19]

In short, the enforcement of IP in NICs has become increasingly dependent on whether those nations can bear the costs. These are in turn dependent on public education, infrastructure development. Developing nations could be co-opted into upholding foreign IP rights and protection if adequate fiscal measures are implemented. Thus, for example, famous marks could pay the accrued costs of protection to the national economies and earn their legal status instead of attempting to push into the developing countries' space surreptitiously or treating them as colonies and barbarians. An appropriate methodology for taxation of foreign IP should be worked out taking into account, among others things:

a. the period of association of the respective IP in the specific nation;
b. the period of protection that the respective IP has enjoyed on the home country before it has sought protection in the specific host country; and
c. the fee structures employed by the home country and the appropriate level of fee payable at the relevant time.

A second front of action would be to address the problem of pricing brand goods beyond the pockets of the average consumer in developing nations, discussed in Chapter 8.[20] Thirdly, foreign companies and countries should find appropriate formulae for reining in their avarice and encouraging piracy abroad with a view to cutting the ground from under the feet of their competitors at home. It should be perfectly legitimate that countries where this has occurred (as reported in China in the past) should be awarded compensation, as they bear the brunt of the criticism and retaliatory actions of the industrial nations at the same time as falling victim to manipulation and illicit activities by multi-national corporations that operate in them.

There are also developments in the developing countries that encourage more attention to IP. Governments are more than ever ready and willing to attract foreign capital and technology. There is a growing perception that the public needs to be educated about the value and relevance of IP to the local economies. An added momentum has been created by a growing movement of local artists, inventors and entrepreneurs for better protection of their own works and activities. Local

19 A Chinese commentator asserted, 'since the anti-terrorism war was launched, people in the Middle East have become increasingly disgusted with US products. Before the United States started war against Iraq, US exports to the Middle East region dropped by 25 percent–40 percent. McDonald's declared that it would close 175 branches in 10 Muslim countries, Coca Cola's sales volume also began to go down.' See, 'Price Paid for Victory of "Hard Strength"', *People's Daily Online*, 13 February 2004. Accessed online from Factiva.

20 For a discussion of efforts in that direction in Asia, see, Chapter 8, at 178–181.

businesses intent on joining up with foreign businesses in ventures of all kinds realize that the gains of stronger protection will serve mutual purposes.

Again, some local businesses have devised private (self-help) forms of protection. In Ethiopia, film makers in local languages have taken the step of not releasing their work until well after the potential audience has had a chance to go to their local 'customized cinemas' and viewed the respective film. This was a development over the earlier practice of releasing copies of their films through rental businesses, which unfortunately led to rampant copying by borrowers and circulation of illegal copies.

Other instruments of self-help are the shaming of recalcitrant infringers through the press, whereby the offenders take and pay for advertising space in which their grovelling apologies are broadcast. The rise of collective societies and private agencies that trail pirates and collect evidence against them has also increased the reach against illegal activities.

Actions through the legal system, even where circumstances did not warrant a positive outcome, have helped raise the profile of proprietors at the same time as sending clear messages to infringers that no stone will be left unturned to tackle the problem.

Conclusion

The persistent pressures of the industrial powers on NICs and countries much lower in their economic standings to enforce their IP laws (and thereby protect, for the most part, the interests of foreign proprietors) has led to pleadings for reason and lenient treatment,[21] on the one hand, and diffidence by some of the NICs on the other hand. The reality of the profound causes for lack of enforcement has not yet forced itself onto the agenda of all nations, let alone helped redefine their respective responsibilities. The more NICs and similarly inclined nations have been pushed to the wall and decried as outlaws and pirates, the less it seems possible that these nations will be convinced of the cause of the industrial powers to have their citizens' rights protected regardless of the NICs' internal circumstances and difficulties.

The solutions for the increasingly dim prospects of any progress in the direction that Western industrial powers expect seem to be reassessing the financial burdens of the task at hand for the NICs. Mainly this will take the shape of reallocating burdens to the proprietors or agencies of Western industrial powers that are outposts of enforcement in the NICs. This might be done through:

21 L.T.C. Harms, 'Offering Cake for the South', 22(10) *European Intellectual Property Review* 451 October 2000, at 451 (appealing to those powers to be considerate towards the 'poor South').

a. a redefined fee structure for recognition of rights by NICs, the earmarking of a portion of the receipts of IP administrative authorities in Western industrial nations and Japan or some other financial outlay that will alleviate the permanent shortfall within NICs; or
b. the Western industrial nations and Japan working for a more comprehensive settlement of the diversity of social, political and economic ills of the NICs and other nations and helping, in their own self-interest, broader and extensive changes to take place.

It would seem that the building up of further pressure applied to NICs might soon reach a breaking point and the entire façade of allegiance to IP legal norms and enforcement in those nations and across the South might collapse entirely. The Western industrial powers and Japan should therefore realize before it is too late that the unending piling of blame and pressure onto NICs and other nations might backfire, with disastrous consequences to their IP owners.

Chapter 10
Free Trade Agreements as Surrogates for 'TRIPS Plus'*

Introduction

For over a century, the path for intellectual property (IP) law-making in the developing countries (DCs) has deviated from that normally attributed to sovereign nations. Instead of providing support for the national economy, political space and cultural and social life, IP law-making has become a means of appeasing powerful external pressures on those nations. The quest of the major industrial nations to open up world trade through numerous bilateral and multilateral treaties culminating in the Agreement Establishing the World Trade Organization (WTO) in 1994 ended by imposing far-reaching IP laws on developing nations. However, that achievement has never fully satisfied the industrial powers, especially the US. The latter has continued to deploy additional devices to induce the DCs into further opening their domestic markets, principally for US goods and services but indirectly also for the industrial nations as a whole.

Inevitably, one of those devices has been to force DCs to transplant more IP laws from the US regardless of whether those laws have any relevance to the local economy and society. DCs have also been coaxed into acceding to a few more (post-TRIPS) multilateral treaties without being given or promised anything substantial in return. Far worse, they have been transformed into unwitting instruments for enforcement of those alien laws, despite the increasing recognition of their deleterious consequences to innovation and growth in DCs.

The most recent saga in harnessing the markets of DCs to those of the industrial countries comprises yet another wave of IP law-making at their expense. This latest wave has taken the shape of free trade agreements (FTAs) signed mainly between DCs and the industrial powers (such as the US and EU). The explosion in the number of 'FTAs' concluded even among DCs may create the impression that all nations must see benefits from them. However, the relatively larger number of FTAs signed by the EU and the US as compared with others as well as the key role they have assigned to IP in their FTAs belies that impression.

This chapter seeks to examine the salient aspects of the IP clauses in FTAs signed to date and their potential repercussions on DCs, including those in Asia.

---

* This chapter originally appeared, in the author's name, as 'Free-Trade Agreements as Surrogates for TRIPs Plus', 28(7) *European Intellectual Property Review* 374–80, 2006.

First the chapter briefly summarizes the evolution of IP law-making across developing nations. Then it highlights the relevant IP provisions in the FTAs and analyses their significance for DCs. Finally, it inquires into the potential difficulties that the FTAs might face in their implementation and their standing vis-à-vis the current debate on IP in the Doha Round.

The chapter concludes that the FTAs have pushed the debate on IP in DCs ever higher on the agenda of international trade and development and that any progress that the EU and US could hope to make in pre-empting dissonance in ongoing multilateral trade negotiations might be short-sighted. It argues that the FTAs will accentuate the fundamental divergence of IP laws from the conditions, requirements and capabilities for enforcement of DCs.

A Brief Sketch of the Evolution of Intellectual Property in Developing Countries

In the area of IP law-making, developing countries (DCs) as a group have suffered from several rounds of unequal treatment and coercion by the developed countries.[1] The first round took place during colonization. DCs were subjected to imposition of alien IP laws although often the process was portrayed as importation by the colonial powers in the purported service of the DCs themselves. The huge disparity in the social and economic standing of the colonizers and the colonized nations was never perceived to be enough cause to stop such transplantation, amongst others, of IP laws. Indeed, the laws were more in tune with the needs and requirements of the colonial trading/commercial outposts established by business interests of the metropolitan powers and were meant to serve them much more than the 'natives'.

The second round was during the so-called decolonization period (late 1950s and 1960s). DCs were cheated out of debunking the alien IP laws, indeed of any laws that had not taken root in the local environment. Instead, they were hoodwinked or compelled into accepting more foreign laws with the promise that those laws were the *sine qua non* for their modernization or westernization.[2] Thus

---

1 For a summary of the developments in Asia, see, C. Antons, 'Legal Culture and History of Law in Asia', in Christopher Heath (ed.), *Intellectual Property Law in Asia*, Kluwer Law International: London, 2003, at 13–35. See also, A. Endeshaw, *Intellectual Property Policy for Non-Industrial Countries*, Dartmouth: Aldershot, 1996, pp. 146–76 (regarding developments in Africa).

2 See for instance, James A. Gardner, *Legal Imperialism: American Lawyers and Foreign Aid in Latin America*, The University of Wisconsin Press: Madison, WI, 1980. See also, Kristin Mann and Richard Roberts (eds), *Law in Colonial Africa*, Heinemann: London, 1991. For a critique of the legal modernisation perspective, see David M. Trubek and Marc Galanter, 'Scholars in Self-estrangement: Some Reflections on the Crisis in Law and Developmet Studies in the Unitied States', 1 *Wisconsin Law Review* 1062, 1974.

in Ghana, where Kwame Nkrumah advocated a radical departure in the life of the nation, the legal system was never touched, let alone revised.[3] Asian legal systems still manifest diverse colonial heritages (Spanish, Dutch, British, Portuguese, French and others) and the resulting complexities.[4]

The third round was in the 1970s and 1980s. The increasing frustrations of DCs with the lack of opportunities to develop their economies and pull themselves out of the mire of disease, poverty and technological backwardness bred fresh initiatives to reform the international IP system in their favour. However, their efforts were blocked at every step and any concessions made to them (such as the 1969 Stockholm Protocol) were nullified by the start of the Uruguay Round of GATT negotiations.

The fourth round started with the passage of the Agreement on Trade-Related Aspects of Intellectual Property Rights (TRIPS) in 1994, as part of the WTO. The TRIPS represented a total shutdown of any prospects of DCs finding suitable paths for encouraging innovation and creativity domestically. The little gains that DCs had made in the international debate in the 1960, 1970s and 1980s as well as some of the openings available to them in the major IP conventions (to inject their domestic requirements into their local laws) were totally obliterated by the TRIPS. Indeed, the efforts of DCs to be able to exercise their sovereign right to devise their own laws to reflect their economic, social and cultural aspirations for transformation began to be seen as desiring to 'weaken' IP,[5] to 'pirate' other nations' IP[6] or any number of other highly emotive charges. Instead, TRIPS began to be propagated by the major industrial powers and champions of 'property rights theory',[7] as if all nations needed to have identical laws and the types of those laws had to be determined by the powerful nations.

Moreover, the new-found role of DCs as conduits for implementation of measures and rules in favour of international economic forces (whose interests the governments of the industrial nations champion) has been propagated as a natural development in international political economy.[8] The gradual abdication of the state in DCs from assuming and executing national economic and political tasks but, instead, espousing foreign economic and political interests has also been viewed as an inevitable development of the latter part of the twentieth century.

---

3 See Endeshaw, note 1, above, at 156.

4 See Antons, note 1, above, ibid.

5 Robert M. Sherwood, *Intellectual Property and Economic Development*, Westview Press: Boulder, CO, 1990.

6 See Marshall A. Leaffer, 'Protecting United States Intellectual Property Abroad: Toward a New Multilateralism', 76 *Iowa Law Review* 273, 1991.

7 See, for instance, Justin Hughes, 'The Philosophy of Intellectual Property', 77 *Georgetown Law Journal* 287, 1988.

8 See generally, Gunther Teubner (ed.), *Global Law Without a State*, Dartmouth: Aldershot, 1997.

The fifth round of unequal treatment and coercion has set in with the rise of FTAs deployed especially by the US as tools for extending, among other things, the IP obligations of DCs beyond those codified in TRIPS, in other words during the last decade. FTAs signed among DCs or between DCs and what are known as 'emerging economies' (such as Chile, Taiwan or Mexico) in the post-WTO period generally make, if at all, nominal references to IP. On the other hand, FTAs formulated by the US and, to a lesser extent, Japan and the EU leave DCs with no choice but to accept more onerous IP and enforcement regimes than they are prepared to put up with.

The US, in particular, is relentlessly negotiating FTAs with all kinds of DCs regardless of the latter's economic or technological base and whatever the implications might be for their pursuit of progress. Indeed, it seems determined to take all DCs 'hostages' first before even starting to initiate any movement towards TRIPS plus with the other major industrial nations. This manoeuvre to have all DCs endorse any TRIPS plus provisions that the US has failed to push through at the multilateral level might eventually lead to a greater number of DCs adopting new IP rules and obligations they would not have done otherwise. As it is, various nations, including those organized as the G20,[9] have expressed their disenchantment with previously concluded treaties, including TRIPS, and with the diverse obligations they view as too onerous even after the passage of 10 years since they were adopted.

While striving to move the goal posts of international trade by tackling DCs one by one and injecting TRIPS plus provisions into the laws of those nations through the mechanisms of FTAs, the US and its major partners have relentlessly pursued ways of scuttling any resistance to their agenda and the intense pressures in the Doha round. After the of failure of the Cancun Ministerial meeting in September 2003, the US Trade Representative was contemptuous of the widespread opposition to the relentless pressure of the EU, US and Japan to open up the market in DCs without any corresponding concessions on their part. He asserted, 'one of the problems we ran into was that a number of countries just thought it was a freebie – they could just make whatever points they suggested, argue, and not offer and

9 This is a coalition of DCs that was formed in reaction to US and EU manoeuvres in trade negotiations in the Doha Round. According to one report 'Just before Cancun, an attempted coup d'etat of sorts, by the US and the EC, in agreeing between themselves and tabling a framework package on agriculture (accommodating each other at the expense of the developing countries), became a putsch – when Brazil and India brought together quickly a coalition of developing countries with offensive and defensive interests in agriculture and leading to the formation of the G20 and their counter to the US–EC package'. See Chakravarthi Raghavan, 'Time Ripe for WTO Transparency, Inclusiveness, Orderly Procedures?' *Third World Network*, 6 August 2004; available at http://www.twnside.org.sg.

give. And now they're going to face the cold reality of that strategy, coming home with nothing'.[10]

One of the contested issues between the US and EU and Japan on the one hand and the DCs on the other relates to the reform of patent law as proposed in the 'substantive patent law treaty' (SPLT). It is to be recalled that many DCs have openly rejected any moves towards expanding the scope of patents; on the contrary, many have sought to remove current obligations such as in the areas of process/product patents for drugs. Yet, it is interesting that, in January 2005, the US, EU, Canada, Australia and Japan held secret meetings in Washington[11] to streamline their positions on advancing their causes in international IP and thwart the emerging demand for a 'development agenda' in WIPO and beyond. As one commentator noted, 'The fear is that the larger economies, and the United States in particular, are trying to show they can take the negotiations outside of WIPO if that organization cannot keep the talks on track by keeping developing countries in check. That would leave developing countries out of any agreement reached by the larger economies'.[12]

The lack of agreement among all parties in the projected global harmonization of national patent systems, including the fact that the WIPO General Assembly decided, in October 2006, to put any further discussion of the draft on hold for 2007, prompted the 'Group B+' countries to forge ahead in their efforts to undertake the same with the hope of foisting it on the rest later on.[13]

Intellectual Property Provisions in Free Trade Agreements

It will not be possible, in the limited space available, to undertake a detailed analysis of the huge number and diversity of FTAs signed over the last decade, even where the topic of interest is an aspect of those FTAs, namely IP. Instead, we will look at the IP provisions in some of the FTAs that the major industrial countries have concluded with DCs before briefly looking at the projects of the emerging economies (Singapore and South Korea) in the same direction.

---

10 Bruce Odessey [Cancun, Mexico], 'WTO Cancun Negotiations Collapse; Trade Deal By 2005 Seen as Unlikely', 14 September 2003; available at [The US Mission to the European Union] http://www.useu.be/Categories/WTO/Sept1403CancunCollapse.html.

11 William New, 'Washington Patent Meeting Stirs Concerns', *Intellectual Property Watch*; available at http://www.ip-watch.org.

12 Ibid.

13 See, William New and Tove Iren S. Gerhardsen, 'Group B+ Draft Patent Harmonisation Treaty Emerges', *Intellectual Property Watch*, 7 November 2006 available at http://www.ip-watch.org.

European Union

In recent years, the EU has concluded a growing number of FTAs (often referred to as 'Association Agreements') with South and Eastern Mediterranean countries: the Palestinian Authority (1997), Tunisia (1998), Israel (2000), Morocco (2000), Algeria (2001), Jordan (2002), Lebanon (2002), Egypt (2004), Syria (2004) and Serbia (2008).[14] Similar agreements are under negotiation, for instance with Canada, South Korea and Saudi Arabia. The agreements include provisions relating to cooperation in intellectual property.

The EU signed a Trade, Development and Cooperation Agreement (TDCA) with South Africa in 1999, creating a Free Trade Area between them. The intellectual property provision in the TDCA (Article 46) expresses the parties' agreement to 'ensure adequate and effective protection of intellectual property rights in conformity with the highest international standards', including TRIPS, and that they 'undertake to improve, where appropriate, the protection provided for under [TRIPS]'.[15]

As if to impress on South Africa the need to adhere to those 'highest standards', the TDCA states that the 'Community and its Member States confirm the importance they attach to the obligations arising' from the 1996 WIPO Treaties.[16] Indeed, the EU seems clearly disinclined to thrust those Treaties on South Africa when it suggests that 'South Africa could favourably consider accession to the multilateral conventions [that is the 1996 WIPO Treaties]'.[17] The same stance of the EU is also evident in Article 46(2): 'If problems in the area of intellectual property protection affecting trading conditions were to occur, urgent consultations shall be undertaken, at the request of either Party, with a view to reaching mutually satisfactory solutions'. Finally, the TDCA stipulates for the EU to 'provide, on request and on mutually agreed terms and conditions, technical assistance to South Africa'.[18]

The EU had signed an Economic Partnership, Political Coordination and Cooperation Agreement (the 'Global Agreement') with Mexico in December 1997 that came into force in October 2000. The IP concern in the EU–Mexico agreement appeared to be to create a means of dialogue and dispute resolution in cases where difficulties might arise. The relevant section is reproduced below.

CONSULTATION MECHANISM FOR INTELLECTUAL PROPERTY MATTERS

Article 40 – Special Committee on Intellectual Property Matters

14 http://europa.eu.int/comm/external_relations/.
15 Article 46(1), of the Trade, Development and Cooperation Agreement (TDCA).
16 Article 46(3), ibid.
17 Article 46(4), ibid.
18 Article 46(6), ibid.

> 1. The Joint Council hereby establishes a Special Committee on Intellectual Property Matters. The Special Committee shall be comprised of representatives of the Parties. The Special Committee shall be convened within 30 days following a request of either Party with a view to reaching mutually satisfactory solutions to difficulties arising in the protection of intellectual property. The office of chairman of the Special Committee shall be held alternatively by each of the Parties. The Special Committee shall report to the Joint Committee.
>
> 2. For purposes of paragraph 1, 'protection' shall include matters affecting the availability, acquisition, scope, maintenance and enforcement of intellectual property rights as well as those matters affecting the use of intellectual property rights.

The FTA that the EU signed with Chile in November 2002, 'The EU–Chile Association Agreement', provides for IP, in Article 32:

> 1. The Parties agree to cooperate, according to their own capabilities, in matters relating to the practice, promotion, dissemination, streamlining, management, harmonisation, protection and effective application of intellectual property rights, the prevention of abuses of such rights, the fight against counterfeiting and piracy, and the establishment and strengthening of national organisations for control and protection of such rights.
>
> 2. Technical cooperation can focus on one or more of the activities listed below:
>
> (a) legislative advice: comments on draft laws relating to the general provisions and basic principles of the international conventions listed in Article 170, copyright and related rights, trademarks, geographical indications, traditional expressions or complementary quality mentions, industrial designs, patents, layout-designs (topographies) of integrated circuits, protection of undisclosed information, control of anti-competitive practices in contractual licences, enforcement and other matters relating to the protection of intellectual property rights;
>
> (b) advice on the ways to organise administrative infrastructure, such as patent offices, collecting societies, etc;
>
> (c) training in the field of intellectual property rights administration and management techniques;
>
> (d) specific training of judges and Customs and Police Officers, in order to make the enforcement of laws more effective; and

(e) awareness-building activities for the private sector and civil society.

Again, as in the IP provision in the EU–Mexico agreement, Article 32 for Chile (above) emphasizes cooperation and refers to the parties' 'own capabilities', as a crucial definer of the assumed obligations. It seems plain that the EU was not intent on forcing either Mexico or Chile to adopt any higher standards of IP than might already be in place in either country. Indeed, the absence of any mention of whether the two 'emerging economies' need to approximate their IP laws to that of EU is symptomatic of the 'persuasive' approach that has already been noticed of the EU during the Uruguay Round negotiations.[19] Moreover, the consideration given to the parties' 'own capabilities' would be indicative of the EU's sensitivity to perceptible imbalances between the contracting parties.

Overall, therefore, the IP clauses in the bilateral arrangements of the EU remain within the domain of enforcement of current obligations rather than, as in the case of the US, an attempt to extend the range or depth of IP rights.

Japan

In comparison with the EU and US, Japan has fewer FTAs and more 'partnership' or cooperation agreements, although it has not failed to inject its concerns about IP in whatever form of agreement it has engaged in. Thus 'The Agreement between Japan and the United Mexican States for the Strengthening of Economic Partnership' (which entered into force in April 2005) refers to IP matters in a peripheral manner (in Articles 8 and 144). Article 8 refers to the parties' agreement on a list of geographic indications for spirits, as per TRIPS. Article 144 ('Cooperation in the Field of Intellectual Property') concerns cooperation. It states as follows:

> The Parties, recognising the growing importance of intellectual property … as a factor of economic competitiveness in the knowledge-based economy, and of IP protection in this new environment, shall develop their cooperation in the field of IP. Such cooperation may include the exchange of information on:
>
> (a) public awareness activities of the importance of IP protection and the function of IP protection systems to their respective nationals;
>
> (b) improvement of IP protection systems and their cooperation;
>
> (c) policy measures conducive to ensuring adequate enforcement of IP rights;

19 F.-K. Beier and G. Schricker (eds), *WIPO or GATT?: New Ways in the International Protection of Intellectual Property*, VCH: Weinheim, 1989.

(d) automation of administrative processes of IP authority in order to enhance its efficiency.

It is apparent that, just as the EU, the Japanese approach banks on persuading Mexico to work together with Japan to build up its intellectual property. There is no mention of any new IP rules that Japan might seek to have Mexico adopt or new expectations to work towards. Instead, the perception seems to be to create a consensus that might be beneficial to both parties. This is a far cry from the well-known US attitudes of hard bargains and tussles.

United States

The US has concluded FTAs with Canada and Mexico (NAFTA), Israel, Jordan, Chile, Singapore, Australia, Bahrain, Morocco, Southern African Customs Union (comprising Botswana, Lesotho, Namibia, South Africa and Swaziland), Panama and the Central American States (Costa Rica, El Salvador, Guatemala, Honduras and Nicaragua) while feverishly working on more (such as with the United Arab Emirates). The largest of these ongoing negotiations is for a 'Free Trade Area of the Americas' to bring together 34 countries of the Western Hemisphere (including Chile and the Central American countries). The US is also intent on extending the Singapore FTA (started in 2000 and put into effect in January 2005) to other ASEAN nations. It had declared its plan through its 26 October 2002 announcement of 'the Enterprise for ASEAN Initiative', and identified the possible candidates as being the Philippines, Thailand, Indonesia and Malaysia.[20] The FTA signed with Korea is currently awaiting approval by Congress while those with Thailand and Malaysia are in the pipeline.[21]

As in the past,[22] the US seems to have taken the current bilateral route (of FTAs) to shorten the long, drawn-out process of multilateral, post-TRIPS negotiations and to overcome the resistance of other countries to US manoeuvres and manipulations.[23] No doubt, the lining up of relatively small or economically marginal states as candidates for the adoption of the US position in international

20 [US]Congressional Budget Office, 'The Pros and Cons of Pursuing Free-Trade Agreements', 31 July 2003; available at www.cbo.gov.

21 See http://www.ustr.gov/Trade_Agreements/Bilateral.

22 For a discussion of the earlier use by the US of bilateral agreements as a means of pre-empting multilateral agreements and undercutting possible wrangles, see, S.P. Ladas, *The International Protection of Industrial Property*, Harvard University Press: Cambridge, MA, 1930.

23 In his statement to the press after the failure of the Cancun Ministerial, US Trade Representative Robert B. Zoellick declared, 'the United States has an agenda on multiple fronts. We're going to keep opening markets one way or another.' See Bruce Odessey [Cancun, Mexico], 'WTO Cancun Negotiations Collapse; Trade Deal By 2005 Seen as Unlikely', 14 September 2003; available at [The US Mission to the European Union] http://www.useu.be/Categories/WTO/Sept1403CancunCollapse.html. Apparently, he had

trade represents a shrewd tactical move. The US has steadfastly pursued the same policy over many decades. As State Department planner George Kennan put it in 1948:

> We have about 50 percent of the world's wealth, but only 6.3 percent of its population … In this situation, we cannot fail to be the object of envy and resentment. Our real task in the coming period is to devise a pattern of relationships which will permit us to maintain this position of disparity without positive detriment to our national security. To do so, we will have to dispense with all sentimentality and day-dreaming: and our attention will have to be concentrated everywhere on our immediate national objectives.[24]

The US singled out Singapore in Asia as a platform to project the new bilateral route of FTAs as the way forward in shaping international trade rules in its favour. Thus the USTR proclaimed, 'The leading edge U.S.–Singapore Free Trade Agreement (FTA) is the first U.S. FTA with an Asian nation and will serve as the foundation for other possible FTAs in Southeast Asia under President Bush's Enterprise for ASEAN Initiative (EAI)'.[25]

The FTAs the US has managed to sign with DCs cover a spectrum of issues that are part of multilateral negotiations begun at the Doha Ministerial in 2001. The TRIPS plus provisions in the US initiated FTAs consist of:

(a) Expansion of the scope of protection available for drugs manufacturers:

(i) extension of the patent term (by compensating time lost in processing patent application or registration of a drug);

(ii) making national drug regulatory authorities assume the tasks of patent enforcement agents – the FTAs impose on such authorities a new obligation to prevent registration (for 'marketing approval') of generic versions of patented drugs,[26] in other words to undertake the work of patent offices surreptitiously;

(iii) further restriction of compulsory licence by prohibition of transfer of test data and related knowhow;

(iv) protection of test data for 5–10 years;

---

stated to the same effect earlier: 'We will solve trade liberalization through bilateralism and regionalism if we need to'. Ibid.

24 See George Kennan, *State Department Policy Planning Study*, cited by Noam Chomsky in *On Power and Ideology: The Managua Lectures*, Black Rose: Montreal, 1987.

25 See USTR website, http://www.ustr.gov.

26 See Article 17.10.2(c) of the US–Chile Free Trade Agreement.

(v) restriction of generic production until the patent expires or the patentee grants consent.

(b) Limitations on parallel importation.

(c) Protection of program-carrying satellite signals.

(d) Removal of exceptions from patentability of life forms.

(e) Incorporation of the contents of obligations arising from the 1996 WIPO treaties.

It is easy to see how the IP provisions in FTAs have become direct means of furthering the US point of view in international trade. The wave of grass-roots protests against poverty, lack of medicines and access to educational materials and technology has inevitably emboldened many DCs to resist any further concessions in the multilateral trading system. The FTA route has therefore appeared to the US to be the only path left to advance its cause of opening the global market. Its status as 'the only superpower' has propelled it further in that direction. Consequently, the FTAs have become, in US hands, means of pre-empting multilateral negotiations which are unlikely to take on board US proposals or to agree to them in a short period of time.

That the US has single-handedly and in a rather arrogant manner thrust FTAs on DCs in much the same way as standard-term contracts used to be foisted on ordinary consumers is demonstrated by the similar structure, layout and contents of the IP provisions in those FTAs. Even the numbering of the chapters for IP incorporated in the agreements betrays an uncanny similarity across them – IP is in either Chapter 14 (Bahrain), 15 (Morocco), 16 (Singapore) or 17 (Australia and Chile) of the respective FTA. The high level of similarity of the provisions cannot be accidental any more than the fact that they largely ignore the diversity in the conditions of the respective signatory nations. Clearly, there must be a better explanation for this acquiescence on a grand scale than the mutuality of interests expressed in the preambles of the respective FTAs.

The emerging economies

Apart from the major industrial powers (the EU, US and Japan), some of the 'emerging economies', like Taiwan, Mexico, Chile, Singapore and South Korea, have initiated FTAs with DCs and among themselves. These groups of countries aspire to generate net inflow of income by participating in the technology trade (and the various forms of IP that control such trade). They have thus started to play the catch-up game by deploying FTAs.

For reasons that have been stated so often by its officials, Singapore is intent on making it to the next level of economic performance, perceived to be driven by the biotechnological revolution. It has also been considered axiomatic for Singapore that a robust IP system should be in place to realize that ambition. This may partly explain why Singapore has engaged in creating FTAs with all kinds of states.

Singapore has thus far concluded 13 FTAs with the likes of the US, New Zealand, Jordan, Australia, the European Free Trade Association, Korea, Japan, Panama and Switzerland.[27] The FTA with Jordan (by all accounts a DC) spells out in Article 8.8, the parties' obligations in IP: 'Each Party affirms its commitments in connection with intellectual property rights under the WTO Agreement'. Clearly, the parties do not intend to extend the existing international IP regime, merely to continue to be bound by them.

Singapore continues to negotiate similar FTAs with others in Latin America, Europe and Asia.[28] The official statement on the 'substantial agreement' reached in the negotiation with Panama disclosed that it 'covered a wide range of issues' and listed them at length,[29] but there was no specific mention of IP; the final agreement did not have any such provision either. This suggests that IP does not play a prominent part in FTAs undertaken by Singapore, perhaps lending credence to the Singapore government's oft-repeated aim of 'trade-liberalization'. The negotiation with Panama was as a matter of fact described as 'a Free Trade Agreement that will bring about greater trade liberalisation between the two countries'.[30]

Singapore's negotiations with Chile and New Zealand towards what has been dubbed 'the Pacific-Three Free Trade Agreement (P3 FTA)' appears to include IP as part of the topics under discussion.[31] Again, there is no indication that Singapore is trying to reach for the sky, following in the footsteps of the US.

South Korea too has started forging its own FTAs with a few countries. The South Korea–Chile free trade agreement was ratified in February 2004, a year after it was signed, partly because of opposition from farmers.[32] The objectives of the agreement in the area of IP has been stated clearly as the provision of 'adequate and effective protection and enforcement'.[33] The extended list of obligations placed in Article 16 of the FTA does no more than detail them. We reproduce below the most general of these:

27 See, http://www.fta.gov.sg/sg_fta.asp.

28 Ibid.

29 [Press Release, Ministry of Trade and Industry], 'Conclusion of the Second Round of the Panama–Singapore Free Trade Agreement, 28 July 2004', 29 July 2004; available at http://app.fta.gov.sg/asp/index.asp.

30 Ibid.

31 [Press Release, Ministry of Trade and Industry], 'Singapore, Chile and New Zealand complete Third Round of Pacific-Three FTA Negotiations', 17 December 2004, ibid.

32 [Reuters] South Korea Passes Chile Free Trade Pact, 16 February; available at http://www.bilaterals.org.

33 Article 1.2, 1(2), of the FTA between South Korea and Chile.

Article 16.1: Obligations

1. Each Party shall provide, in its territory, to the nationals of the other Party adequate and effective protection and enforcement of intellectual property rights, while ensuring that measures to enforce intellectual property rights do not themselves become unnecessary barriers to legitimate trade.

2. To provide adequate and effective protection and enforcement of intellectual property rights, each Party shall faithfully implement the international conventions it has acceded to, including the TRIPS Agreement.

Article 16.2: More Extensive Protection

A Party may implement in its domestic law more extensive protection of intellectual property rights than is required under this Agreement, provided that such protection is not inconsistent with this Agreement and the TRIPS Agreement.

Clearly, these are obligations that the parties already have under the various treaties and conventions. Consequently, South Korea is not pushing any hidden agenda. Even Article 16.2 which might, on the face of it, prompt TRIPS plus measures is only a repeat of the TRIPS provision to the same effect. To that extent, therefore, the particular FTA does not place South Korea in a different league from Singapore. The only slight difference in the FTA is the apparent concession of South Korea to Chile's pursuit of recognition of geographic indications (a detailed list of which has been attached to the FTA).

All in all, it would seem that the engagement of Singapore and South Korea in the area of FTA tilts more toward opening up markets for their goods and services than any future ambitions of ascendancy on the technology ladder and establishment of a TRIPS plus framework with their trading partners. Where IP figures as a provision in their respective FTAs, the intention appears to be to express commitment to the observance of current international obligations rather than TRIPS plus extensions.

The Problems IP Provisions in FTAs Present to Developing Nations

Much of the criticism of the FTAs revolves around the trade imbalance that already exists between the industrial and developing country signatories and the probability of that imbalance worsening as a result of the implementation of the FTAs. In relation to Morocco, for instance, a commentator had this to say:

The FTA clause will mainly benefit US products subject in Morocco to 20 percent custom duties, compared to 4 percent restrictive tariffs on Moroccan products

> entering the US. This was reflected by a March 2 press release by the office of the US Trade Representative, saying: 'This is the best market access package negotiated yet with a developing country in a US free-trade agreement.'[34]

The widespread opposition to FTAs for all practical purposes imposed on DCs does not often spot the problems that the TRIPS plus clauses might pose to such nations. Thus while pointing to the negative impacts that FTAs might have on the export trade of such countries, the IP clauses are mentioned merely as one of the problems. Even then, the reference may be to a limited area of IP. In relation to Morocco, for instance, according to the commentator cited above, 'The deal's most controversial aspect remains the two titles in the clause on the enforcement of intellectual property rights relating to generic medicine. They could complicate and delay the access of pharmaceutical industries to generic molecules once they enter the public domain'.[35]

Yet, the FTAs that the US has signed with DCs deliberately incorporate the spectrum of IP laws already on the statute books of the US. Unlike the EU, Japan and the emerging economies which seek to persuade their trading partners to live up to their existing IP commitments and help them achieve them, the US wields its colossal power, as ever, to push every signatory to adopt anything it considers necessary for its businesses. In its zeal to prise open the markets of DCs, the US has engaged in untrammelled use of the carrot and the stick to expand IP rights in DCs beyond the latter's internal (domestic) requirements. The widening gap between their internal IP requirements and those imposed on them to advance the wishes and demands of the major ICs has no doubt contributed to the problem of enforcement in DCs.

The imbalance between DCs and industrial powers that have signed FTAs is such that the former's acquiescence to onerous terms without at the same time gaining an equivalent benefit breeds discontent across all sectors of the population. Neverthless, public sensitivities in the DCs is perennially ignored both in the manner of imposition of foreign-induced IP laws and in the pressure to have those laws enforced regardless of the ultimate consequences to the social and economic fabric of DCs. The major industrial countries do not seem to sense that the FTAs might be the last straw in pushing DCs to the limit and that they might lead to a total collapse of the IP system. Ironically, Japan and the EU are reticent about deploying similar tactics as the US but opportunistically watch while the US forges ahead with TRIPS plus formulae in disregard of widespread opposition and well-grounded arguments that even the current system may not be sustainable.

As regards the specific possible impacts, on DCs, of the IP clauses enshrined in the FTAs, it needs to be noted that there is an abundant commentary on their

34 Khatoun Haidar, 'Moroccans Unsettled by Free-trade Deal with US', *The Daily Star*, Beirut, 18 March 2004; reproduced in http://www.bilaterals.org.

35 Ibid.

harmfulness to creativity and innovation, even within the US.[36] We would merely confine our remarks here to the implications, to DCs, of the expansion of rights in favour of the drugs manufacturers.

The FTA route of empowering drug administration authorities to refuse registration of generic drugs erodes the role of patent offices and provides easy and cheap leeway for proprietors to block generic drugs even when their patents may have expired or cannot stand up to scrutiny. Until the current attempt to twist their roles, the regulatory authorities did not have any competence other than to check for the safety, effectiveness or quality of the drugs. TRIPS never envisaged such a course of action either.

The US has injected another avenue for blocking competition from generic drugs by seeking to lock away data supplied by its companies applying for registration of their drugs at national regulatory authorities. While in the past generic manufacturers would only present to the national regulatory authorities the performance of the equivalent drugs they sought to introduce to gain marketing approval, the US move will prevent them from doing so because they will have to use their own test data. The imposition of a five-year moratorium on use of the test data supplied by the US companies effectively serves as a patent. Far worse, if the originator US companies gain approval for marketing in the US, they could just as well prevent any generic competition in signatory countries (such as Morocco which has acceded to such a provision) by simply asserting the data exclusivity from the time that approval was given in the US, and refuse to market the relevant drug in the signatory country. Any possibility of issuing a compulsory licence by the signatory country will be curtailed as the data exclusivity will prevent any registration.

Conclusion

The explosion of the FTAs may be viewed as an expression of the desire of nations to open up markets to the export trade and foreign investment, but that is not the full story. Beneath the flurry of negotiations and signings, there lie brutal realities that DCs need to examine before committing themselves to any further obligations, particularly in the IP field.

It is tragic that even DCs that have been given an extension of time to comply with TRIPS (2016) might be losing that extension through FTAs. Most of the states targeted by the US for its FTAs are DCs ravaged by poverty (40–50 per cent of Africa), disease (38 per cent of the population in Botswana is afflicted by AIDs)

36 See Michael A. Heller, 'The Boundaries of Private Property', 108 *Yale Law Journal* 1163, 1999 (arguing that earlier inventions tagged by rights present a stumbling block for later innovation). Compare Ejan Mackaay, 'The Economics of Intellectual Property Rights in Civil Law Systems', in Aristides N. Hatzis (ed.), *Economic Analysis of Law – A European Perspective*, Edward Elgar: Cheltenham, 2008.

or various forms of underdevelopment. Paradoxically, this has not stopped the US from exerting its sheer global power to push through FTAs right and left without any thought of the repercussions to other countries, particularly the DCs. Surely, the US authorities must understand that they can command virtually any DC into submission on all fronts and that no DC can singly stand up to the US or EU even where vital national interests might be jeopardized by any FTAs. The appearance of comity and mutual interest with signatory states that the US expresses in the FTAs cannot delude anyone anymore.

Ultimately, the critical issue for DCs remains the same as ever. Do they wish to renounce their desire to devise laws and policies suitable to their internal requirements? Would their governments have to abandon their roles as guardians of the national interest and, instead, become virtual tools of foreign powers and multinational companies forever enforcing foreign laws and policies?

The US government as well as those of DCs need to heed the voices of reason among the general public. There is growing recognition of and outcry against the possible adverse impacts of further expansion of IP, particularly in DCs. Thus, one writer in Singapore queried the appropriateness of further revision of the copyright law:

> stronger and tighter IP laws may not necessarily increase the incentive to create … In the course of the review, I hope the Intellectual Property Office of Singapore will act independently of the IP laws in the United States, some of which are limiting and controversial, and may not work to the benefit of a small country like Singapore where our technology (for example, information technology and biotech) and media/entertainment industries are not as developed as the US. Sufficient leeway should be provided to ensure that small homegrown companies, where innovation will likely come from, will have ample room to benefit from the revised laws.[37]

37 Tay Eng Wah, 'Too Much Reach and Copyright Stifles Creativity', *The Straits Times* [Forum] [Singapore], 29 May 2003, at 18.

Chapter 11
Do Asian Nations Take Intellectual Property Rights Seriously?*

Introduction

Nowadays, no media report is complete without a story relating to intellectual property (IP) featuring prominently and competing for attention among the welter of current news and views. IP developments in single countries, regions or around the globe are recorded continuously and in detail by all sorts of media outlets. Some of the electronic media engage entirely in reporting IP-related events and activities on a daily basis.

Amidst the multiplicity of IP resources and the volume of information they release, one indubitable fact stands out. Whether by design or unconsciously, confirmation of the ascent of countries in global, economic league tables seems to be announced through the appearance of repeated news of their ill-deeds in the IP field. A Japanese study thus commented, 'In connection with the advancement of industrial technology in China, Taiwan, Korea and other places in the Asian Region, infringements of not only the trademark and design rights but even infringements of patent rights are increasing'.[1] Ironically, it has become a rare feat for such countries and similar ones in the rest of the world to receive a welcoming review of their efforts to introduce more IP law and implement them. Indeed, reports of any changes in IP among the newly industrializing nations, such as those in Asia, are thus replete with calumny and backhanded attacks of deficiencies and wilful dereliction of obligations on their part. The Intellectual Property Task Force created by the US Justice Department in 2004 thus commented:

> While developing countries in Asia have increased their manufacturing capacity for legitimate goods, the region has also become a major manufacturer of counterfeit products. Factories in China, Taiwan, and Hong Kong produce numerous counterfeit designer goods and other products protected by United States trademarks. Factories in Singapore and Thailand produce large amounts of counterfeit software and movies that are exported to the United States,

---

* An earlier version of this chapter appeared, in the author's name, as 'Do Asian Nations Take Intellectual Property Rights Seriously?' 4(2) *SCRIPT-ed* 166, 2007; available at http://www.law.ed.ac.uk/ahrc/script-ed/vol4-2/endeshaw.asp.

1 Japan Patent Office, *FY2004 Survey Report on Losses Caused by Counterfeiting*, March 2005; available at http://www.jpo.go.jp.

> sometimes before the films are released to the general public. Consequently, many intellectual property offences in the United States are traced to manufacturing plants and bank accounts in Asia. In fact the United States Trade Representative has identified several Southeast Asian countries, such as China, Malaysia, Thailand, Taiwan, Indonesia, and the Philippines as countries that do not adequately or effectively protect intellectual property rights.[2]

Such a scathing critique that denies any positive progress in South East Asia may be puzzling, even a shock, to many, not least in governments and academia across Asia. Yet, accounts of IP laws and practices in Asia in the regular press as well as the learned journals in the West barely relate to the economic and social upheavals that lie in the background. Instead, a self-serving comparison is played up before the reader, namely between 'deficiency' in enforcement of laws in these countries and the (presumably 'exemplary'?) practice in Western Europe and North America to suggest the pointlessness of having the laws in the first place. The uninformed observer might even be persuaded to think that the situation must have got worse as the years went by.

Undoubtedly, the story of IP law-making and implementation in Asia has not always been glorious. For that matter, neither have other countries (Germany, the US and Switzerland, among them) demonstrated anything to the contrary while pursuing their respective goals of achieving industrialization and social progress in past centuries. Still, painting a gloomy picture of Asian IP, usually in the interests of foreign proprietors, or denying any of its deficiencies, as happens with some domestic political and economic interests in Asia, will fail to explain adequately the paradox of more laws being placed on their statute books while, as constantly claimed by their critics, there might be less progress in their implementation. A more sound approach would appear to us to be an assessment of the state of IP law in Asia or elsewhere by reference principally to the internal factors that necessitated its emergence and continue to define or redefine it. This paper attempts to examine recent developments in IP law Asia with such an approach.

The chapter discerns three main tendencies in current Asian IP law: an attempt by nations to keep abreast of any additional demands of the industrial powers and to introduce all manners of new laws or revision of old ones considered to be important for foreign investors; a continuation of Asian reluctance to confront foreign nations (chiefly the US and EU) as regards the forms and contents as well as enforcement of such laws; and a desire to keep costs of the IP system down and help local businesses benefit from better access to such a system. Each of these tendencies will be addressed in turn in this chapter. It will also address the inevitable question of the likely course of future developments. The chapter concludes that foreign, particularly US, criticism and attendant heavy-handed moves to compel

2 See US Justice Department, Office of the Attorney General, *Report of the Department of Justice's Task Force on Intellectual Property*, October 2004, at 32.

Asian nations to implement IP laws are being viewed more and more through Asian eyes as crossing the boundaries of propriety and might easily backfire.

Laws Galore but Instability Persists

Although nearly all the Asian nations have declared the compliance of their laws with the Agreement on Trade-Related Aspects of Intellectual Property Rights (TRIPS), they continue to promulgate new laws or amend old versions.[3] For reasons of space, we will confine ourselves to three countries, namely South Korea, Taiwan and Singapore. South Korea amended its Copyright Act in 2003 to incorporate changes prompted by the WIPO Copyright Treaty and joined the latter in June 2004. It also joined the Trademark Law Treaty in February 2003 as well as the Madrid Protocol in April 2003. In October 2004, it agreed to take part in the US Strategy Targeting Organized Piracy (STOP!). South Korea again amended its copyright-related laws in January 2005, among other things extending exclusive transmission rights to sound recording producers and performers. Taiwan amended all its laws in 2003 but did the same again to its patent law in July 2004 and to its copyright law in August 2004. In January 2005, Taiwan's legislature passed a law that protects pharmaceutical test data for new drugs for five years. Singapore also amended its laws on patents, trademarks and plant varieties protection in July 2004 and its copyright law in January 2005. Singapore joined the WIPO Copyright Treaty and the WIPO Performances and Phonograms Treaty on 17 April 2005.

This phenomenon of unstopping IP law-making characteristic of most Asian nations over the last decade has resulted from a straightforward cause. Asian nations have for long behaved as if the question of whether they should add more IP laws to those they already possess was out of their hands. This was a reflection, in large measure, of their huge dependence on the industrial powers of the US, EU and Japan for their exports and source of foreign investment. Indeed, Asian nations raced against each other to embrace any laws and measures thrown at them by the US or, to a lesser extent, the EU and Japan. Nations that showed any semblance of doubt in the permanent transplant of IP law or even attempted to buck the trend were viewed by the industrial powers as prevaricating or heretical. The upshot of this has been the growing number of nations that deeply resent the avalanche of foreign IP law placed on their statue books but do not speak out in public against it or demonstrate their desire to stop it.

In spite of the growing resentments, often expressed only through the local print media, the US, Europe and Japan maintain that any scrutiny into the existing IP system to make it more responsive to local conditions will lead to dilution of that system and therefore remain adamant that no changes of that nature should

---

3 See Asia–Pacific Economic Cooperation, 'IPR Policy Progress Mapping and Follow-up Report on Comprehensive Strategy on IPR in APEC', submitted by Japan to the 20th Intellectual Property Experts' Group Meeting, Seoul, Korea, 22–3 February 2005.

be allowed. The US in particular has been engaged in a new round of bilateral agreements (known as 'free trade' agreements, or FTAs) with developing countries across the world to lock those countries into an IP regime modelled very much on its own domestic laws. However, even those nations that have signed up to an FTA with the US are not exempt from further pressures. Thus the International Intellectual Property Alliance had cause to be annoyed with Singapore's choice to allow parallel imports and to seek to reverse it:

> [T]he relaxation of parallel imports has resulted in an influx into Singapore of pirated product masquerading as legitimate imports. Because of police reluctance to accord priority to such infringement, industry must resort to expensive and lengthy civil litigation in order to keep such pirate products out of the market. The Government of Singapore should reconsider its position on this issue given these changing developments, and should either add an exclusive right to authorize imports, or in the alternative, should, as neighboring countries and territories have done, provide a window of time from the release of a copyright title before allowing parallel imports into the market.[4]

An inevitable consequence of the constant harangue of the US and industry bodies with stakes in global IP is the creation of instability in the Asian IP system, a continuing erosion in the efficacy of even those rules already in place. The plethora of measures proposed each year by the United Stated Trade Representative (USTR) and the International Intellectual Property Alliance (IIPA) are suggestive not only of the liberty they take with the affairs of other nations but also of the little respect they have for the institutions and efforts of others. Thus, for instance, addressing Indonesia, the IIPA commanded: 'To ensure that adequate resources are devoted to the piracy problem on a year-round basis, the President must sign and implement the National Task Force Decree, and assign sufficient numbers of officers to tackle copyright piracy and bring piracy rates down.'[5] As regards Taiwan's efforts, after acknowledging that disappearance of pirated optical discs and 'illegal factory production', the same organization commented, 'Taiwan continues, however, to be world's largest supplier of blank recordable media to pirate operations globally and, to date, Taiwan has not prosecuted factories that "knowingly" supply blank product to affiliate pirate operations abroad'.[6] The IIPA declared similarly,

> By the end of 2005, China must

4 See International Intellectual Property Alliance, *2006 Special 301 Report*, 13 February 2006; available at http://www.iipa.com.

5 Ibid.

6 See International Intellectual Property Alliance, *2005 Special 301 Report*; available at http://www.iipa.com.

> - Through amended copyright legislation or regulations, correct the deficiencies in China's implementation of the WCT and WPPT, and ratify the two treaties.
>
> - Significantly ease evidentiary burdens in civil cases, including establishing a presumption with respect to subsistence and ownership of copyright and, ideally, permitting use of a U.S. copyright certificate, and ensure that evidentiary requirements are consistently applied by judges and are available in a transparent manner to litigants.
>
> Each of the measures noted above is necessary to strengthen China's intellectual property enforcement regime. The true test, however, is the impact of China's actions and policies on U.S. sales and exports of copyrighted works.[7]

The frustration of Asian nations with the high-handed manner of the industrial powers and allied institutions in their unrelenting drive to impose layers upon layers of IP laws and measures on them has surfaced from time to time. Koreans were recently vocal about the potential impact of opening to foreign proprietors further access to the local film industry.[8] One prominent film actor was reported as saying, 'South Korean movies will now walk the path toward collapse without measures to guard against Hollywood's dominance'.[9] Public demonstrations of 'some 1,500 South Korean movie producers, actors and directors' with placards reading, 'Stop humiliating negotiations that will allow a cultural invasion',[10] took centre stage in the debate over whether the domestic film industry could withstand competition from Hollywood. The South Korean government, on the other hand, iterated, 'The current situation is that we cannot survive unless joining the worldwide free trade trend and that has frequently demanded our screen quota system be changed'.[11] Clearly the government was not oblivious to the looming dangers for the local film industry but sought, just as much as other Asian nations, to factor them into the overall scheme of its engagements with, and dependence on, the US.

---

7 Ibid.

8 South Korea apparently required local cinemas, from as far back as 1966, to show local movies for 146 days a year. As part of ongoing negotiations with South Korea for a free trade agreement, the US had pushed for a reduction by denouncing 'the quota system as an unfair trade practice and major hurdle'. The South Korean government subsequently agreed to reduce the restrictions to 73 days a year. See Jae-Soon Chang, 'South Korea Cuts Homegrown Movie Quota', *Associated Press* [Seoul], 26 January 2006; available at http://www.mercurynews.com; accessed 20 February 2006.

9 Ibid.

10 See, 'Korea anti-Hollywood Demos' at http://p2pnet.net/story/7874, 9 February 2006; accessed 20 February 2006.

11 See note 8, above, ibid.

Shying Away from Confrontation

The attitudes of Asian nations towards post-Doha issues in IP have been arguably embryonic. Even where they were expressed, they

> remained limited to such disjointed aspects as biodiversity, compulsory licensing and extension of protection to geographic indications to cultural or other artefacts in Asia. The obvious lack of a unified perspective across Asian states prevents the emergence of articulate positions on major IP issues that could command broader appeal among governments, civil society, the professional groups and consumers.[12]

When the Friends of Development (FOD), led by Argentina and Brazil, put forward proposals for a 'Development Agenda' for the World Intellectual Property Organization (WIPO),[13] one could have guessed that Asian nations would play a peripheral role, just as they had done at Doha in 2001 and since then. Singapore spoke on behalf of the 'Asian group' at the Inter-Sessional Intergovernmental Meeting (IIM) on a Development Agenda for WIPO on the first day (11 April 2005) expressing support for the proposal and emphasizing that 'mainstreaming development dimension into all WIPO's work is imperative' and that 'IP is not an end in itself'. It also spoke against the 'one size fits all approach' as being inappropriate; instead, it asserted that there should be respect for the 'policy space' of developing countries and a weighing of costs of IP against the benefits.[14]

When Singapore again addressed the WIPO inter-governmental meeting on a 'development agenda', this time on behalf of the Association of Southeast Asian Nations (ASEAN), it merely iterated, in diplomatic language, support for strengthening WIPO's activities, glossing over the serious issues on the table.[15] It stated, 'ASEAN believed that the proposal to establish a Development Agenda offered WIPO an opportunity to explore and identify additional measures, which could strengthen WIPO's role in promoting development and enhancing the

12 See A. Endeshaw, 'Asian Perspectives on Post-TRIPS Issues in Intellectual Property', 8(2) *The Journal of World Intellectual Property*, 211–35, March 2005.

13 WIPO, 'Proposal by Argentina and Brazil for the Establishment of a Development Agenda for WIPO', Geneva, 27 August 2004; WO/GA/31/11. The proposal was later elaborated through a further document; see WIPO, 'Proposal to Establish a Development Agenda for WIPO: An Elaboration of Issues Raised in Document WO/GA/31/11', Geneva, 6 April 2005; IIM/1/4.

14 See, the Electronic Frontier Foundation (EFF), Deeplinks, Blogging WIPO's Development Agenda Meeting – Day 1, 11 April 2005; available at http://www.eff.org; accessed 20 February 2006. See also WIPO, Inter-sessional Intergovernmental meeting on a development agenda for WIPO: Report, First Session, Geneva, 11–13 April 2005; IIM/1/6, 31 July 2005, at paragraph 40.

15 See, WIPO, note 14, above, ibid., at paragraph 41.

development dimension into its work'.[16] Indeed, its expression of gratitude towards WIPO for help extended to ASEAN in all manners of activities outweighed any glib support that group extended to the 'development agenda'. Neither did it clearly identify which side of the debate ASEAN sought to stand. Considering the vociferous statements made by the Philippines and Myanmar at Cancun,[17] it makes one wonder whether those countries had changed stance in the short time since then.

The Singapore delegation itself expressed something different from the view it stated on behalf of Asia. It asserted,

> a development dimension had always been an integral part of the Organization [WIPO] since its incorporation into the family of the UN agencies in 1974 … [and that] WIPO possessed the competence and initiative to measure up to this task in a transparent and effective manner within its existing mandate. Hence, it did not see the need to change the WIPO convention, nor establish new procedures or bodies to integrate the development dimension into the work of the Organization.[18]

Needless to say, all of this echoed the US proposal which Singapore viewed 'could help WIPO to sharpen the focus of its cooperation for development projects'.[19] One must note here that the US position was antithetical to that of the FOD and Singapore's association with that position ran counter to its statement on behalf of Asia.

Indonesia stated quite bluntly its gratitude to the WIPO for helping it develop the IP system in Indonesia and for its technical assistance, although it also quipped that 'intellectual property alone could only contribute to providing part of the solution'.[20] South Korea affirmed that 'intellectual property would increasingly become important in the development strategies of all countries' but confined itself to a call for 'the rational use of resources … to avoid a negative impact on the budget of the parties involved'.[21] In short, it did not find anything worth changing both in the activities of WIPO or the IP system as a whole.

China initially demonstrated that same tendency of looking on while others battled for or against the status quo in IP. In the first session of the inter-governmental deliberations mentioned above, the Chinese delegation pointed out, 'WIPO's concern about development' should not be confined to technical

16 Ibid.

17 See Endeshaw, at note 12, above, ibid.

18 See, WIPO, note 14, above, ibid., at paragraph 90.

19 Ibid.

20 Ibid., at paragraph 93.

21 WIPO, Inter-sessional Intergovernmental Meeting on a Development Agenda for WIPO: Report, Second Session, Geneva, 20–22 June 2005; IIM/2/10, 1 September 2005; at paragraph 40.

assistance,[22] that 'in identifying priorities and setting-up of IP norms, WIPO would fully take development into account' as well as 'the real capacity of Member States'.[23] During the second session, China declared some support for the proposals of the FOD indirectly by citing approvingly the explanations offered by the FOD.[24] Thus it referred to the pressure brought to bear on countries during multilateral or bilateral trade talks to accede to TRIPS plus provisions to point to the impact of norm-setting activities in WIPO on developing countries. It added, 'it supported more norm-setting activities in WIPO, including those harmonization activities for the purpose of encouraging innovation'.[25] It sought to push for application of 'the concept of users in norm-setting activities' with a view to including all parties and not just rights holders.[26] In the end, China remained uncommitted to the contents of the proposals of the FOD, seeking instead to speak on a single aspect of the deliberations, even then making a dubious point without taking sides or seeming to support any of the protagonists.

When Thailand spoke at the second session of the WIPO intergovernmental meeting, on behalf of the ASEAN group, it iterated what Singapore had stated on behalf of ASEAN during the first session.[27] Thailand simply repeated that 'development had always been an important aspect of WIPO's work' and expressed its gratitude towards WIPO's assistance.[28] It declared, '[t]he Development Agenda offered WIPO the opportunity to further enhance and strengthen its role in promoting development and contribute to the realization of the millennium development goals'.[29]

In the end, with the exception of India,[30] which declared its full support for the proposal of the FOD, no country from Asia openly embraced that proposal, least of all formally joined the ranks of the FOD. Considering the long-standing Asian practice of quietly acceding to the demands of the industrial powers to expand the type and scope of IP they adopted as well as enforce it, it may come as no surprise that no Asian nation portrayed itself as part of the general movement of developing countries to claim a 'policy space' for themselves.

On the other hand, as would be expected, Japan was forthright in its support for the US and other industrial powers which maintained that no new 'dimension' would be necessary for WIPO as it has always played that role.[31] Japan expressed

---

22 See WIPO, note 14, above, ibid., at paragraph 52.

23 Ibid.

24 See WIPO, note 21, above, ibid., at paragraph 191.

25 Ibid.

26 Ibid.

27 Ibid., at paragraph 28.

28 Ibid.

29 Ibid.

30 Statement by Debabrata SAHA, Deputy Permanent Representative of India [at the United Nations, Geneva], 1 October 2004; available at www.cptech.org/ip/wipo/india10012004.html; accessed 31 January 2006.

31 See WIPO, note 14, above, ibid., at paragraph 45.

its support for improving the technical cooperation and capacity building activities of the WIPO in much the same way as the US, UK and other countries had done. Remarkably, Japan did not explicitly reject the proposals of the FOD; it skirted around them by iterating such standard statements as the need to increase 'awareness of intellectual property systems' to enhance 'the effectiveness of WIPO's activities related to development'.[32]

Building the IP Infrastructure

Until very recently, the institutional trappings of IP implementation and enforcement in Asia had not received adequate attention. The promulgation of laws was not often accompanied by the creation of institutions, other than the traditional registries of patents and trademarks, that could realize the potentials of IP to transform the economic and technological conditions of the respective nations. This was simply because the widely assumed role of IP as a means of attracting foreign technology and capital was perceived to have been achieved as soon as the laws were promulgated and registration offices opened their doors to discharge their routine functions. That perception has changed in recent years to such an extent that countries have swung around to experimenting with all kinds of formulae they believe to be expediting the exploitation of the innovations protected by the respective laws. Thus, there was a proposal in China for establishing a separate ministry to spearhead IP protection.[33] The use of the IP infrastructure as a means of generating resources to self-finance related activities has become a subject of sets of plans and operations. Singapore took the more ambitious stance of committing itself 'to developing into a regional and global hub for the creation, commercialization and management of IP as part of its work-plan for the future'.[34] Malaysia has also embarked on transforming the administration of IP into a self-financing enterprise, thereby offloading a basic function of the state.

In terms of improving the efficiency of the administration of IP, the deployment of electronic means has become a growing trend in Asia. Singapore introduced such from 2003. By 2004, Hong Kong implemented electronic filing and publication for trademarks as well as patents and designs. China did the same from 12 March 2004. Taiwan and Thailand have all introduced electronic searches and plan to implement application systems as well.

32 Ibid.

33 Dow Jones, Beijing, 'China Scholar suggests creating antipiracy Ministry', Dow Jones International News, 26 November 2003; available from Factiva (global.factiva.com), accessed 8 February 2004.

34 See Asia-Pacific Economic Cooperation, *Report on the Enforcement Best Practices in APEC Economies to Combat Optical Disk Piracy*, submitted by Singapore to the 21st APEC Intellectual Property Experts' Group Meeting, Manila, Philippines, 2–3 August, 2005.

Public education is another aspect of the institutionalization of IP in Asia. The creation of public awareness of IP rights has become one of the major themes of activity, whether by government departments, the local IP offices or international agencies and interest groups. This happens all the time and across many Asian countries,[35] although the form and frequency of such activities widely differ.[36] In any case, an ethical dimension has been injected into the IP discourse in Asia on the apparent premise that legal sanctions alone might not suffice and that attitudes in Asia towards IP need to change to enhance its enforcement in the day-to-day context. Although awareness campaigns will no doubt raise the profile of IP in the society and send the message that illegitimate use will not be tolerated, it cannot be certain that the general public will be persuaded to be equally sympathetic towards domestic and foreign forms of IP for the simple reason that the latter remain dominant in most parts of Asia.

A further aspect of the institutionalization process is the emergence across the economically significant countries in Asia (Hong Kong, Taiwan, Thailand, Korea, Malaysia, Philippines and Singapore) from 1999[37] of a single coordinating body for enforcement activities. These countries have increased the number of agencies and investigators dealing with enforcement of IP; most of them have also established schemes to pay informers substantial sums in return for information leading to conviction of illegal operators.[38] China established in April 2004 a National Working Group on IP Protection led by Vice Premier Wu Yi and comprising ministries, agencies and the courts. The expressed aim is to achieve results by 'harmonizing the enforcement work between administrative agencies and judicial bodies, streamline giving directives for national crackdown actions and providing public education and propaganda activities'.[39] The Philippines also established the Philippine Anti-Piracy Team (PAPT) in 2005 to stamp out 'software piracy'. Indonesia is similarly expected to sign into law a National IP Task Force Decree which establishes an inter-departmental task force on IP enforcement comprising of representatives of the relevant government departments.

The US has not viewed such steps as sufficient and sought to tighten them up further by opening a special office (under an 'Intellectual Property Law Enforcement Coordinator', IPLEC) in its embassies. On the face of it, establishing IP Attachés, branches of the FBI or some other outfit in foreign lands might seem

35 Ibid.

36 For Hong Kong, see Bien Perez, 'Educating to Counteract Software Piracy', *South China Morning Post*, 18 November 2003, at 3; available from Factiva (global.factiva.com), accessed 8 February 2004 (discussing how the IP Department, Customs and Excise and the Business Software Alliance plan to undertake such a campaign).

37 See, Asia–Pacific Economic Cooperation, note 34, above, ibid.

38 Ibid.

39 See, Asia–Pacific Economic Cooperation, IPR Policy Progress Mapping and Follow-up Report on 'Comprehensive Strategy on IPR in APEC', submitted by Japan to the 20th Intellectual Property Experts' Group Meeting, Seoul, Korea, 22–3 February 2005.

a remarkable idea. However, the obvious disregard for national sensitivities, not to say sovereignty, might backfire. The efficiency to be gained in the enforcement of IP rights by flying in foreign experts and investigators might be outweighed by a general feeling of dejection that might set in among local institutions and operatives as well as the public at large.

Mixed Signals

In spite of the vociferous demands of the US, and to a lesser extent the EU and Japan, to subject Asia, as a matter of fact all developing countries, to forced marches in adopting and implementing a mirror-image of their domestic IP systems, Asia remains condemned by history and inertia to plod along at its own pace. This has not been part of any wilful plan of Asian governments or discernible by the protagonists of the 'Asian Miracle'. The variety of opposed forces and tendencies at play makes it difficult to arrive upon any easy prognosis of developments.

For instance, local enterprises are beginning to demand enforcement of rights not necessarily to exploit any such rights but simply to preserve their market standing from illegitimate producers. This has been very true of the music and film industries. Fake products have also stirred up domestic resentment in another way – counterfeit medicines have caused deaths and no less an authority than the World Health Organization has launched a campaign to stamp out such practices in six Asian countries.[40]

In the software industry, however, pirated copies may trigger the opposite reactions to that normally expected. Microsoft reaps benefits from such a practice in China as the market becomes hooked on its products, illegally available for practically nothing, rather than purchasing the alternative software developed domestically.[41] In that sense, then, local software developers would find it essential to enforce the existing rights to guarantee their very existence. Conversely too, foreign IP owners would do better by joining forces with local brands and interest groups rather than undermining them. The encouragement of local industry and protection of IP seem to go hand in hand with the extent of protection that foreigners are likely to gain. Any attempt to drive off local brands from the market might have the undesirable consequence of local businesses and (ultimately their governments) washing their hands of the enforcement of the IP system.

On a general level, too, there may appear to be a divergence of Asia from the rest of the world. The reactions of developing nations elsewhere to the inflexibility of Western governments in trying to hold on to the advancing wave of IP harmonization has not been to abandon any hope of change or withdraw

---

40 'Fakes are for Real – But Stronger Asian brands may Help to Combat Piracy', *Financial Times*, 13 November 2003, at 12; available from Factiva (global.factiva.com), accessed 8 February 2004.

41 Ibid.

their demands for a 'policy space' in their law-making and implementation. Their incipient but growing movement is generating more sympathy from special interest groups (such as Oxfam and Medicins Sans Frontiers) and the general public in the West. On the other hand, the population and business community in the developing nations increasingly view the state of dissension as a signal of the demerits of the system and its illegitimacy. Curiously, Asia might not appear to manifest such a development.

The more forceful the external pressure directed at Asian nations, the less reticent they have become in initiating measures that could respond to internal demands for change. The more responsive Asian nations were to those pressures and acceded to new laws and measures, the more homogenous and undifferentiated the local laws and practices have become. Indeed, the more pressure has been exerted to force Asia onto the IP bandwagon, the less authoritative and effective the latter have appeared before the populace. Thus US persistence (such as through the FTAs) in turning Asian IP into an identical copy of its own and to subject every decision and practical movement to local detachments of its own enforcement machinery will end as a hollow victory. The deployment of FBI or similar officers to supervise entry and exit ports in Asian countries as well as the passage of overall control to 'Intellectual Property Attachés' or 'Intellectual Property Enforcement Officers' stationed at its foreign embassies[42] will signal the end of any local initiatives in taking responsibility for the making and implementation of laws. This is a slippery path for the US to tread. Clearly, Asian acquiescence to foreign pressures on the IP front will continue in so far as they are in the grip of economic and geo-political dependence on the US and the other two main industrial powers, the EU and Japan. The US will therefore never receive any signs for when to stop.

Furthermore, developments in IP law in Asia continue to be mediated by non-IP factors. For one thing, the fact that China and the Asian Tigers are displacing manufacturing in the US and EU with products similar in quality but costing less

42 The first such appointment was made for Asia when an 'Intellectual Property Law Enforcement Coordinator (IPLEC)' was announced on the recommendations of the Intellectual Property Task Force created by the Justice Department in 2004. See, US Department of Justice, News Release, 'Attorney General Alberto R. Gonzales Announces Appointment of Intellectual Property Law Enforcement Coordinator For Asia', 5 January 2006; available at www.doj.gov. The task of such an officer is 'Coordinating investigations and prosecutions of intellectual property offenders located in the region; Developing relationships with foreign law enforcement agencies and prosecutors in the area; Providing legal and technical assistance to foreign law enforcement agencies on intellectual property enforcement; Assisting federal prosecutors in the United States working on intellectual property cases involving Asia; and Examining intellectual property crime trends in the region'. Ibid. Attorney General Gonzales added, 'Protecting intellectual property rights in the United States and throughout the world is one of the highest priorities of the Department of Justice. My appointment of an Intellectual Property Law Enforcement Coordinator for Asia is an important step in coordinating enforcement efforts in a critical region of the world.' Ibid.

fuels a love–hate relationship. Meeting consumer demands and thus diffusing the concerns of protectionists in the West go hand in hand with the strident voices of those intent on tightening the screws on Asian exporters and extracting any available concessions whether in ordinary trade terms or in IP. While Asian nations have had to cave in to demands of the US to introduce further IP laws through FTAs, the surplus they generate through their exports to the US sustains US budgetary deficit and debts.[43]

In the mean time, Asian nations are ever on the lookout for cushions and support to sustain their drive to maintain and expand export markets. The recent evidence of China taking advantage of distrust between the US and Latin American nations and rising Anti-Americanism to forge business links, create and open up markets, and pour in investment in the latter has fomented fear and consternation among US leaders.[44] While the US is still bogged in expanding and fortifying a pan-American trading bloc, China is creating with Latin American nations economic relationships not coloured by any political ambitions.[45] China's indiscriminate alliance with all sorts of governments in the developing world, including in Africa, with a view to carving out a trading zone in anything but name, may provide to those nations a space within which to manoeuvre for better terms and benefits than those offered by the traditional industrial powers. China too is gaining breathing space and an opportunity to reduce its trading dependence on the US as well as possibly stave off strident criticism of its IP.

Conclusion

The stance of the industrial powers on Asian IP has evident flaws, not only in terms of policy but also in the manner of the absorption of the legal system into the Asian body politic. The apparently overriding foreign concerns of making Asian IP laws

43 John Schmid, 'Two Cars and One View: U.S. Taken for a Ride', *The Milwaukee Journal Sentinel*, 25 January 2004, 1A; accessed through Factiva on 7 February 2004 (discussing the implications of Chinese increased access to the US market, job losses and why the US has been lax about not taking serious action).

44 Saul Landau, 'Chinese Influence on the Rise in Latin America', *Foreign Policy in Focus*, June 2005; available at www.fpif.org; accessed 20 February 2006. Landau writes, 'In November 2004, Chinese President Hu Jintao signed 39 commercial agreements with five Latin American nations. Chinese investments in Argentina alone totalled some $20 billion … At the end of 2004 and the beginning of 2005, China offered more than $50 billion in investment and credits to countries inside the traditional Monroe Doctrine's shield.' Ibid.

45 'Is Washington Losing Latin America?', *The New York Times*, 1 February 2006; available online at http://www.nytimes.com; accessed 20 February 2006. *The New York Times* commented, 'China is still a long way from threatening or even really competing with the influence of the United States in Latin America. But as in other parts of the world, China is pragmatically and aggressively seeking economic and political advantages there.' Ibid.

into mirror-images of those in the US, Japan and EU as well as moving towards establishing enforcement agencies under the direct control of foreign institutions and government departments will, in the long run, cause incalculable damage to the interests of Western corporations and IP owners. One might indeed sense something of a backlash brewing in Asia against the constant harping on 'piracy' of well-known foreign brands and products,[46] while the state of local innovation remains relatively lower than, and far behind from, those hailing from the EU, US or Japan. Sooner rather than later, this might translate into widespread 'piracy', boycotting of 'branded' western goods and the like.[47]

Furthermore, although the debate regarding the rights of sovereign nations to legislate in accordance with their social and economic aspirations is still raging, the nexus between the legitimacy of IP rights and general human rights remains unarticulated in the interest of Asian nations. The industrial nations who rage against the lack of enforcement of IP rights in Asia treat as being of lesser significance the trampling of human rights in general. Indeed, the perception that IP rights can be enforced regardless of the absence or down-playing of human rights seems to be a self-serving facade put up by Western powers to look after their corporations ahead of the general interests of Asians and, indeed, of people in developing countries. Clearly such a stance will not endear foreign corporations to Asians over the long term. Enforcement of special rights for foreigners without due regard for the general rights of citizens in Asia not only generates suspicion and hatred but also ends in fomenting opposition to those special rights. Ultimately, the current tendencies of forcing nations into TRIPS plus regimes might have

46 A very recent case in the UK is the attempt to boycott Coca-Cola by the National Union of Students (NUS) in retaliation for the corporation's unethical practices in Colombia: 'It is alleged that The Coca-Cola Company and its bottling partners in Colombia colluded with paramilitaries to murder, intimidate and harass trade union members.' See, 'Coca-Cola Update', http://www.nusonline.co.uk. Coca Cola's sponsorship of the Winter Olympic Games in Turin was a subject of debate when reportedly 'two municipal councils in Rome have decided to ban [the Olympic torch] from passing through their streets in protest at what they say is the bad treatment of Coca Cola workers in Colombia. The leaders of the campaign say more than three hundred other councillors across Italy back them.' See BBC World Service, 'Olympic Torch Controversy', 7 November, 2005; available at http://www.bbc.co.uk/worldservice.

47 The practice of boycotting 'a company's products in order to make a political statement' is already in full swing, not least in the US, in protest against those companies' support for the Republican Party. See, 'Consumer Guide and Brand List for the top 25 Republican Party Donors with Consumer Brands'; available at http://www.boycottbush.net/consumers.htm. The particular boycott was initiated by *Ethical Consumer* magazine (UK-based) in reaction to the 'rejection by President Bush of the Kyoto Agreement on global warming' and because he 'continues to be the single biggest obstacle to an intelligent human response to this threat.' Ibid. See also Mark Tran, 'Branded', *Guardian Unlimited blogs*, 1 September 2005 (discussing the results of an online opinion poll of 15,500 consumers in 17 countries on major brands and found strong attitudes against Nike, Coca Cola, McDonald's and Nestlé).

the unfortunate effect of fostering rebellion in the streets and shops of Asia, thus robbing the fledgling IP system of any legitimacy it might otherwise have been building up.

Chapter 12
Intellectual Property and the 'WIPO Development Agenda'*

Introduction

The persistent attempts of the major industrial nations to press ahead with the newly initiated (Doha) round of international trade negotiations under the auspices of the World Trade Organization (WTO) have met with resistance from the developing countries (DCs). The failure of the WTO Ministerial meeting in Cancun and the slow pace of trade negotiations both prior and subsequent to this meeting are potent proof of that resistance. Moreover, the anti-globalization demonstrations that have erupted everywhere (Seattle and Prague, amongst others) have highlighted the problems of economic and social transformation in DCs. The worsening impacts of mass poverty and the spread of the Aids pandemic on DCs have fuelled their repeated calls for reform of the global trading system. The pressure for change has become so overwhelming that even the major industrial powers have joined with other nations in various fora[1] to begin to address the problems of economic development and technology transfer that afflict DCs.

By comparison, the role of intellectual property (IP) in the development of non-industrial nations has received very little attention from any quarter.[2] This is because, on the one hand, the value and impact of IP were considered a settled issue once virtually all nations had joined the WTO Agreement on Trade-Related Aspects of Intellectual Property Rights (TRIPS). On the other hand, the major

---

* An earlier version of this chapter appeared, in the author's name, as 'Intellectual Property and the "WIPO Development Agenda"', 1 *Journal of Information, Law and Technology* 2006 (Special Issue: IP); available at http://www2.warwick.ac.uk/fac/soc/law/elj/jilt.

1 Among them are the following: the Millennium Development Goals adopted by the United Nations, the Johannesburg Declaration on Sustainable Development, which was issued by the World Summit on Sustainable Development, and the Sao Paulo Consensus adopted at UNCTAD XI.

2 The UK government's Commission on Intellectual Property attempted to look at the problem but its recommendations fell short of calling for a through revision of the IP system for the benefit of DCs. See Commission on Intellectual Property Rights, *Report of the Commission on Intellectual Property Rights: Integrating Intellectual Property Rights and Development Policy*, London, September 2002. It is interesting that even the Commission's suggestions for a few concessions to the DCs were rejected outright, prompting the government to distance itself from the Commission's recommendations and putting an end to its existence.

industrial nations were reluctant to concede that the implications of IP might merit scrutiny at the international level. Every time DCs demanded that the WTO Ministerials re-examine the link between IP and development, reconsider the TRIPS and allow relevant adjustments in their favour, the major industrial nations always expressed the view that any outstanding issues should be left to the TRIPS Council and resolved in line with the provisions of the TRIPS Agreement.[3] This meant, in essence, that the industrial powers were unwilling to re-examine TRIPS because they suspected that such a step might result in 'a lowering of standards' or 'weakening of IP'. Indeed, the TRIPS itself does not allow any reservations for nations that accede to it and firmly rejects the adoption by members of any form of IP that does not lead to further extensions of the scope of rights enshrined in it.[4]

The DCs have persisted in their demands to have the new round of WTO trade negotiations revisit the role of TRIPS in their economies and cultures. Still, apart from the pronouncement on access to drugs made at Doha,[5] the general expectations of the DCs that the new Doha round could resolve the problem of the impact of TRIPS on their economies and societies have failed to be met. This has prompted DCs, whether singly[6] or in groups,[7] to express their disappointment with and desperation for review of the situation even more loudly. Brazil and Argentina (on behalf of the 'Group of Friends of Development' or FoD) took the extra step of articulating a 'development agenda' ('DA') for the World Intellectual Property Organization (WIPO) and formally submitting their proposal, on 26 August 2004, to the WIPO General Assembly. The General Assembly subsequently adopted a decision, on 4 October 2004, to consider their submission as well as additional proposals that other members might have on the same topic. Since then, the US, UK and Mexico have submitted their responses and positions.

This chapter examines the various proposals within the framework of the historical roles of IP and the social-economic conditions of DCs. It starts off by

3 The Council is in charge of examining the unresolved issues in TRIPS, the so-called 'built-in agenda', as well as making proposals for 'modification or amendment' of TRIPS.

4 Article 72, TRIPS.

5 WTO, 'The Declaration on the TRIPS Agreement and Public Health', 20 November 2001, WT/MIN(01)/DEC/2.

6 The Philippines, for instance, presented a proposal for re-examination of the impact of WTO-linked obligations on DCs. See, WTO, General Council, Preparations for the 1999 Ministerial Conference, 'Proposal for a Declaration on Developing Countries, Communication from the Philippines', WT/GC/W/393, 25 November 1999.

7 The Africa Group, certain countries from South America as well as Asia asserted, among other things, 'the rights of members (pursuant to Article 8.2) to take measures to prevent the abuse of intellectual property rights by right holders or the resort to practices which unreasonably restrain trade or adversely affect the international transfer of technology'. See WTO, TRIPS Council, 'Submission by the African Group, Barbados, Bolivia, Brazil, Cuba, Dominican Republic, Ecuador, Honduras, India, Indonesia, Jamaica, Pakistan, Paraguay, Philippines, Peru, Sri Lanka, Thailand and Venezuela', IP/C/W/296, 29 June 2001.

summarizing the negative experiences of DCs in their failed attempts to reform the IP system both on an international level and locally. Then it picks up the recent (post-TRIPS) exploits of the DCs in pushing for some form of revision of TRIPS as part of the new (Doha) round of international trade negotiations. Next it examines the proposal for a 'WIPO Development Agenda' put forward by Argentina and Brazil (as part of the FOD). Finally, it looks at the reception of that proposal by the major industrial powers as well as other DCs, and assesses its chances of success. The chapter concludes by highlighting the fallacious assumptions that permeate the 'WIPO Development Agenda', namely that the international IP system culminating in TRIPS can still facilitate the transformation of DCs and that it possesses sufficient flexibility to meet the needs of such nations.

The Failure of Developing Countries to Reform the Intellectual Property System

Starting from the 1960s, the developing countries (DCs) have sought to reshape their international relations. In particular, they set out to reform the international intellectual property (IP) system by removing certain features which they believed to be barriers to their economic and technological development and to transform it into a vehicle that could further their aspirations for change and growth. Their proposals for reform of the IP system concentrated on extending free or permitted use in copyright, and the revocation of rights for lack of use or, where abuse occurred, the imposition of compulsory licensing on all forms of IP where the proprietors of the respective rights failed to supply a reasonably priced, adequate volume of products to satisfy local demand.[8]

The initial attempt of the DCs was to inject their proposals into the Paris and Berne conventions by way of amendments. Predictably, the major industrial countries presented a robust defence of the status quo and refused to entertain virtually all of the proposals for reform that the DCs put forward. Although certain concessions were promised and seemed destined to be adopted by the members of the Conventions,[9] they were all sidelined and eventually abandoned. Indeed, by the beginning of the Uruguay Round of GATT negotiations (1986), the reform movement had lost virtually all its momentum. The delay tactics deployed by the major industrial powers and the lack of fresh ideas that could recharge the movement put paid to any further advances in the cause of the DCs.

The failure of the DCs to reform the international IP system did not spring solely from their weakness in mustering sufficient bargaining power. Above all, the reform movement was fraught with conceptual fallacies and tactical blunders. The conceptual fallacies which continue to imbue the IP debate, put forward

8 See, A. Endeshaw, *Intellectual Property Policy for Non-Industrial Countries*, Dartmouth: Aldershot, 1996, at 105–108.

9 An example is the Stockholm Protocol to the Berne Convention.

even, as we will see below, by the proponents of the latest call for reform, Brazil and Argentina, arise from the perception that IP should be a universal vehicle and that all nations need to adopt identical or undifferentiated forms of IP. The major IP writers and commentators in the US, UK and Germany have raised this fallacious proposition to the level of ideology and propagated it regularly through scholarly publications, government policy documents and the mass media. The DCs' formulation of the reform of the international IP system was consequently a by-product of that approach. In other words, having embraced the universality of IP (involuntarily during colonialism and uncritically afterwards) and knowing full well that the international IP system was fundamental to the making of the major industrial powers, DCs were inevitably trapped into seeking only to reform that system as a whole rather than piercing the ideological façade and digging up novel solutions. In particular, DCs should have woken up to the fact that IP had evolved over the centuries under conditions specific to Western Europe and later the US, and should therefore always be formulated by reference to the cultural, socio-economic and technological conditions of a society. The persistent ignorance of policy-makers and so-called experts in DCs of the fact that the forms and scope of IP need to be congruent with the level and type of cultural, socio-economic and technological substructure within a society has left them prey to transplants of laws and rules that fulfil the needs of only the most industrially developed nations.

Indeed, the governments of DCs were deluded into thinking that every form of IP copied from the industrial countries of Western Europe and North America would be relevant to their circumstances. In most instances, they sought to fill any perceived gaps in their laws by transplanting similar solutions already on the statute books of the developed industrial nations. The predominant view in international IP circles equated this to modernization and considered it to be an inevitable part of the economic and technological transition that DCs desired to achieve. The United Nations was coopted into fostering these misconceptions under the guise of helping DCs. The WIPO and the United Nations Conference on Trade and Development (UNCTAD) have become key organizations in charge of proselytizing the 'universalist' notion of IP in DCs and in making sure that the DCs' laws kept pace not with their domestic needs and circumstances but with those of the developed industrial countries. As a consequence, virtually all DCs have retained the gamut of IP laws that were imposed on them from colonial times, buttressed from time to time by the WIPO from without and national legislatures from within to bring them into line with the IP laws of the most industrially developed countries.

It is ironic that even at the height of their movement to reform the international IP system, the DCs could not grasp that their aspirations were in diametric opposition to the pressures and activities of the industrial nations to extend that system and even deepen it. While the DCs failed to discover alternative paths for their pursuits, the major industrial nations were critical not only of the DCs' proposals for reform of the international IP system but also their domestic implementation of existing obligations under the major conventions. The DCs' desire for reform was perceived by the industrial powers as an attempt to claw back the frontiers of that system and to weaken it in order to deprive their multinational corporations of adequate protection in the DCs. The reform movement was therefore doomed to fail.

The DCs could never succeed in reforming the international IP system, principally because it was made by, and served the purposes of, the industrial powers. If the system did not work for the DCs it was because it was not meant to. The rationale and aims of international IP protection were precipitated by the growth of international trade in manufactured goods, and not of raw materials and agricultural products, among the industrial nations. The fact that DCs largely export primary, that is unprocessed or semi-processed, goods means that they were, and still are, in no state to influence the making or implementation of the international IP system.

Short of a total withdrawal of the DCs from the international IP treaties and charting their own paths from scratch, the only realistic chance that the DCs had of reforming anything depended on a grasp of the conceptual foundations of IP law, its purposes and relevance for DCs within the context of their international obligations. This would have implied that any notion of reform should be directed at their local IP laws. However, as their IP laws were in conformity with the thinking and practice that prevailed in the industrial nations, even reforms of the local IP laws would lead to collision with their obligations under the international treaties. Nonetheless, DCs never really digested the seriousness of the underlying issues, let alone reforming their own internal IP laws. Even the most vocal critics of the international IP system and proponents of reforms such as India,[10] Brazil[11] and Mexico[12] (individually or as part of the Group of 77) never really understood the need for internal or local reforms.

We now know that the DCs not only failed in reforming IP both in the domestic context and on an international level, but also found themselves victims of a further surge in the demands of the major industrial powers, particularly the US, to expand the scope and enforcement of IP. The superimposition of TRIPS on the international IP system in the face of the DCs' fierce resistance killed off any lingering hopes of reforming that system. This was done through the simple formula of christening IP law and enforcement as an aspect of international trade. The treatment of international IP protection as a trade issue and introduction of minimum (universal) standards for all forms of IP, far beyond the requirements under the major conventions, put paid to any national (domestic) attempts to work out alternative paths. The momentary concessions that DCs had obtained

10 See Terence P. Stewart (ed.), *The GATT Uruguay Round: A Negotiating History (1986–1992), Volume II: Commentary*, Kluwer Law and Taxation Publishers, 1993, at 2271 (regarding India's contention that countries should be free to formulate laws appropriate to themselves and they should be granted more favourable treatment in the international IP system).

11 See Stewart, ibid., on Brazil's proposal for compulsory licence over patents.

12 Mexico contended that overprotection of IP prevents DCs from securing access to modern technology. Ibid., at 2267.

in international forums in the 1960s and 1970s were virtually eliminated and the relentless pressure to further extend the IP system and its implementation came into in full swing. The ultimate consequence to IP law-making in DCs, and for that matter in industrial nations, may be summarized as follows:

> [More and more] the fundamental question that lies at the core of national IP law, namely conformity with the socio-economic conditions of the nations that introduce or adopt it, seemed irrelevant. It was, and had to be, conveniently ignored by the major industrial nations once they got away with TRIPS, under the leadership of the US. Any further progress in the scope and nature of IP protection would only be on their terms. Simply put … the dominant trading nations could seek further changes in the existing IP regime, at will, to suit their purposes. Thus, although TRIPS might be the minimum standard for all *trading* nations, that is members of WTO at the moment, the very fact that the major ICs [industrial countries] can wield their standings in WTO to push ever higher standards means that, henceforth, a general adoption of the highest common denominator is likely to become the way forward for international IP.[13]

There is abundant proof for the further extension of IP rights since TRIPS in the WIPO treaties relating to copyright, patent and trademark as well as the injection of higher standards of IP law and enforcement (dubbed 'TRIPS plus') through the device of free trade agreements deployed, chiefly, by the US.

New Quests of Developing Countries in Intellectual Property: Doha to Cancun

During the preparations for a new round of WTO negotiations, the developing countries (DCs) once again expressed their hopes that the impact of TRIPS on their prospects for development would be reviewed. At any rate, they contended that such a review is called for under specific provisions of TRIPS[14] as well as pursuant to the 'built-in agenda' in TRIPS.[15] The major industrial powers, however, bluntly rejected any calls for such a revision. They eschewed any proposals for the grant of certain concessions to the DCs that would promote transfer of knowledge and

---

13 A. Endeshaw, 'The Paradox of Intellectual Property Lawmaking in the New Millennium: Universal Templates as Terms of Surrender for non-Industrial Nations; Piracy as an Offshoot', 10(1) *Cardozo Journal of International and Comparative Law*, 47–77, Spring 2002, at 58.

14 See, Article 27(3), TRIPS, on the protection of plant varieties.

15 See, Articles 23(4) and 24(1) on geographical indications; and Article 64(2) and (3) on discontinuation of the 'non-violation' provision of WTO as a form of dispute resolution.

technology to the mutual advantage of both DCs and the industrial powers.[16] On the other hand, the ongoing review by the TRIPS Council of the implementation of obligations of WTO member states,[17] the examination of the unresolved issues in TRIPS (the 'built-in agenda'[18]) as well as the permissibility of submitting proposals for 'modification or amendment' of TRIPS did not produce anything substantial, or of interest to DCs. The TRIPS Council remained incapacitated by the web of proposals and counter proposals emanating from diametrically opposed groups of countries, the major industrial powers on the one hand and the DCs on the other. In the event, it is no coincidence that it became more of a battlefield of ideas and less a forum for consensus and practical action.

The most important development, from the point of view of DCs, was the declaration on the nexus between IP and state intervention during national emergencies, particularly in the context of national health. Supported by a worldwide clamour for cheaper drugs to assist AIDS sufferers, the DCs snatched a major concession during the 2001 Doha Ministerial meeting in the shape of the declaration on the permissibility of state intervention in health emergencies to sidestep rights of IP owners.[19] Apart from the fact that such powers of the state were explicitly incorporated in TRIPS and that any additional assurance by the major industrial nations that they would not impose sanctions on DCs that exercise their rights was therefore unnecessary, the demands of DCs to receive such assurance indicated beyond any doubt their morbid fear of the latent power of retaliation that the big industrial nations possessed. The Declaration hence constituted a mere restatement of the existing rules in TRIPS and represented no compromise, leave alone erosion, of IP rights that pharmaceutical manufacturers

---

16 See Frederick M. Abbott, 'TRIPS in Seattle: The Not-So-Surprising Failure and the Future of the TRIPS Agenda', 14 *Berkley Journal of International Law* 165, 2000.

17 Article 68, TRIPS.

18 These are Article 24.1, on entering into negotiations for increasing the protection of individual geographical indications; Article 24.2, on reviewing the application of the TRIPS provisions for geographical indications; Article 23.4, on undertaking negotiations for establishing a multilateral system of notification and registration of geographical indications for wines; Article 27.3(b), on reviewing after four years from entry into force of TRIPS, of members' measures to protect plant varieties and any exclusion from patentability they might make; Article 64.3, on establishing modalities for non-IP complaints five years from entry into force of the WTO Agreement; Article 71.1, on reviewing the implementation of TRIPS by developing nations, post-2000.

19 Paragraph 6 of the Doha Ministerial Declaration 2001 partly reads: 'We recognize that under WTO rules no country should be prevented from taking measures for the protection of human, animal or plant life or health, or of the environment at the levels it considers appropriate, subject to the requirement that they are not applied in a manner which would constitute a means of arbitrary or unjustifiable discrimination between countries where the same conditions prevail, or a disguised restriction on international trade, and are otherwise in accordance with the provisions of the WTO Agreements'. See note 5, ibid.

in the major industrial nations might have – despite the profuse references to the 'breakthrough' achieved or the victories scored by DCs and their supporters.

Furthermore, the 'Declaration on the TRIPS Agreement and Public Health' was fraught with all kinds of restrictions and practical hurdles. For one thing, it restricts products made under compulsory licence to those destined 'predominantly for the supply of the domestic market'. Secondly, resort to compulsory licence would be allowed 'only in the case of a national emergency or other circumstances of extreme urgency or in cases of public non-commercial use'.[20] Thirdly, the additional requirements of disclosure, registration and administration of licensed products make the exercise so burdensome that DCs have in effect elected to ignore its use in practice. To date, there are no records of any imports/exports of generic drugs by DCs in conformity with the Declaration.

It is interesting that, apart from the declaration on health, the major industrial powers were forced to pronounce a Doha Development Agenda,[21] which promised to place the 'needs and interests' of DCs 'at the heart of the Work Programme adopted in this Declaration'.[22] Still, the Doha Ministerial did not produce any policy statements regarding the revision of TRIPS in the manner that the DCs had demanded. It merely gave instructions to the TRIPS Council to examine 'the relationship between the TRIPS Agreement and the Convention on Biological Diversity, the protection of traditional knowledge and folklore, and other relevant new developments raised by members pursuant to Article 71.1'.[23]

Subsequent to the Doha Ministerial, the TRIPS Council has been busy collating and distributing the views of the WTO members on the problem of protecting and exploiting indigenous or traditional knowledge as well as the extension of protection to geographical indications other than wines and spirits. DCs have submitted a diversity of views and engaged heavily in the negotiations.[24] Yet, the coalition of major industrial nations and a few DCs ranged against them in the negotiations does not bode well for any outcome before too long. Indeed, the DCs' undying hopes for reconsideration of TRIPS appeared, despite the momentary concessions on generic drugs, more illusory than ever. The major industrial nations have expressly reiterated their rejection of any reconsideration of TRIPS

---

20 Decision of the WTO General Council of 30 August 2003, 'Implementation of Paragraph 6 of the Doha Declaration on the TRIPS Agreement and Public Health', WT/L/540, 1 September 2003, paragraph 1.

21 WTO, The Doha WTO Ministerial Declaration 2001, 20 November 2001, WT/MIN(01)/DEC/1.

22 Paragraph 2, ibid.

23 Paragraph 19, ibid.

24 For example, see, WTO, Council for TRIPS, 'The Relationship Between the TRIPS Agreement and the Convention on Biological Diversity and the Protection of Traditional Knowledge' (communication from Brazil, on behalf of China, Cuba, Dominican Republic, Ecuador, India, Pakistan, Peru, Thailand, Venezuela, Zambia and Zimbabwe), IP/C/W/356, 24 June 2002.

and sought to interpret the 'built-in agenda' as a straightening out of any remaining *minor* issues.

One would have expected that the preparations of the DCs for the September 2003 Cancun conference could have included the expression of fresh views on the state and direction of their desire to see a revision of TRIPS. In their 2003 meeting, leaders of the Non-Aligned Movement expressed the need to work out a framework for special and differential treatment of DCs and called for a 'Review [of[the TRIMs and TRIPS Agreements from a developmental dimension with a view to neutraliz[ing] the negative aspects of these agreements on the development of the developing countries and stressed the importance of implementing, and interpreting the TRIPS Agreement in a manner supportive of public health and access to medicines for all'. [25]

According to the stated views of their delegations at the opening of the ill-fated Cancun Conference, however, DCs had all but abandoned any notion of revision of TRIPS or its extension to cover additional geographic indications and traditional knowledge. They expressed their principal expectations at Cancun in terms of gaining market entry for their products through the removal of agricultural subsidies and other barriers in the markets of Western Europe and North America.[26] The only exception seemed to be Myanmar, which argued

> harmful practices such as economic coercive measures, trade sanctions, linkage to trade preferences, development aids or debt relief initiatives are being used by some major developed countries are [sic] contrary to the multilateral trade rules [and] that [sic] negatively affect the socio-economic lives of the people and also slow down the development process. We strongly believe that developing countries have the right to choose the path of development in accordance with their national priorities and objectives.[27]

In the end, the failure of the Conference left even the trade issues on the back burner. It is only with the proposals to consider the relationship between IP and development – submitted by Brazil and Argentina to the WIPO – that global IP issues have found fresh impetus.

---

25 Final Document of the XIII Conference of Heads of State or Government of the Non-Aligned Movement Kuala Lumpur, 24–5 February 2003.

26 Thus the Philippines demanded special and differential treatment for DCs to be able to pursue 'rural development and food security'. See, Ministerial Conference, Fifth Session, Cancun, 10–14 September 2003, Statement by the Honourable Manuel Roxas, Secretary of Trade and Industry, World Trade Organization, WT/MIN(03)/ST/63, 10 September 2003.

27 Ministerial Conference, Fifth Session, Cancún, 10–14 September 2003, Statement by H.E. Brigadier General Pyi Sone, Minister for Commerce of Myanmar, World Trade Organization, WT/MIN(03)/ST/105, 12 September 2003.

The Proposed 'WIPO Development Agenda'

The initiative of Brazil and Argentina (as well as other 12 developing countries)[28] to place IP at the heart of the development discourse has come in the wake of failures of all previous attempts by DCs to impress on the major industrial nations the necessity of 'granting' specific exceptions or exemptions from obligations imposed on them through the sprawling international IP regime. The proposal states, at the outset,

> The role of intellectual property and its impact on development must be carefully assessed on a case-by-case basis. IP protection is a policy instrument the operation of which may, in actual practice, produce benefits as well as costs, which may vary in accordance with a country's level of development. Action is therefore needed to ensure, in all countries, that the costs do not outweigh the benefits of IP protection.[29]

It may be pointed out that the broad generalization on the supposed costs and benefits of the IP protection does not refer just to DCs but to all countries. This is symptomatic of the widespread and ideologically based illusion that all nations require, and will be served by, the same set of IP laws. Hence, the proposal does not question whether some nations might not need any IP at all. Moreover, the proposal fails to indicate why if, as it asserts, IP protection is a 'policy instrument', its formulation cannot be at issue? As we will see from the contents of the proposal, it does not seem that Brazil and Argentina grasp the basic, intractable problems of IP for DCs – that current forms not only do not reflect their internal requirements for economic and technological development, but also block such development.

The proposal has four basic components. The proposal first addresses the role of WIPO and suggests that it needs to go beyond 'the promotion of intellectual property protection'[30] and be 'fully guided by the broad development goals that the UN has set for itself, in particular in the Millennium Development Goals'.[31] The proposal thus seeks for WIPO become an instrument for the implementation of UN policies and suggests for that purpose the amendment of the WIPO Convention to reflect the integration of the 'development dimension' into its activities.

A second aspect of the proposal concerns new treaties, such as the draft Substantive Patent Law Treaty (SPLT), that are currently being drafted or

---

28 WIPO, 'Proposal by Argentina and Brazil for the Establishment of a Development Agenda for WIPO', Geneva, 27 August 2004; WO/GA/31/11. The proposal was later elaborated through a further document; see WIPO, 'Proposal to Establish a Development Agenda for WIPO: An Elaboration of Issues Raised in Document WO/GA/31/11', Geneva, 6 April 2005; IIM/1/4.

29 Proposal by Argentina and Brazil, note 28, ibid.

30 Ibid.

31 Ibid.

negotiated. As regards the SPLT, it asserts that it 'would considerably raise patent protection standards, creating new obligations that developing countries will hardly be able to implement'.[32] It thus suggests that the views of the DCs expressed through proposed amendments be incorporated into the draft to make it 'more responsive to public interest concerns and the specific development needs of developing countries'.[33] It exhorts members to 'strive for an outcome that unequivocally acknowledges and seeks to preserve public interest flexibilities and the policy space of Member States'.[34] The proponents do not seem to realize that all previous advances in IP law-making were done in the interest of the pace-setters and without regard to the special circumstances of the least developed countries. Even when the minimal standards of the major conventions were endorsed, in the nineteenth century, against the proposals for universal or extensive standards applicable to all, it was not out of sympathy for the lesser developed but as a consequence of the deep division among the pace-setters themselves.

As part of the same concern for 'safeguarding public interest flexibilities', the proposal then refers to 'access to information and knowledge sharing' as 'essential elements in fostering innovation and creativity in the information economy' to argue that extending IP protection 'to the digital environment would obstruct the free flow of information and scuttle efforts to set up new arrangements for promoting innovation and creativity, through initiatives such as the "Creative Commons"'.[35] It therefore suggests that any treaties in relation to the digital environment need to address the 'interests of consumers and the public at large' and 'safeguard the exceptions and limitations existing in the domestic laws of Member States'.[36] It urges WIPO to consider the potential value of open access models such as the Human Genome Project and Open Source Software 'for the promotion of innovation and creativity'.[37] These proposals seem to assume that all nations will be affected by the expansion of IP to the same degree and require identical solutions. Yet, not all nations, least of all DCs, have transited to the 'information economy'. Thus, while the industrial nations might need to rethink their IP system in light of advances in information and communication technologies (ICT), the same cannot be said of DCs. The nature of the economic, technological problems DCs face are so different from those of the industrialized countries that their engagement with the catch-up game with the industrial nations will not be helped either by such rethinking or by a reversion to the utopian notion of 'common heritage of mankind'. The DCs cannot be party to a further attempt of the industrialized nations to foist forms of IP on all nations yet again while they

32 Ibid.
33 Ibid.
34 Ibid.
35 Ibid.
36 Ibid.
37 Ibid.

themselves continue to suffer from their past experience of 'received' or imported laws made by those industrialized nations.

A third element of the proposal questions the efficacy of Articles 7 and 8 of TRIPS, namely that it would facilitate 'transfer of technology' to DCs. It contends that the DCs 'lack the necessary infrastructure and institutional capacity to absorb such technology'.[38] It adds that 'higher standards of intellectual property protection' have not led to transfer of technology even in those countries possessing 'a degree of absorptive technological capacity'.[39] It concludes, 'In effect, corrective measures are needed to address the inability of existing IP agreements and treaties to promote a real transfer of technology to developing countries and LDCs.'[40]

The proposal suggests the creation of a body under WIPO 'to ensure an effective transfer of technology to developing countries, similarly to what has already been done in other fora such as the WTO and the UNCTAD'. It cites as an example the introduction of a 'Treaty on Access to Knowledge and Technology' that promotes 'access by the developing countries to the results of publicly funded research in the developed countries'.[41] This aspect of the proposal resuscitates the debate in the 1970s and 1980s, ending with the failed draft treaty on transfer of technology that DCs managed to push through UNCTAD relying on their majority ('Group of 77') in that forum. Although the current proposal relates only to publicly funded research, leaving out privately held proprietary knowledge that was included in the previous debate, the industrial nations that rejected it then will not necessarily be convinced that the fundamental arguments they put forward have lost their relevance today.

A fourth element of the proposal is enforcement of IP. It contends that IP enforcement should be approached 'in the context of broader societal interests and development-related concerns, in accordance with Article 7 of TRIPS'. It also asserts, 'The rights of countries to implement their international obligations in accordance with their own legal systems and practice, as clearly foreseen by Article 1.1 of TRIPS, should be safeguarded'.[42] It comments that the Advisory Committee on Enforcement (ACE), established by WIPO in 2002 should not confine itself to the perspective of right holders or to infringement issues, but should also consider their obligations as well as 'the need to ensure that enforcement procedures are fair and equitable and do not lend themselves to abusive practices by right holders that may unduly restrain legitimate competition'.[43] It refers to Articles 8 and 40 of TRIPS respectively as supporting measures 'to curb practices that may adversely

38 Ibid.
39 Ibid.
40 Ibid.
41 Ibid.
42 Ibid.
43 Ibid.

affect trade and the international transfer of technology' or to address 'anti-competitive practices in contractual licenses'.[44]

Clearly, the proposal seeks to introduce standards of use of IP by rights holders under the guise of curbing abusive practices. One might recall that throughout the evolution of IP, particularly during the mercantilist era, the main concern of the state was the lack of use or implementation of the object of rights. The obligation on patentees to work their inventions, prominent during the earliest phase (e.g. in Venice), was gradually eroded until it became a point of conflict between DCs and the major industrial powers in the 1960s and 1970s. Regardless of whether the proponents are aware of the historical impasse preceding TRIPS, the current proposal is hence an attempt to revive the debate. TRIPS sealed the fate of any such demands by rejecting the introduction of any preconditions in domestic legislation for the use of IP or even their recognition. No nation can deny registration of patents or trademarks by reference to lack of domestic use or in the traditional phrase, 'working'.

The proposal to balance the rights of proprietors with their obligations seems therefore an attempt to open old wounds without providing fresh arguments as to how this might become plausible. As a matter of fact, it is rather odd that such a suggestion has been made while the conditions of DCs have deteriorated in every department: their national IP systems have fallen under the absolute domination of foreign rights holders and their share in the world economy has been in precipitous decline. The reference to 'abusive' or 'anti-competitive' practices might suggest that the proponents did not differentiate the two sets of problems, namely lack of working vs use or the fallouts from use (working). While economists constantly questioned the inherently anti-competitive nature of IP but always came to the conclusion that such an outcome was a necessary evil, IP law was ill-equipped to address the problems of 'overuse' or 'abuse' For, the deployment of IP rights extends beyond IP *per se* into contract law, competition law and human rights. Consequently, any attempt to contain the problem within IP will not lead to viable solutions. Still, 'overuse' or 'abuse' is hardly a problem prevalent in DCs alone.

A fifth element of the proposal concerns the provision of technical assistance and its availability both in breadth and in quality. It goes off on a tangent, however: 'This is important to ensure that in all countries the costs of IP protection do not outweigh the benefits thereof. In this regard, national regimes set up to implement international obligations should be administratively sustainable and not overburden scarce national resources that may be more productively employed in other areas.'[45] There seems to be a number of contradictory claims here. On the one hand, the proposal does not make it clear why, if nations have set up a system to administer IP, those systems cannot be run in a 'sustainable' way. If the state concerned did not wish to put up the finances for the established system, either the state was aware all along that such a system was for face-saving purposes, to create the impression

44 Ibid.

45 Ibid.

that it was discharging its international obligations and the like, or that the state was fully reliant on foreign assistance. In both cases, the state would not seem to have been convinced of the utility of such a system to the national economy or that the nation might benefit from supporting it to the hilt. The truth, however, is further from this: the IP machinery erected in DCs serves international rights holders a lot more than domestic proprietors. In fact, the system would collapse forthwith were it not for the income received from foreign applications and the fear of the government officials that the absence of the trappings of the capitalist economy and industrialization might adversely impact on foreign investment and aid. Thus the proposal should have owned up fully to the reality of IP administration in DCs and called on the major industrial countries to pay for the upkeep of a system they largely benefit from or would not want to see collapse. Indeed, the promise of technical assistance is not altruistic at all – it is a channel the industrial nations have adopted for disbursing funds in DCs for services to be rendered to their IP rights holders. If the WIPO Development Agenda now insists that more of this should be available, it does not in any way diminish the stake the major industrial powers have in the IP systems of DCs. Quite the contrary – the proposal is only a coded reminder to those powers that those systems have always served their rights holders and that it is up to them to maintain and extend it further.

The proposal also asserts that 'WIPO's legislative assistance should ensure that national laws on intellectual property are tailored to meet each country's level of development and are fully responsive to the specific needs and problems of individual societies. It also must be directed towards assisting developing countries to make full use of the flexibilities in existing intellectual property agreements, in particular to promote important public policy objectives.' Whilst extending technical cooperation to meet the needs of nations might be within WIPO's remit, it is not clear how it should also engage in the formulation of IP laws appropriate to DCs. Would it not indeed be more appropriate for the respective DCs themselves to assume such a responsibility with or without the assistance of WIPO? Moreover, the assertion that DCs can still manage to formulate laws in keeping with 'each country's level of development and are fully responsive to the specific needs and problems of individual societies' contrasts sharply with the current reality of IP rights as being firmly fixed on global levels and therefore operating in a universal framework. Clearly, not only the logic of the proposal but also its very language is a relapse into the dead past.

A sixth element of the proposal concerns participation of civil society in the work of WIPO, 'including in all norm-setting activity'. The proposal calls for a change in current practice of inviting only representatives of IP right holders and admitting non-governmental organizations (NGOs) to represent 'the public interest'. It argues for participation of such NGOs 'to ensure that in IP norm-setting a proper balance is struck between the producers and users of technological knowledge, in a manner that fully services the public interest'.[46]

46 Ibid.

All in all, the proposal is a rehash of well-known perspectives that totally lacked a grasp of the reality of IP law in DCs as well as on an international level and ideas rejected by the major industrial powers as attempts to dilute or weaken IP rights. It puts a gloss on the real problems that DCs face in formulating and executing an IP policy that reflects their domestic needs as sovereign nations.

The Reception of the 'WIPO Development Agenda'

The proposal submitted to the WIPO General Assembly in September 2004 by Argentina and Brazil and cosponsored by 12 other DCs (all of whom have adopted the group name of 'the Friends of Development') has not been embraced by all DCs. Notable absentees are India and China, indeed the DCs of the entire Asian continent. It seems also that the G-20 group of nations[47] that crystallized during the Cancun WTO Ministerial Meeting has not endorsed the DA proposals as such. It is puzzling why the FOD did not merge with the G-20, if not to avoid fragmentation in the level of support for change in international trade rules, at least to consolidate the efforts of the DCs and create a broad-based pressure on the developed industrial nations.

Two counter-proposals were submitted to WIPO by two major industrial nations, the US and the UK. The EU, Japan and Canada did not reveal their views until after the first inter-sessional intergovernmental meeting of the WIPO devoted to the DA was held on 11–13 April 2005 and the second from 20 to 22 June 2005. Mexico's views, largely echoing those of the US and UK, were in stark contrast to that country's position on IP at the Uruguay Round. Interestingly, although India did not join the ranks of the FOD, it openly stated its opposition to the status quo in IP.[48]

Apart from the above, other nations have expressed their views in the course of the discussions during the Inter-Sessional Intergovernmental Meeting (IIM) on a Development Agenda for WIPO. Some nations, Australia and Japan among them, have expressed their agreement with the US view that implementation of a 'development agenda' has always been an integral part of WIPO's mission. Others have supported the stance of the FOD. Still others have sought to add to the DA, by way of further elaboration; a case in point is Chile. The rest of DCs in Africa

47 Notwithstanding the fluctuation in membership (currently at 21), the group comprises Argentina, Bolivia, Brazil, Chile, China, Costa Rica, Cuba, Ecuador, Egypt, El Salvador, Guatemala, India, Mexico, Nigeria, Pakistan, Paraguay, Philippines, South Africa, Thailand and Venezuela. See http://www.g-20.mre.gov.br.

48 Statement by Debabrata SAHA, Deputy Permanent Representative of India, 1 October 2004; available at www.cptech.org/ip/wipo/india10012004.html; accessed 31 January 2006.

and the Middle East expressed their opinions (through Morocco[49] and Bahrain,[50] respectively) in support of the contrasting positions of the FOD and that of the US and the UK. We will presently examine the set of views that were expressed in written submissions and are therefore more accessible to us.

United States

By far the strongest and earliest opposition to the DA came from the US.[51] As a matter of fact, the reactions of the US to the proposal could not have been unexpected. The US countered that WIPO had engaged in 'a robust "development agenda" in all of its work for a long time, delivering high-quality development activities to Member States on a demand-driven basis'.[52] It insisted that WIPO should continue with its defined role of promoting IP rather than attempting to take on additional development concerns that are within the ambit of other UN agencies. The US asserted further that IP alone 'cannot bring about development and can contribute only part of the solution'; that it is 'simply one part of the necessary infrastructure needed to stimulate development'.[53] The US proposed, instead, to strengthen WIPO's role through a 'WIPO Partnership Program' – an Internet-based facility 'to match specific needs with available resources' more effectively and in a transparent manner.[54]

Clearly, the US did not appear to have been impressed by the repeated calls for injection of a 'development dimension' into the operations of WIPO. Neither did it seem to appreciate the significance of the renewed demands for a rethink of the international IP regime, particularly its relevance to DCs. It merely reiterated the well-known views in industrial nations about the role and continuity of technical assistance programme as extended to DCs by the WIPO. Inevitably, the evident gap between the demands and expectations of the FOD and their supporters, on the one hand, and the dismissive approach apparent in the US (and some of its supporters), on the other, will lead to further disappointments among DCs and an even stronger desire to recast the international IP regime in a manner 'more responsive to public interest concerns and the specific development needs of developing countries'.[55]

49 WIPO, 'The African Proposal for the Establishment of a Development Agenda for the World Intellectual Property Organization (WIPO)', Geneva, 18 July 2005, IIM/3/2.

50 WIPO, 'Proposal by the Kingdom of Bahrain on the Importance of Intellectual Property in Social and Economic Development and National Development Programs for the Inter-Sessional Intergovernmental Meeting on a Development Agenda for WIPO', Geneva, 14 June 2005, IIM/2/2.

51 WIPO, 'Proposal by the United States of America for the Establishment of a Partnership Program in WIPO', Geneva, 18 March 2005, IIM/1/2.

52 Ibid.

53 Ibid.

54 Ibid.

55 Proposal by Argentina and Brazil, note 28, ibid.

United Kingdom

The UK proposal[56] reiterated the US view that IP policy is only one aspect of the development process. It pointed to 'the development of an indigenous scientific and technological capacity' as crucial for such a process and to the IP system as 'an important element in developing that capacity'.[57] The UK then argued that assistance should be directed at building the DCs' capacity in science and technology. It also showed a willingness to depart from the outright rejection of the DA by the US. On the one hand, the UK relied on the recommendations of the Commission on Intellectual Property Rights it had established in 2001 to concede that 'IP regimes can and should be tailored to take into account individual country's circumstances within the framework of international agreements such as TRIPS'.[58] Not that such a position represents anything radically different from the status quo, anchored as it is to unqualified support for TRIPS – the very premise that the DA looks more and more to be pitting itself against. Yet the UK's eagerness to endorse concerns of 'development' as expressed in the DA – by calling for the need to give 'explicit recognition to both the benefits and costs of IP protection and the corresponding need to adjust domestic regimes in developing countries to ensure that the costs do not outweigh the benefits'[59] – demonstrated an inclination to appease the increasingly strident voices of the FOD.[60]

On the other hand, the UK argued that WIPO's activities should be guided by the need to integrate IP policies with the development objectives of countries – very much akin to one of the demands in the DA. The UK declared that 'if WIPO is unable to do this within its existing mandate then that mandate should be changed … We are however not as yet persuaded that WIPO's existing mandate is such that it is prevented from effectively integrating development objectives into its activities.'[61] Unlike the US, therefore, the UK seemed ready to reconsider whether the WIPO has not lived up to the expectations placed on it and to agree to changes, if so convinced.

In the area of technical assistance, the UK expressed the view that something must be done to enhance 'capacity to facilitate the development of balanced IP-related policies'.[62] It wondered whether WIPO has managed to draw up and execute the requisite action plans in the context of the broad objectives of development in countries or regions. It called for examination of WIPO's activities and past record in order to redefine its programmes on development. Ultimately,

56 WIPO, 'Proposal by the United Kingdom', Geneva, 7 April 2005, IIM/1/5.

57 Ibid.

58 Ibid.

59 Ibid.

60 WIPO, 'Proposal to Establish a Development Agenda for WIPO: An Elaboration of Issues Raised in Document WO/GA/31/11', Geneva, 6 April 2005, IIM/1/4.

61 See note 56, ibid.

62 Ibid.

it sought to reinforce the existing provision of the technical assistance to DCs by all parties, including individual governments, through further rationalization and coordination. It thus welcomed the proposal of the US for a new facility to coordinate and match needs with the available assistance.

As regards the issue of further harmonization of patent laws, the UK maintained that common rules, even in restricted aspects such as on novelty and inventive steps, will benefit all nations by reducing costs and time for processing applications in multiple jurisdictions. It conceded, however, that in 'countries where there is little or no domestic demand for patents, further harmonization is unlikely to bring any direct benefit to offset the costs of further amending their patent laws. For such countries it may be appropriate to explicitly provide in any harmonization proposal an extended transition period or even a clear opt out.'[63]

While the UK's largesse of allowing deferred obligations in future harmonization activities may be commendable, one wonders why such an approach cannot be applied across the board to all DCs who have not directly benefited from TRIPS – the very premise of the current demands for DA, though unarticulated and still vaguely kept in the background. Indeed, the UK's attempt to warm to the DA while remaining silent about the intransigence of the US casts doubts on its motives. By pushing for a reinvigoration of WIPO's 'Permanent Committee on Cooperation for Development' as the ultimate tool to rectify the perceived deficiencies of the IP system,[64] it shrinks from upholding the broad reform of the same system according to its analysis of tailoring a system in conformity with the specific circumstances of DCs. Both the US and its other industrial allies and the FOD must be wondering what the UK has actually offered as the way forward.

On the question of technology transfer, the UK referred to current activities under the WTO, following from the Doha Ministerial in 2001, as being a more proper forum for discussion.

Mexico

In its proposal,[65] Mexico took the view that the most important consideration in the current debate should be rationalization of resources. It asserted, 'resources are not in plentiful supply and must be used rationally even where they come from external sources'.[66] Mexico pointed to the absence of knowledge by the general population of the relevance and benefits of the IP system as 'a cause of inefficiency as well as an obstacle to development'.[67] It contended that 'The sanction of conduct which infringes intellectual property is of no use, if it is not complemented by appropriate

63 Ibid.

64 WIPO, 'Proposal by the United Kingdom', Geneva, 14 June 2005, IIM/2/3.

65 WIPO, 'Proposal by Mexico on Intellectual Property and Development', Geneva, 1 April 2005, IIM/1/3.

66 Ibid.

67 Ibid.

dissemination and understanding of the system.'[68] Consequently, Mexico proposed that dissemination be integrated into WIPO's activities in DCs.[69]

Mexico did not stop at suggesting the creation of awareness among the general public in DCs. It endorsed the current international IP system and demonstrated its alliance with the developed industrial countries in no uncertain terms: 'The viability and success of the national systems require an international standard-setting framework based on clear, predictable and non-discriminatory rules, as well as minimum protection standards not subject to modifications resulting from the political, economic, social and even cultural changes generated by the members of the international community'.[70] Now, this is a declaration not only in favour of the existing international IP regime but also a rejection of any attempts to 'modify' national systems at all. Although Mexico is a member of the G-20 that is presently seeking to modify the current international trade regime and to implement the Doha Development Agenda, its rebuttal of the DA newly formulated by the FOD is bewildering. Considering its determined opposition to TRIPS at the Uruguay Round, one would have thought that, at the very least, Mexico could express some sort of support to the DA.

India

India's response rested on its opposition to any further harmonization by citing 'all the damage that TRIPS has wrought on developing countries'.[71]It asserted that DCs need a flexible IP regime, a 'national policy space', just as much as 'today's developed countries had when they themselves were at a comparable stage of development'.[72] It argued further that 'higher and higher levels of IP protection, inherent in any harmonization exercise that takes no account of the circumstances of each country, are extremely detrimental to developing countries'.[73] In India's view, any further harmonization of IP will only 'serve the interest of rent seekers, who are predominantly in developed countries, rather than that of the public in developing countries'.[74] Accordingly, India called on the industrialized powers to respect 'the national policy space' of DCs when seeking to add to their international obligations.

With regards to the DA, India declared its full support but sought to define the direction of desirable changes somewhat differently by calling for the 'need to take into account any possible negative impact on the users of IP, on consumers at large, or on public policy in general'.[75] It asserted that IP protection was 'meant,

68 Ibid
69 Ibid.
70 Ibid.
71 See, note 48, ibid.
72 Ibid.
73 Ibid.
74 Ibid.
75 Ibid.

first and foremost, to promote societal development by encouraging technological innovation' and hence a country should be able to calibrate the kind of incentive it wishes to create 'in the light of its own circumstances, taking into account the overall costs and benefits of such protection'.[76] In a sense, then, India stands for a total halt to an IP harmonization at an international level so long as that harmonization leads to further obligations being placed on DCs. Although not explicitly, India also seems to desire the unravelling of the TRIPS. It would appear that the ambiguity and wishful thinking in the DA, on the one hand, and the absence of clear intentions in the DA about what needs to be done to TRIPS, on the other, may have put off India from cosponsoring that proposal.

In the area of transfer of technology, India sought to make it an obligation of developed countries as a quid pro quo for IP protection that DCs provide to 'western rights holders'. It asserted that without such an obligation being imposed on the developed industrial nations, consumers in DCs will hardly benefit from IP protection.[77] India must surely know that this strange proposal finds no support in logic or theory. Were rent outflows to be the basis of evaluating the benefits of the IP system, all countries save a handful would qualify for the bounty that India has suggested. However, such a measure would be tantamount to abolition of the international IP system, precisely because it is the framework for transfer of incomes ('rent') from one country to another, not just only between DCs and industrial nations.

Bahrain

Bahrain produced a lengthy document,[78] on behalf of the Middle East countries,[79] iterating general views on the value of an IP system in the abstract, the benefits it received from WIPO's help and its proposals to improve the technical assistance system. Thus, it did not seize upon any of the grounds for a critique of the past roles of WIPO expressed by the proponents of the DA. Indeed, Bahrain seemed determined to add its voice to the US and other countries which saw no need to establish a 'development dimension' to WIPO's current role, only some improvements in the form of cooperation and coordination of the technical assistance.

76 Ibid.

77 Ibid.

78 WIPO, 'Proposal by the Kingdom of Bahrain on the Importance of Intellectual Property in Social and Economic Development and National Development Programs for the Inter-Sessional Intergovernmental Meeting on a Development Agenda for WIPO', Geneva, 14 June 2005, IIM/2/2.

79 These are: Jordan, Lebanon, United Arab Emirates, Qatar, Yemen, Oman, Saudi Arabia, Kuwait, Syria and Libyan Arab Jamahiriya.

Morocco

Morocco, representing the African group, reiterated the importance of IP as 'one mechanism among many for bringing about development', but that it should not be 'detrimental to individual national efforts at development'.[80] Morocco demanded that 'the existing international IP architecture should be made more democratic and responsive to the needs and aspirations of developing and least developed countries, especially in matters that are vital to the needs and welfare of their citizenry.'[81]

In terms of the specific issues presented in the DA, Morocco declared that 'knowledge has no bounds or confines, and has never had one single source', ignoring the fact that IP mediates the boundaries of where publicly available and 'private' knowledge meet. This view paints Morocco's approach of how WIPO should be reformed to serve the DA: to enable countries 'to gain access to technology at reasonable cost'; and to facilitate 'access to foreign patented information on technology and technical resources'.[82] It then added, 'Relaxation of patent rules should therefore, be considered as a policy option for developing and least developed countries to facilitate their drive towards technological and scientific development.'[83] Clearly, Morocco does not seem to appreciate the nature of the international IP regime that stands guard over the subject-matter of its proposals or the fact that similar demands in the 1970s and 1980s fell on deaf ears. Instead of repeating the failed demands, therefore, Morocco should have stepped up to the challenge of formulating IP strategies conducive to technological and social development in DCs, regardless of whether the international regime allows it or the developed industrial nations welcome it.

That Morocco is oblivious to the current IP regime across the world is proved by its limited concerns in the area of norm-setting. Amidst all the argument for reforms of the status quo, Morocco could only put forward a proposal for a treaty 'on the protection of genetic resources, traditional knowledge and folklore'.[84] Again, although it also called for an impact assessment study to be conducted into 'technical assistance, technology transfer and impact of new treaties on developing and least developed countries',[85] it did not countenance any need for reform in the domestic IP laws of DCs.

Finally, Morocco sought to involve the WIPO in conducting studies into the obstacles for IP protection in the context, particularly, of the informal sector in Africa as well as the 'tangible costs and benefits' of such protection for the sector 'especially with regards to generation of employment'.[86] Its proposals encompassed

80 WIPO, 'Proposal by Mexico on Intellectual Property and Development', Geneva, 1 April 2005, IIM/1/3.

81 Ibid.

82 Ibid.

83 Ibid.

84 Ibid.

85 Ibid.

86 Ibid.

virtually all aspects of the development process: strengthening the roles of small and medium enterprises; 'bridging the digital divide'; reversing the brain drain; and creating better 'access to essential medicines and food, and also to information and knowledge for education and research'.[87]

Chile

Chile submitted its proposals for an appraisal of the public domain, the creation of a complementary systems to IP and an assessment of what the appropriate levels of IP might be to each country by reference to its particular situation and the degree of development and institutional capacity in that country.[88] As regards the public domain, Chile urged WIPO to undertake a study to look into its implications and benefits and to 'draw up proposals and models' for its protection and access.[89]

In relation to the second, Chile argued that 'economic policy instruments' such as 'competitions, tax benefits, direct contributions, work commissions and public procurement' stimulate creativity.[90] Chile thus proposed that WIPO set up 'a permanent area for analysis and discussion' of these incentives 'in addition to the intellectual property system'.[91]

As regards the third, Chile suggested that a study of the development dimension be conducted not only 'to demonstrate the benefits and impact of intellectual property systems' but also to identify the costs and appropriate levels of IP protection congruent to the particular circumstances of a country but within the framework of 'the minimum standard' established by TRIPS.[92] For all the apparent desire to re-examine the three specified issues, Chile has not grappled with the crux of the current debate: whether or not to create or inject a shift in the international IP system to facilitate development as demanded by DCs. It is not easy to understand why else Chile would propose an independent study of the relationship between IP and competition, the extent of exceptions and limitations to IP that DCs might need to facilitate innovation.[93]

Conclusion

Commentators, policy-makers and government officials in the industrial nations might be amused by the new attempt of the FOD to cast doubt on the benefits of the international IP regime to DCs. Exactly 10 years after the adoption of a

87 Ibid.
88 WIPO, 'Proposal by Chile', Geneva, 12 January 2006, PCDA/1/2.
89 Ibid.
90 Ibid.
91 Ibid.
92 Ibid.
93 Ibid.

global standard of IP by all members of the WTO, it might never have seemed that questions of appropriateness and relevance of that standard to the DCs would return to haunt them. As it is, many have made a career out of promoting IP for DCs, to the extent of turning the adoption or rejection of IP in DCs into an ideological divide between those who stand for progress and those who oppose it. The WIPO had been busy, since its inception, transplanting IP to all DCs, and has clung tenaciously to an unchanging template for that purpose. Any form of differentiation among national IP laws was a taboo subject even among academic circles.

However, with the rise in awareness of the economic and social decay that many DCs suffer under the weight of what are broadly perceived to be unfair world trade rules and the willingness of sections of the population in the industrial nations to come to the aid of the suffering majority, the tide has started to turn. Many seem ready to see that the critique of the current international IP system generally or in the DCs is neither about the abandonment of that system altogether, nor about promoting theft or piracy. The proposals of the FOD have ignited fresh debate into the role of IP in the development of DCs and generated sympathetic responses overall.

The success or failure of the current attempt to transform the WIPO into a tool of development in the interest of DCs will, nevertheless, depend on whether Brazil and Argentina (the FOD) can muster enough support among DCs and gather around themselves countries like China and India who have the experience, resources and clout to win the argument in the face of intransigence from some of the industrial countries, in particular the US. For one thing, the forays of the US into pulling DCs into some form of free trade agreement, with uniform TRIPS-plus provisions, will deprive them of more and more countries that might opt for a fundamental reversal in the IP system – the relatively favourable stance of the EU notwithstanding.

Secondly, the FOD have yet to define the kind of changes they desire to bring about in the IP field. As it stands, their proposals are, in many ways, illusory or utopian; they seek to appeal to, and draw on, the increasing sympathy that some governments and the general public in the West express for the provision of massive relief to DCs. The proposals seek to take advantage of the constant portrayal, in the media, of mass poverty, rampant disease, interminable conflicts and repression in DCs as well as the weakening of the administrative and infrastructural capabilities of the DCs to fortify arguments for a largely undefined 'development dimension'.

Clearly, they need to move away from battling the international system and concentrate on the formulae suitable to DCs. The rationale for this is simple. Just as the industrial nations strive to protect their IP everywhere in the world, DCs too should seek to promote innovation and build their economies through a suitable form of IP. To that extent, devising an appropriate form of IP is, first and foremost, an internal matter for both groups of nations although the industrial countries attempt to portray IP as something that needs to be treated as a common concern transcending national interests and boundaries. This is exemplified by the aggressive stance of the US in the last two decades.

Ultimately, if the FOD intend to make an impact, they should insist on the exercise of their sovereign rights to legislate and implement laws appropriate to their needs. Should any country desire protection for its IP beyond its borders, that again should depend on the consent to which those countries are entitled as sovereign nations. It is a matter of historical record that most of the present-day DCs were coopted into the major conventions without their consent (because they were colonies or unable to stand up to the pressures put on them by the industrial powers). Lacking the fundamental attributes of sovereignty, namely acting on consent reflecting the expressed wishes of its population, no DC can be held to live up to the obligations enshrined in the major conventions. DCs should exercise such a right now and allow their populations to express their views on the long-standing shackles placed on their businesses, creative communities and the wider society. If democracy is the byword for the twenty-first century, surely such a course should be welcome by the major powers and other industrial countries.

Finally, the FOD needs to transcend the false sermon that the door is still open for DCs to tinker with TRIPS and modify its deleterious impacts. An example is Reichman, who advises DCs that Articles 7, 8, 31 and 40 of TRIPS 'arm developing and least-developed countries with legal grounds for maintaining a considerable degree of domestic control over intellectual property policies in a post-TRIPS environment, including the imposition of compulsory licenses'.[94] However, the apparent concessions to DCs are conditional on adherence to substantive rules of TRIPS and hence any deviation ostensibly allowed is merely theoretical. The paralysis of many DCs to act in favour of their population in facing the AIDS pandemic because of the fear of retaliation from the major industrial powers attests to the reality of the underlying power of TRIPS. In short, the lack of legislative space for DCs that TRIPS entails is indisputable. The rush of DCs to inject the standards of TRIPS into their domestic legislation is testimony to that phenomenon. Even when DCs seek to take advantage of the specified provisions (such as compulsory licence in relation to pharmaceuticals), there is no lack of writers and interest groups who seek to show this as an attempt to weaken the IP system or free ride on others' IP.[95]

94 See J.H. Reichman, 'Universal Minimum Standards of Intellectual Property Protection under the TRIPS Component of the WTO Agreement', 29 *International Lawyer* 345–88, 1995, at 357–8.

95 Thus Leaffer asserts rather sharply that 'In Third World countries, the piracy of intellectual property is justified by an ideology of development. Ready access to intellectual property is viewed as important to development, whereas the enforcement of intellectual property law is considered a burden on development.' See Marshall A. Leaffer, 'Protecting United States Intellectual Property Abroad: Toward a New Multilateralism', 76 *Iowa Law Review* 273, 1991, at 282.

Chapter 13
Intellectual Property and the 'Digital Divide'*

Introduction

The literature in the social sciences relating to the information and communication technologies (ICT) addresses aspects of the problem of the digital divide. Unfortunately, very little has been written on the legal dimension of the same problem. Even then, the focus has been on policy and regulatory issues surrounding access to ICTs.[1] Far less significance has been given to the problem in the intellectual property (IP) literature, although some of the debate on the continuing expansion of IP indirectly touches on it.

This chapter aims to examine how IP might contribute towards the digital divide and the possible ways and means of reversing its negative impact. As already mentioned, the ongoing debate on the further expansion of IP to cover ('propertise') every imaginable form of information and calls to curtail or revise such expansion indirectly link with the urge to lessen whatever impact IP might have on the digital divide. While the literature critiquing IP expansion towards the end of the twentieth century has largely developed in the context of concerns for the continuity of creativity and innovation as well as cultural progress in the industrially advanced societies, this chapter seeks to scrutinize the narrower problem of how IP might have impinged on the digital divide. This can be achieved by moving beyond the general denunciation of current IP as somehow outdated and as a mere stranglehold over innovation and human progress; instead, the chapter explores the nature of IP and the manner of its evolution over the centuries within the framework of the demands and expectations of economies and societies, whether industrial or non-industrial. The benefits of such an approach are that the critique of the system will be grounded in the history, economics and technologies of countries and nations that gave rise to it as well as that any proposals for validating, reforming or overthrowing the system will not appear whimsical or utopian.

---

* This article originally appeared, in the author's name, as 'Intellectual Property and the Digital Divide' 1 *Journal of Information, Law and Technology* 2008; available at http://www2.warwick.ac.uk/fac/soc/law/elj/jilt.

1 Andres Guadamuz Gonzalez, 'The Digital Divide: It's The Content, Stupid: Part 1', *Computer and Telecommunications Law Review*, 73–77, 2005, at 73.

The chapter is organized in four sections. The first defines the concept of 'digital divide'. The second outlines whether and how IP law has coped with the digital revolution. Then the perspectives of the relevant stakeholders in stemming the digital divide are reviewed: the OECD and the WSIS; global corporations such as Microsoft; NGOs and the 'Friends of The Intellectual Commons'. The final section brings together, and critically assesses, the various strands of views on possible way(s) of bridging the digital divide in terms of current IP law and policy and in light of any emerging trends. The chapter concludes that, while IP does contribute to the digital divide, some of its critics fail to recognize the paramount role of the economic and social environment within which it has developed; consequently, any proposals for overthrowing IP while leaving that environment intact will remain fanciful.

The 'Digital Divide' Defined

The term 'digital divide' has become a popular shorthand to refer to any perceived inequality in the use of ICT; however, no clear consensus has emerged in defining it.[2] More often, the term is used broadly to denote the gap between the technology haves and have-nots as a whole. One commentator refers to the 'unequal patters of development' arising from the unequal access to the 'new world of instant communications and infinite information on demand'.[3] He argues, 'In a world governed by information, exclusion from information is as devastating as exclusion from land in an agricultural age'.[4] Occasionally, there is a tendency to view the concept as equivalent to the gap in information, in other words, not just in access to facilities alone.

A report prepared for UNESCO, by contrast, views gaps in the level of ICT introduced by countries, 'between "ICT-haves" and "have-nots"' as a measure of 'the digital divide';[5] indeed, it used a Digital Divide Index to 'track the diffusion and uptake of ICTs over time and across economies and regions'.[6] Norris takes the 'digital divide' to mean 'a multidimensional phenomenon encompassing three distinct aspects': gaps between the industrial and developing countries ('global divide'); the information rich and poor within each nation ('social divide'); and 'the

---

2 Ibid.

3 Titus Alexander, *Unravelling Global Apartheid: An Overview of World Politics*, Polity Press: Cambridge, 1996, at 195.

4 Ibid.

5 See, George Sciadas (ed.), *Monitoring the Digital Divide ... and Beyond.* Orbicom: Montreal, 2003; available at: http://www.orbicom.uqam.ca/projects/ddi2002/2003_dd_pdf_en.pdf; at 1.

6 Ibid., at iii.

difference between those who do and do not, use the panoply of digital resources to engage, mobilize and participate in public life' ('democratic divide').[7]

Paré disagrees with the 'binary conceptualisation of the digital divide', which looks to the rate of access as the sole determinant and proposes the use of 'socio-economic variables such as capability/skills, content, literacy, income and culture as well as the nature of commercial and regulatory environments, that account for the absorptive capacity of societies toward technological innovations'.[8] Presenting their findings of a study of the problem within the US, Mosseberger et al. similarly point out that 'having access to a computer is insufficient if individuals lack the skills they need to take advantage of technology'.[9] They add, 'Access is undeniably important, but the real policy question is how well society will be able to take advantage of the opportunities offered by technology'.[10] To answer that question, they looked at the 'skills divide', the 'economic opportunity divide' and 'the democracy divide' as being crucial to their studies.

At the background of any determination of the digital divide are the differing levels of access to information resources or facilities in some countries or communities as compared with others. Indeed, the degree of penetration of ICT (and elements of such) in all countries has been regularly monitored to assess whether countries, communities or groups within them have moved further ahead than, or fallen behind, others. Leagues of tables have been regularly issued by various organizations[11] and deployed in analysis of trends and issues.

Regardless of the differences in approaches or terminologies used in diagnosing the nature of the problem of the digital divide, it would seem reasonable to hold that issues relating to affordability and availability of the basic infrastructure for ICT that lie within the competences of governments and private businesses differ greatly from those of resources that communities, groups and individuals may or may not muster to take advantage of that infrastructure and deploy them for their everyday needs. Yet all of these in turn depend ultimately on the level of industrialization and commercial standing, or lack thereof, of the relevant country vis-à-vis other countries. Any tale, therefore, of a digital divide which does not link achievements or failures to the standing of a country within the global economic and technological dynamics would not only be futile (as lacking in an

---

7 Pippa Norris, *Digital Divide: Civic Engagement, Information Poverty and the Internet Worldwide*, Cambridge University Press: Cambridge, 2001, at 4.

8 See Daniel Paré, 'The Digital Divide: Why the "The" is Misleading', in Mathias Klang and Andrew Murray (eds), *Human Rights In The Digital Age*, Cavendish Publishing: London, 2005, pp. 85–97, at 88.

9 Karen Mosseberger et al., *Virtual Inequality: Beyond the Digital Divide*, Georgetown University Press: Washington, DC, 2003, at 1.

10 Ibid., at 5.

11 See, for example, UCTAD, *Information Economy Report 2006: The Development Perspective*; available at http://www.unctad.org; 'Internet World Stats' at http://www.internetworldstats.com.

essential perspective), but also devoid of logic (by ignoring the relativism inherent to comparisons of divergent cultures, geographic locations and histories).

It is also the author's contention that any meaningful discourse on the digital divide should concentrate on the impact of the digital revolution on nations' or communities' successes or failures, at most, since the late 1980s. To extend any such studies to times and technologies beyond the onset of the digital revolution will not only lead to confusion but end up restating the obvious conclusions that development theories (especially the dependency school) on the post-War years have long ago reached: developing countries (DCs) are at the bottom of the pile without much real prospect of getting out of their decay.[12] Merely to translate those long-standing conclusions into digitalspeak, stack them up as the ever-widening digital divide and come out thundering against the 'information rich' or 'technology haves' will be to rehash a paltry truth everybody has known all along.

On the other hand, an investigation of the digital divide in terms of the incidence and spread of elements of ICT, such as the Internet[13] or cyberspace, in countries, communities or groups or per head of population without any reference to the prevailing disparity in economic, technological and other forms before the onset of such elements would merely lead to tautological conclusions. Surely, the adverse or other impacts of the digital revolution could be established properly if such an investigation took account of the prevailing disparity among countries, groups and communities before its onset. Moreover, a determination of the existence or otherwise of the digital divide should require a perusal of all elements of ICT across the board rather than one or a set of them.

Intellectual Property and the Digital Revolution

There is very little controversy over what constitutes 'intellectual property' (IP), although occasionally confusion arises about its boundaries and the legitimacy of private, non-commercial use of such property. In theory, all forms of creative works that have been fruits of labour and 'perspiration' and proved to have established a modicum of novelty over and above that currently available to society can claim protection under the law (see Figure 13.1) and in the name of the creator. In theory, therefore, any work embodying a quantum of creativity, Q, is eligible for a form of protection for a period of time, T, regardless of which category it falls under.[14] The grant of a proprietary status to such works under specific forms of legislation or by

12 See, generally, Samir Amin, *Unequal Development – An Essay on the Social Formation of Peripheral Capitalism*, The Harvester Press: Brighton, 1976.

13 See Gonzalez, note 1, above, where the frame of reference is content issues on the Internet. See, also, Norris, above, note 7.

14 For a fuller discussion, see A. Endeshaw, 'Reconfiguring Intellectual Property for the Information Age: Towards Information Property?', 7(3) *The Journal of World Intellectual Property*, 327–64, May 2004.

the courts has developed into an unquestionable facet of every industrial society for the past 150 years or so.

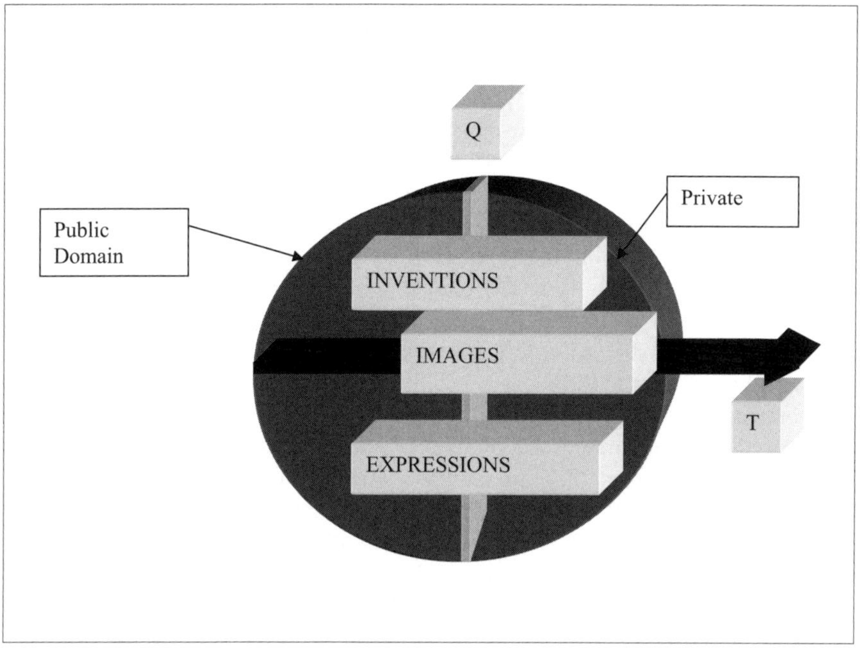

Figure 13.1 Principal categories of IP

IP has traditionally been classified into four categories: patent, copyright, trademarks and designs. All save copyright ('expressions') arise from registration of the respective form of creative work (invention, signs and appearances) with government authorities (previously called the patent office but increasingly changed to intellectual property office) and the issue of a certificate by the same authorities specifying a named person's right to use the creative work on an exclusive basis. The right holder decides whether to apply the creative work to produce goods or services for sale or licence it to others to use the said work towards the same objectives. This right enables the creator to recoup expenses incurred in the course of the creative process that led to the work, such as research and development (R&D) in the case of inventions. This is particularly important for huge companies such as pharmaceuticals that engage in continuous and expensive R&D. A lot of commentary has asserted that, were inventors not allowed to keep the right to exploit their inventions to themselves, the stock of new ideas generated in societies might dry up. Other views have also contested the relevance of patents for inventions although those views are heard less and less these days.

The nature of copyright differs from the 'industrial property' categories, largely because the creative process takes on a passive form, leading to no transformation of material surroundings it captures as its setting.[15] Thus a painting remains a reflection of the person or thing it is presumed to capture in lines and colour without anything happening to the person or thing as such. This contrasts with the physical transformation of a person through plastic surgery and possibly leading to claims of a design or an invention. The overall provision in copyright for expressions of whatever form has enabled it to provide refuge for all sorts of non-industrial, non-material or, in short, passive activities extending from poetry to dramatic episodes to mime to stage performances (musicals, circuses, acrobatics) to electronic circuitry (software).

Any serious opposition to the grant of rights to ideas in the forms that have come to pass emerged from the second half of the twentieth century from previously colonial countries that sought to modify it to reflect their economic and cultural needs. It was only since governments and legislature in industrial nations revised, updated and extended IP in many directions, both through the Trade-Related Aspects of Intellectual Property (TRIPS) and afterwards in the urge to cope with the impacts of the digital revolution, that disquiet on the renewed status of IP within these nations too has gained ground. Today, both groups of nations have found advocates, respectively, for change and rethinking of the post-TRIPS status quo.

The disquiet in the DCs relates chiefly to the inappropriateness of the forms of IP that have been transplanted to them during colonialism and afterwards and the huge pressure mounted against them not to change them to reflect internal/domestic economic, cultural and technological needs. It is now an established fact that any post-TRIPS changes can only be upwards (reinforcements, upgrading, deepening, etc.), whereas the demand of most DCs from the decades prior to TRIPS was for an overhaul of the IP system as a whole to work out how it might be customized to serve their economic, technological and cultural requirements. At the height of the clamour to make generic drugs available to DCs to fight the HIV/AIDS epidemic untrammelled by IP that pharmaceutical companies strove to erect against them, the 2001 Doha Declaration seemed to pave the way for change. Yet it only provided a momentary reassurance to DCs of an allowance which was already part of the workings of patent law. In other words, the pretence of accommodating the demands of the DCs was in reality a restatement of existing law and no more.

The repeated plea to rethink IP even in the industrial nations arises from the assessment that post-TRIPS extensions in IP, in the wake of the digital revolution and the rapid advances of biotechnology, have deleterious consequences to

15 Ibid., at 357–8.

innovation,[16] culture, the economy and even democracy.[17] Thus the patenting of human genes has been viewed as not only unethical in commodifying the human body and in appropriating naturally existing substances but also as being harmful to public health and to research.[18] Patenting of business methods as well as other trivia, traditionally considered outside the bounds of patent law, has triggered objections to the clogging of patent offices with all kinds of claims for registration[19] as well as a possible gridlock of the Internet resulting from the diversity of patent grants for software (application programs) enabling online transactions.[20]

---

16 In connection with the latest attempt to revise US patent law, through the Patent Reform Act of 2007, Chandler, Mark (senior vice president and general counsel of Cisco Systems) has reportedly commented that 'our patent system is broken. Patents are increasingly used not as shields to protect the fruits of creativity from misappropriation, but as weapons to extract money from the productive part of society and transfer it to entrepreneurial speculators whose only innovation is new ways to game the system'. See, 'Patent Reform ... or Ruin?', *The Washington Times*, 1 August 2007, quoted in http://www.patentfairness.org/media/in_the_news.cfm. Bruce Sewell, general counsel for Intel Corporation, wrote, 'The U.S. patent system is beginning to show its age; outpaced by the swift evolution of technology and commerce, it increasingly favours speculators over innovators, impeding innovation and economic growth.' See Bruce Sewell, 'Patent Nonsense', *The Wall Street Journal*, 12 July 2007; quoted in ibid.

17 Thus Fred H. Cate wrote, 'Without access to information and the freedom to express ourselves, citizens cannot elect their leaders and oversee the activities of the government ... The consent of the governed is the only legitimate source of sovereign power in a democracy, and it is only meaningful if informed.' See Fred H. Cate, 'The Commodification of Information and the Control of Expression', *AMICUS CURIAE Journal of the Society for Advanced Legal Studies*, September/October 2002.

18 Lori B. Andrews, 'Genes and Patent Policy: Rethinking Intellectual Property Rights', 3(10) *Nature Reviews Genetics*, 803–808, 2002.

19 The US alone has reportedly a backlog of 1 million patents which would require 2.5 years to clear; at the same time new applications will continue to be received. See Tove Gerhardsen, 'WIPO: "Explosive Growth" in Patent Filings Strains IP System', *Intellectual Property Watch*, 10 August 2007; available at http://www.ip-watch.org.

20 One of the contests in the EU took the shape of vigorous opposition to the proposed software patent directive (named the 'European Computer-Implemented Inventions Directive'). On 28 April 2003, scientists from around Europe signed a petition to the European Parliament against it, contending that such a move will not only impact on how software will be developed in EU, but also lead to the squeezing out of smaller businesses by the larger corporations very much like the practice in the US. See Matthew Broersma, 'Scientists Protest EU Software Patents', *CNET News.com*, 28 April 2003. Later, the Foundation for a Free Information Infrastructure led a one day shut down of websites displaying this in three languages: 'This page is temporarily closed in protest against software patents. Web sites may soon be closed down regularly due to software patents. Software patents can get you prosecuted for publishing texts you wrote yourself.' See John P. Mello Jr, 'Software Patent Protest Moves from Street to Internet', 26 August 2003, at http://www.technewsworld.com/story/31431.html; accessed 29 October 2007.

In the realm of trademarks, a growing extension of current forms of protection under the rubric of anti-dilution law (in the US) or 'likelihood of confusion' (in its UK variant) portends to erect a protective ring around famous marks way beyond the expectations under the Paris Convention or, indeed, TRIPS. It should be noted that the recent push for increased protection for famous marks was intended as part of the groping towards a solution for domain name disputes that emerged first in the US. Now, we have the additional instrument in the US of the anti-squatting law.

The general perspective that has taken hold everywhere is that of erecting a defence for established marks, particularly against their misuse as domain names. In other words, domain names are still not considered proper subject matter for protection in their own right. The approach of incorporating 'dilution' rather than the loose 'likelihood of confusion' standard in the UK for resolving domain name disputes may appear more appropriate; however, the issue is deeper than the adoption or non-adoption of existing protective formula for general or famous marks. Domain names are arguably a species of marks but their impact necessitates more than tinkering with existing rules and procedures devised for trademarks. It is interesting to note that neither the Internet Corporation for Assigned Names and Numbers (ICANN) nor the World Intellectual Property Organization (WIPO) have recognized this or given it any serious thought.

The most popular controversy regarding the relevance of IP to the digital age was, nonetheless, born amidst the information glut that the Internet spawned. Some saw the huge potential for the Internet to allow the creation, exchange and dissemination of information as the end of copyright.[21] Others saw the phenomenon as leading to the divorce between content and medium so that, in their view, 'information wants to be free' and cannot any longer be bottled under any law to remain proprietary. The debate continues to rage over whether the creative works that authors produce will be deprived of legal protection even if the means of distribution and exchange appear to have been transformed infinitely more than the printing revolution sparked by the Gutenburg Press. Clearly, there is a need to make adjustments to the scope of copyright and the extent of the permissibility for individual users and society at large to share in the fruits of others' labour but calls for the abandonment of copyright remain illusory.

Perspectives of Stakeholders in Bridging the Digital Divide

While there is growing consensus among governments, corporations and the general public that the digital divide needs to be narrowed, if not eliminated, the attitudes of the different stakeholders towards its nature and the ways in which it can, or must, be tackled vary greatly. In that sense, the approach towards bridging

21 John Perry Barlow, 'The Economy of Ideas: Selling Wine Without Bottles', *Wired*, March 1994; available at http://www.wired.com/wired/archive/2.03/economy.ideas.html.

the digital divide appears to be just like arresting global warming. As regards the latter, there is almost universal agreement that global warming needs to be stopped and even clawed back for the good of humanity but the problem of whether and how that can be done continues to be as thorny as ever.

The World Summit on the Information Society (WSIS)

The World Summit on the Information Society (WSIS), probably the largest and most representative global body that could address the problem of the digital divide, adopted a Declaration and an Action Plan (Geneva, 2003). It recognized that 'the benefits of the information technology revolution are today unevenly distributed between the developed and developing countries and within societies' and expressed its commitment to turn 'this digital divide into a digital opportunity for all, particularly for those who risk being left behind and being further marginalized'.[22]

In order to achieve these goals, WSIS sought to mobilize governments, 'the private sector, civil society and international organizations', in other words everybody, to express 'strong commitment' and 'digital solidarity, both at national and international levels'[23] as iterated through the *Digital Solidarity Agenda* within the *Plan of Action*. As usual with international fora and agencies, the major plank of the planned effort to bridge the gap takes the shape of calls for more aid and assistance from all the stakeholders, amongst others, through the proposed 'voluntary Digital Solidarity Fund'.[24] If one were to reread the documents of the UN Conference on Trade and Development (UNCTAD) on the contentious issue, in the 1960s and 1970s, of how to effect transfer of technology (TOT) to DCs, by inserting ICT in place of TOT, one would find a striking resemblance. The parallels of the declared commitment to promote access to, and use of, ICTs today with the equivalent hopes and urges to do the same for TOT three decades ago, leave one in no doubt about the identical nature of the problems.

Even where the general approach towards tackling the *current* problem of the digital divide appears to be a throwback to the *past*, one might hope that the WSIS would supply a few points of departure in the realm of IP. WSIS states, instead,

> Intellectual Property protection is important to encourage innovation and creativity in the Information Society; similarly, the wide dissemination, diffusion, and sharing of knowledge is important to encourage innovation and creativity. Facilitating meaningful participation by all in intellectual property

22 International Telecommunications Union, *WSIS Outcome Documents*, December 2005, Geneva; paragraph 10 of its Declaration of Principles.

23 Ibid., paragraph 17.

24 Ibid., paragraph 61.

> issues and knowledge sharing through full awareness and capacity building is a fundamental part of an inclusive Information Society.[25]

In effect, WSIS is reaffirming existing forms of legal recognition available to creators of new works while at the same time calling on them to engage in 'knowledge sharing'. This is clearly an attempt to take no side in the growing dispute between proprietors increasingly bent on more stringent demands for protection and enforcement, on the one hand, and end-users and the general public, on the other, who have sought to shift the balance in their favour by narrowing down the scopes of protection,[26] lessening the burden on under-resourced communities, groups or individuals[27] or even throwing certain forms of information open to use by anyone.[28]

As if to deflect criticism of the one-sided approach of sanctifying a steady course in IP just as proprietors would have expected it to, WSIS has inserted some bland notions of sharing information and knowledge in the Geneva Plan of Action. While seeking to prompt governments and other stakeholders to create for the public 'affordable or free-of-charge access' to ICT and provide help for such, it does not fail to mention the necessity of 'respecting Intellectual Property Rights (IPRs) and encouraging the use of information and sharing of knowledge'.[29] Yet, this approach of paying homage to the status quo betrays a total lack of will to acknowledge the problems that IP faces from the digital revolution as well as the swathe of opinion on the need for change in IP that is sweeping the world, including the corridors of corporate powers and governments. Constituted as it is of governments and other bodies with a spectrum of varying (and at times diametrically opposed) views on all the attendant factors that impinge on the digital divide, the WSIS could not conceivably have openly recognized, leave alone agreed, to settle the numerous issues that bedevil IP in the information society. Yet, one would have expected of it, at least, a clear statement of the nature of the problems that will continue to haunt it and fuel the digital divide. Yet that has not happened. The WSIS has merely followed the beaten track of the UNCTAD and will probably not escape the fate of the latter either – hovering between outright annihilation and irrelevance.

---

25 Ibid., paragraph 42.

26 See, for instance, M. Khor, 'Rethinking Intellectual Property Rights and TRIPS', in P. Drahos and R. Mayne (eds), *Global Intellectual Property Rights: Knowledge, Access and Development*, Palgrave Macmillan: Basingstoke, 2002, pp. 214–24.

27 Ibid.

28 The National Human Genome Research Institute (NHGRI) issued its policy, 'NHGRI Policy for Release and Database Deposition of Sequence Data' on 21 December 2000, to have all genome sequences generated by the Human Genome Project to be deposited into a public database freely accessible by anyone. See http://www.genome.gov/10000910.

29 International Telecommunications Union, note 21, above; Number 10 (d) of the Geneva Plan of Action 2003.

The Organization for Economic Cooperation and Development (OECD)

The OECD does not seem to recognize any form of digital divide among or within its members, although it acknowledges the existence of differences in the levels of impact on productivity and diffusion of ICTs between countries and the need to 'facilitate access by disadvantaged groups as well as by people living in remote areas'.[30] Crucially, it maintains the remedy for this to lie within market forces:

> Market reforms to reduce the costs of new technology can facilitate access by disadvantaged groups as well as by people living in remote areas. The development of infrastructure is the key to greater inclusiveness. Competition is important for this to happen, but may not be sufficient in all cases. If governments want to ensure that all areas and social groups eventually have access to high speed Internet services, they must do this in a least-cost way that does not distort market forces.[31]

Inevitably, while it indirectly seeks to address inequality of access to ICTs within its members, the focus of its recommendations to its member states is to exhort them to adopt strategies to harness ICT for the further growth of their economies. The 2003 report, therefore, dwells on implementing measures and policies to further entrench ICT in the economies of OECD countries. The OECD considered the problems that afflict DCs only in passing. Even then, the OECD merely seeks to replicate in DCs the policies it considers to be appropriate to its member states:

> Many of the policies recommended in this report apply to developing countries as well. Moreover, development co-operation policies have a key role to play in helping developing countries create the right policy environment to attract ICT investment and build the required capabilities to make use of ICT as part of achieving their broader economic and social goals.[32]

The OECD's stance resonates with that of the Global Economic Forum's 'Global Digital Divide Initiative Taskforce' (GDDI).[33] In spite of its expressed commitment to address the problems of the digital divide, the GDDI has shown a reluctance to propose any measures beyond manipulating the operation of the market: loosening up regulatory barriers in the acquisition and distribution of ICTs. The GDDI has not at any point raised any notion of tackling the possible barriers that IP might present to access to ICTs and diffusion of knowledge.

---

30 OECD, *Meeting of the OECD Council at Ministerial Level: Seizing the Benefits of ICT in a Digital Economy*, 2003, at 23.

31 Ibid.

32 Ibid., at 23–4.

33 See http://www.weforum.org.

Not surprisingly, the global ICT corporations have adopted a similar perspective to that the OECD. They have sought to demonstrate their appreciation of the problem of the digital divide although their responses largely remain limited to the provision of technical assistance and reduction of prices in certain respects. Sun Microsystems, for instance, routinely makes statements on bridging the digital divide without expounding any corporate policy as such.[34] Most of the statements are in connection with new resources it has made available in the market to the buying public across the world. In essence, the repeated references to the 'digital divide' are mere marketing ploys and bear no relation to the urge to take account of the widening gap and provide means of narrowing it down more specifically in under-resourced parts of the world. Even when mention is made of offers and grants by the corporation to certain schools and communities, these are invariably in terms of computers and minimal amounts of technical assistance in a limited fashion.

Microsoft likewise boasts of the variety of forms of assistance it provides to 'more than 139 countries across' Europe, Middle East and Africa.[35] Thus it states, by reference to the Middle East:

> We are working with governments, NGOs and others in the region to explore fresh and innovative ideas that will remove barriers to work and help governments take advantage of the global knowledge economy. Together we are investing in ICT to streamline government services and building high-quality systems of education that will empower youth, women and the unemployed with the skills and knowledge they need to realize their potential.[36]

In connection with Africa, Microsoft declares:

> At Microsoft we are committed to playing our part in Africa's development by forming partnerships to build the local knowledge economy: enabling ICT access and skills development and the creation of localised content for African communities, teachers, students, governments and businesses.[37]

Microsoft, nevertheless, appears to reject any notions of radical changes in the status quo regarding the roles of IP in the digital divide. Bill Gates reportedly

---

34 See Sun Microsystems, 'Sun Bridges the Healthcare Digital Divide', October 2006; available at http://www.sun.com/solutions/documents/articles/hc_digital_divide.xml.

35 Microsoft, *Realizing Potential in Europe, the Middle East and Africa*, 2005; available at http://download.microsoft.com/download.

36 Ibid.

37 Ibid

castigated those who seek 'to reform and restrict intellectual-property rights'[38] as follows:

> I'd say that of the world's economies, there's more that believe in intellectual property today than ever. There are fewer communists in the world today than there were. There are some new modern-day sort of communists who want to get rid of the incentive for musicians and moviemakers and software makers under various guises. They don't think that those incentives should exist.[39]

In his view, only piecemeal changes to the system, such as fine-tuning the patent system, could be appropriate. As for the role of IP, he contends 'when people say they want to be the most competitive economy, they've got to have the incentive system. Intellectual property is the incentive system for the products of the future'.[40]

International non-governmental organizations (NGOs)

The position of international NGOs as regards tackling the problem of the digital divide appears to be to favour reforms that could address the needs of deprived groups within the industrial nations and DCs in general without committing to exactly what sort of reforms would be acceptable.

One of these NGOs is ActionAid, which welcomed the report of the Commission on Intellectual Property Rights in 2002 for 'acknowledging that intellectual property rights legislation has a detrimental effect on poor countries'.[41] It saw the report as exposing the monopoly over biotechnology that patents allow big business to exercise, 'thereby prioritising profit over the needs of poor farmers'.[42] It urged the UK government to follow up the report by initiating a 'radical' reform of TRIPS and the adoption of 'a system that protects the rights of poor farmers and supports development worldwide'.[43] It warned, 'If this report is cast aside, it will be a disaster for millions of poor farmers'.[44]

ActionAid has gone further to characterize current copyright law as leading to 'excessive pricing, limited adaptability and unavailability of suitable learning

38 Michael Kanellos, 'Bill Gates: Restricting IP Rights is Tantamount to Communism', *CNET News.com*, 6 January 2005.

39 Ibid.

40 Ibid.

41 Alex Kirby, 'Intellectual Property Rights "harm poor"', BBC News, 12 September 2002; available at http://news.bbc.co.uk/1/hi/sci/tech/2253270.stm.

42 Ibid.

43 Ibid.

44 Ibid.

materials' in the 'South' and hence adding its voice to the 'access to knowledge' (a2k) campaign.[45]

Oxfam looked at the broader picture of the role of IP in 'the control of knowledge' by major corporations and the 'damaging' consequence of this, particularly 'in poor countries'.[46] It saw the impacts of TRIPS to be the exclusion of 'poor people from access to vital "knowledge goods" such as medicines, seeds, and educational materials' through the 'higher prices' it empowers corporations to impose.[47] Above all, it perceives TRIPS to 'exacerbate the technological divide' already existing 'between rich and poor countries' mainly because the latter are 'net importers of the kinds of high-tech goods and know-how protected by TRIPS' as well as being subjected to higher prices and licence fees.[48]

As regards whether the IP system might in the long term be beneficial to DCs, Oxfam argues to the contrary: that it 'restricts the ability of poor countries to innovate and participate effectively in global markets' through prohibition of imitations and adaptation of new technologies. It also notes that 'the lack of technological capacity [within DCs] means that foreign companies will capture most of the benefits of stronger IP protection.'[49]

In terms of overall objectives, Oxfam appears to champion 'outright abolition' of TRIPS although, as a matter of campaign strategy, it believes that piecemeal reforms (in other words, 'salami' tactics) have a better chance of getting popular acceptance and serving as a means of stopping the major industrial countries and their corporations from 'bullying poor countries over their patent laws'.[50] In practice, therefore, Oxfam prefers reviews of TRIPS in certain respects such as allowing 'longer transition periods for developing countries to comply with TRIPS', and more flexibility in the manner of granting and the scope of patents as well as exemption from them for medicines, for instance.[51]

Oxfam aims, in the long run, to build up 'the pressure for change' without necessarily proposing any alternatives to the TRIPS. Its dilemma is reflected in the question it posed at the beginning of its position paper: 'Will knowledge be monopolized by corporate interests for private profit, and shaped by the markets of rich consumers, or will it be kept within the public domain, and used to help end poverty, hunger, and disease?'[52] Its objection to knowledge being controlled by corporations is as dubious as its hope that even proprietary knowledge could

45 ActionAid, 'Intellectual Property Rights: Copyright Law and its Affect on Education'; available at http://www.actionaid.org/main.aspx?PageID=134.

46 Oxfam, *Intellectual Property and the Knowledge Gap*, Oxfam Discussion Paper 12/01, December 2001.

47 Ibid.

48 Ibid.

49 Ibid.

50 Ibid.

51 Ibid.

52 Ibid.

be 'kept within the public domain' is a pipe dream. The fact of the matter is that the major proprietary stakeholders in IP (and governments that back them to the hilt) cannot be convinced that they would gain more from placing their IP in the public domain. It should also be noted that Oxfam's view of turning IP held by major Western corporations over to the public domain for the purpose, essentially, of ending 'poverty, hunger, and disease' in DCs is unbelievably naive. Not only is this a repeat of the failed demand of the UNCTAD-led movement in the 1970s to make all knowledge 'the common heritage of mankind' and benefit DCs through a massive TOT but has yet to find support even for the benefit of the industrial countries themselves. Oxfam's apparently altruistic urges to rescue the DCs from problems they face in the IP field therefore remain hollow.

The 'Friends of the Intellectual Commons'

The brief survey of the diverse perspectives of the stakeholders will not be complete without a reference to the activities and standpoint of certain groups (initiated by academics and self-confessed 'hackers') sharing no particular identity but probably classifiable as the 'Friends of the Intellectual Commons' (FIC).[53] The main characteristic defining these groups is their advocacy of the maximum reform of IP to release what might otherwise be proprietary knowledge into the public domain (or the 'intellectual commons', as they prefer to call the resulting new body of publicly available knowledge). They consider such a measure to be necessary to meet the demands of societies both in the industrial and developing nations, now as well as in the future, for free access to information. Some even tend to veer towards pushing for the total abolition of the IP system or some of its categories, the most popular candidate for axing being copyright. McKenzie Wark thus contends that, in order to produce new information, hackers need access to information unfettered by 'private property and the commodity form'.[54]

In terms of the substance of their contentions, the FIC broadly hold that 'The redistribution of property rights in the case of information feudalism involves a transfer of knowledge assets from the intellectual commons into private hands'.[55]

53 This label seems to be appropriate in light of previous use of 'Friends of IP' by the major industrial nations who pushed IP onto the agenda of the Uruguay Round and produced TRIPS, as well as more recently by 'the Friends of Development', who seek to place the re-examination and revision of TRIPS at the centre of the Doha Round multilateral trade negotiations.

54 McKenzie Wark, *A Hacker Manifesto*, Harvard University Press: Cambridge, MA, 2004, at paragraph 195.

55 Peter Drahos with John Braithwaite, *Information Feudalism: Who Owns the Knowledge Economy?* Earthscan: London, 2002, at 2. They assert further, 'Patent law … has become one of the main mechanisms by which public knowledge assets have been privatised'. Ibid., at 150. Again, 'Information feudalism is a regime of property rights that is not economically efficient, and does not get the balance right between rewarding innovation and diffusing it. Like feudalism, it rewards guilds instead of inventive individual citizens. It

While it is true that the role of technological (and hence self-help) measures deployed by ICT corporations to lock in whatever information (proprietary or non-proprietary) they lay their hands on and keep them out of the reach of non-paying potential end-users is growing, the generalization expressed in the quoted statement is unjustified. Indeed, it represents a key fallacy, propagated by sections of the FIC, that IP has allowed the appropriation of the intellectual commons. We will return to this fallacy later.

In support of their views, the FIC point to the growing trend (notably among hackers) of 'sharing' creative works, in particular software and literature, that is taking shape in the digital environment. Bays and Mowbray comment: 'Individual Internet users donate content for other Internet users to use free of charge. In return, each individual receives access to all the content made available by others. The amount an individual receives is much more than they could ever produce.'[56] An aspect of the activity of this supposedly carefree new community is the release of software developed by its participants for sharing among the public. The 'free' or 'open source' software movement lets programmers and users acquire software together with the source code for free, under a licence,[57] with the expectation that later modifications to the source code will also be made freely available to all.[58] While differences have emerged between the proponents of 'free software' (the earliest project[59]) and 'open source software' (coined later to refer to the

makes democratic citizens trespassers on knowledge that should be the common heritage of humankind, their educational birthright. Ironically, information feudalism, by dismantling the publicness of knowledge, will eventually rob the knowledge economy of much of its productivity.' Ibid., at 219.

56 See Hillary Bays and Miranda Mowbray, 'Cookies, Gift-Giving, and the Internet', 4(11) *First Monday*, 1 November 1999; available at http://firstmonday.org/issues/issue4_11/bays.

57 This has been termed a 'Copyleft licence' and defined as 'a general method for making a program or other work free, and requiring all modified and extended versions of the program to be free as well'. See http://www.gnu.org/copyleft. The intended contrast obviously is with copyright. The copyleft licence is hence viewed as 'a legal instrument that gives everyone the rights to use, modify, and redistribute the program's code *or any program derived from it* but only if the distribution terms are unchanged'. Ibid. The reversal of the name from 'copyright' into 'copyleft' is to suggest this difference.

58 Maureen O'Sullivan, 'Making Copyright Ambidextrous: An Expose of Copyleft', 3 *Journal of Information, Law and Technology* 2002.

59 See, www.fsf.org, which defines 'free software' by reference to 'four kinds of freedom, for the users of the software', namely 'to run the program, for any purpose'; 'to study how the program works, and adapt it to your needs', access to the source code being a precondition for this; 'to redistribute copies so you can help your neighbour'; 'to improve the program, and release your improvements to the public, so that the whole community benefits', again access to the source code being a precondition for this. In addition, they stress that '"Free software" does not mean "non-commercial"'.

same[60]), more particularly regarding the nature of 'freedom' underlying each and the extent to which commercialization of such software will be permissible, both see themselves ranged against proprietary software. There is no doubt that the practical impact of the free or open source software movement has been growing; some have viewed it as 'challenging the hegemony of proprietary software in some fields, while it dominates in others'.[61] It is even argued that, without free software 'the Internet would virtually grind to a halt'.[62]

Of potentially greater importance in the context of the digital divide is the fledgling 'open access' movement which seeks to make content available to users online, free of charge and without the normal restrictions of copyright. To safeguard online content from being appropriated commercially but enable users to enjoy all forms of use without restriction, the scheme operates a licence. In that sense, the free access relies on a waiver of copyright that authors might otherwise claim over their works. Such a scheme is consequently more applicable to circumstances where authors do not earn royalties (as in peer-reviewed journal articles) and do not depend on such income for their living.[63]

Other schemes include the Berlin Declaration on Open Access to Knowledge in the Sciences and Humanities[64] and the Budapest Open Access Initiative.[65] The Berlin Declaration urges the creation of a 'global and accessible representation of knowledge' whereby '[c]ontent and software tools must be openly accessible and compatible'. It characterizes 'Open access' as

> a free, irrevocable, worldwide, right [granted by authors and right holders to 'all users'] of access to, and a license to copy, use, distribute, transmit and display the work publicly and to make and distribute derivative works, in any digital medium for any responsible purpose, subject to proper attribution of authorship … as well as the right to make small numbers of printed copies for their personal use.[66]

Budapest Open Access Initiative regards 'open access', as 'free and unrestricted online availability'.[67] Its focus is the literature that 'scholars give to the world

---

60 See, www.opensource.org. 'Open source' is defined as including access to the source code as well as additional criteria such as free distribution (without any royalties or fees); the source code to be made available even when a part of a product; modifications and derivative works to be allowed. Ibid.

61 O'Sullivan, note 58, above, ibid.

62 Ibid.

63 See Peter Suber, 'Creating an Intellectual Commons through Open Access'; available at http://dlc.dlib.indiana.edu/archive/00001246; accessed 8 November 2007.

64 See, http://oa.mpg.de/openaccess-berlin/berlindeclaration.html.

65 See, http://www.soros.org/openaccess.

66 See, note 64, above, ibid.

67 See, note 65, above, ibid.

without expectation of payment' and includes peer-reviewed articles as well as comments and notes.[68] It describes the extent of 'open access' to this literature as

> its free availability on the public internet, permitting any users to read, download, copy, distribute, print, search, or link to the full texts of these articles, crawl them for indexing, pass them as data to software, or use them for any other lawful purpose, without financial, legal, or technical barriers other than those inseparable from gaining access to the internet itself.[69]

Both sets of schemes place restrictions in terms of requiring users to acknowledge authors as well as maintain the integrity of their works. They also recognize the cost implications of providing open access. However, they fail to address how the challenge that such costs represent particularly for under-resourced communities and groups should be overcome.

A parallel movement has also emerged in the shape of 'the Creative Commons' (as well as the 'Science Commons'[70]initiated in 2005 to cater for scientific works), which seeks to make works freely available to the public under a licence that protects the IP in the works. The basic idea is to create an 'intellectual property conservancy' that 'will serve to protect works of special public value from exclusionary private ownership and from obsolescence due to neglect or technological change'.[71] It is apparent that the resort to IP to preserve 'the commons' departs from the anti-proprietary stance of FICs. Indeed, this fact is openly acknowledged: 'A Creative Commons license is based on copyright'.[72]

The Creative Commons licence comprises four key terms: the attribution of the relevant work to the author or licensor; the restraint against using the work 'primarily' for commercial ends; the making of only 'verbatim copies of the work' without therefore adapting or changing it; and allowances for making 'derivative works' on condition that they are licensed 'under the same Creative Commons license terms'.[73] In a sense, the purpose of this mechanism is 'to enable creators and licensors to license their works on more flexible terms' such that licensees benefit from using a work 'without having to ask for permission' as long as they 'use it consistent with the license terms'.[74] Indeed, the ease of using (sheltering under) the scheme to gain access to works without suffering any legal action from rights holders may have contributed to its adoption by a number of organizations. Thus the British Broadcasting Corporation (BBC) has come up with its 'Creative Archive' initiative that would 'allow people to download clips of BBC factual

68 Ibid.

69 Ibid.

70 See http://sciencecommons.org/about/; accessed 8 November 2007.

71 See http://wiki.creativecommons.org/Legal_Concepts; accessed 8 November, 2007.

72 Ibid., FAQ.

73 Ibid.

74 Ibid.

programmes from bbc.co.uk for non-commercial use, keep them on their PCs, manipulate and share them, so making the BBC's archives more accessible to licence fee payers'.[75]

The proliferation of schemes and experiments to provide freely and publicly accessible material has been regarded as signalling the end of IP. One commentator thus contends, 'The fact that people continue to post content online has to constitute hard evidence against some of the classic mantras expressed in the utilitarian justification for intellectual property'.[76] He asserts further that 'people are willing to create without hope of remuneration, and caring little for the strength of protection awarded by laws that protect intellectual creations'.[77] Another writer argues that, in the new environment, new elites or 'netocrats', 'defined by the fact that they manipulate information rather than managing property or producing goods', are taking over the power from 'the old capitalists' obsessed with money, titles and the like.[78] According to him, the new status 'requires entirely different characteristics: knowledge, contacts, overview, vision'.[79] The new asset is consequently not control over information as such but '[t]he ability to network and gain an overview of large amounts of information that is sought after by everyone [and] cannot be copied or stolen'.[80] It would appear, hence, that the notion of property in ideas or knowledge is doomed.

Intellectual Property and the 'Digital Divide'

The above review of the perspectives of the OECD, global ICT corporations and industrial governments that back them has predictably revealed a steadfast affirmation of IP and its continued role in spite of any perceived digital gaps opening up in any society. Any allowances they make for change in IP are of a piecemeal nature, in effect to modify its application when the technological medium prompts such. The only serious support for reform, even abandonment, of IP to bridge the digital divide hailed from international NGOs and the FICs.

The author has already argued that the NGOs have yet to articulate their views fully and move beyond general pronouncements. Essentially, they have failed to show how the 'rich North' can afford to strip the proprietary basis of information

75 See Press Office, BBC, 'BBC Creative Archive Pioneers New Approach to Public Access Rights in Digital Age', 2 May 2006; available at http://www.bbc.co.uk/pressoffice/pressreleases/stories/2004/05_may/26/creative_archive.shtml; accessed 8 November 2007.

76 See Andres Guadamuz Gonzalez, 'The Digital Divide: It's The Content, Stupid: Part 2', 11(4) *Computer and Telecommunications Law Review*, 113–18, 2005, at 115.

77 Ibid., at 116.

78 Alexander Bard and Jan Söderqvist, *Netocracy: The New Power Elite and Life After Capitalism*, Pearson Education: London, 2002, at 132.

79 Ibid., at 198.

80 Ibid., at 255.

vital for the health, education and culture of the 'poor South'. Until they do that, it is submitted that their loud demands for change in international IP, particularly their espousal of the abolition of TRIPS, will always have a hollow ring to them.

The FICs do not fare better either; their pursuit of a total reversal of IP is not borne out either theoretically or through their practice. Thus, in spite of his antipathy to IP and his preference for its abolition, mentioned above, Wark bends over backwards to recognize the basic needs of the hackers through IP:

> To maintain their autonomy, hackers need some means of extracting an income from the hack, and thus from some limited protection of their rights … In the short term, some form of intellectual property may secure some autonomy for the hacker class … but in the long run, the hacker can realise its virtuality through the abolition of intellectual property as a fetter on the hack itself.[81]

Wark's admission that hackers might inevitably resort to IP as a means of earning income, be it for a limited time, while their ultimate desire is the total abolition of IP, betrays the FIC's fundamental dilemma, namely, whether jettisoning IP entirely can be a viable project in a world where creativity is predominantly harnessed by big capital in the furtherance of the age-old motive for profit and even threatens to snap up any voluntary abandonment of property rights in newly created works such as 'free software'.

Nonetheless, the FIC's contention that the major corporations have been able to use IP to appropriate the intellectual commons has gained notoriety. In order to understand the scale of confusion that the contention has generated, one needs to consider two distinct aspects of this problem: the nature and scopes of rights granted under IP laws as well as the extent to which public domain matter could become linked to, or absorbed in, the subject-matter of rights.

It is common knowledge that the boundary of claims that IP holders, even applicants, put up under all categories is always elastic and, were the system lacking in means of denying or averting unjustified claims, the constant blurring of distinctions could make the IP system meaningless. Indeed, this is one of the principal issues that the courts have to address repeatedly in contests between warring claimants. While the variations in subject-matter may present more or less difficulty for determining the appropriateness of a grant, the IP administrators as well as the courts always seek to strike down claims that are not backed by the level of creativity and uniqueness required in the appropriate field to qualify for a grant. Moreover, the same process works to keep public domain materials from being appropriated in the guise of new claims or as part of the scope of claims.[82]

81 See Wark, note 54, above, ibid., at paragraph 196.

82 Zermer contends that the public as a 'collective' contributor to copyrighted works (and hence as authors) needs to be allowed a share in the recognition of rights which presently appears to be bestowed on individuals alone. See Lior Zermer, *The Idea of Authorship in Copyright*, Ashgate: Aldershot, 2007. However, this view fails to see the

The constant battle in front of the administrative agencies and the courts to reject or slim down claims unsupported by evidence of significant advance in technology or form of expression or both is recorded in so many forms that one fails to understand why the allegation is made that the public domain is being transferred to private hands, just as during the enclosure movement in English history. Even when, as pointed out already, the digital revolution has opened up possibilities for appropriation of public domain information, willy-nilly, this has not been necessarily through the IP system. That IP continues to recognize claims to creative works and grants rights to persons or corporations even in the digital era is not a manifestation of any inherent defect in the law. That is what IP was supposed to do from early on. The question therefore turns into whether the application of IP law to digital products has been supplanted by other extra-legal practices and processes, thus overthrowing the assumption that only creative works newly produced by persons and corporations can be granted proprietary status. In that sense, the FIC should look beyond current IP law and work out how prevailing access to public domain materials in analogue form could be maintained in the context of digital forms and content in whatever medium they may be found.

In the event, the principal solution that appears to have evolved in response to the demands and practices of ICT corporations is to legitimize their use of technological measures and devices in locking away non-copyright materials for their paying clients only. For that purpose, the prevailing provisions of IP law that covered data bases have been revised across Europe to incorporate protection of essentially non-proprietary matter provided that the relevant database business had invested resources to establish and maintain such. Arguably, the concerns expressed of the lack of adequate protection under the prior law for non-copyright materials in digital databases could have been addressed under some form of 'unfair competition' rules which proscribe not access but direct imitation. However, this has not been the approach taken in the US, or in Europe, although the latter had plenty of opportunities to find innovative solutions, rather than follow the US for purposes purely of narrowing the comparative advantages that US corporations could have over their EU counterparts.

Indeed, the EU could have trail-blazed in this area of law by rejecting the obvious uncertainty created in adopting a quasi-copyright solution for non-copyright stuff merely because it has been digitized and kept in electronic 'libraries'. Secondly, the EU could have left the new digital power houses to their own devices, namely

---

problem underpinning current copyright, namely that its scope has not been adequately demarcated and its ostensible basis in the creativity of expressions has not been consistently or rigorously upheld by the courts. In other words, a reform of copyright would hardly be necessary in the direction indicated by Zermer as in theory even current copyright bestows or is supposed to bestow rights in original expressions. Where therefore the public's contribution has wilfully or in advertently been claimed (over-claimed) by individuals, as happens in patent applications, the failure of the system/users or the market to rectify it is no indication of the failure of copyright as such.

maintaining their locks and other forms of security. In any event, that would be what the ICT corporations in the business of electronic databases and other products could have been doing.[83] Clearly, these approaches would not even scratch the thorny question of how to replicate current forms of access to analogue materials, through the fair use provisions, to be available for digital matter.

A possible solution along this line would have been to make businesses that produce digital goods provide to the public access to their resources which originate in, and remain in large part, public domain. However, this would not be, to say the least, warmly received by database establishments and the like; nor would it be possible to enforce such a law. The truth of the matter is that, in as much as there is a market for such goods, private establishments would continue to produce them and keep them under lock and key, regardless of any outcry against the appropriation of the intellectual commons or such like. As Gonzalez remarks, 'The end result of this trend towards privatisation of content is that the web might become a two-tier environment, with high-content sites locked away by subscription fees, while the public web contains less valuable information.'[84]

This realization may explain why the EU, faced by the dilemma of either following the US, which had already stolen a march in this area of activity, or imposing some form of regulatory control, thereby erecting further arbitrage against its businesses, opted for the former. If ever any thought of tightening a grip on locking up public domain materials in electronic forms had emerged in Europe, the fear of handing over to the US all the opportunities must have dissuaded it from adopting such a path.

Curiously, even the FIC, with no ostensible vested interests to uphold, have yet to formulate this problem properly, least of all face it. In spite of their declared preference for the abolition of any proprietary basis in electronic networks and information, we have yet to learn from them how this proposal can overcome the globally entrenched interests and become operational in a day-to-day setting. Instead of the high-flown rhetoric, however, the FIC lauds the birth of a new movement that seeks to address the problem of access in a way unconnected with overthrowing the law directly or replacing it with other rules.

A further weakness of the FIC is that they do not distinguish between the needs of economies and cultures in the West from those of others in Africa, Asia or Latin America. While most critics of the IP system accept the necessity of addressing the grave conditions in the 'Third World' under some form of 'preferential treatment' in the IP field, the radical view of overthrowing IP proposed by the FIC seeks to achieve that feat everywhere.

83 As Gonzalez rightly comments, 'There cannot be any doubt that companies that provide services will have a valid interest in recouping their investment by selling their content, but the result of this may be to increase the digital divide'. See Gonzalez, note 75, above, ibid., at 113. In addition, 'even if the people in these countries could access the internet, almost half of them could not understand what is on the screen'. Ibid.

84 Ibid.

Conclusion

The debate concerning the impact of the digital revolution on IP in general and, conversely, the effects of an extended form of IP on the long-acknowledged technology divide between the industrial and developing nations, currently popularized by the term 'digital divide', has become polarized in recent years. On the one hand, those calling for reform, if not rethink, of the IP system continue to produce mountains of arguments from a diversity of perspectives: economics, technology and innovation, science and culture, ethics and human rights. The increasingly emotive voices heard in conferences have begun to overflow to the courts and the streets across the world.

On the other hand, proponents of piecemeal adaptations of IP to the prevailing technological advances recognize no serious hurdles in this traditional process of legal change. They do not view any loopholes in the current law as justifying a total revamp of the IP system as a whole. Indeed, some contend that the loopholes are symptoms of the failure to strengthen and extend IP beyond the parameters introduced through TRIPS and in recognition of rapid technological advances.

At the head of those who continue to push for a rapid adjustment of the current forms of IP to the digital age and beyond are the global information corporations. Even public organizations with core tasks of information archiving and diffusion such as the British Library engage in the same manner. The British Library has thus expressed, through its IP Manifesto,[85] the urgency of closing the loopholes that have been created in copyright law since the incidence of digitization and the Internet. One such loophole is the extent to which users might rely on 'fair use' provisions so far available to them in the non-digital context to digital works. The British Library referred to their emerging experience of licensing agreements concerning digital materials presented to them undermining such provisions. It therefore pleaded that 'if unchecked, this trend will drastically reduce public access, thus significantly undermining the strength and vitality of our creative and educational sectors – with predictable consequences for UK plc'.[86] It thus called for extension of '[e]xisting limitations and exceptions to copyright law ... to encompass unambiguously the digital environment'.[87]

In the mean time, global ICT corporations continue to view the resolution of any problems attendant on their deployment of IP (such as the digital divide, unavailability of medicines, educational and cultural materials for people in developing nations) as achievable through the traditional means of letting market

85 British Library, 'Intellectual Property: A Balance – the British Library Manifesto', 25 September 2006; available at http://www.bl.uk/news/pdf/ipmanifesto.pdf.; accessed 8 November 2007.

86 Ibid.

87 Ibid.

forces decide.[88] They contend that only allowing the laws of competition and limiting government intervention from seeking to influence, or determine, the provision of access would have counter-productive consequences. Although bringing down the costs of ICT infrastructures through subsidies, the introduction of more appropriate devices (such as the stripped down laptops or software) and deploying alternative methods, such as mobile phones rather than the Internet, have proved popular and effective in certain countries (e.g. Bangladesh[89]), these corporations have yet to endorse them fully. Indeed, in many cases, they oppose these measures.[90] Only international organizations, such as the ITU, have maintained a certain level of assistance in all kinds of directions (equipment, capacity building and the like).

As far as the DCs are concerned, the basic problems of literacy[91] and the fact that '43 per cent of web users do not speak English at all'[92] ultimately make any increased access to the Internet to bridge the digital divide quixotic. Moreover, as newly developed digital educational materials remain for the most part proprietary or subject to high subscription charges out of the range of even available government resources, nations will have to embark on a strategy of developing content domestically to fill the vacuum so created and enable entire communities to produce vitally needed materials for their cultural progress and for their schools.[93]

---

88 Thus Chaney writes, by reference to the conditions in the US, 'If the digital divide is purely a question of economics, then it won't take long for market forces to solve it. Propelled by both the profit motive and philanthropic goals, high-tech companies are bringing the benefits of technology to low-income communities at a rapid pace. Numerous studies show that Internet access is quickly spreading to the low-income population.' See Helen Chaney, 'How the Hig-tech Sector is Bridging the "Digital Divide"', Fall 2000, at 5; available from www.pacificresearch.org.

89 Through the concept of the 'telephone lady' offering mobile payphone services, sponsored by the Grameen Bank in Bangladesh. See, Stuart Weinstein and Charles Wild, 'Closing the Digital Divide: Who will Invest in Universal Access?', 4(1) *Hertfordshire Law Journal*, 2–11, at 7–8 [no date].

90 As Morrison explains, 'In Thailand, the reality is that less than five percent of the one million people with HIV and AIDS have access to antiretroviral therapy. Multi-national pharmaceutical companies have responded by asserting that public health policy rather than price and trade barriers is the key reason that there is limited access to affordable essential medicines for HIV and AIDS in developing countries.' See, C. Morrison, 'Rethinking Intellectual Property Rights: Accessing Essential Medicines for HIV and AIDS in Thailand', *Int Conf AIDS*, 7–12 July 2002, at 14: Abstract no. G12628; available at http://gateway.nlm.nih.gov/MeetingAbstracts/102251074.html; accessed on 9 November 2007.

91 Gonzalez comments that 'even if the people in these countries could access the internet, almost half of them could not understand what is on the screen'. See Gonzalez, note 76, above, ibid., at 113.

92 Ibid.

93 Ibid., at 114.

Chapter 14

Towards Alternative Policy Frameworks

Introduction

As repeatedly pointed out throughout this book, the dominant jurisprudence in intellectual property (IP) views IP to be universal and therefore capable of being implemented in all countries regardless of time and conditions.[1] It equates the failure in implementation of IP laws in developing countries (DCs) in general and the emerging economies in particular to lack of political good will or a desire to free-ride on the technological achievements of industrial countries.[2] The major industrial nations have acted on these pronouncements to put pressure on DCs,[3] directly or indirectly, to implement their IP laws to the satisfaction of those industrial nations. The US has taken the lead through its threats of trade sanctions

1 See, generally, F.K, Beier, 'The Significance of the Patent System for Technical, Economic and Social Progress', 11 I.I.C. 569, 1980; R. Michael Gadbaw and Timothy J. Richards (eds), *Intellectual Property Rights: Global Consensus, Global Conflict?* Westview Press: Boulder, CO, 1988; and Robert M. Sherwood, *Intellectual Property and Economic Development*, Westview Press: Boulder, CO, 1990.

2 See, Marshall A. Leaffer, 'Protecting United States Intellectual Property Abroad: Toward a New Multilateralism', 76 *Iowa Law Review* 273, 1991; and Robert M. Sherwood, 'The TRIPS Agreement: Implications for Developing Countries', 37 *IDEA* 491, 1997. By contrast, other writers have contended that the IP laws in DCs are not rooted in their social–economic conditions and, consequently, their role will remain peripheral. See, Edith T. Penrose, *The Economics of the International Patent System*, John Hopkins Press: Baltimore, MD, 1951; Helge E. Grundmann, 'Foreign Patent Monopolies in Developing Countries: An Empirical Analysis', 12 *Journal of Development Studies* 186, 1976; A. Samuel Oddi, 'The International Patent System and Third World Development: Reality or Myth?', 1987 *Duke Law Journal* 831, 1987; P.S. Sangal and Kishore Singh (eds), *Indian Patent System and Paris Convention: Legal Perspectives*, Ashoka: Delhi, 1987; A. Endeshaw, *Intellectual Property Policy for Non-Industrial Countries*, Dartmouth: Aldershot, 1996; and Keith E. Maskus and Jerome H. Reichman, 'The Globalisation Of Private Knowledge Goods And The Privatisation Of Global Public Goods', 7 *Journal of International Economic Law* 279, June 2004.

3 See, generally, Paul C.B. Liu, 'U.S. Industry's Influence on Intellectual Property Negotiations and Special 301 Actions', 13 *UCLA Pacific Basin Law Journal* 87, Fall 1994.

routinely announced every year.[4] The EU[5] and Japan,[6] on the other hand, have tended to apply persuasion by pointing to deficiencies of the DCs in IP law-making or enforcement and asking for explanations or changes.

Some independent voices have called for mounting awareness campaigns in those nations. Others have also proposed pumping more aid into DCs to upgrade the latter's IP laws and institutions. Groups like Oxfam and Médecins Sans Frontières have sought to lobby for changes (such as in the marketing and distribution strategies of pharmaceutical companies) and to involve the general public in the West towards that end. In all respects, the introduction and development of IP laws in DCs have been increasingly wrested from the hands of local governments and interested domestic groups and turned into intensely contested spheres of activities where external forces stake their claims to undiminished authority. In recent years, for instance, the US has made its views known on this score by issuing, through its embassies, to governments in DCs an 'Action Plan' for IP in a specific country.[7] Lately, the US has moved to inject huge chunks of its IP law into bilateral agreements with other (mostly developing) nations under the rubric of further liberalization of trade. The grafting of IP laws of the US onto the laws of DCs through the mechanisms of Free Trade Agreements (FTAs) has sparked off debate and resentment as to the propriety of this approach to pre-empting multilateral negotiations.

Nevertheless, regardless of the FTAs, the mounting pressures and threats of supposedly retaliatory action against DCs by some of the advanced industrial countries, most DCs still fail to implement the laws they readily place on their statute books. The leading industrial nations routinely rebuke the DCs for failing to implement their IP laws and portray them as 'pirates' deserving of retaliatory action (usually sanctions). The DCs persistently deny any intentional lapse in

4 See the *National Trade Estimate Report on Foreign Trade Barriers* prepared by the Office of the United States Trade Representative for the various years at http://www.ustr.gov/reports/nte.

5 See [European Commission] 'Survey on Enforcement of Intellectual Property Rights in Third Countries, July 2003'; available at http://europa.eu.int/comm/trade/issues/sectoral/intell_property/survey_en.htm. The survey was viewed by the EC as 'a diagnostic allowing DG Trade, and the Commission services to act more efficiently and to develop a clear strategy to tackle the growing problems caused by violations of IPR and by the deficient enforcement of such rights in third countries'. Ibid.

6 [Ministry of Economy, Trade and Industry, Japan] *The Report of the Task Force on Industrial Competitiveness and Intellectual Property Policy*, 5 June 2002; available at http://www.jpo.go.jp. The same ministry states that 'Japan has been approaching countries and regions where counterfeit infringement is grave by asking them to improve the situation. Japan has helped developing countries to enrich their intellectual property systems by such means as cooperation in training for intellectual property-related human resources.' Ibid.

7 Thus Indonesia and the Philippines were issued with such 'Action Plans' in May and August 2002, respectively. See [USTR], *2003 National Trade Estimate Report on Foreign Trade Barriers*; available at http://www.ustr.gov/reports/nte/2003/index.htm.

enforcing their laws. However, the tension between the two groups of countries persists. The trade negotiations in the Doha Round (launched in November 2001) have borne marks of disappointment and grudges of the respective bloc of nations despite the concessions of the major industrial powers to ease the problems of access to drugs for public health purposes in DCs as well as to extend them assistance for transfer of technology and economic development. The debacle of many WTO Ministerial Meetings (since 2001), the simmering discontent among DCs and the dilemmas of the major industrial nations as regards the way forward in multilateral negotiations compound the urgent necessity for alternative policy frameworks to promote international trade and economic development.

The search for alternative policy frameworks in global trade and economic interdependence as well as in trans-border environmental issues has preoccupied academics and policy-makers, as well as governments and civil society groups. The account of post-TRIPS developments in IP in recent years in Asian emerging economies undertaken in this book has underscored the need to conduct a similar search in order to address the impasse in the IP field between the industrial and developing nations and find ways of overcoming it.

The Rationale for Alternative Policy Frameworks in Intellectual Property

It is worth stressing that the persistent drive, chiefly by the US, to establish universal standards in IP far beyond those already enshrined in TRIPS has not been welcomed without reservations even among the major industrial economies. A growing resentment has set in against governments and groups of industrialists and businesses that seek to bolster such a drive. The fear, even uproar, expressed lately about the 'enclosure movement' of sorts in cyberspace, epitomized, for instance, by the digitization of entire libraries by Google for commercial gain[8] and by the proposed further extension of the boundaries of the criminal law as espoused in *Digital Britain*[9] reveal a desire to curb the unrelenting push for universalization.

Yet, there have been no clear alternative paths drawn up by, or for, the major actors, the EU, Japan or the US, to slow down the pace, at the very least. In spite of the growing army of opponents of propertization of all forms of cultural and scientific achievements in these nations and beyond, the boundaries of the permissible and impermissible have continued to be blurred, even erased, in favour of the proprietors. In the meantime, emerging countries in Asia and elsewhere as well as DCs in general have not desisted from continuing to import externally motivated or formulated IP rules without any significant modification or objection.

8 This has been reiterated in many fora, including the media. See Ian Traynor, 'Brussles Launches Copyright Campaign to Counter Google', *The Guardian* [London], 8 September 2009, at 31.

9 See [UK] Department for Culture, Media and Sport, *Digital Britain: The Final Report – 16 June 2009*; available online at http://www.culture.gov.uk.

Policy makers and the legislature in these countries take it for granted, or succumb to the predominant thinking, that policies, laws and practices in IP are, or should be, identical for all nations.

However, nothing seems further from the reality. Although IP laws in all lands have become alike, even uniform, the practices have remained either totally apart or have evolved in confusingly different directions. The despair that proprietors from industrial nations express in the lack of protection for their intangible assets in DCs is matched by the antagonism that the latter feel towards IP laws they view increasingly as being irrelevant, not to say inimical, to their own (domestic) needs. Both are equally manifestations of a misconception that has taken root in IP policy and implementation.

No one seems to doubt that the social and medical ills of any country should be tackled through solutions and approaches informed by the specific characteristics, culture, geography and general environment of those countries. Even the application of technologies in different contexts has always been perceived to be subject to 'appropriateness', culture and social factors. For a long time, the debate on 'appropriate technology' had a significant influence on the quest of DCs to attain progress in that field. However, the law that directly impinges on, and defines, the respective rights and obligations of proprietors and users of technology has become disentangled from that essential concern and attained a status of 'universality' both in space and time.

Theories of 'property rights' which attribute pre-human ('natural') existence to such rights or, at any rate, assert that they stretch back to the time when humans started roaming over the earth have gained ascendancy over other theories which seek to link IP forms to specific social and economic configurations. As a result, the differentiation that needs to be maintained in the making or implementation of laws across countries and cultures has been trampled underfoot. All nations are expected to think alike and behave alike in IP terms, if not in others as well.

It seems highly irrational that people should expect similarities where none could exist in reality. However, that is how IP has been framed and pushed to become over the last 15 years. No nation can take stock of its own internal peculiarities, needs or problems any longer and set out to craft a legal and institutional structure in tune with its own state of social and economic conditions. The threat of trade sanctions, political and military pressure has compelled nations to abandon making their own laws and, instead, copy versions of the laws of the major industrial nations. Indeed, many DCs have to work hard to establish what is expected of them across a range of policies, laws and institutions.

Over time, the attempts of DCs to fake compliance with the wishes and demands of the industrial nations have taken precedence over working out *autonomously* policies and laws appropriate to their requirements and in line with their capabilities. Preoccupied with the perennial pressure to copy IP laws and institutions of the industrial nations, DCs could not effect any real changes in their own domestic laws and institutions. This has generally resulted in a state of paralysis in developing nations. One would have thought that the breakdown in the traditional route of law-making and enforcement, namely national authorities responding to local needs and aspirations without ignoring legitimate international concerns, could turn out to be counter-productive at some stage. However, the continuous rise in expectations of IP owners in the industrial nations, particularly the big powers, that the rapid spread of their laws to DCs amounts to a promise to execute them instantly, has generated illusions. For many a multinational company operating in DCs, the state of IP enforcement has remained patchy or non-existent. They bring their influence to bear on governments such as those of the US and EU to continue to put pressure on DCs to implement the IP laws on their statute books. Yet DCs have discovered that they can hardly afford, or willingly commit, to implement laws that do not conform to their requirements. They have begun to realize the implications for their economic and technological transformation of bending to pressure exerted on them on behalf of proprietors in the rich and affluent nations and not, as often claimed, in both groups of countries.

Who would blame the DCs then if the requisite political goodwill, infrastructure, judicial and policing machinery ever remain short of the desirable because of the widespread feeling among them that what is expected of them is implementation of what is effectively foreign law in the services of foreign entities and individuals? The industrial powers' perception that treaties should be upheld, that governments should fulfil their obligations lest they fall prey to trade sanctions and external political pressure serves only to heighten the state of misunderstanding between the two sides. The confrontation is made worse by the attitude of most IP writers (some taking positions on an ideological level), which ignores the specific problems that afflict the enforcement of IP in the non-industrial nations of the world. If one were to listen to them and endorse their views wholeheartedly, there would be no way out of the impasse.

Some writers have adopted a sympathetic tone towards the problems of the DCs without necessarily overcoming the limitations of the ideologically inclined. Writers well-disposed towards DCs hold the view that the problems are temporary and that some of them will play a full role once those problems have been overcome. The lack of education is thus cited by these groups of writers as one of the most important problems in IP enforcement. Others refer to institutional shortcomings (absence of a proper judicial system, policing and transparency). Their prescriptions are hence for reforms that are bound to be piecemeal and come to an end shortly after barely scratching the surface.

There is growing recognition that the transformation of the DCs in the economic and technological fields may be desirable even for the industrial nations. The crises that bedevil the world economy every so often could be averted or overcome through an expansion of the market in DCs and ultimately the global market. The impasse in the IP field could also be resolved if both industrial and developing nations accept the necessity for a joint approach to achieve mutual benefits.

The Nature and Scope of the Research Agenda

It has been reiterated throughout the book that most of the Asian countries possess IP laws inherited or borrowed from European nations. They have managed to set up the necessary legal and institutional structure for IP and yet for decades they have been portrayed as pirates and earmarked for retaliatory punishment (usually sanctions) by the major industrial nations (US, mainly, and the EU and Japan, to a lesser extent). The Asian countries have exerted themselves to live up to the expectations that the latter group of countries place on them. Yet, it has become clear that the IP system already in place in Asia has failed to be translated fully into reality. A cursory look at the USTR's annual reports reveals that nearly all these countries have been routinely placed on one 'Watch List' or another every year.

It is the author's considered view that any serious research to resolve the impasse in IP between the industrial and developing nations (including those in Asia) should focus, above all, on re-examining the validity of the dominant jurisprudence in IP (referred to above), particularly its relevance to the latter groups of countries as a whole and the emergent economies especially. The principal aims of such a search should be to establish the key causes for the failure in implementation of IP laws in DCs in general and emerging economies in particular, as well as the relative significance of those causes, and to suggest possible reforms in IP policy and practice.

While the literature constantly refers to the problems of enforcement of IP in general terms and seems to suggest that they have got worse since the injection of TRIPS into international trade rules, detailed studies into the factors that influence, or plague, implementation remain unavailable. Frequent estimates of rising levels of 'piracy' in DCs, issued by organizations representing IP proprietors in the West (such as the International Intellectual Property Alliance and the Business Software Alliance or even the USTR) merely assert the existence of the problem without pinpointing specific causes for the alleged state of affairs or providing any empirical evidence to sustain their claims. Research should therefore be undertaken to fill that gap and provide a fresh perspective on the fundamentals of IP law-making and enforcement in the context of DCs with a focus on the emerging economies.

The review of the literature pertaining to the IP system as well as its evolution in specific Asian countries, exposed in Chapter 8, has thrown up the potent factors that might have an impact on law-making and enforcement of IP: the social and cultural environment; government policies (economic, technological and legal, especially IP); the state of infrastructure and financial resources for IP administration and implementation; and marketing strategies of, and competition among, foreign companies in relation to IP protected (or brand) products. Consequently, research should focus on examining the following:

1. the level of contributions (sunk costs and recurrent expenses as well as other commitments) of IP owners and governments (both local and foreign)

to law enforcement, public education, development of infrastructure and procedures as well as human capacity building in the specific field of IP;
2. the pricing of IP protected goods;
3. the conflicts of interests among and between foreign and local businesses in the making and implementation of IP laws; and
4. the attitudes of businesses, consumers, local artists and inventors, publishers and entrepreneurs of all types towards the IP system and its implications.

These bands of inquiry could be broken down further into detailed items about which data can be collected with a view to eliciting attitudes of different sectors of the society in each nation, including artists, writers, inventors and publishers as well as policy makers, law-enforcement agencies and the business community (both local and international). The research should also cover the spectrum of concerns that IP owners in the major industrial nations express regarding recognition of rights, the system of protection and the judicial and administrative avenues for redress.

The research output will be an understanding of the factors holding back the enforcement of IP in Asia and their relative significance as well as recommendations for the benefit of both Asian countries and their major international trading partners. The findings will hopefully lead to a drawing up of strategy and policies as well as to mapping out alternative plans of future action that governments and civil society would be expected to engage in vis-à-vis the following outstanding issues:

- whether innovation in DCs and the emergent economies calls for specific forms and levels of IP and other policy and institutional props;
- whether such countries can find room within the international IP system to be able to manoeuvre for their own ends or establish their own alternative means of IP protection;
- whether those countries can opt out of the international IP system and yet remain within the WTO mechanism.

Ultimately, the research will lead to the development of fresh perspectives in an area of study that has slumbered long except for the occasional sideshow it has occupied in past and current IP research. It will invigorate researchers to undertake more concerted attempts at understanding the problems better and finding appropriate solutions rather than borrowing cut and dried approaches and tips from studies in the state of IP in countries like the UK and the US. As well, the consequent rise in number of IP specialists on problems that plague DCs could gradually begin to influence government and private business policies and lead to improvements on the ground: better understanding and implementation of laws, more appropriate institutional mechanisms and an increase in human capacity. The abilities of governments and businesses to overcome current problems that bedevil international trade and commerce will thereby multiply. It will lead to a win–win situation for all countries and businesses.

References

Abbott, F.M, 'Symposium on Global Competition and Public Policy in an Era of Technological Integration: The New Global Technology Regime: The WTO TRIPS Agreement and Global Economic Development', 72 *Chicago-Kent Law Review* 385, 1996.

——, 'TRIPS in Seattle: The Not-So-Surprising Failure and the Future of the TRIPS Agenda'. 14 *Berkeley Journal of International Law* 165, 2000.

ActionAid, 'Intellectual Property Rights: Copyright Law and its Affect on Education'; available at http://www.actionaid.org.

Alexander, T., *Unravelling Global Apartheid: An Overview of World Politics*, Polity Press: Cambridge, 1996.

Alford, W.P., 'How Theory Does – and Does Not – Matter: American Approaches To Intellectual Property Law In East Asia', 13 *UCLA Pacific Basin Law Journal* 8, Fall 1994; available online from Lexis-Nexis.

——, *To Steal a Book is an Elegant Offense: Intellectual Property Law in Chinese Civilization*, Stanford University Press: Stanford, CA , 1995.

Allison, J.R. and Lin, L., 'The Evolution of Chinese Attitudes Toward Property Rights in Invention and Discovery', 20 *University of Pennsylvania Journal of International Economic Law* 735, Winter 1999.

Amin, S., *Unequal Development – An Essay on the Social Formation of Peripheral Capitalism*, The Harvester Press: Brighton, 1976.

Andrews, L.B., 'Genes and Patent Policy: Rethinking Intellectual Property Rights', 3(10) *Nature Reviews Genetics* 803, 2002.

Ang, K.H., 'The Existing Patent System in Singapore and its Contemplative Development – as Seen from the Viewpoint of the Registry', in *Seminar on Patent and Trademark Licensing Singapore*, 10–12 December 1980, WIPO.

[Anonymous] 11 *World Intellectual Property Report* 3, 88, March 1997.

——, 'Indonesia: Parliament Strengthens IP Legislation', *IPAsia* 13, December 2000/January 2001.

——, 'Piracy Remains a Problem in China, U.S. Says', *The Wall Street Journal*, 24 January 2002; available online from the Dow Jones Interactive.

Antons, C., 'Legal Culture and History of Law in Asia', in *Intellectual Property Law in Asia*, C. Heath (ed.), Kluwer Law International: London, 2003, at 13–35.

Antons, C., Blakeney, M. and Heath C. (eds), *Intellectual Property Harmonisation Within ASEAN and APEC*, Kluwer Law International: London, 2004.

Appelbaum, R.P. and Henderson, J., *States and Development in the Asian Pacific Rim*, Sage Publications: Thousand Oaks, CA, 1992.

Asia-Pacific Economic Cooperation, 'IPR Policy Progress Mapping and Follow-up Report on "Comprehensive Strategy on IPR in APEC"', submitted by Japan to the 20th Intellectual Property Experts' Group Meeting, Seoul, Korea, 22–3 February 2005.

——, 'IPR Policy Progress Mapping and Follow-up Report on "Comprehensive Strategy on IPR in APEC"', submitted by Japan to the 20th Intellectual Property Experts' Group Meeting, Seoul, Korea, 22–3 February 2005.

——, 'Report on the Enforcement Best Practices in APEC Economies to Combat Optical Disk Piracy', submitted by Singapore to the 21st APEC Intellectual Property Experts' Group Meeting, Manila, Philippines, 2–3 August 2005.

Balat, M.A.E. and Mohamed M.H., 'The TRIPS Agreement and Developing Countries: A Legal Analysis of the Impact of the New Intellectual Property Rights Law on the Pharmaceutical Industry in Egypt', 2 *Web Journal of Current Legal Issues* 1 [2004].

Bard, A. and Söderqvist, J., *Netocracy: The New Power Elite and Life After Capitalism*, Pearson Education: London, 2002.

Barlow, J.P., 'The Economy of Ideas: Selling Wine Without Bottles', *Wired*, March 1994; available at http://www.wired.com.

Beier, F.K., 'The Significance of the Patent System for Technical, Economic and Social Progress', 11(5) *IIC* 569, 1980.

Beier, F.K and Schricker, G. (eds), *GATT or WIPO? New Ways in the International Protection of Industrial Property*, VCH: Weinheim, 1989.

Board of Trade, *The British Patent System, Report of the Committee to examine the Patent System and Patent Law*, HMSO: London, 1970.

British Library, 'Intellectual Property: A Balance – The British Library Manifesto', 25 September 2006; available at http://www.bl.uk/news/pdf/ipmanifesto.pdf.

Callan, B., 'US and European Efforts to Enhance Intellectual Property Protection in Asia: A Logic in Cooperation', *IPAsia*, 35–8, November 1997.

Cate, F.H., 'Symposium: Introduction: Sovereignty and the Globalization of Intellectual Property', 6 *Indiana Journal of Global Legal Studies* 1, Fall 1998.

Chanda, A., 'Copyright Cases Involving American Commercial Icons Highlight Chinese Intellectual Property Issues', *WMRC Daily Analysis*, 9 January 2004.

Chaney, H., 'How the Hig-tech Sector is Bridging the "Digital Divide"', Fall 2000, at 5; available from www.pacificresearch.org.

Chiappetta, V., 'The Desirability of Agreeing to Disagree: The WTO, TRIPS, International IPR Exhaustion and a Few Other Things', 21 *Michigan Journal of International Law* 333, Spring 2000.

Chow, D.C.K., 'Counterfeiting in the People's Republic of China', 78 *Washington University Law Quarterly* 1, Spring 2000.

Chung, H.C., 'Protection of Artists' Rights Under the Korean Copyright Law', 12 *Pacific Rim Law and Policy Journal* 179, January 2003.

Cohen J.A. and Dixon, T.A., 'Intellectual Property in China', *IPAsia* 24, March 1996.

Cohen, M.A. et al. (eds), *Chinese Intellectual Property Law and Practice*, Kluwer Law International: London, 1999.

Correa, C.M., 'Transfer of Technology in Latin America: A Decade of Control', 15 *Journal of World Trade Law* 388 (1981).

Correa, C.M. and Yusuf A.A. (eds), *Intellectual Property and International Trade: The* TRIPS *Agreement*, Kluwer Law International: London, 1998.

Crispin, S.W., 'Innovation', *Far Eastern Economic Review*, 8 January 2004, at 30.

D'Amato, A. and Long, D.E. (eds), *International Intellectual Property Law*, Kluwer Law International: London, 1997.

Djaic, D., 'Why does the Enforcement of Indonesia's Intellectual Property Laws Continue to be a Problem?', 22(10) *European Intellectual Property Review* 454, October 2000.

Drahos, P., with Braithwaite, J., *Information Feudalism: Who Owns the Knowledge Economy?* Earthscan: London, 2002.

Drahos, P. and Mayne R. (eds), *Global Intellectual Property Rights: Knowledge, Access and Development*, Palgrave Macmillan: Basingstoke, 2002.

Economic Council of Canada, *Report on Intellectual and Industrial Property*, Ottawa, 1971.

Endeshaw, A. *Intellectual Property Policy for Non-Industrial Countries*, Dartmouth: Aldershot, 1996.

——, 'A Critical Assessment of the US-China Conflict on Intellectual Property', 6(2) *Albany Law Journal of Science and Technology* 295–338, 1996.

——, *Intellectual Property In China: The Roots of the Problem of Enforcement*, Acumen Publishing Company: Singapore, 1996.

——, 'The Asian Approach in Responding to Developments in Intellectual Property', in *Asian Communications Handbook 2001*, A. Goonasekera and L.C. Wah (eds), Asian Media Information and Communication Centre and Schools of Communication Studies, Nanyang Technological University, 2001, at 269–77.

——, 'The Paradox of Intellectual Property Lawmaking in the New Millennium: Universal Templates as Terms of Surrender for non-Industrial Nations; Piracy as an Offshoot', 10(1) *Cardozo Journal of International and Comparative Law* 47–77, Spring 2002.

——, 'Reconfiguring Intellectual Property for the Information Age: Towards Information Property?', 7(3) *The Journal of World Intellectual Property* 327–64, May 2004.

——, 'Asian Perspectives on Post-TRIPS Issues in Intellectual Property', 8(2) *The Journal of World Intellectual Property* 211–35, March 2005.

Fong, W.S., 'Protection of Intellectual Property in Malaysia', ASEAN Law Association 1982 General Assembly, Report, 25–9 October 1982, Kuala Lumpur.

Gadbaw, R.M., 'Intellectual Property and International Trade: Merger or Marriage of Convenience?', 22(2) *Vanderbilt Journal of Transnational Law* 223, 1989.

Gadbaw, R.M. and Richards, T.J. (eds), *Intellectual Property Rights: Global Consensus, Global Conflict?*, Westview Press: Boulder, CO, 1988.

Gardner, J.A., *Legal Imperialism: American Lawyers and Foreign Aid in Latin America*, The University of Wisconsin Press: Madison, WI, 1980.

Gerhardsen, T., 'WIPO: "Explosive Growth" in Patent Filings Strains IP System', *Intellectual Property Watch*, 10 August 2007; available at http://www.ip-watch.org.

Gillespie, J., 'Law and Development "in the Market Place"', in *Law, Capitalism and Power in Asia: The Rule of Law and Legal Institutions*, K. Jayasuriya (ed.), Routledge: London, 1999.

Gonzalez, A.G., 'The Digital Divide: It's the Content, Stupid: Part 1', *Computer and Telecommunications Law Review* 73–7, 2005.

——, 'The Digital Divide: It's the Content, Stupid: Part 2', 11(4) *Computer and Telecommunications Law Review* 113–18, 2005.

Griffin, E.M., 'Stop Relying on Uncle Sam! – A Proactive Approach to Copyright Protection in the People's Republic of China', 6 *Texas Intellectual Property Law Journal* 169, 1998.

Grundmann, H.E., 'Foreign Patent Monopolies in Developing Countries: An Empirical Analysis', 12 *Journal of Development Studies* 186, 1976.

Gutterman A. and Brown, R. (eds), *Intellectual Property Laws of East Asia*, Sweet & Maxwell Asia: Malaysia, 1997.

Halbert, D.J., *Intellectual Property in the Information Age: The Politics of Expanding Ownership Rights*, Quorum: Westport, CT, 1999.

Hamilton, M.A., 'The TRIPS Agreement: Imperialistic, Outdated, and Overprotective', 29 *Vanderbilt Journal of Transnational Law* 613, May 1996.

Hansen, H.C., 'International Copyright: An Unorthodox Analysis', 29 *Vanderbilt Journal of Transnational Law* 579, May 1996.

Harding, A., 'Global Doctrines and Local Knowledge: Law in South East Asia', *International and Comparative Law Quarterly*, January 2002.

Harms, L.T.C., 'Offering Cake for the South', 22(10) *European Intellectual Property Review* 451, October 2000.

Heath, C. (ed.), *Intellectual Property Law in Asia*, Kluwer Law International: London, 2004.

Heller, M.A., 'The Boundaries of Private Property', 108 *Yale Law Journal* 1163, 1999.

Hicks, L.L. and Holbein, J.R., 'Convergence of National Intellectual Property Norms in International Trading Agreements', 12(5) *American University Journal of International Law and Policy* 769, 1997.

Hughes, J., 'The Philosophy of Intellectual Property', 77 *Georgetown Law Journal* 287, 1988.

Innes, J. and Turpin, T., *Intellectual Property Legislation and Innovation in Asia-Pacific Economies: Case Studies of Intellectual Property Law in Australia, China, Indonesia, Korea, the Philippines and Thailand*, Hybrid: Ormond, Victoria, 1999.

[Institute of Development Studies, University of Sussex] 'Intellectual Property Rights', Trade & Investment Background Briefing No. 6, no date.

International Intellectual Property Alliance, *2005 Special 301 Report*; available at http://www.iipa.com.

——, *2006 Special 301 Report*, 13 February 2006, available at http://www.iipa.com.

International Telecommunications Union, *WSIS Outcome Documents*, Geneva, December 2005.

[Japan, MITI] The Report of the Commission on Intellectual Property Rights in the Twenty-first Century, 'Toward the Era of Intellectual Creation, Challenges For Breakthrough', 7 April 1997; available at http://www.jpo-miti.go.jp.

[Japan Ministry of Economy, Trade and Industry] *The Report of the Task Force on Industrial Competitiveness and Intellectual Property Policy*, 5 June 2002.

——, *2003 Report on the WTO Consistency of Trade Policies by Major Trading Partners*, 28 March 2003.

Japan Patent Office, *FY2004 Survey Report on Losses Caused by Counterfeiting*, March 2005; available at http://www.jpo.go.jp.

Jenckes, K.S., 'Protection of Foreign Copyrights in China: The Intellectual Property Courts and Alternative Avenues of Protection', *Southern California Interdisciplinary Law Journal* 55, 1997.

Kaehlig, C. and Churchill, G.J., *Indonesian Intellectual Property Law*, P.T. Tatanusa: Jakarta, 1993.

Kanellos, M., 'Bill Gates: Restricting IP Rights is Tantamount to Communism', *CNET News.com*, 6 January 2005.

Kawagoe, T. and Sekiguchi, S. (eds), *East Asian Economies: Transformation and Challenges*, Center for Asian and Pacific Studies, Sekei University: Tokyo; and Institute of Southeast Asian Studies: Singapore, 1995.

Kearney, R.P., *The Warrior Worker: The Challenge of the Korean Way of Working*, Henry Holt and Company: New York, 1991.

Kennan, G., *State Department Policy Planning Study*, cited by Noam Chomsky in *On Power and Ideology: The Managua Lectures*, Black Rose: Montreal, 1987.

Khaw, L.T., *Copyright Law in Malaysia*, Butterworths Asia: Hong Kong, 1994.

Khor, M., 'Rethinking Intellectual Property rights And TRIPS', in P. Drahos and R. Mayne (eds), *Global Intellectual Property Rights: Knowledge, Access and Development*, Palgrave Macmillan: Basingstoke, 2002.

Kim, B., 'Licensing and Technology Transfer', in C. Heath (ed.), *Intellectual Property Law in Korea*, Kluwer Law International: London, 2003.

Kolle, G., 'Computer Software Protection – Present Situation and Future Prospects', 13(70) *Copyright* 9, March 1977.

Kuny, K., 'The PRC is Going to Put into Effect their Patent Law', *China Patents and Trademarks*, Issue 1, April 1985.

Ladas, S.P., *The International Protection of Industrial Property*, Harvard University Press: Cambridge, MA, 1930.

Landau, S., 'Chinese Influence on the Rise in Latin America', *Foreign Policy in Focus*, June 2005; available at www.fpif.org.

Lara, G., 'The Piracy Of American Films In China: Why The U.S. Art Form is not Protected by Copyright Laws in the People's Republic Of China', 2 *UCLA Journal of International Law and Foreign Affairs* 343, Fall 1997/Winter, 1998.

Leaffer, M.A., 'Protecting United States Intellectual Property Abroad: Toward a New Multilateralism', 76 *Iowa Law Review* 273, 1991.

Lee, I., 'Culturally-Based Copyright Systems?: The U.S. and Korea in Conflict', *Washington University Law Quarterly* 1103, Winter 2001.

Lee, K., 'General Introduction', in C. Heath (ed.), *Intellectual Property Law in Korea*, Kluwer Law International: London, 2003.

Lessig, L., *The Future of Ideas: The Fate of the Commons in a Connected World*, Random House: New York, 2001.

Liu, P.C.B., 'U.S. Industry's Influence on Intellectual Property Negotiations and Special 301 Actions', 13 *UCLA Pacific Basin Law Journal* 87, Fall 1994.

Machlup, F., *An Economic Review of the Patent System*, US Congress, Senate Committee on the Judiciary, Subcommittee on Patents, Trademarks and Copyrights, Study No. 15, Government Printing Office: Washington, DC, 1958.

Mackaay, E., 'The Economics of Intellectual Property Rights in Civil Law Systems', in *Economic Analysis of Law – A European Perspective*, A.N. Hatzis (ed.), Edward Elgar: Cheltenham, 2008.

Mandeville, T.D. et al., *Economic Effects of the Australian Patent System: A Commissioned Report to the Industrial Property Advisory Committee*, Australian Government Publishing Service: Canberra, 1982.

Mann, K. and Roberts, R. (eds), *Law in Colonial Africa*, Heinemann: London, 1991.

Mantle, R.A. et al., *Intellectual Property Law of China*, Juris: Huntington, NY, 1999.

Martosewojo, W., 'Protection of Intellectual Property in Indonesia', ASEAN Law Association 1982 General Assembly, *Report*, 25–9 October 1982, Kuala Lumpur.

Maskus, K.E., *Intellectual Property Rights in the Global Economy*, Institute for International Economics: Washington, DC, 2000.

Maskus, K.E. and Reichman, 'J.H., The Globalisation of Private Knowledge Goods and the Privatisation of Global Public Goods', 7 *Journal of International Economic Law* 279, June 2004.

May, C., *A Global Political Economy of Intellectual Property Rights: The New Enclosures?* Routledge: New York, 2000.

Microsoft, *Realising Potential in Europe, the Middle East and Africa*, 2005; available at http://download.microsoft.com.

Morrison C., 'Rethinking Intellectual Property Rights: Accessing Essential Medicines for HIV and AIDS in Thailand', *Int Conference on AIDS*, 7–12 July 2002.

Mosseberger, K. et al., *Virtual Inequality: Beyond the Digital Divide*, Georgetown University Press: Washington, DC, 2003.

Mossinghoff, G.J. and Kuo, V.S., 'World Patent System circa 20XX A.D.', *Intellectual Property Review 1999*, 1999.

Naya, S.F. and Iboshi, P.I., 'A Post-Uruguay Round Agenda for APEC: Promoting Convergence of North American and Asian Values', in Chia Siow Yue (ed.), *APEC: Challenges and Opportunities*, Institute of Southeast Asian Studies: Singapore, 1994.

New, W., 'Washington Patent Meeting Stirs Concerns', *Intellectual Property Watch*; available at http://www.ip-watch.org.

New, W. et al., 'Group B+ Draft Patent Harmonisation Treaty Emerges', *Intellectual Property Watch*, 7 November 2006; available at http://www.ip-watch.org.

[Non-Aligned Movement] 'Final Document of the XIII Conference of Heads of State or Government of the Non-Aligned Movement', Kuala Lumpur, 24–5 February 2003.

Norris, P., *Digital Divide: Civic Engagement, Information Poverty and the Internet Worldwide*, Cambridge University Press: Cambridge, 2001.

Oddi, A.S., 'The International Patent System and Third World Development: Reality or Myth?', *Duke Law Journal* 831, 1987.

——, 'TRIPS – Natural Rights and a "Polite Form of Economic Imperialism"', 29 *Vanderbilt Journal of Transnational Law* 415, May 1996.

OECD, *Meeting of the OECD Council at Ministerial Level: Seizing the Benefits of ICT in a Digital Economy*, 2003.

Ordish, R. and Adcock, A., *China Intellectual Property – Challenges and Solutions: An Essential Business Guide*, Wiley: Chichester, 2008.

O'Sullivan, M., 'Making Copyright Ambidextrous: An Expose of Copyleft', 3 *Journal of Information, Law and Technology* 2002; available at http://www2.warwick.ac.uk/fac/soc/law/elj/jilt.

Oxfam, *Intellectual Property and the Knowledge Gap*, Oxfam Discussion Paper 12/01, December 2001.

Paré, D., 'The Digital Divide: Why the "The" is Misleading', in *Human Rights In The Digital Age*, M. Klang and A. Murray (eds), Cavendish Publishing: London, 2005.

Penrose, E.T. *The Economics of the International Patent System*, Johns Hopkins Press: Baltimore, MD, 1951.

Pistor, K. and Wellons, P.A. et al., *The Role of Law and Legal Institutions in Asian Economic Development 1960–95*, Oxford University Press: New York, 1998.

Prebluda, D.E., 'Countering International Trade in Counterfeit Goods', 12(2) *Brooklyn Journal of International Law* 339–67, March 1986.

Radhie, T.M., 'Harmonization of Laws: Issues and Prospects in ASEAN Law, Technology and Development', 1(2) *ASEAN Law and Society Journal* 50–61, July–December 1986.

Raghavan, C., 'Time Ripe for WTO Transparency, Inclusiveness, Orderly Procedures?', *Third World Network*, 6 August 2004.

Reichman, H., 'Universal Minimum Standards of Intellectual Property Protection under the TRIPS Component of the WTO Agreement', 29(2) *International Law* 345 Summer, 1995.

Reichman, J.H., 'Compliance with the TRIPS Agreement: Introduction to a Scholarly Debate', 29 *Vanderbilt Journal of Transnat'l Law* 363, May 1996.

Ricketson, S., *The Law of Intellectual Property*, Law Book Company: Sydney, 1984.

Sangal, P.S. and Singh, K. (eds) *Indian Patent Sytem and Paris Convention: Legal Perspectives*, Ashoka Printers: Delhi, 1987.

Sarnoff, D., 'A World Patent System, Kettering Award Address to the Tenth Annual Public Conference', 10 *IDEA* 143, 1966.

Sayoc, J.S.J., 'Protection of Intellectual Property in the Philippines', *Report*, ASEAN Law Association General Assembly, 25–9 October 1982, Kuala Lumpur, 1982.

Scherer, F.M., 'Taking Stock: The Law and Economics Of Intellectual Property Rights: The Pharmaceutical Industry and World Intellectual Property Standards', 53 *Vanderbilt Law Review* 2245, November 2000.

Sciadas, G. (ed.), *Monitoring the Digital Divide ... and Beyond*, Orbicom: Montreal, 2003; available at: http://www.orbicom.uqam.ca/projects.

Seidman, R.B., *The State, Law and Development*, Frances Pinter: London, 1978.

Sherwood, R.M., 'The TRIPS Agreement: Implications for Developing Countries', 37 *IDEA* 491, 1997.

——, *Intellectual Property and Economic Development*, Westview Press: Boulder, CO, 1990.

Siwek, S.E., *Engines of Growth: Economic Contributions of the U.S. Intellectual Property Industries* [November 2005] (commissioned study for NBC Universal).

Sodipo, B., *Piracy and Counterfeiting: GATT*, TRIPS *and Developing Countries*, Kluwer Law International: London, 1997.

Stewart, T.P. (ed.), *The GATT Uruguay Round: A Negotiating History (1986–1992), Volume II: Commentary*, Kluwer Law and Taxation Publishers: London, 1993.

Su, E., 'The Winners and The Losers: The Agreement On Trade-Related Aspects Of Intellectual Property Rights and its Effects On Developing Countries', 23 *Houston Journal of International Law* 169, Fall 2000.

Suber, P., 'Creating an Intellectual Commons through Open Access'; available at http://dlc.dlib.indiana.edu/archive.

Sun, A.Y., *From Pirate King to Jungle King: Transformation of Taiwan's Intellectual Property Protection*, Occasional Papers/Reprints in Contemporary

Asian Studies, No. 6 (143). School of Law, University of Maryland: College Park, MD, 1997.

Taylor, C.T. and Silberston, Z.A., *The Economic Impact of the Patent System: A Study of the British Experience*, Cambridge University Press: Cambridge, 1973.

Teubner, G. (ed.), *Global Law Without a State*, Dartmouth: Aldershot, 1997.

Tiefenbrun, S., 'Piracy of Intellectual Property in China and the Former Soviet Union and its Effects Upon International Trade: A Comparison', 46 *Buffalo Law Review* 1, Winter, 1998.

Trubek, D.M. and Galanter, M., 'Scholars in Self-estrangement: Some Reflections on the Crisis in Law and Development Studies in the United States', *Wisconsin Law Review* 1062, 1974.

[UK] Commission on Intellectual Property Rights, *Report of the Commission on Intellectual Property Rights: Integrating Intellectual Property Rights and Development Policy*, London, September 2002.

UNCTAD, 'The Role of the Patent System in the Transfer of Technology to Developing Countries', UN Doc. TD/B/C. 6/12, UN: New York, 1975.

——, *Information Economy Report 2006: The Development Perspective*; available at http://www.unctad.org.

Upoff, E. *Intellectual Property and US Relations With Indonesia, Malaysia, Singapore, and Thailand*, Southeast Asia Program, Cornell University: Ithaca, NY, 1991.

US Congress, Office of Technology Assessment, *Intellectual Property Rights in an Age of ElectroDCs and Information*, Robert E. Krieger Publishing Company, Malabar, FL, 1987.

US Congressional Budget Office, 'The Pros and Cons of Pursuing Free-Trade Agreements', 31 July 2003; available at www.cbo.gov.

US Justice Department, Office of the Attorney General, *Report of the Department of Justice's Task Force on Intellectual Property*, October 2004.

US Report of the President's Commission on the Patent System, *To Promote the Progress of ... Useful Arts: In an Age of Exploding Technology*, Washington, DC, 1966.

——, International Trade Commission, 'Foreign Protection of Intellectual Property Rights and the Effect on U.S. Industry and Trade', ITC Pub. No. 2065, February 1988.

——, The President's Commission on Industrial Competitiveness, *Global Competition, the New Reality*, Washington, DC, 1985.

——, *Report of the President's Commission on Industrial Competitiveness*, Volume II, Washington, DC, 1985.

US Trade Representative (USTR), 'National Trade Estimate Report on Foreign Trade Barriers'; available at http://www.ustr.gov/reports/index.shtml.

Wade, W., *Governing the Market: Economic Theory and the Role of Government in East Asian Industrialisation*, Princeton University Press: Princeton, NJ, 2000; quoted in Nagesh Kumar, 'Intellectual Property Rights, Technology and Economic Development: Experiences of Asian Countries', Research and Information System for Non-aligned and Other Developing Countries, RIS DP No. 25-2002, May 2002.

Wark, M., *A Hacker Manifesto*, Harvard University Press: Cambridge, MA, 2004.

Wei, G., *The Law of Copyright in Singapore*, Singapore National Printers, 1989.

Weinstein, S. and Wild, C., 'Closing the Digital Divide: Who Will Invest in Universal Access?', 4(1) *Hertfordshire Law Journal* 2–11 [no date].

Wineburg, A., 'Jurisprudence in Asia: Enforcing Intellectual Property Rights', 5 *University of Baltimore Intellectual Property Law Journal* 25, Fall 1996/Spring 1997.

WIPO (ed.), *Introduction to Intellectual Property: Theory and Practice*, Kluwer Law International: London, 1997.

——, 'Proposal by Argentina and Brazil for the Establishment of a Development Agenda for WIPO', Geneva, 27 August 2004; WO/GA/31/11.

——, 'Proposal by the United States of America for the Establishment of a Partnership Program in WIPO', Geneva, 18 March 2005, IIM/1/2.

——, 'Proposal by Mexico on Intellectual Property and Development', Geneva, 1 April 2005, IIM/1/3.

——, 'Proposal to Establish a Development Agenda for WIPO: An Elaboration of Issues Raised in Document WO/GA/31/11', Geneva, 6 April 2005; IIM/1/4.

——, 'Proposal by the Kingdom of Bahrain on the Importance of Intellectual Property in Social and Economic Development and National Development Programs for the Inter-Sessional Intergovernmental Meeting on a Development Agenda for WIPO', Geneva, 14 June 2005, IIM/2/2.

——, 'Proposal by the United Kingdom', Geneva, 14 June 2005, IIM/2/3.

——, 'The African Proposal for the Establishment of a Development Agenda for the World Intellectual Property Organization (WIPO)', Geneva, 18 July 2005, IIM/3/2.

——, 'Inter-sessional Intergovernmental Meeting on a Development Agenda for WIPO: Report, Second Session', Geneva, 20–22 June 2005; IIM/2/10, 1 September 2005.

Wright, S.E., 'Copyright in Singapore: Some Recent Developments', 1 *Malayan Law Journal* cviii-cxviii, 1 April 1986.

WTO, General Council, 'Preparations for the 1999 Ministerial Conference, Proposals on IPR Issues', *Communication from India*, WT/GC/W/147, 18 February 1999.

——, TRIPs Council, 'Non-Violation Nullification or Impairment Under the Agreement on Trade Related Aspects of Intellectual Property Rights (TRIPs)', Proposal from Cuba, the Dominican Republic, Egypt, Indonesia, Malaysia and Pakistan, IP/C/W/141, 29 April 1999.

——, General Council, 'Preparations for the 1999 Ministerial Conference, Proposals Regarding the TRIPS Agreement in terms of Paragraph 9(a)(i) of the

Geneva Ministerial Declaration', Communication from India, WT/GC/W/225, 2 July 1999.

——, General Council, 'Preparations for the 1999 Ministerial Conference, Proposal for a Declaration on Developing Countries', Communication from the Philippines, WT/GC/W/393, 25 November 1999.

——, TRIPs Council, 'Communication from India', Documents IP/C/W/196, 12 July 2000.

——, TRIPs Council, 'Protection of Biodiversity and Traditional Knowledge – the Indian Experience', Submission by India, IP/C/W/198, 14 July 2000.

——, TRIPs Council, 'Communication From Bulgaria, The Czech Republic, Egypt, Iceland, India, Kenya, Liechtenstein, Pakistan, Slovenia, Sri Lanka, Switzerland and Turkey', Document IP/C/W/204/Rev. 1, 2 October 2000.

——, TRIPs Council, 'Review of the Provisions of Article 27.3(B) – Japan's View', Communication from Japan, IP/C/W/236, 11 December 2000.

——, TRIPs Council, 'Proposal From Bulgaria, Cuba, The Czech Republic, Egypt, Iceland, India, Jamaica, Kenya, Liechtenstein, Mauritius, Nigeria, Pakistan, Slovenia, Sri Lanka, Switzerland, Turkey and Venezuela', Document IP/C/W/247/Rev. 1, 17 May 2001.

——, TRIPs Council, 'Submission by the African Group, Barbados, Bolivia, Brazil, Cuba, Dominican Republic, Ecuador, Honduras, India, Indonesia, Jamaica, Pakistan, Paraguay, Philippines, Peru, Sri Lanka, Thailand and Venezuela', IP/C/W/296, 29 June 2001.

——, TRIPS Council, 'Submission by the African Group, Barbados, Bolivia, Brazil, Cuba, Dominican Republic, Ecuador, Honduras, India, Indonesia, Jamaica, Pakistan, Paraguay, Philippines, Peru, Sri Lanka, Thailand and Venezuela', IP/C/W/296, 29 June 2001.

——, 'The Declaration on the TRIPS Agreement and Public Health', 20 November 2001, WT/MIN(01)/DEC/2.

——, The Doha WTO Ministerial Declaration 2001, 20 November 2001, WT/MIN(01)/DEC/1.

——, 'Amendment of the TRIPS Agreement – Extension of the Period for the Acceptance by Members of the Protocol Amending the TRIPS Agreement', 21 December 2007.

Youm, K.Y., 'Copyright Law in the Republic of Korea', 17 *UCLA Pacific Basin Law Journal* 276, Fall 1999/Spring 2000.

Yu, P.K., 'From Pirates to Partners: Protecting Intellectual Property in China in the Twenty First Century', 50 *American University Law Review* 131, 2001.

Zermer, L., *The Idea of Authorship in Copyright*, Ashgate: Aldershot, 2007.

Zhang, N., 'Intellectual Property Law Enforcement in China: Trade Issues, Policies and Practices' 8 *Fordham Intellectual Property, Media and Entertainment Law Journal* 63, Fall 1997; 13 March 2001.

Zheng, C., with Pendeleton, M.D., *Chinese Intellectual Property and Technology Transfer Law*, Sweet & Maxwell: London, 1987.

Index